JAPAN

Japan

THE PRECARIOUS FUTURE

Edited by Frank Baldwin and Anne Allison

A Joint Publication of the Social Science Research Council
and New York University Press

NEW YORK UNIVERSITY PRESS

New York and London

www.nyupress.org

ISBN: 978-1-4798-8938-9 (hardback)

ISBN: 978-1-4798-5145-4 (paperback)

For Library of Congress Cataloging-in-Publication data,
please contact the Library of Congress.

New York University Press books are printed on acid-free paper, and their binding
materials are chosen for strength and durability. We strive to use environmentally
responsible suppliers and materials to the greatest extent possible in publishing our
books.

Manufactured in the United States of America

c 10 9 8 7 6 5 4 3 2 1

Also available as an ebook

References to Internet websites (URLs) were accurate at the time of writing. Neither
the author nor New York University Press is responsible for URLs that may have expired
or changed since the manuscript was prepared.

Contents

Acknowledgments

This book was inspired by the resilient people of the Tōhoku region of Japan, which was struck by a megaearthquake, tsunami, and meltdowns at the Fukushima nuclear power complex in March 2011. Craig Calhoun and Mary McDonnell at the Social Science Research Council (SSRC) envisioned research by social scientists to look beyond the disaster at Japan's near future. The project also commemorates the twentieth anniversary of the Abe Fellowship Program, a collaboration between the Japan Foundation Center for Global Partnership (CGP) and the SSRC. Eight Abe Fellows and a member of the Abe Program Committee contributed to this volume and participated in a public symposium in Tokyo in July 2012 on Japan's future.

We are grateful to the Japan Foundation Center for Global Partnership for financial support. We also want to thank several individuals who assisted us at various stages. Former CGP executive director Akio Nomura recognized the lasting contribution of research to the legacy of 3/11. Takuya Ozaki helped shape this volume and administered the project from its inception through thick and thin. Jean-Francois Roof created the graphics and resolved countless computer problems. David Slater and Andrew DeWit made valuable contributions as discussants at a workshop in Hayama, Japan, in 2012. Susan Schmidt and Elisabeth Magnus gave unerring advice on stylistic matters. Two anonymous reviewers made very useful critiques.

The Editorial Department of the SSRC provided excellent support, in the early stage by Paul Price and thereafter by Alyson Metzger and Michael

Simon. Our editor at New York University Press, Ilene Kalish, watched over the manuscript from its inception.

Working on this project has been a rewarding experience thanks to the contributions of our authors. We deeply appreciate their scholarship and dedicated willingness to meet a harsh publication schedule.

All Japanese names (and Korean and Chinese names) in the manuscript are according to Western convention: given name followed by surname. The one exception is in chapter 11, where the name of Fukuzawa Yukichi, a historic person, has the family name first, in accord with standard Japanese usage. In short-form citations in the notes authors are identified by surname.

Introduction: Japan's Possible Futures

Frank Baldwin and Anne Allison

Japan was in economic trouble long before Lehman Brothers collapsed in September 2008. The bursting of the real estate and stock market bubble in the early 1990s brought the Lost Decade (now two Lost Decades) of deflationary retraction, unemployment, and shattered dreams. Paradoxically, Japan weathered the acute financial shock relatively well; financial institutions were not heavily invested in subprime mortgage–backed securities. Yet as the world's third-largest economy, Japan could not dodge the global recession that damped its economic growth and undermined social institutions designed to provide security and predictability. By February 2011 trade surpluses were falling and the suicide rate had been on the rise for a decade. A sluggish economy translated into abandoned plans for marriage and a family, national budget deficits, and underfunded social security programs. Japan was becoming a precarious society.

To these woes was added a staggering natural disaster. At 2:46 p.m. on March 11, 2011, a 9.0 earthquake off the northeast coast triggered a tsunami that battered three coastal prefectures, killed 15,891 people with 2,579 missing, displaced about six hundred thousand, and caused damage estimated at ¥16.9 trillion. The meltdown of three reactors at the Fukushima Daiichi nuclear plant caused radiation leakage that continued in 2014. About eighty thousand nearby residents were evacuated, and for a time Tokyo was at risk of airborne contamination. The government has earmarked up to ¥35 trillion for reconstruction over a five-year period. Journalists and scholars have written extensively about the triple disaster.[1]

Unlike earlier volumes in the Possible Futures series, this book is centered not on the global financial crisis but on an array of systemic and structural issues that determine a country's well-being. Adapting the series' guidelines, we considered how "past history and current challenges shape possible futures." Would recovery mean a retrofitting of earlier patterns or portend genuine change?[2] Assuming that long-range forecasts have limited utility, we set the time in the near future—three to five years. The papers presented here are not predictions or prescriptive blueprints (except perhaps for the chapter on demography); authors were not expected to hazard scenarios of the future, a fool's errand. They were asked to use their analytical skills and knowledge of Japan and East Asia to look over the horizon. Participants gathered at a conference in Hayama, Japan, March 30 to April 1, 2012, to discuss preliminary papers. As the papers were under revision, the Liberal Democratic Party (LDP) came to power in December 2012 with an ambitious policy agenda to change Japan's course. The LDP strengthened its mandate with successes in the House of Councillors election in July 2013 and a snap election in December 2014 and may be dominant until 2018. Several chapters were revised again to cover developments in 2014, including those on nuclear policy and political leadership. Events have no respect for the schedule of edited volumes.

Where is Japan headed? Broadly speaking, one possible future is that the country recovers from 3/11, sustains modest GDP growth through its industrial and scientific prowess, and remains a democratic midlevel power with increased attention paid to those suffering the effects of economic and social precarity today. A less sanguine possibility is that Japan declines, shrunken by insoluble demographic dilemmas and its inability to resolve such problems as energy, gender inequality, and rising disparity. Overshadowed by China, Japan might become a mere shadow of the country once touted as a global leader.[3] However tantalizing it would be to imagine Japan decades from now, such speculation is beyond the scope of this volume. As the Japanese proverb warns, "Speak of next year and the devil laughs."

Then what is the outlook for the near future? First of all, the participants show that hard times lie ahead for the disadvantaged as social inequality grows. Second, can a high-tech industrial society limp along with a makeshift energy policy or shift from nuclear to alternative sources? Until 3/11 few people thought so. Third, if Japan hemorrhages manufacturing and innovative capacity for another five years, the drop in trade balances will undermine its ability to care for an aging population and provide other services. Last, the longer that naval and air patrols from Japan and China play "chicken" near disputed islands in the South China Sea, the greater the probability of a serious incident.

On the other hand, the authors in this volume also show that Japan has impressive strengths: enormous financial assets, low unemployment, a skilled, resilient population, and strong institutions. The national health system works, and Japanese corporations are competitive internationally. Although there are no outright Cassandras among the authors, several are guardedly pessimistic while others are tentatively optimistic. It is fair to say there is a shared sense of incremental slippage in social capital and of crises ahead if effective action is not taken. The canary in the coal mine is short of breath.

In chapter 1, Sawako Shirahase analyzes what is a major demographic transformation facing Japan: a falling birthrate, the rapid rise of the proportion of elderly, and a population projected to decline by 2060 to 80 million from 128 million today. In 2014 the fertility rate stood at 1.4, far below the replacement rate, while life expectancy for women was the highest in the world. Extensive media coverage of these trends has contributed to apprehension about the country's future. No European industrialized country has undergone such a rapid demographic change. Caused mainly by a reduction in the fertility rate, it is due both to fewer young people marrying and to married couples having fewer children. The effects on economic inequality and changes to family structure—with the resultant implications for caregiving of the elderly—are considerable. Yet to date government policies to reverse these trends have not worked, and Shirahase does not expect future initiatives to be more effective. If population size itself—with the possibility that Japan may experience a labor shortage in the future—is the issue, immigration should be more progressively embraced. This does not appear imminent, however, and neither political leaders nor the public are ready for a national debate. She concludes that only by changing its socioeconomic orientation to become a "blended society" that better accommodates diverse lifestyles and immigrants can Japan navigate its demographic destiny.

The concept of "precarity" introduced by Anne Allison in chapter 2 helps explain changes in the labor market, demography, and economic security as well as in social living and well-being. She notes that one-third of the population live alone, and as fewer marry, have their own family, or are steadily employed, more and more feel disconnected from the social attachments that conferred status and belonging in the family-corporate system under "Japan

Inc." beginning in the 1960s. A sense of not belonging and of isolation has spread in what Japanese call a "relationless society" dramatically characterized by lonely deaths—people who die alone and whose bodies are found only later. Many phenomena are linked to social disaggregation: a high rate of suicide, social withdrawal, directionless youth, homelessness, and underemployment. Allison calls this social precarity and argues that what distinguishes it in Japan is the disintegration over the last twenty years of the family-corporate system, which has served as the country's de facto welfare scheme, prop to state capitalism, and template for social belonging and citizenship in the postwar era. But just as older forms of social connectedness fray, Allison finds that hopeful new ways of being and belonging in society have arisen, such as volunteerism after 3/11 and local mutual support organizations that are redesigning sociality away from the narrow confines of family and work.

Complementing Allison, Machiko Osawa and Jeff Kingston in chapter 3 document significant shifts in employment patterns over the past two decades. The proportion of the workforce hired as nonregular employees has doubled. The rise of the precariat is primarily due to corporate cost cutting and government deregulation of the labor market. Lacking job security and benefits, the precariat accounts for one-third of the labor force and half of young workers. And unstable employment correlates with other disturbing socioeconomic trends: the rise in poverty, growing economic disparity, and discouraged youth. Osawa and Kingston argue that precaritization of employment contributes to other problems facing policy makers as they plan for Japan's possible futures, including income disparities, an inadequate safety net, and weakening social cohesion. Not encouraged by the efforts to date by the government or employers, they warn that failure to better incorporate women or immigrants into the labor force epitomizes the precarity of a future Japan.

The need for Japan to diversify the categories and patterns for people to work, live, and reproduce is also discussed by Ayako Kano in chapter 4. Japan ranks at the bottom of Organisation for Economic Co-operation and Development (OECD) countries in terms of gender equality, a standing that hinders not only the rights of women but also the nation's capacity to confront the challenges of socioeconomic viability. In a theme echoed by several authors in this volume (Osawa and Kingston, Shirahase, Allison), Kano sees gender traditionalism—a rigid bifurcation of gender roles, with men as breadwinners, women as housewives, and both expected to marry and reproduce families that replicate the same gendered division of labor—as complicit with many social issues. Given the difficulties in balancing family and work, those who lack regular employment, men as well as women, find it difficult to marry and have children. The government has been cognizant of the need to promote a "gender-equal society" and has instituted a number of progressive policies since the 1990s. But by the turn of the new century such initiatives met with a fierce backlash within conservative and neonationalist circles. Today, the very concept of a gender-equal society has shifted to emphasis on the participation of men in child care versus equality for women in society and the workplace.

The Great East Japan Earthquake and Tsunami triggered a meltdown at the Fukushima Daiichi nuclear reactor that might have been expected to produce a radical change in Japan's nuclear policy, as it did in other countries such as Germany. Jacques Hymans shows in chapter 5 that although no nuclear reactors are operating today compared with fifty-four prior to 3/11, reform of Japan's nuclear safety system and energy policy has been remarkably slow. Certain changes have occurred, including creation of an independent safety watchdog agency and the announcement of a zero nuclear power generation policy by 2040. But credibility and carry-through are questionable, leading to a de facto post-Fukushima nuclear policy gridlock. Hymans says policy makers have failed to coalesce around a viable long-term nuclear program because veto players with different strategic interests have created an extremely fractionalized policy-making arena. Pessimistic about a resolution in the near future, he sees danger ahead not only for Japan's environment and economy but also for public confidence in the country's political institutions. A cleanup is likely to take decades and cost up to $500 billion.

In chapter 6, William Siembieda and Haruo Hayashi outline the history of disaster management in Japan, particularly since the 1995 Kobe Earthquake, when the central government took on new responsibilities, and 3/11, when a weak reconstruction agency faltered badly. They untangle the web of Japan's decentralized and compartmentalized disaster management system—nuclear safety was handled separately—and contrast Japan's centralized responses to calamity to those of Chile, New Zealand, and China. Although seismologists cannot foretell events precisely, a grim consensus predicts major earthquakes in the Tōkai and Tokyo areas in the next few decades. In Tōkai alone, the estimated losses—up to 320,000 casualties over thirty prefectures—and economic damage could stagger the nation. Although constrained by the new demographic and economic realities described by other authors in this book, planners must try to minimize the projected hardship with limited resources. The denial and wishful thinking that characterized some assessments before 3/11 have given way to new safety standards and organizational arrangements. Siembieda and Hayashi anticipate a less rule-bound holistic approach to disaster management that engages the business community and civil society with a more agile and adaptive central government. Despite the foreboding outlook for megadisasters, the authors believe the lessons learned from 3/11 may pave the way for a less vulnerable future.

Saori Katada and Gene Park ask in chapter 7 when Japan will have to face the music for its lack of fiscal discipline. Given that it is strapped by high public debt and endless budget deficits, not only is the social security system for an aging population shaky but so is the ability to fund security needs in the rivalry with China. The authors review on-again, off-again attempts at fiscal consolidation when the government has been able neither to curb spending nor to raise taxes enough to fill the gap. Certain assets offset profligacy: no foreign debt, a high domestic savings rate, and positive trade balances (now slipping away). Helped by official intervention, major banks survived reckless speculation in the real estate and stock bubble of the 1990s and emerged from the Big Bang shocks of the 1990s in good shape, albeit with their numbers thinned to a few megabanks. The silver bullet is Japanese government bonds and the willingness of now risk-averse bankers to buy them in large quantities. The authors conclude that the uneasy status quo is sustainable in the near future but that Japan will have to borrow abroad in a decade or so. Enter new prime minister Abe, who boldly rolled the dice to stimulate growth by changing monetary and fiscal policy. Now the question is whether Abenomics will mitigate the economic malaise or harm Japan's credit rating and solvency.

To Takahiro Fujimoto, the wholesale relocation of manufacturing plants overseas is shortsighted and threatens the nation's future. In chapter 8, he advocates public policy to retain a strong manufacturing sector in Japan. His analysis rests on a neo-Ricardian theory of comparative advantage—Japan's industrial productivity—combined with rigorous empirical observation of factories and design centers. A domestic industrial base is the source of innovation, commercial success, and favorable trade balances, according to Fujimoto. This perspective from the shop floor is not popular in boardrooms or the media. Attracted by the siren's song of low wages in China and other emerging economies, especially since the financial crisis of 2008, corporate managers have moved hundreds of plants abroad, losing the precious synergy of design and blue-collar skill available in Japan. The mass media echo boardroom groupthink and exaggerate cyclical trends into a doomsday scenario for Japanese factories. Rather than accepting a race to the bottom in wages and deindustrialization as the inevitable outcome of global trends, Fujimoto argues that preservation of efficient manufacturing sites is essential for economic recovery. Eschewing protectionism, he recommends tax and environmental policies that reward efficient plants and management. The US experience of massive trade deficits, offshoring, and rust belts is a cautionary tale for Japan.

In chapter 9, Masaru Yarime examines the role of science and technology in Japan, from the creation of modern industrial and military establishments through an abrupt shift to civilian priorities after World War II and the later transition to a postindustrial economy driven by research and development. Government policies shaped the rapid economic growth of the 1960s and 1970s and still sway the national agenda today. When the economy faltered in the 1990s, Japan borrowed the concept of an "entrepreneurial university" from the United States to transfer science and technology from academia to industry, with inconclusive results so far. Japan's R&D spending, mostly from the private sector, remains among the highest for industrialized countries and has impressive achievements in big science and technology, from bullet trains and the K computer to Nobel prizes. Favorable trade balances over the years owe much to basic and applied research. Yet Japan now lags behind in such critical indicators as research publications, patents, and international collaboration. Old patterns no longer work, Yarime says, pointing to a new paradigm of innovation that cuts across conventional boundaries. Although institutional reform is proving difficult, he contends that Japan can lead the way to integrated solutions to complex problems.

China is the four-hundred-pound gorilla in the room when Japanese strategists ponder security. Hiroshi Nakanishi in chapter 10 recounts how in 2010 the Kan administration scrapped the static Cold War mission of the Self-Defense Forces (SDF) as a supplement deterrent (to the United States) against Russia and adapted a "mission leap" of defense of the sea and air space around Japan, including responses to attacks on offshore islands. Additional steps were taken in 2011–14 toward military cooperation with the United States, the United Kingdom, and Australia. Restrictions on arms sales were removed and defense spending was boosted. The game changer was reinterpretation of the constitution in July 2014 to allow the SDF to engage in military operations overseas. A broad bipartisan consensus underlies this shift, says Nakanishi, although the public does not yet grasp the full implications. Japanese public opinion imputes hostile intentions and increased military capability to China's actions in the dispute over the Senkaku Islands; meanwhile, negative Chinese public opinion toward Japan has surged in recent years. China has repeatedly tested Japan's resolve with naval and air patrols that skirt Japanese territory and has hinted at an irredentist claim to Okinawa. Nakanishi recommends that Japan avoid escalation and respond in a way commensurate with the provocation, while trying through diplomacy to dissuade China from its goal of projecting naval power globally. Relations with the United States remain the keystone of Japan's security; badly bungled in 2009, they have improved under the Abe administration. Managing that bilateral relationship, expanding military ties with other nations, and reaching an accommodation with China make up the near-term security agenda. Counterterrorism was added to the agenda when the Islamic State beheaded two Japanese hostages in January 2015.

Claude Meyer assays the intense rivalry between Japan and China for leadership in Asia and ventures a long-run forecast. Unlike many contemporary observers, he does not see the race as already half over and China the certain victor. Japan is too strong—with formidable financial and industrial assets complemented by national resiliency—to fall by the wayside soon. China has sprinted past Japan in manufacturing exports, for instance, but is an also-ran in soft power and other fields. Meyer sees, rather than a clear winner in the near future, a mutual economic dependency prevailing over nationalistic assertiveness. Although China has settled many territorial disputes, he finds worrisome its escalation of disputes over maritime rights such as that with Japan over the Senkaku/Daioyu Islands. For the next decade an antagonistic geopolitical standoff of grudgingly shared leadership is most likely. Meyer concludes that from about 2030 China's economy will be four times that of Japan's and that Beijing may dominate the rest of Asia. On the other hand, if a nascent Asian Community of shared democratic values is formed, Japan and India could counter China's influence.

Ellis Krauss and Robert Pekkanen in chapter 12 take on the vexed issue of leadership, explaining why the country has been so plagued by turnstile prime ministers over the past two decades. Given the challenges facing Japan today, they decry—as does the public in general—the instability of leadership at the top, which they track in terms of the prime ministership, noting its long legacy in the postwar era as a weak office. In what has been a bureaucracy-strong parliamentary democracy, two reforms instituted between 1994 and 2001 provided at least the potential for a stronger prime ministership. But in their assessment, only Jun'ichirō Koizumi realized this potential, for reasons that include his ability to cultivate a popular image through the mass media and his willingness to be a maverick in exercising radical reforms. Both before and after him have come a string of short-term, ineffective prime ministers. In considering possible futures of Japan, Krauss and Pekkanen argue that another transformational leader like Koizumi is desperately needed and conclude that Shinzō Abe, after a remarkable political comeback and three electoral victories, may be such a leader, for better or worse.

Lawrence Repeta and Colin Jones in chapter 13 examine what strong leadership by Prime Minister Abe is likely to mean for the 1947 Peace Constitution, "imposed" by US Occupation officials to implant a legal framework that would sustain demilitarization and democracy. The new charter replaced imperial authority with popular sovereignty—"We, the Japanese people"—and made the once-divine emperor a symbol of the nation. Other provisions guaranteed basic rights of speech, assembly, and religion that a public long denied freedom and weary of militarism supported, particularly the "No War" Article 9 that restricts Japan's use of military power. Conservatives bowed to force majeure and adjusted to the alien values and language, but they were restively longing for a constitution "Made in Japan." Emboldened by a sweeping electoral victory in December 2012, the LDP announced plans to revise the constitution and submit it to a public referendum. The LDP draft constitution, Repeta and Jones write, is ideologically nationalistic and authoritarian and rejects universal concepts of human rights, for example, in favor of vague nativist precepts. LDP success in the July 2013 Upper House election cleared the way for a factious battle over revision, and the party threw down the gauntlet in 2014 by reinterpreting Article 9.

Japan: The Precarious Future opens with a sobering review of demographic projections and widening economic inequality. The first set of papers show how as prospects of steady employment and a middle-class lifestyle dissolve for an increasing number of Japanese, so do an ethos of egalitarianism and an expectation of security upheld in postwar times. What has emerged today is a social system of winners and losers and a national mood of nagging unease. As the population literally shrinks, fear rises that Japan is in decline and that the toll will be heavy on those most vulnerable by reason of age, gender, ethnicity, and underemployment. Shifting focus, the next set of papers concerns Japan's strengths and opportunities, from its formidable financial assets and improved disaster planning to a dynamic industrial sector and world-class science and technology. From the perspective of infrastructure and reaction to crises, the tone is guardedly optimistic about the near future. The final four chapters look at political leadership in national security and domestic politics. Adroit management of ties with Beijing would improve Japan's security, but mutual brinksmanship and nationalistic grandstanding may edge the rivalry toward confrontation. At home, with a conservative coalition apparently ascendant, the prime minister may stay in office long enough to accomplish transformative changes. The ongoing radiation crisis at Fukushima and the lack of an energy policy suggest a turbulent tenure. Whether a bitter struggle over constitutional revision leads to domestic stalemate and regional isolation remains to be seen.

Notes

1. Two books by Jeff Kingston capture much of the horror and response. See Jeff Kingston, ed., *Tsunami: Japan's Post-Fukushima Future*, Kindle ed. (Washington, DC: Foreign Policy, 2011), and Jeff Kingston, ed., *Natural Disaster and Nuclear Crisis in Japan* (Routledge: London, 2012).

2. Richard J. Samuels, *3.11: Disaster and Change in Japan* (Ithaca, NY: Cornell University Press, 2013). In a brilliant analysis of three major policy areas, Samuels contends that 3/11 was not a "game changer." Three years after the disaster, more change is apparent, including the Liberal Democratic Party's domestic political and regional security goals.

3. Ezra Vogel, *Japan as Number One: Lessons for America* (Cambridge, MA: Harvard University Press, 1979). The theme of Japan's decline is explored in a series of articles collected by Sheila A. Smith at the Council on Foreign Relations website: "Is Japan in Decline?," November 28, 2012–January 18, 2013, www.cfr.org/projects/world/is-japan-in-decline/pr1628.

CHAPTER ONE

Demography as Destiny: Falling Birthrates and the Allure of a Blended Society

Sawako Shirahase

Demography is the study of population, the ebbs and flows formed by the life courses of individuals.[1] Today, Japan is undergoing a major demographic transformation marked by both a decline in fertility and a rapidly aging population. Fertility, the main determinant of demographic structure in any society, has declined in Japan for about four decades and in 2010 stood at 1.39, far below the replacement rate. At the same time, the elderly proportion (aged sixty-five years and above) has dramatically increased since the mid-1980s because of declined fertility and increased longevity; in 2010 it was 23.04 percent.[2]

Such a demographic transformation increases the gap between the productive and postproductive generation, which has a number of consequences. The social security system, for example, is strained because of the imbalance between the working-age generation who contribute to it and the retired generation who receive its benefits. In addition to this gap, the labor market has worsened since the late 2000s, particularly for young people who are delaying marriage or choosing not to marry at all. At the other end of the demographic spectrum, the elderly have drastically altered their living arrangements; the number of one-person and couple-only households has increased and that of three-generation households has declined. The welfare system, however, is premised on a familial structure (of men who work, women who take care of children and aging parents, and living arrangements based on extended or nuclear families) that is becoming outdated. Coupled with the generational gap between those contributing to, and those withdrawing from, the social security system, this means that the welfare system is getting stretched and is failing to protect more and more Japanese. One consequence is the increase in poverty, particularly among families with young children.

No European industrial country has undergone such radical shifts in demography and family structure in such a short period of time. And both the speed and depth of these changes in Japan have produced a number of social problems for which, in my estimation, no clear solutions have yet emerged. In this chapter, I discuss this demographic crisis from a sociological perspective, focusing on two specific issues: the change in family structure and the effect—of this as well as other demographic, social, and economic changes—on socioeconomic (in)equality.

Rising Inequality

Japan was the first Asian country to industrialize, and the rapid economic growth after World War II transformed its industrial structure. The primary sector shrank while the secondary and tertiary sectors expanded.[3] A wave of migrants from the countryside sought jobs in the city, and the number of white-collar workers rapidly increased. An urban lifestyle emerged, and families downsized from extended (three generations) to nuclear (parents and children).

According to the *Economic Survey of Japan* in 1953, the nominal national income in 1951 was thirteen times larger than in 1946.[4] The Income Doubling Plan launched by the Ikeda cabinet in 1960 reached its goal well ahead of the target date, earning kudos from around the world for Japan's success. Examining how this "economic miracle" was achieved, foreign researchers began to write positively about Japan's "lifetime employment" system.

In Japan, these economic achievements correlated with what was a widespread perception from the 1970s into the 1980s that the country had become a predominantly middle-class society—a characterization that was not entirely true, as we shall see. As the average per capita income continued to rise (despite the slight decrease in the overall economic growth after the spurt in the 1960s), people could afford automobiles and household electrical appliances (televisions, refrigerators, washing machines). Home ownership was no longer just a dream, and a middle-class consumer lifestyle became a reality for a majority of Japanese. It now became easier to buy clothes and accessories advertised in national magazines in almost every city, and this increase in consumer power across the nation blurred what had earlier been a clear urban/ rural distinction. In a comparative study of income distribution in 1976, the Organisation for Economic Co-operation and Development (OECD) found Japan to be the most egalitarian country of all the industrialized nations.[5] Japanese took this as further evidence of exceptionalism; the self-image of a middle-class and homogeneous society encouraged the stereotype of everyone having a middle-class consciousness and sharing a common lifestyle.[6]

In 1984 Yasusuke Murakami declared that Japan had become a new middle-mass society where lifestyle and worldview were widely shared and class differences had faded away.[7] But these confident assertions of Japan as an egalitarian society started to erode by the late 1980s as evidence of inequality started to emerge. In 1998, economist Toshiaki Tachibanaki's best seller *Economic Inequality in Japan* documented that income inequality in Japan was of an order similar to that of the United States. Sociologist Toshiki Sato joined the debate with *The Unequal Society*, an analysis of social inequality in Japan, that found a limited degree of mobility into the upper white-collar class. Sato argued that Japan was becoming more rigidly stratified.[8]

Yet this contention—of Japan becoming unequal and class divided in the 1990s—assumes that Japan was once a society with a high degree of equality, and the evidence that would support this, as well as the claim of a historical devolution toward inequality in Japan, has been contested by a number of scholars.[9] On the basis of his analysis of microdata concerning social status between the 1970s and 1990s, Kazuo Seiyama, for example, dismissed the assertion of Japan's original equity as more myth than reality. According to him, there was no empirical evidence to prove that Japanese had ever achieved as widespread socioeconomic equality as it was perceived to have or that there was an explicit trend toward increasing social inequality, including a pattern of social mobility.[10] Economist Tsuneo Ishikawa also cast doubt on the notion that Japanese society had ever been as egalitarian and homogeneous as was commonly supposed, on the basis of his own study of income inequality.[11]

The recent resurgence of interest in inequality is tied to a rising instability in the labor market that has been verified by a number of facts. For example, the number of nonregular workers has surged since the recession of the 1990s, as shown by Machiko Osawa and Jeff Kingston in chapter 3 of this volume. Youth have fallen on hard times, particularly those without college degrees. Unemployment for young people aged fifteen to twenty-four in 2011 was 11.5 percent for those with only compulsory education (middle school), while the corresponding figure for those with higher education was 8.2 percent.[12] Forty-seven percent, almost half of these young people, were nonregular workers. In 2010 the proportion of non-regular workers among young workers aged fifteen to twenty-four was 45.8 percent; the corresponding figure twenty years ago was 20.2 percent, less than half.[13] Not only attaining work but attaining sustainable work has become difficult for young people as the putative norm of career-long tenure with a stable employer is becoming replaced by a labor force sharply divided between those with and those without regular employment. Given how much value, and pressure, is still placed on having a stable income and job, it is not surprising that young people with blurry prospects for the future have a hard time finding a marriage partner or being willing to marry themselves. The same applies to having children.

Declining Birthrate and Recession

The main driving force behind Japan's rapidly aging population is the continuous decline in the fertility rate, which in 2011 was 1.39, far below the replacement rate of 2.08.[14] When the population as a whole started to decline in 2006, policy makers and business leaders voiced concern about economic growth and social stability in the future. Two factors largely explain the decrease in the total fertility rate: the increasing number of young people who shy away from or postpone marriage and the declining birthrate among married couples, with the latter more important in explaining the decline in the total fertility rate since the mid-1990s. The completed fertility rate for married couples was 1.96 in 2010, down from 2.23 in 2002.[15] The decline was primarily a result of fewer couples having three or more children. There has not been a large increase in the proportion of married couples without children. Only 6.4 percent of couples who have been married for fifteen to nineteen years are childless, a 3 percent increase from 2002, but still insignificant.[16]

The fertility rate has been below the replacement rate for more than thirty years. The so called "1.57 shock" in 1990 was the tipping point when the government took official notice of the problem and began to introduce social policies to support families with young children. The measures included maternity leave and a family-care leave system for caregivers of children or frail family members (1991),[17] as well as the Angel Plan (1994) to make companies and the government (central and local) more involved in child care.[18]

Subsequently, other measures were taken to address the decline in birthrate and marriage rate and to reconcile child rearing with work. The thinking

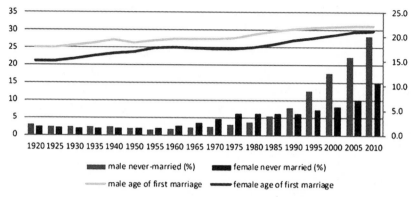

FIGURE 1.1   Trends in the average age of first marriage and the percentage of those who have never been married. (National Institute of Population and Social Security Research, *Population Statistics of Japan 2012* [Tokyo, 2012], 108.)

in these plans also became more complicated and expansive. The new Angel Plan (1999), for example, factored in not only child care outside the home but also the employment system and education as complicit in fertility rates.[19] To date, however, these policies have not yet boosted the total fertility rate. One reason for this is undoubtedly the continuation of instability in the labor system.

Until the mid-1990s, the decline in fertility was explained mostly in terms of the increasing number of unmarried people. Because only 2 percent of children are born out of wedlock in Japan, marriage and childbirth are closely related.[20]

Figure 1.1 shows trends in the average age of first marriage for men and women and changes in the proportion of people who never marry. For both men and women, there is an increased tendency to marry later (if at all). From 1960 to 2010, the average age at first marriage rose by roughly five years for men and six years for women. More recently we have also seen a narrowing of the age gap between husband and wife, roughly halving from a peak of about 3.7 years in 1985 to 1.5 years in 2010. The proportion of people spending their whole life unmarried rose sharply in the 1990s. Until the 1980s more women than men never married, but that pattern was reversed in the late 1980s, and the never-married rate has continued to climb steeply for men ever since. The never-married rate of men was 20.1 percent and that of women was 10.6 percent in 2010.[21] Among the overall population of unmarried men, those in their forties and fifties remain a minority, but this is the fastest-growing demographic.

Family Policies on Child Rearing

By far the most common reason for having fewer children is the excessively high cost of child rearing and education, cited by nearly two-thirds of survey respondents. Having children is simply too expensive, they say. If that is the case, a bold program of cash incentives might well be effective in promoting childbirth. Indeed, in April 2006 the scope of child allowances was extended from preschoolers to cover all children in elementary school as well.[22] In 2007 the monthly payment was increased to ¥10,000 for children under the age of three and the income ceiling was eased.[23]

In Japanese electoral politics there is rarely public discussion of policy. In 2009, however, the Democratic Party of Japan (DPJ) differentiated itself from the long-dominant Liberal Democratic Party (LDP) by promising in its manifesto (platform) to introduce a "universal" family policy for children: a ¥26,000 monthly allowance for every child aged fifteen or younger to all child-rearing families regardless of family income. This addressed the cost of child rearing, was popular with voters, and brought the DPJ to power in August.

The DPJ also raised child poverty as a serious social problem that the LDP had long ignored. The Hatoyama cabinet in 2010 formulated a set of policy goals that shifted the main focus from the decline in fertility to the issue of child welfare.[24] The legislation's three main provisions were the concept of "children first" policies, a shift from emphasis on the birthrate to support of children, child care, and a life/work/child care balance. The DPJ commendably tried to separate child welfare from the population issue and made a universal child allowance—thought to have great public appeal—a core election strategy. However, the party failed to explain sufficiently the basic principle of a child allowance—whether the agenda was to benefit child welfare, reduce the economic burden of child rearing on parents, or encourage adults to have more children. Consequently, there was confusion about the goal of its proposed welfare policy. Was it driven more by concern for child welfare or by concern about Japan's declining fertility? More importantly, the DPJ's failure to provide a workable budget for the plan—an extraordinary lapse by a new ruling party—led to an unfortunate ending. After intense political bargaining with opposition political parties, the DPJ accepted an income cap on allowances and dropped the universal provision. Still, the amended Child Allowance Act of 2012 provided larger allowances for a longer period of time.[25]

The DPJ also overpromised and fumbled the issue of gender equality, a key concept that could reshape the country's demographic destiny. But gender—and its relation to both the economy and demography—is embedded in the division of labor fostered by the sustained burst of economic growth in the 1950s and 1960s.[26] The male breadwinner/female housewife model shored up the social economy.[27] Full-time housewives enabled husbands to work long hours without having to tend to their children.[28] Jane Lewis categorizes societies into three types based on the degree of adoption of the male breadwinner model: (1) a model in which the division of labor is embedded in social systems where the dependency on unpaid work done by married women is quite high, (2) a modified model in which the role of the family in child rearing is partially shared with the government in response to increased labor force participation by married women, and (3) a model in which the government takes the lead in sharing the responsibility to raise children and the society is the least dependent on unpaid work performed primarily by women.[29] Mari Osawa contends that the third model is crucial for gender equality.[30] But in Japan housework, including caring for family members, is performed primarily by married women, whose work pattern remains intermittent despite the increase in the number of women who have attained higher education. The proportion of women in managerial positions is still very small, and the gender wage gap is large when compared with that in Europe and the United States.[31] Although more than a half century has passed since the stage of rapid economic growth, the gender division of labor has not significantly changed. That the fundamental norm of social relations is still based on gender helps to explain why marriage has become a less attractive lifestyle option for young people. And this, in turn, is tied to the income and employment precarity so many face today.

The gendered division of labor has a negative impact on men as well as women, it should be noted. Men are expected to be the breadwinner of the family and to be responsible for its economic well-being. However, in a long-term economic recession, young men find it increasingly difficult to get full-time jobs and are unable to form and support a new family. According to the Japan Life Course Panel Survey conducted by the Institute of Social Sciences, University of Tokyo, young men today are more likely not to marry because of a lack of financial security than was the case in the 1970s and 1980s.[32] Women are more likely to give as their reason for not marrying that they do not want to lose freedom. On the one hand, women who want to pursue a career face discrimination at many levels. On the other, the normative gendered division of labor justifies their expectation that men will perform the conventional role of family breadwinner.

The Third Plan for Gender Equality, approved by the cabinet in December 2010, emphasized women's role in society.[33] As noted here—and elsewhere in this volume by Ayako Kano (chapter 4), and Machiko Osawa and Jeff Kingston (chapter 3)—vitalization of women at work is critical in the smaller labor force in the future (that is, without recourse to immigration as another possible solution). But the intermittent working pattern of women continues mainly because women are forced to choose between employment and raising a family. These normative expectations for engendering marriage, family, and work also result in low fertility rates.

Japan has been characterized as the least favorable work environment for women among industrial countries, as exemplified by the discontinuous work pattern among mothers, the large gendered wage gap, and the very low proportion of women holding managerial positions.[34] Approximately 70 percent of mothers stop working when they give birth to their first child, and their working profiles after that become intermittent. Nearly the same percentage of all married women say mothers should devote themselves to child rearing while their children are young,[35] and the younger generation agrees as well. Meanwhile, the financial contribution of married women to the household is limited, and the strong male breadwinner model of employment established sixty years ago remains in place even though the economic climate has changed entirely. Average working hours in Japan are still very long, and employees in managerial positions work even longer. This pattern, too, dates from the 1950s despite the decline in economic growth.

In the Fourteenth National Fertility Survey conducted by the National Institute of Population and Social Security Research in 2010, a large majority of unmarried men and women declared their intention to get married, although fewer and fewer are actually tying the knot.[36] The number of people who expect to get married within a year varies by employment status, especially among men; full-time workers are more likely to express an intention to marry than those in nonstandard jobs. Men working full-time jobs actively seek a partner and maintain a positive attitude about marriage, while those working part time have fewer opportunities to meet possible partners.[37] For women, by contrast, the difference in work status has far less impact on the desire to marry. Women working full time or part time show a strong desire to get married,[38] reflecting, I speculate, the deep-rooted norm of gendered roles in contemporary Japan: that men should be the breadwinners and women should be supported.

The persistence of this gendered division of labor is closely related to the low fertility rate in Japan. If the decline in fertility were the result of individual choice in fertility behavior and of couples' reluctance to have children, there would not be much we could do about it. However, since a large majority of the younger population say they want to get married and have children, the discrepancy between individuals' intentions and their actual behavior is a serious social problem that, in my view, must be addressed. Individual women are forced to make a choice: stay in the labor force or get married and have children.

An Aging Population and Generational Imbalance

Japan's aging population is one consequence of the striking decline in fertility during the 1950s. This is also linked to social inequality. According to one analysis, the increase in income inequality since the mid-1980s is largely due to aging.[39] As argued by Fumio Ōtake, the higher proportion of elderly households in which income inequality is greater than in younger households leads to the rates of increasing inequality nationwide. The relationship between the increase in income inequality and the aging population is evident when we look at the degree of inequality both between and within age groups.

Figure 1.2 shows the extent of income inequality calculated by mean log deviation (MLD) by the age group of the head of the household. Because the unit of income data is usually the household, the extent of income inequality is calculated on that basis, not that of the individual.[40] The proportional distribution of the household head's age changed from the 1980s to the 2000s.[41] While the pattern of income inequality by age group has not differed greatly in the last two decades, the extent of income inequality among elderly households is larger than that among working middle-age household heads. The increase in income inequality thus correlates with the aging population. However, within the age group of household heads, we see different patterns of change in income inequality. Income inequality among young household heads has become larger since the mid-1980s, while among older household heads, particularly those aged seventy and over, it has declined since 1986. Even so, the recent increase in income inequality is primarily due

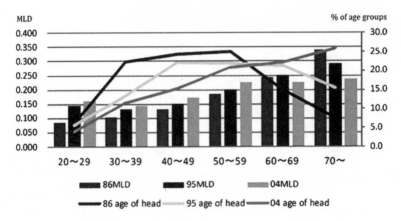

FIGURE 1.2   Trends in income equality (mean log deviation [MLD]) and the age distribution of household heads. (Ministry of Health, Labor, and Welfare, "Comprehensive Survey of People's Living Conditions," 1986, 1995, and 2004.)

to the increased number of older heads of households and not an expansion of income inequality across all age groups. This then may change in the future considering the changes in household. Still, in summary, income inequality is closely related to changes in the demographic structure of the household.

On the other hand, income inequality among elderly households has decreased since the mid-1980s. Why has this happened? The answer lies in household structure and income package. In the mid-1970s, the majority of those aged sixty-five and over were living in three-generation households and 13 percent were living with only their spouse. One-person households were a small minority, accounting for less than 10 percent. In 2010, the proportion of elderly living in three-generation households dropped to less than 20 percent, while the percentage of elderly living in one-person households grew to 23 percent, with couple-only elderly households rising to 30 percent. The majority of elderly households are now either a couple or one person.

Compared with other OECD societies, Japan had the highest degree of income inequality among elderly households in the mid-1980s and the mid-1990s, mainly because of the large difference in economic well-being by the type of household in which the elderly reside.[42] If the elderly co-reside with their younger generation, usually the family of their eldest son, they are economically better off; by contrast, if they live alone, they are most likely to suffer economic hardship. Elderly women living alone showed a very high poverty rate.[43] Depending on whether they live in multigeneration households

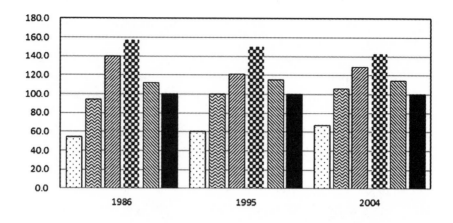

□ one-person ▨ couple-only ▨ parents with unmarried kids ⩫ three-generation ◩ other ■ total

FIGURE 1.3   Income gap by type of household with elderly members (total = 100). (Ministry of Health, Labor, and Welfare, "Comprehensive Survey of People's Living Conditions," 1986, 1995, and 2004.)

or live alone, the economic well-being of the elderly is vastly different. In Europe, where most elderly live with their spouse or alone, the difference between household types is not as large as in Japan.

However, the household structure for the elderly in Japan has become more similar to the European pattern than it used to be, and the difference in economic well-being by household type is not as large as before. To determine the extent to which differences in economic well-being based on household structure explain income inequality among households, I compare here the medium equivalent income of households by type among those with elderly members. Figure 1.3 shows the differences in median equivalent disposable income of households with elderly members in the mid-1980s, mid-1990s, and mid-2000s. The level of economic well-being among elderly one-person households used to be extremely low, and the difference between them and those in three-generation households was largely responsible for income inequality among households with the elderly. The narrowing of the gap between types correlates with the decline in income inequality among the elderly. Whether the elderly live alone or with their offspring, there is less disparity than before.

The improvement in the average economic level of the elderly living alone reflects higher benefits provided under the public pension system. The 1985 pension reform guaranteed similar basic pensions to men and women, raising the economic level of female one-person households. In looking at the distribution of public pensions among elderly one-person households (figure 1.4A), we found that in the mid-1980s more than 60 percent earned less than ¥800,000 per year. In the mid-2000s the corresponding figure was less than 30 percent, while those who received more than ¥2,000,000 increased from 6 percent in 1986 to 23 percent in 2004. The income package for elderly couple-only households (figure 1.4B) shows that in 1986 about one-third received less than ¥800,000 but that about twenty years later the corresponding figure had dropped to less than 10 percent and that about 20 percent—ten times higher than in 1986—received a public pension of more than ¥3,600,000.[44] Improvement in the public pension system contributed to raising the income of the elderly, particularly those who live alone.[45]Although the poverty rate of widowed pensioners living alone remains very high (48.6 percent in 2004), the 1985 pension reform gave women the right to receive basic pension benefits regardless of their marital status).[46]

We have confirmed the improvement in the economic well-being of the elderly, particularly those living in one-person households. On the other hand, the financial situation among young households has declined compared to their parents' generation largely because of the increase in unemployment and nonregular employment among youth. Furthermore, as noted above, because the number of young households has declined because of delayed marriage, the impact on overall income inequality appears limited. Young people cannot afford to leave home to form new families and are likely to be hidden behind their parents' household in assessments of their economic well-being. In fact, the majority of unmarried young people live with their parents and must rely on their family as a shelter from economic hardship.[47] The intergenerational gap in economic well-being is also hidden behind the micro-level relationship within the household.

Before turning to the future, let's review the demographic pattern in Japan since World War II. At the macro level, the population aged and the household structure changed in response to people's way of life—when they got married, when they had children, and how they lived in their later years. Income inequality increased from the mid-1980s as the population grew older (more precisely, heads of households got older). Income inequality among elderly households is relatively larger than that among middle-aged households; the higher the proportion of older households, the higher the degree

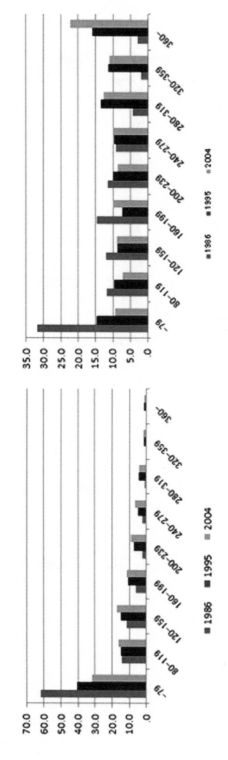

FIGURE 1.4A Distribution of public pensions among the elderly living alone (¥10,000). (Ministry of Health, Labor, and Welfare, "Comprehensive Survey of People's Living Conditions," 1986, 1995, and 2004.)

FIGURE 1.4B Distribution of public pensions among the elderly living with a spouse (¥10,000). (Ministry of Health, Labor, and Welfare, "Comprehensive Survey of People's Living Conditions," 1986, 1995, and 2004.)

of income inequality. Income inequality has risen among young households, but they carry less weight in the age structure, and this has less impact at the macro level. The decline in the number of young households echoes the continuous drop in the fertility rate as young people postpone marriage and stay with their parents. The intergenerational relationship at the micro level, particularly within the household/family, appears to be more important in supporting not only the elderly who used to be taken care of through multi-generational coresidence but also young people who have difficulty obtaining economic security and future prospects. How to prepare for the old-old age of the current elderly as well as the soon-to-be-elderly who are less secure economically after retirement is an urgent issue for Japan.

The lifestyle Japanese can expect today and anticipate for tomorrow is completely different from what it was fifty years ago. Young people can no longer count on a stable full-time job upon graduation from school and incremental pay increases throughout a career. The number of unemployed who cannot make the mandatory social security insurance payments has increased, as has the number of elderly retirees who need benefits. Five decades ago, no one predicted either a huge aging population or a long economic recession. Outdated assumptions about society and the social welfare system must be drastically revised—as the public is coming to recognize.

Population Projection: Japan's Possible Futures?

Let's consider what the future will look like if the current situation does not dramatically change. In January 2012 the National Institute of Population and Social Security Research announced the latest population projection based on the 2010 Japan Census.[48] Projections usually combine assumptions about mortality, fertility, and international immigration. Their main purpose is not quite to predict the future but to project it on the basis of present circumstances. In other words, they show the demographic outlook on the basis of the situation where the social welfare system or the fundamental concepts governing the social system, including social security, remain as they are now. Figure 1.5 presents the latest projection of Japanese population based on a medium-range estimation of fertility and mortality.

The population of Japan in 2010 was 128.06 million.[49] In twenty years from 2010 it will be 116.22 million, in 2048 less than 100 million, and in 2060 86

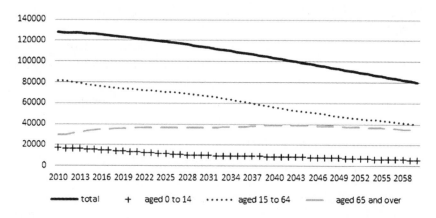

FIGURE 1.5 Population projection from 2010 (1,000 persons). (National Institute of Population and Social Security Research, *Population Projection of Japan 2012* [Tokyo, 2012], 15.)

million. If we look at the population structure of those aged 0 to 14, this number started to decrease in the 1980s, dropped to 16.87 million in 2010, and will be 7.91 million by 2060 (figure 1.5). The elderly numbered 29.48 million in 2010 and will increase to 34.64 million by 2060. The proportion of the elderly, 23 percent in 2010, will be 39.9 percent in 2060. Almost one out of every 2.5 persons will be in the elderly age group[50]—a fact that has been much played up in media coverage, which has stressed the increased burden on the working-age population. In the future one working-age person will need to support one elderly person; in the past, four working-age people supported each elderly person. Along with a rise in the proportion of the elderly, the size of the population began to drop in 2008. A smaller population in itself is not necessarily a calamity for Japan given its relatively small land area; more space per capita could be beneficial. The real problem is the imbalance in population structure.

The decrease in overall population size and the skewing of the older generation are occurring simultaneously, but not uniformly across Japan; depopulation varies greatly in speed and extent by region. The population projection, based on the 2005 census data, shows the outlook by prefecture.[51] Population size started to decline in thirty-two prefectures from 2000 to 2010 and will be under way in all forty-six prefectures by 2015. According to a 2008 population projection by municipality, municipalities with a population of less than five thousand will increase to 20.4 percent in 2035 from 12.4 percent in 2005.

Although the population will decline quickly in rural areas, the decrease will be relatively small in the Tokyo area and larger cities.

The very high proportion of the elderly in a shrinking population presents a particular demographic dilemma. It took twenty-four years to bring the proportion of the elderly in Japan from 7 percent up to 14 percent, which is less than a fifth the time—124 years—it took in France for the elderly population to reach the same proportion. The tremendous speed of change in the population calls for fundamental reforms of the social welfare system, especially social security. As noted above, during the period of rapid economic growth there were relatively large numbers of young people paying into the system and a small number of the elderly who were expected to receive benefits. Economic growth kept unemployment low, and the relatively small size of the elderly population compared with the large number of people working—the population bonus—kept the system in balance.

However, we are now in very different socioeconomic circumstances from fifty years ago. Facing a new demographic era demands new strategies and orientations. One option is immigration.

The Revolving Door: Immigration Policy in Japan

In 2010 there were 2.13 million foreigners registered in Japan, almost double the number twenty years earlier, yet their percentage of the total population was only 1.67 percent.[52] The great majority (674,879) of registered foreigners were Chinese. The other major distinct alien groups were Koreans (545,401), Brazilians (210,032), and Filipinos (209,376). The number of permanent foreign residents (out of total registered foreigners) was 565,089, which was 26.5 percent, a very low figure compared to other developed countries. Unlike the United States, for example, Japan is not an immigrant society and has a long history of resisting immigration and serious discussion of immigrants and foreign workers. This has changed recently, prompted by demographic necessity.

From after World War II to the 1980s, the Justice Ministry's policy toward immigration was designed to maintain an ethnically homogeneous society and rigorous control of those foreigners allowed in the country, thereby preventing illegal entrants. For example, Koreans born on Japanese soil were pressured to leave or to assimilate by renouncing their nationality and identity. Eventually most Koreans were given the status of Special Permanent

Resident, and, over time, an uneasy accommodation was reached. In general, foreign migration has been related to labor shortages. For example, during the speculative bubble from 1986 to 1992 the number of foreigners in Japan almost doubled, from 2,021,450 to 3,926,347.[53]

In the first national employment plan (1967), the government declared that Japan would not rely on foreign workers during the era of rapid economic growth. Former minister of labor Takashi Hayakawa claimed there was no compelling necessity for foreign workers because the Japanese labor market was distinct—unlike Europe and the United States—and, more importantly, because employment opportunities had to be preserved for middle-aged and older Japanese.[54] The second (1973) and third (1976) basic employment plans adhered to the same policy. In the early 1980s, after two decades of dynamic economic development, when a labor shortage loomed and industry wanted inexpensive unskilled workers (more Japanese youth were seeking higher education), the government started to consider foreign workers.[55] The relatively high standard of living and wages in Japan attracted job seekers from abroad. The immigration control policy was changed, first by encouraging ethnic repatriates, migrants from Brazil and Peru who were the descendants of Japanese immigrants. Attracted by assurances of permanent residence in the "homeland," by 1990 a total of 59,371 Brazilians and Peruvians were living in Japan.[56]

All other foreign workers were admitted on the basis of a short-term employment contract and were expected to return home when it ended. Japan's projection of an image of a overcrowded country uninterested in multiculturalism dissuaded many would-be migrants. But the number of unskilled alien workers increased in the 1990s as "ethnic repatriates (front door), trainees (side door) and irregulars (back door)" entered the country.[57]

The Commission on Japan's Goals in the Twenty-First Century, under the initiative of the late prime minister Keizō Obuchi, issued the first progressive report on immigration in 2000. Entitled "The Frontier Within: Individual Empowerment and Better Governance in the New Millennium," the report endorsed favorable treatment of foreign immigrants.[58] Ethnic diversity would enhance social vitality and enable Japan to survive international competition, the report said. But who were appropriate immigrants? The commission wanted highly qualified foreigners who could contribute to Japan's next stage of development. Japan's explicit "immigration and permanent residence system" had a double standard: receptive to highly qualified professionals and resistant to low-skilled workers. Unfortunately, debate on this report was halted by Obuchi's untimely death.

Nevertheless, attitudes changed at the Justice Ministry regarding some long-term alien residents and their contribution to Japanese society. Officials encouraged many to apply for permanent residence—equivalent to a green card in the United States—a proactive solicitation unthinkable a few years earlier. Permission to stay in Japan was no longer tied to an employer; well-to-do aliens could consider spending a lifetime in Japan. In 2010, 565,089 foreigners had permanent resident status.[59]

At the same time, to keep a sizable pool of unskilled foreign labor in Japan the Justice Ministry looked the other way at employed illegal aliens (mainly visa overstayers), who reportedly numbered about three hundred thousand in 2010, and flawed official trainee programs (exploitation and abuses led to highly publicized incidents). But the global financial crisis triggered unemployment among aliens and Japanese alike. Now a liability, the newcomers from Brazil and Peru were offered one-way tickets "home," and the combined total of ethnic repatriates fell 91,660 in three years.[60] In early 2012 the Ministry of Justice announced a new program of preferential treatment for "highly skilled foreign professionals" that offers a fast track to permanent residence. Although the ministry cites population decline, the low birthrate, and the aging population as a rationale, the program reportedly has a modest target figure of two thousand.[61] To sustain the working-age population, Japan (without taking other measures such as increasing female employment or raising the retirement age) would have to admit almost four hundred thousand replacement migrants annually until 2050.[62] Opponents often charge that an inflow on that scale would affect cultural values and alter Japan's national identity. And immigration of this magnitude is clearly untenable unless the country embraces ethnic diversity and multiculturalism.

There has been no serious debate in Japan about immigrants and immigration because of the widespread antipathy still held against living with large numbers of non-Japanese and constructing a "Japanese" society of people from various ethnic backgrounds. This antipathy against immigration/multiculturalism held by Japanese is reflected in public policy. Yasuyuki Kitawaki claims that there is no comprehensive policy that encompasses the whole process of immigration: entry, short-term stay, long-term residency, permanent residency, and naturalization. And devising such a policy is an obvious first step,[63] not merely toward controlling immigrants—what Japan has long had in the way of policies—but toward integrating immigrants into the society and building, with them, a new kind of social entity. This, in my view, is what Japan desperately needs. The inability of the country, and its citizens, to yet do that stems, in part, from the disconnect between the perception and reality of immigrants in Japan, and the woeful ignorance of so many Japanese regarding how immigrants live, work, and survive.[64]

A Blended Society and Demographic Destiny

Japan faces possible futures with demography as destiny—an aged population and a low birthrate—unless the fundamental social system, including social norms, can substantially change. Yet there is widespread resistance to the kinds of changes, such as greater social heterogeneity, that are required. Although foreign workers contribute to Japanese society, for example, they are not seriously regarded as part of Japan's future (or present), and the same is true of unconventional groups like one-parent families and people who never marry. The recent increase in income inequality among young households with small children is closely related to unconventional lifestyles.[65]

The family, as the basic unit of society, has provided economic security in Japan, and the welfare state has been largely implemented through it. However, the increase of both people who never marry and marriages that end in divorce raises the question of how well the conventional family framework accords with contemporary Japan. As Anne Allison points out in chapter 2 of this volume, we can no longer expect the family to play the same role that it did in the past.

Getting divorced, becoming a single mother, marrying a foreigner, and being a foreigner have all been stigmatized in Japan. Yet it is essential, in my view, to adopt new arrangements—for belonging, residing, laboring, and reproducing—in Japan that will tolerate, and actively promote, an increasing number of persons with varied ethnic backgrounds as well as different types of families.

One possible future of Japan is a blended society. Japanese used to think of themselves as culturally "unique," distinct from advanced Western capitalist societies, as well as ethnically and socioeconomically homogeneous. Today, Japan shares social problems such as inequality and poverty with Europe and North America, and the population is becoming more diverse. Immigration will be the next urgent social issue: how to treat foreigners not just in utilitarian terms of filling labor or demographic shortages, but in terms of integrating them into Japanese society. Merely admitting people from different cultures into a preexisting national mix, the strategy of multiculturalism, will not suffice. To build a blended society (that is, a society not only ethnically but socially, and in multiple other ways, diverse) we need to reshape the country's common culture into one that makes acceptance of difference a core value.

There is much work to be done if Japan is to navigate its demographic "destiny." We cannot avoid this demographic destination totally or perhaps even change it dramatically. But we can change, I believe, our socioeconomic orientation in significant ways to better accommodate the high proportion of elderly and a low birthrate for future generations.

Notes

1. The research for this chapter was supported by Grant 25000001 from the Japan Society for the Promotion of Science. I want to thank Anne Allison and Frank Baldwin for their help.

2. National Institute of Population and Social Security Research, *Latest Demographic Statistics 2013* (Tokyo: National Institute of Population and Social Security Research, 2013), 30.

3. Kazuo Okochi, Bernard Karsh, and Solomon B. Levine, eds., *Workers and Employers in Japan: The Japanese Employment Relations System* (Tokyo: University of Tokyo Press, 1993).

4. Keizai Shingichō, *Sengo no kokumin shotoku* [Economic survey of Japan], no. 1 (Tokyo: Gakuyo Shobo, 1953).

5. Malcolm Sawyer, *Income Distribution in OECD Countries* (Paris: OECD, 1976).

6. In fact, according to the Public Opinion Survey on People's Lives (Kokumin seikatsu ni kansuru yoron chōsa) conducted by the Cabinet Office of Japan, about 90 percent of respondents claimed in 1970 that they were situated in the middle strata; "Kokumin sekatsu ni kansuru yoron chōsa" [Public opinion survey concerning people's lifestyles], 1970, http://survey.gov-online.go.jp/index-ko.html.

7. Yasusuke Murakami, *Shin-chūkan taishū no jidai: Sengo nihon no kaibōgaku* [The new middle-mass society: The anatomy of postwar Japan] (Tokyo: Chūō Kōronsha, 1984).

8. See Toshiki Satō, *Fubyōdo shakai nihon: Sayōnara sochūryū* [Unequal Japan: Farewell to the middle-mass society] (Tokyo: Chūō Kōron Shinsha, 2000); Toshiaki Tachibanaki, *Nihon no keizai kakusa: Shotoku to shisan kara kangaeru* [Economic inequality in Japan: An analysis of income and assets] (Tokyo: Iwanami Shoten, 1998).

9. Hiroshi Ishida, "Shakai idō kara mita kakusa no jittai" [Social inequality and social mobility], in *Nihon no shotoku bunpai to kakusa* [Income disparity and distribution in Japan], ed. Takashi Miyajima (Tokyo: Tōyō Keizai Shinpō Sha, 2002).

10. Kazuo Seiyama, "*Kaisō saiseisan no shinwa*" [The myths of status reproduction], in *Nihon no shotoku kakusa to shakai kaisō* [Income differentials and social stratification in Japan], ed. Y. Higuchi (Tokyo: Nihon Hyōronsha, 2000), 85–103.

11. Tsuneo Ishikawa, *Shotoku to tomi* [Income and wealth] (Tokyo: Iwanami Shoten, 1991); Tsuneo Ishikawa, *Nihon no shotoku to tomi no bunpai* [Income and wealth distribution in Japan] (Tokyo: University of Tokyo Press, 1994).

12. Japan, Ministry of Internal Affairs and Communications, "Rōdōryoku chōsa nempō 2011" [Annual labor survey, 2011], 2012, www.stat.go.jp/data/roudou/report/2011/index.htm.

13. Japan, Ministry of Internal Affairs and Communications, "Rōdōryoku chōsa shōsai shūkei 2010" [Detailed results of labor survey, 2010], www.stat.go.jp/data/roudou/rireki/nen/dt/pdf/2010.pdf.

14. Japan, Ministry of Health, Labor, and Welfare [hereafter MHLW], "2011 Jinkō dōtai tōkei (kakuteisū) no gaikyō" [Basic results of statistics 2011], 2012, www.mhlw.go.jp/toukei/saikin/hw/jinkou/kakutei11/dl/00_all.pdf.

15. The completed fertility rate is calculated from the number of children born to couples who have been married for fifteen to nineteen years.

16. National Institute of Population and Social Security Research, "Fourteenth National Fertility Survey," 2011, www.ipss.go.jp/ps-doukou/j/doukou14/doukou14.asp.

17. MHLW, Act on the Welfare of Workers Who Take Care of Children or Other Family Members Including Child Care and Family Care Leave, 1991, http://law.e-gov.go.jp/htmldata/H03/H03HO076.html.

18. MHLW, "Kongo no kosodate shien no tame no shisaku no kihonteki hōkō ni tsuite" [Support of child rearing for the future], 1994, www.mhlw.go.jp/bunya/kodomo/angelplan.html.

19. MHLW, "Shin enzeru puran ni tsuite" [The new Angel Plan], 1999, http://www1.mhlw.go.jp/topics/syousika/tp0816-3_18.html.

20. National Institute of Population and Social Security Research, "2014 Population Statistics," 2014, www.ipss.go.jp/syoushika/tohkei/Popular/Popular2014. asp?chap=0, table 4-18.

21. The never-married rate is the percentage of those who have never been married at the age of fifty.

22. National Institute of Population and Social Security Research, "2012 Population Statistics," 2012, www.ipss.go.jp/syoushika/tohkei/Popular/Popular2012. asp?chap=0, table 6-23.

23. MHLW, "2007 Jidōteate seisaku gaiyō" [Child allowance policy 2007], 2007, www. mhlw.go.jp/bunya/kodomo/jidou-teate.html.

24. Japan, Cabinet Office, *Kodomo, kosodateno bision: Kodomo no egao ga afureru shakai no tame ni* [Child rearing: A society of smiling children], 2010, http://www8.cao. go.jp/shoushi/vision/pdf/honbun.pdf.

25. The universal child allowance was replaced in 2013 by an allowance with income restrictions. The income cutoff to receive the child allowance is ¥9.6 million before taxes.

26. Chizuko Ueno, *Kafuchōsei to Shihonsei: Marukusu Shugi Feminizumu no Chihei* [Patriarchy and capitalism: Marxist feminism] (Tokyo: Iwanami Shoten, 1990).

27. Mari Osawa, *Kigyō Chūshin Shakai o Koete* [Beyond the firm-oriented society] (Tokyo: Jiji Press, 1993).

28. Emiko Ochiai, *21-seiki Kazoku e* [The twenty-first-century Japanese family] (Tokyo: Yūhikaku, 1994).

29. Jane Lewis, "Gender and Welfare Regimes," *Journal of European Social Policy* 2, no. 3 (1992): 59–171.

30. Mari Osawa, *Gendai nihon no seikatsu hoshō shisutemu* [The contemporary Japanese livelihood security system] (Tokyo: Iwanami Shoten, 2007).

31. Sawako Shirahase, *Social Inequality in Japan* (London: Routledge, 2013).

32. Sawako Shirahase, *Ikikatano fubyōdō: Otagaisama no shakai ni mukete* [Inequalities in life courses: Seeking a mutually supportive society] (Tokyo: Iwanami Shoten, 2010).

33. The plan is available at the Gender Equality Bureau, "The third basic plan for gender equality," 2010, www.gender.go.jp/kihon-keikaku/3rd/index.html. For the English version, see www.gender.go.jp/english_contents/category/pub/whitepaper/pdf/3rd_bpg.pdf.

34. OECD, *Closing the Gender Gap: Act Now* (Paris: OECD Publishing, 2012), http://europedirect.pde.gov.gr/images/pubs/Closing-the-gender-gap.pdf.

35. National Institute of Population and Social Security Research, *Fourth National Family Survey*, 2008, www.ipss.go.jp/ps-katei/j/NSFJ4/NSFJ4_yoshi.pdf.

36. National Institute of Population and Social Security Research, *Fourteenth National Fertility Survey*, 2011, www.ipss.go.jp/ps-doukou/j/doukou14_s/point14_s.pdf.

37. Hiroshi Ishida et al., "Daily Lives, Dating, and the Understanding of the Rights of Workers: The Results of the Japanese Life Course Panel Survey (JLPS) 2009," University of Tokyo, Institute of Social Sciences, Panel Survey, Discussion Paper Series 30, 2009, http://ssjda.iss.u-tokyo.ac.jp/panel/dp/PanelDP_030Ishida.pdf.

38. Hiroshi Ishida et al., "Inequality, Marriage and Social Security: The Results of the Japanese Life Course Panel Survey (JLPS) 2011," University of Tokyo, Institute of Social Sciences, Panel Survey, Discussion Paper Series 53, 2012, http://ssjda.iss.u-tokyo.ac.jp/panel/dp/PanelDP_053Ishida.pdf.

39. Fumio Ōtake, "1980-nendai no shotoku/shisan bunpai" [Income and wealth distribution in the 1980s], *Kikan Riron Keizaigaku* 45, no. 5 (1994): 385–402.

40. If an elderly woman lives with her son's family and he is head of the household, she is indirectly counted in his household. In this section, I examine income inequality on the basis of the household head.

41. The data analyzed here are from the Comprehensive Survey of People's Living Conditions, conducted by the MHLW in 1986, 1995, and 2004. We examine inequality, following the OECD method, through disposable income, which is derived by subtracting the direct tax and social insurance from the total household income and dividing it by the square root of the number of household members in order to take into account the household size.

42. Sawako Shirahase, "Nihon no shotoku kakusa to kōreisha setai: Kokusai hikaku no kanten kara" [Income inequality and households with elderly members: A cross-national comparison], *Japan Labor Research Journal* 500 (2002): 72–85; Shirahase, *Social Inequality in Japan*.

43. Sawako Shirahase, "Kōrei-ki o hitori de kurasu to iukoto" [Living alone in later life], *Kikan Riron Keizaigaku* 41, no. 2 (2005): 111–21.

44. The consumer price index (2010 base year) was 88.4 in 1985, 101.2 in 1994, and 100.7 in 2003, according to Japan Bureau of Statistics, "Outline of the 2010-Base Consumer Price Index," www.stat.go.jp/english/data/cpi/pdf/2010base.pdf. The MHLW's "Comprehensive Survey of People's Living Conditions" (1986, 1995, 2004) gives income for the year just previous to the survey year.

45. We cannot overlook the high risk of economic hardship for elderly one-person households, even if the poverty rate declines. The median equivalent disposable income of elderly people living alone is less than 70 percent that of total households.

46. Atsushi Seike and Atsutoshi Yamada, *Kōreisha shūgyō no keizaigaku* [The economics of elderly employment] (Tokyo: Nihon Keizai Shinbun Sha, 2004). Before 1985,

when a couple divorced the husband received the pension; there was no way for the wife to be economically secure in later life.

47. Shirahase, *Social Inequality in Japan.*

48. The latest population projection is available at "Nihon no shōrai suikei jinko" [Population projection for Japan], www.ipss.go.jp/syoushika/tohkei/newest04/sh2401top.html (accessed January 30, 2012).

49. The primary results of the 2010 Census of Japan are presented at www.stat.go.jp/data/kokusei/2010/kihon1/pdf/youyaku.pdf.

50. This projection is primarily based on birth and mortality data with no significant change in the immigrant factor. However, as the economy becomes globalized, the number of foreign workers and immigrants will increase. The figure for fifty years hence will have to be revised to some extent.

51. National Institute of Population and Social Security Research, *Nihon no shōrai suikei jinkō* [Population projection for Japan], 2012, www.ipss.go.jp/pp-fuken/j/fuken2012/gaiyo.pdf.

52. Ministry of Justice, "Tōroku gaikokujin tōkei tōkeihyō" [Statistics for registered foreigners], 2011, www.moj.go.jp/housei/toukei/toukei_ichiran_touroku.html.

53. Hiroshi Murashita, *Gaikokujin rōdōsha mondai no seisaku to hō* [Foreign workers: Law and policy] (Osaka: Osaka University of Economics and Law Press, 1999).

54. Hiromasa Mori, "Nihon ni okeru gaikokujin rōdōsha mondai no kenkyū dōkō" [Foreign workers in Japan], *Journal of Ohara Institute for Social Research* 528 (2002): 31–41.

55. Takao Shimizu, "Gaikokujin seisaku no hensen to kakushu teigen" [Proposals regarding foreigners in Japan], in *Sōgō chōsa, jinkō-genshō shakai no mondai* (Tokyo: Kokuritsu Kokkai Toshokan), 1–25.

56. Tsukasa Sasai and Akira Ishikawa, "Japan's International Migration and Its Impacts on Population on Projections for Japan," *Journal of Population Problems* 64, no. 4 (2008): 1–18.

57. Atsushi Kondo, *Citizenship in a Global World: Comparing Citizenship Rights for Aliens* (London: Palgrave Macmillan, 2001).

58. Prime Minister's Commission on Japan's Goals in the Twenty-First Century, "The Frontier Within: Individual Empowerment and Better Governance in the New Millennium," 2000, www.kantei.go.jp/jp/21century/report/htmls/index.html.

59. Ministry of Justice, *Tōroku gaikokujin tōkei* [Statistics of registered foreigners], 2011, 16, www.moj.go.jp/content/000078095.pdf.

60. Takashi Yamazaki, "Gaikokujin rōdōsha no shūrō/koyō/shakai hoshō no genjō to kadai" [Foreign workers: Jobs, employment, and social security], *Refarensu* 10 (2006): 18–43.

61. MHLW, *Pointo seido shikō ni tomonau gaikokujin koyō jōkyō todokede ni tsuite* [A point system for foreign workers], 2012, www.mhlw.go.jp/bunya/koyou/gaikoku-jin-koyou/dl/g120424.pdf. By comparison, the US Diversity Visa Program authorizes fifty thousand permanent resident visas per year. "Instructions for the 2014 Diversity Immigrant Visa Program (DV-2014)," 2014, http://travel.state.gov/content/dam/visas/DV_2014_Instructions.pdf.

62. Robert Dekle, "Financing Consumption in an Aging Japan: The Role of Foreign Capital Inflows and Immigration," *Journal of Japanese and International Economies* 18 (2004): 506–27.

63. Yasuyuki Kitawaki, "Nihon no gaikokujin seisaku" [The lives of foreigners in Japan], *Tagengo Tabunka: Jissen to Kenkyū* 1, no. 3 (2008): 5–25.

64. Kondo, *Citizenship in a Global World*.

65. Shirahase, *Ikikatano fubyōdō*. See also Aya Ezawa and Chisa Fujiwara, "Lone Mothers and Welfare-to-Work Policies in Japan and the United States: Towards an Alternative Perspective," *Journal of Sociology and Social Welfare* 32, no. 4 (2005): 41–63; Aya Abe, *Kodomo no Hinkon* [Children's poverty] (Tokyo: Iwanami Shoten, 2008).

CHAPTER TWO

Precarity and Hope: Social Connectedness in Postcapitalist Japan

Anne Allison

Postwar Japan was a nation-state of high economic growth, sustained productivity, and global acclaim as a postindustrial power. In this era of "Toyota-
ism," quality circles and just-in-time production method lent Japanese firms
a competitive edge across the globe. At home, core workers were flexibly
utilized, and, hired more to the firm than to any particular job, they stayed
long term. Under what was called the "Japanese management style," durability—continuity and security over time—became the normative ideal. Such a
notion of work was part of "lean production" or, more accurately, "lean and
dual":[1] a system that gave core workers (mainly men) lifelong jobs but also
profited from the expendability and low wages given a peripheral labor force
of women and contracted male workers.

Postwar Japan is sometimes nicknamed "Japan Inc." for government-busi-
ness collusion and the corporatization of its social ideology of attaching to a
workplace/company until retirement. Even though not all male workers ever
received lifetime employment, this was the normative model—giving one's
all to a company in a relationship that extended long term and expanded to
more than just a job. Working in the present then was a project about the
future: about staying connected, advancing slowly, building security. But
this long-range work plan also demanded total commitment in the here and
now. Gendered as the male role par excellence, worker-bee men absented
themselves from home where women—hard at work raising the next generation—provided an important role in the social factory of economic productivity. Everyone worked hard in the present for a future both promised and

deferred: women at home, men at work, and children commuting between school and cram-school.

The family-corporate system, along with its logics of time and security, is disintegrating in post-Bubble Japan, as I will lay out in this chapter. My argument is that both the genesis and the degeneration of this system have shaped the very specific form of precarity experienced by Japan/ese today as well as how hope is conceptualized (or not) for the future. This system that socialized people into wanting and expecting a certain stability in everyday life whose reference point was the future—a futurity reproduced out of present productivity (at home, school, and work)—lingers as a lost fantasy for many today. This is a longing for what is not—stable, secure, possible for themselves or their country for the future. But the postwar system of entwining family with work had an underside as well: it skewed everyday life so much toward productivity that little time was left (even at home) for people to take care of one another. The emergence of loneliness, isolation, and disconnectedness characterizes twenty-first-century "de-social Japan" (or "the relationless society"—a term that has gained great salience recently in Japan) and yet these desocialities have been more exposed than caused by the economic precaritization starting in the 1990s. In this sense, the slowing down of the economy presents an opportunity for people to reassess their values and rhythms of social life. Until the crisis of the Great East Japan Earthquake and tsunami and the associated nuclear accident, however, hopefulness about the chance to remake social priorities was not a common reaction to the times. Yet 3/11 has shocked Japanese into reassessing the values of life and the necessity of working "together" to overcome the recent disaster. What such efforts—of volunteerism, mutual support, antinuclear protests—suggest for the possibilities of future socialities will be taken up at the end of this chapter.

The Postwar Period: Rapid Economic Growth, Corporate Familism, "My-Homeism"

It was after its defeat in the Second World War that Japan replaced empire building overseas with an economy of rapid growth and material prosperity at home. Rebuilding itself as an industrial producer of high-tech manufacturing, Japan succeeded in becoming a world economic power by the 1970s. The state organization of its "enterprise society" around the three pillars of family, corporation, and school was supplemented and enforced by the mass consumer culture emerging at the same time. This system not only boosted Japan's economy as an industrial producer (and an economic power) but also supplied Japan's middle class with secure jobs, steady incomes, and high-priced consumer lifestyles. Indeed, by the end of the 1970s, a vast majority of citizens self-identified as middle class, even though, as pointed out by Sawako Shirahase in the previous chapter, the reality was far more uneven, with greater socioeconomic inequality across the country than commonly acknowledged. Still, there was a vision of a good life shared by a great many people. A designation closely linked to a heteronormative and increasingly nuclearized family, the good life was defined in large part by familial roles. This meant, for a man, providing for family; for a woman, raising children and running the home; and for a child, excelling academically and acquiring a job and family of one's own as an adult.

In the buildup of corporate capitalism, the family also boosted consumption because it was the site of a new kind of home: a privatized, domestic space filled with consumer electronics—washing machines, electric fans, and a family car parked outside.[2] Called "my-homeism," this arrangement operated as at once a consumer dream and a social contract—what people came to desire and what they received in return for working hard. It also operated according to strict gender roles: the financial running of the household depended on the man's wage while the domestic management of its every-dayness fell to the woman. The enterprise society ran similarly on gender performance: core workers were hired for the long term, and their tenure was rewarded with calibrated salary increases intended to support the families they were (supposed to be) having. This meant that core workers, given a "family wage," were primarily men. This also meant that corporate capital-ism, intertwined with the family, constituted a "family corporate system" that benefited from the pool of cheap labor provided by women—confined, when they did work, to low-paid, mainly part-time jobs.[3]

The feeling of moving forward and progressively improving (as a nation, a family, an individual) infused the national ethos and hopes of the times. Certainly, not everyone had a job with lifelong employment or was married to someone who did; no more than about 30 percent of working men had these mainly white-collar positions in middle- to large-sized corporations. Yet by 1970 75 percent of household heads identified as *sararīman*: a term meaning "salaried worker" that underscores the ideological centrality of the middle-class, heterosexual citizen-worker in postwar Japan.[4] These jobs in or close to corporate Japan signaled a sense of accomplishment and identification even with the state. A salaryman didn't work for Toyota, he *belonged* to Toyota. And belonging gave the male worker his (social) place; having a job became his identity and affiliation that also consumed ever more of his actual life.

The family corporate system linked a particular structure of work to one of family and home, operating on a principle of "reproductive futurism." At the heart of the modern polity, this is the notion that hard work today yields a better tomorrow: the modernist belief in progress staked on "the child as the obligatory token of futurity."[5] In postwar Japan, this was corporate familism operating as blueprint for the nation-state—economic productivity driving (and driven by) (re)productivity at home. Such an ideology undergirds those in the normative center but consigns those who fail to measure up to the social dustbin. When the child embodies the telos of the social order and the very logic "within which the political itself must be thought," the failure to (re)produce gets read as being doomed to "no future."[6] The prospect of no futurity for a shrinking nation-state will have resonance later when we consider how the complicity of family and corporation has imploded in recent times in such precarious forms as social withdrawal (*hikikomori*): youth who, failing to be (re)productive outside the home, withdraw into solitary existences that would seem the ultimate perversion of Japan, Inc. In the case of a withdrawn offspring, the home has failed to produce a productive child who—by becoming a salaryman or "education mama" (mother who ensures that her children study hard and achieve high academic performance)—takes part in the national contract of economic growth. The specter of "no future" for Japan provokes anxiety, some of which is intentionally and ideologically provoked.

When it worked, though, the family-corporate system drove the social economy. It accompanied Japan's rapid urbanization and postindustrialization in the second half of the twentieth century. With the demand for a highly educated workforce, child raising revolved around fewer children and schooling them well. The 1955 family size of five members declined to 3.19 by 1987 (foreshadowing the even lower birthrate of today), and the extended family became a nuclear one (60.5 percent of households in 1987). Division of labor was gendered: breadwinner male and caregiver female. Men worked and brought home the paycheck. Women, in turn, stayed home and managed children and house—their "reproductive bargain."[7] Though the number of working women increased over time (and by 1989 more wives of white-collar workers were working than not), it was typically in part-time jobs, particularly after women had resumed work subsequent to leaving it at childbirth or marriage—a practice that 80 percent of Japanese women still follow today upon having a child.[8]

In the form it developed following the Second World War, the family not only embedded socioeconomic relations but served as the "hidden capital of the Japanese economy."[9] It was family (along with the corporation) that became the basis of Japan's welfare society, assuming this responsibility so the state could cut back on welfare spending.[10] It was family that modeled, and sustained, Japan's emerging enterprise society—work relations that were family-like and allowed men to work uncommonly long hours (making them virtually nonexistent at home).[11] And it was family that also yielded a source of cheap labor in the form of married women, who, when returning to the workforce while raising children, did so in low-paid jobs—a peripheral and locally bred labor force performing the low-status work largely assumed by foreign migrants in other industrialized countries. In all three ways—in terms of Japanese welfare, Japanese management style, and a peripheral labor force—the family constituted an important asset to the postwar capitalistic state.

Dependency, performance, and affect melded in a very particular architecture in these "Japanese" relationships of nestled (family/corporate) belonging. Men worked at companies ideally for life, entering a bond whose responsibilities bled beyond work to the personal and everyday. A company man would devote not only long hours to work but also evenings, weekends, and vacations to "leisure" (drinking, golf) spent in the company of fellow workers. At once a duty and perk, such work-sponsored entertainment affectively blurred the boundaries between labor and life.[12] Such outings also kept a man from home, where complementary webs of duty and dependence were spun around mother and child(ren). Women gained recognition for (re)producing children who achieved high academic performances. But being a mother was a full-time job that seeped into everything from the elaborate lunchboxes taken to school to the games played before bed.[13] Routine caregiving became embedded with this second nature: using and embellishing everyday rituals as a means to extract and reward output.

Just as in the work sphere, the home knitted an affect of care with that of duty and performance. And the two spheres played off one another, fusing social relations—of leisure, loyalty, love—to those of capital, labor, and school. As the sociologist Chie Nakane famously claimed in her book *Japanese Society* (1970), which was published during the zenith of Japan's miracle economy, the postwar workplace operated just like a family.[14] Cemented by kinlike bonds, (male) workers were married to their companies (and coworkers) for decades. According to Francis Fukuyama, who admires it as culturally Japanese, this dynamic ensures trust in the workplace.[15] And, modeled on the family, the affect of dependence (*amae*) (expecting to be taken care of by, in this case, the mother) is transferred to the workplace, thereby, in the thesis proposed by psychiatrist Takeo Doi, assuming special saliency and longevity in Japan.[16]

After the Bubble, a New Era of "Japanese Management Style"

By the late 1990s, Japan's dependency culture had lost its expediency. Seeing it as an obstacle to economic growth, neoliberal reformers like Prime Minister Jun'ichirō Koizumi urged a rethinking of Japanese-style management. But the indictment went deeper, charging that dependency culture created unhealthy "interdependent relationships that hinder individuals from exercising initiative and developing entrepreneurship."[17] Under its new banner of "risk and individual responsibility," the government asked its citizens to remake their subjectivity and become strong and independent individuals "capable of bearing the heavy weight of freedom."[18] Such a makeover to a leaner cultural style applauds risks. But as the interdependencies that once grounded work and well-being get undone, this leaves a lot of people feeling precarious and insecure. Meanwhile, the state has yet to pick up the slack left by the decline of the old family corporate system—which had been assigned responsibility for welfare at the onset of its high-growth economic surge.

By the 1990s, the superstable society started morphing into a socioeconomic environment generally considered to be far less safe; political scientist Motoaki Takahara calls this Japan's "era of unsafe nationalism."[19] Shifts from one work model (long-term, regular employment) to another (shorter term, more nonregular employment) are at the heart of this. Even though flexible labor wasn't entirely new, it increased after the Bubble burst in 1991.[20] As stagnation and recession set in, companies began to downsize, restructure, or merge. Layoffs and unemployment rose, and as hiring of regular employees fell, that of irregular workers sharply increased. Temporary work, sparking in the 1980s, continued to grow in the 1990s.[21] In what was called a "glacial age of hiring," youth were particularly hard hit, becoming the "Lost Generation" in Japan's "Lost Decade" (decade of national decline when youth, coming of working age, cannot find jobs). What replaced the job-for-life, family-based model of work was a model of more flexible, results-based employment: the new era in Japanese-style management. Applauding the flexibilization of the country's labor force, the government adopted other signature tendencies of neoliberalism: deregulation of labor policies, heightened reliance on the privatization of social services, and an ideological endorsement of individual responsibility. Under this new regime of labor, what is productive of and for capitalism is no longer the family or the long-term employment of company workers. Rather, it is the detached, flexibly adaptable, and self-responsible individual.

The Neoliberal Millennium: Structural Reform in Labor and the Home

A decade after the collapse of the Bubble, things hadn't yet bounced back. The economy showed no signs of improving, and crises on other fronts were multiplying as well. The Liberal Democratic Party (LDP) started to lose its hold. And in the wake of a series of scandals involving a number of powerful ministries and compounded by divisive party politics, a mood set in of political chaos.[22] A number of social trends stoked fears as well. The low birthrate continued to alarm the public, as did concern about the strain this placed on the national pension fund, future productivity, and caregiving for the world's fastest-aging population. Kindled by the economic downturn and insecurity over jobs, levels of panic, depression, and anxiety rose nationwide, and the rate of suicide rose dramatically in 1998 (to about 33,300 deaths a year—a number that remained at this level until 2012, when it dipped to below 30,000 for the first time in fifteen years). A moral panic raged around youth—around news stories of young girls engaged in "compensated dating," youth violence, hedonistic consumer spending, significant numbers of socially withdrawn and NEET (not in education, employment, or training) youth, the lifestyle of young adults who lived "parasitically" off parents for years (code-named "parasite singles"), and the "freeter" work pattern (of non-regular or flexible labor)—who tended to get blamed for the precarity of the new economic order and the nonproductivity of Japan itself.[23] And, with two startling events mid-decade—the sarin gas attacks by the religious cult Aum

Shinrikyō on Tokyo's subway system, which killed thirteen people, and the Kobe Earthquake two months earlier, with 6,434 casualties—the very fabric of everyday life at the turn of the twenty-first century seemed to be getting ripped asunder.

It was also a time when a chasm opened up in the ontology of place, where and to whom people connect and what attachments accord recognition and identity. In a society where "the family is the place where people live," as sociologist Masahiro Yamada observed about postwar Japan, this dynamic is shifting to one where the family is less a safeguard from risks than risky itself.[24] As the family disarticulates from work, and both become riddled by insecuritization, the contradiction between the (former) family system and the (current) economic system strains the social placeness of family/work.[25] This produces what Yamada takes to be precarious social deformations—neither good for society nor good for the person—such as the young freeters who don't marry and the rising ranks of NEET who don't find (or even look for) work.[26] As Yamada observes, all of this was exacerbated by the structural reforms (deregulating labor and public service under a neoliberal rhetoric of opening the "free market") that Prime Minister Jun'ichirō Koizumi initiated in 2001. As Koizumi anticipated, the public would feel "pain," and indeed higher levels of precarity hit the Japanese at once. Yet, as noted by activist Makoto Yuasa, much of this was initially hidden by making certain segments of the population shoulder the burden.[27] Those most at risk—and most likely to become irregular workers—are youth, women, those with less impressive academic credentials (and, related to this, those from lower-class backgrounds and from single-parent households), foreign migrants, and, increasingly, men in their fifties. In 2012, one-third of all workers but one-half of all youth were irregular workers: a significant shift even from the end of the 1990s. As Machiko Osawa and Jeff Kingston demonstrate in their essay for this volume (chapter 3), irregular workers are prey to precarity (and, in a word used first by activist Karin Amamiya in Japan, they are the "precariat" or precarious proletariat). The wage disparity between regular and irregular employment sharply rose after 1992;[28] annual wages for irregular workers average ¥1,950,000 ($24,000) for men and ¥1,730,000 ($21,314) for women, which is below the poverty line.[29] Deregulation has also allowed companies to hire workers to do what is essentially the work of regular employers, paying them significantly less.[30] Given that contract work can now be extended for three years (without a pay raise or insurance), irregular workers are kept on in lieu of hiring permanent workers.

Stuck at a low pay level, irregular workers are often unprotected at the workplace as well; since they are easily fired and replaced, their rights are minimal at best. This is particularly true for female workers, who experience the worst gendered wage disparity of all industrialized countries, as Ayako Kano notes in her essay on gender for this volume (chapter 4). Seventy percent of irregular workers are women, and their treatment is not much better even in regular employment, where—on the premise of the male breadwinner—they make only 67.1 percent of male salaries. Eighty percent of working women receive less than ¥3,000,000 per year ($37,000). It is also still the case that, unless they have a job that pays well or parents willing to support them, women without (working) husbands are particularly disadvantaged. And working mothers who leave the job market to raise children are penalized by both the national pension system (which kicks in only after twenty-five years of contributions by a worker) and the social security system (into which a worker and company each contribute half but only, in the case of part-timers, if they are working three-quarters time).[31] Needless to say, single households are one of the poorest segments of the population today, though 87.3 percent of single mothers work part time. Notable as well is the fact that only 2 percent of children in Japan are born out of wedlock.

Those on the lower end of job/life security today are far less likely to marry, have children, or be in a position to either give or receive care when they are old or going through hard times.[32] In short, while the overall social trends are away from marriage and family (divorce is up, childbirth is down, and more are marrying later or not at all), all of this is particularly true for those in the least secure jobs today. Studies show that, because of economic insecurity, women are loath to marry a freeter, and male irregular workers are half as likely as regular workers to get married. Those in a position to have what once constituted the social contract of postwar Japan tend to be limited to those with regular employment.

What was such an ordinary lifestyle has now become a privilege of a diminishing minority (who, even then, often need both spouses to work, a situation that poses its own problems of balancing work/life with children if there are any). But my-homeism still signifies belonging and place, the comforts of "being somewhere" and being normal—a utopianism all its own, as Lauren Berlant notes, about the longing for aspirational normativity when the chance of achieving this is ebbing fast.[33] Such a home evokes "hope," according to Yamada,[34] and as home eludes the grasp of more and more Japanese, so does the capacity to be hopeful—what he calls "a society of hope disparity." Japan is becoming a place where hope has become a privilege of the socioeconomically secure. For the rest of them—the widening pool of "losers"—even the wherewithal to imagine a (different) there and then beyond the (precarious) here and now stretches thin.

Relationless Society

On January 31, 2010, the public Japan Broadcasting Corporation (NHK) aired a television special on Japan's "relationless society." At the center of the report was the statistic that thirty-two thousand Japanese died at home all alone in 2009. This phenomenon, labeled "lonely death," has risen in recent years along with the rise of single households; currently one-third of the population lives alone, including 23 percent of the elderly (aged sixty-five and above). As the NHK special elaborated, when Japanese die "lonely deaths" their bodies often remain undiscovered for days, weeks, or months. Almost daily now there are stories of decaying or mummified remains discovered in a room or apartment where someone had lived unknown and disconnected for years. As unnoticed by neighbors in death as in life, those who die lonely are typically estranged from family as well. When notified of their deaths by the city municipal office, family members often refuse to claim the remains. Instead, a commercial cleanup service comes in, disposing of any belongings and sending the body to a Buddhist temple with a special repository for "relationless souls."[35]

It was this state of social life, and death, that NHK reported on. Lonely death was its iconic example, but the documentary pronounced the decay or dissolution of social bonds to be a much broader condition of life for twenty-first-century Japanese. This is a condition of Japanese living increasingly on their own, and—as reflected in the demographic of a shrinking population on account of low childbirth—declining to marry or have children. It is also a condition of the isolation from others and from mechanisms for care and support that hit Japanese hard in times of hardship and old age. The NHK special generated shock in the public. And as the phrase "relationless society" caught on as a catchword of the times, Japan's broken sociality is now getting debated and discussed across the country. The *Asahi Shimbun* launched a series on what it called Japan's "tribeless society" (a society where no one joins groups any more).[36] Countless essays and conferences have taken up the topic ever since. The words for "ties," "bonds," and "relationships" appeared everywhere in response to the Tōhoku disaster in March 2011. And in light of the high rate of lonely deaths that occurred in the temporary shelters following the Kobe Earthquake, interventions against its occurrence have been put into place in temporary shelters today.

Throughout this discourse on the relationless society, the family—whether its dissolution is bemoaned or alternatives are sought to replace it—is central. That is, a certain notion of family and home still indexes social health as it did during the decades of strong economic growth. This means that when (and for whom) the family is at risk, so is social life itself. Masahiro Yamada says a majority of young Japanese subscribe to this in the equation they make between being married and acquiring social status, economic security, and existential hope. This is certainly the position held by a number of precariat who, as irregular workers, feel frustrated in low-paid jobs that offer no long-term stability, potential for future betterment, or social credentials. Deprived of affiliation to workplace and the means to get married and have a family of one's own—the markers of adulthood—the precariat are socially precarious or, as activist Karin Amamiya puts it, disposable workers and human beings.[37] After having worked ten years as a freeter making a monthly income of ¥100,000 (well below the poverty line), Tomohiro Akagi described his life in similarly despairing tones.[38] Still living at home with his parents and angry at his inability to move out and start his own family, Akagi called his conditions of life "unbearably humiliating," not those of a "human who can live having hope." The article he wrote in the journal *Ronza*, "Hope Is War," is an incendiary attack on the nation-state for failing to protect young Japanese like himself and for allowing an entire generation (the "Lost Generation" who came of working age during the "Lost Decade" of the 1990s, when many failed to secure regular employment) to remain essentially stuck as children for the rest of their lives. According to Akagi, a life with no future is like social death.

But what he claims to desire so much, and to feel so hopeless about ever attaining, is a very particular notion of family and home: children of his own, a wife who would presumably stay home to raise them, a consumerist lifestyle including an automobile and ownership of a house. In short, this is my-homeism: a legacy of the era of Japan Inc. and its family-corporate system. According to a number of studies, this is precisely the image of marriage/home that remains a symbol of hope and aspiration to young Japanese today.

In a popular opinion survey conducted in 2008, half of all young people in their twenties agreed with the statement that a married woman should stay home and raise children while the man works and brings home the paycheck. Respondents in their forties, by contrast, were the fewest to agree with this statement.[39] And, in his own research with young single women, Yamada reports that 40 percent say they hope to marry a man who earns more than ¥6 million per year—a status that only 3.5 percent of young Japanese men have currently achieved.[40] The discrepancy between hope and reality here is striking, suggesting how much a fantasy this notion of family/marriage has currently become. But the fantasy also reflects a basic desire for stability and security—and how tied this still is to an aspirationally normative notion of money, success, and gendered roles.

The psychiatrist and social critic Tamaki Saitō calls Japan a "family-dependent society" whose dependency is severely strained today. But if the family/marriage has been Japan's primary social unit, welfare institution, and prop to corporate capitalism under Japan, Inc., there have also been tensions and pressures in its functioning that have had their own negative effect on the social health of Japanese. It is not only those without or estranged from family/marriage who fall prey to the risks of socioeconomic precarity and the relationless society. For example, Kōji Tsukino writes in *Homeless inside Home* that it was the pressures placed on him by his own family to excel academically and become a salaryman like his father that led him to become an alcoholic and socially withdrawn.[41] In his midforties and successful today as the head of a performance group (the Broken People) and the author of several books, Tsukino spent a number of years in his twenties psychically isolated when he lived at home but incommunicative with other humans, including his parents. This is the official definition of social withdrawal: someone who does not communicate with others and does not go to school, go to work, or enter the social world beyond the premises where he or she lives for six months or more. The statistics on social withdrawal are unreliable, but reportedly there are between 750,000 and 1,000,000 today that meet this definition of a phenomenon that started gaining recognition around the year 2000. Overwhelmingly male, they often start by refusing to go to school at age fourteen or fifteen, around the time of intense studying for entrance exams into high school (when bullying also intensifies), and remain withdrawn for years or even decades.[42] And associated with, if not equivalent to, social withdrawal is the phenomenon of NEET, which characterizes a reported 2,500,000 people in Japan today.[43]

Theories diverge on the causes of, and correctives to, social withdrawal and NEET, but many see the relationship between family/home and work/productivity as critical—critically out of sync today and critical to reestablishing health and order. Some, such as psychiatrist Shunsuke Serizawa, who works with troubled youth, find the family, and the pressure exerted there on children to academically perform, contributing to a competitive ethos in Japan that is stifling for everyone and particularly young people who are growing up too one-sidedly geared to productive output. This was the experience of Tsukino, who felt that home was as much a pressure zone as school and one where he was berated for not being a better student.

Others view the problem differently, finding those prone to withdrawal or becoming a NEET to be insufficiently nourished or attended to by parents—not only in the form of love and warmth (something Tsukino found absent as well) but also in the form of nurturing children's ambitions, imaginations, and horizons of expectation.[44]

This is one of the findings of labor economist Yūji Genda in his work in the Hopology program he established at Tokyo University. When children grow up encouraged by parents to cultivate goals and ambitions and to stick with them, they are far more likely to be hopeful—about themselves, the future, the world they live in. According to Genda, these goals need not adhere to the normative rubric of graduating from a prestigious university, getting married, and becoming a salaryman (or marrying someone who is).[45] Rather, goals could be anything—mastering the flute or helping the homeless. But working toward something one can both do and be acknowledged for is key to acquiring the social wherewithal and confidence to navigate adulthood—what seems missing in the case of at least some *hikikomori* and NEET. And, as Genda points out, one can't be or become a socially healthy adult on one's own. Children need nurturance from parents, and adults need recognition, interaction, and support from others as they age.

The absence of such a support system or social intimates is what characterizes those who die lonely deaths. And like the phenomena of social withdrawal and NEET, the awareness of lonely death has arisen in the context of twenty-first-century Japan, contributing to an unease over not only economic decline but shrinking population and troubled sociality. According to a scholar who works on lonely death, the incidence tripled from 1,123 in 1987 to 3,395 in 2006. Today twenty such deaths occur nationwide every day, with the rate double for men, higher in the cities, and with the discovery of male bodies averaging twelve days after death compared to six days for women. Those most susceptible are single, un(der)employed men in their fifties and sixties who have never married or have lost their wives from death or divorce and are either on welfare or scraping by with precarious jobs. The profile is of a man who has lost connection to society, has severed ties with any family members, and, with no stable workplace now, has also lost touch with former coworkers and friends. Inhabiting a small room or apartment in a cheap apartment building, he stays inside all the time, hoarding garbage, drinking sake, and living off instant ramen.[46] The implosion of a work/family model of sociality—exacerbated by economic decline and an ethos of self-responsibility—is complicit in the syndrome of lonely death.

Popular culture is a useful lens for seeing how social problems register in the national imagination. And it is interesting that lonely death was fictionally portrayed in a movie released a few months after 3/11. Set against the backdrop of sunflowers, which became a symbol of the rebirth of Japan because they grow fast as well as tall and absorb radiation from contaminated soil, *The Dog Who Protects the Stars* tells the story of two socially solitary men: one whose dead body is discovered in his parked car in a forest preserve and the other a worker in a city municipal office in Hokkaido who investigates his death. The older man, as we eventually learn, was once happily married and gainfully employed. But once he loses his job through restructuring, he loses his equilibrium in the world: he bickers with his daughter and wife, can't manage to do much of anything including look for work or help around the house, and agrees to a divorce when his wife asks him for it. Without a family or home any more of his own, "Father" packs up his car and, taking the family dog ("Happy"), hits the road. The story, for him at least, ends when his money runs out and the scavenging he has done with his dog can no longer keep him alive. It is the typical scenario of lonely death: a single, middle-aged man, un(der)employed, who, disconnected from the world, dies unable (or unwilling) to find anyone to help him.

Work and marriage correlate here. The durability/precarity of the family is tied to the man's job, and, for Father at least, the idea of family is unthinkable when the primary breadwinner is unemployed. But without workplace and family, he is left all alone; the condition of social solitude is exacerbated by an attitude of pride or moral reluctance to seek help from anyone else. Such a mind-set—not wanting to be a burden or depend on anyone—is strong among the elderly living alone, as recent research has shown; 32 percent in one study say they wouldn't seek help from family or relatives even in an emergency,[47] and only 4 percent in another (where 70 percent have children) say they hope to live with family in the future. The rest say they don't want to be a burden.[48] But Tomoyuki Takimoto, the director of *The Dog Who Protects the Stars*, did not intend the movie to be exactly hopeless. Father dies, but he has had a dog who "protects" him from loneliness. And, upon uncovering this story, the other solitary man befriends a teenage girl and acquires a dog of his own: social relationships beyond the sphere of both family and work. Such alternatives and rearrangements of a family-dependent sociality are key to possible futures of Japan/ese moving beyond a relationless society.

Possible Futures and Hope

Notwithstanding the implications of much social theorizing that time is constant, unfolding predictably, in fact, the social is made in its punctuation by crises.[49]

The natural disaster and accompanying nuclear accident on March 11, 2011, triggered a national crisis. It hit the northeastern coast of Japan in the three prefectures of Miyagi, Iwate, and Fukushima, and the damage was severe: over eighteen thousand dead, 350,000 displaced, and trillions of yen in damage of property and costs for compensation, relief, and reconstruction. This generated an incredible outpouring of support, assistance, and volunteerism from across the country.[50] In everything from donating clothing and food to going to Tōhoku to shovel mud or empty debris, Japanese of all ages and from all walks of life responded with an energy and goodwill that got marked—in the press and by public figures—as a resurgence of Japanese collectivity. The mottos "Japanese united as one" and "Japan, hang in there!" appeared literally everywhere. The emperor, too, asked citizens to help one another out, and the words for "ties" and "bonds" circulated widely in an atmosphere of promoting, and recognizing, the need to socially (re)connect. A number of commentators, such as novelist Ryū Murakami and pop cultural (*otaku*) guru Hiroki Azuma, saw in this the return of hope to the country, as if, shocked by natural/national crisis, Japanese had regained their sociality.

The reality is more complex. But 3/11 posed a crisis that, while affecting those in the northeast the hardest, also struck all Japanese with the enormity of the destruction, the threat of radiation, and the damage to the country. This was a precariousness felt by everyone and not just those (precariat, unemployed, socially solitary or withdrawn) on the underside of a bipolarized, divided society. It was also a precariousness that provoked action of a collaborative, innovative kind, drawing on existing ties and relationships but also creating new ones involving nonprofit organizations (NPOs), local initiatives, and networks of people across (and beyond) the country. These new(er) forms of sociality that have arisen in response to the precariousness of the times bear seeds of hope for possible futures of Japan/ese. For if the social script has been too narrowly contained to family, and family of a very aspirational, exclusionary sort, then new social designs for being, belonging, and helping one another out are needed to go beyond Japan's era of a relationless society and to reclaim hope—hope out of precarity.

In the wake of the crisis, hundreds of thousands of Japanese were immediately displaced. Many lost everything: family members, homes, the fields and boats they had used to subsist. Living in evacuation shelters sometimes close to the damaged nuclear plants, those with families often split up, with men staying back to seek work and women and children resettling with relatives elsewhere in Japan. Alongside such "diaspora families" were high numbers of elderly already living alone and a random mix of people from different neighborhoods and prefectures. As evacuees started moving into temporary shelters three months after 3/11, these jumbled living arrangements often continued for people dislocated multiple times. One year later, 41,236 were still living in these shelters, some anticipating a stay of far more than the two years originally predicted. Yet multiple initiatives sprang up to help mitigate the alienation and discomfort facing those stranded in temporary shelters. In over 60 percent of the shelters, for example, self-run councils were established within seven months.[51] In others, residents took the initiative to move in together; in Nagahora, a small fishing village in Rikuzentakata (Iwate Prefecture) entirely washed away by the tsunami, the entire community decided to move into a temporary shelter en masse. In another case, people who had found themselves on the same floor of an evacuation shelter decided to move to the temporary shelter as a unit. Taking the initiative meant they had to inhabit a less popular site, but according to the appointed leader of the eight households this created a new kind of social tie—"somewhere between family and friend."[52]

In Sumita (Iwate Prefecture), at a slight remove from where the tsunami struck, it was the town itself that came forward to help build temporary shelters for evacuees from neighboring towns, to pay the extra costs to make these wood instead of metal, and to help on a daily basis in providing services. And here too,

NPOs have been actively involved: painting play equipment for children, helping arrange craft-making (and craft sales) among the women, and mediating between townspeople and residents to carry out festivals (which become hybridized in the process). In the "community garden" at one of these shelters anyone could plant vegetables, and in the shelter for household residency families planted flowers in front of their units. A space both for family and beyond family opened up. There were also interventions for those who might be in danger of lonely death.[53] The town of Ōfunato (Iwate Prefecture) provides an emergency service on cell phones for all residents of temporary shelters. If someone is in danger, or just needs to talk, he or she can reach an operator any time of the day or night. The incidence of lonely death is proportionately far less after the 3/11 earthquake than it was in the wake of the Kobe Earthquake (thirty-three reported by July 2012 compared to forty-six the first year alone following Kobe),[54] probably because of such measures taken to ward against it. And interventions happen elsewhere (and predate 3/11); an NPO has given residents of a large apartment building in Shinjuku, Tokyo, where many elderly live alone a similar service on their cell phones. A small contingent of nurses now provide services in the Sanya district of Tokyo, where many day laborers and unemployed men live, and sit by those dying so no one dies alone. And some local neighborhoods in Tokyo have now instituted night patrols to be on the lookout for elderly people needing help.

If "the last function of family is to provide a space where one belongs," as Hiroki Manabe—in his book on the state of the family following 3/11—has written, then the challenge facing those without such a space is to find, or make, new spaces.[55] The word Manabe uses here is *ibasho* (which means a place where one feels comfortable and at home)—a word that one hears widely in Japan used to reference its absence or loss; speaking of the socially withdrawn with whom he works, Shunsuke Serizawa, for example, says they lack an *ibasho*.[56] Karin Amamiya has noted the same about members of the young precariat who, disaffiliated from an ongoing workplace and sometimes family and friends, lack a sense of recognition or acceptance from others.[57] It would seem that, in the wake of 3/11, volunteering in Tōhoku or joining, sometimes starting, an NPO has provided a sense of belonging and purpose, even hope, for a number of younger, and older, Japanese. Whether this is sustainable and for what percentage or segment of the population is difficult to tell. But it dovetails with another sociological trend that has grown since 3/11—distrust and suspicion of the national government for its complicity with Tokyo Electric Power Company, owner of the Fukushima nuclear plants, and its failure to better safeguard citizens against nuclear meltdown and adequately inform the public of the dangers when they did occur. As in the upsurge of antinuclear protests, one sees citizens more willing to criticize authorities, to take the initiative in monitoring radiation levels and making decisions about safety, and to envision a different future (non-nuclear, less affluent) for Japan. It is arguably at the local level that one sees the most innovation in the way of social designs for the future—initiatives taken to provide alternative means (to family, workplace, locale) for being, belonging, and self/mutual-help.

There is a nationwide movement to establish "regional living rooms" (*chiiki no chanoma*), for example: spaces, often in converted houses, that serve as drop-in centers where anyone can spend the day (and sometimes stay overnight) drinking tea, eating lunch, and enjoying "mutual contact." It targets those who are isolated and lonely with its form of flexible, inclusive sociality: a place for anyone. Another cooperative initiative that is a type of care bank, Nippon Active Life Club, was started in 1993 with 135 branches and now has twenty thousand members across the country. Volunteers donate time (in caring for those who need it) and bank it as hours of care labor that they can later withdraw when they need care themselves. Targeting those in need of everyday help but lacking the human or financial means to acquire it, the club serves as a type of substitute family. Share-houses are also a new trend; people who, starting off as strangers, live cooperatively in a shared space to save on costs and be available to one another as a mutual support system.[58] The explosion of social media (net sites, chat rooms) expands portals for contact and communication as well.[59] Some young people say that this is their primary site of/for sociality (though it opens up possibilities for bullying as well as intimacy), and techno-companions, such as the virtual pet tamagotchi (a big craze in 1997), provide a portable *ibasho* for their owners.[60] And at the local level one sees some of the most aggressive initiatives intended to provide support for young people suffering from social withdrawal and un(der)employment: Niigata City has an entire facility to support young people and has recently added personal counselors to give individualized "coaching" to anyone who seeks it.

A sense that sociality is changing, or coming undone, is hardly unique to twenty-first-century Japan/ese. But there is also something quite particular to both the place and the time. This is the challenge over the last two decades to Japan's family-corporate system, what had been previously (in postwar Japan) the country's de facto welfare system, prop to state capitalism, and template for social belonging and citizenship. Those who experience this most precariously are un(der)employed, without a human safety net, and socially alone. And this correlates with family/work; given that these ties have been the safeguard for living securely, those most insecure today are those stranded from either or both. The very phenomenon of lonely death—something I've been told rarely happens even in the poorest of shantytowns anywhere else—is a sign of a country's very particular kind of sociality and a symptom of its precarity. That such a phenomenon has become newsworthy in Japan and that people are beginning to rethink the boundaries and exclusions of a social rubric that excludes too many (people) and too much (in the way of caregiving) is hopeful. But much more needs to be done to alleviate the problem of social isolation. This means not merely making work and family life more sustainable but also coming up with alternatives to social living and belonging beyond workplace and family (of a heteronormative couple plus children). The hope of a postprecarious Japanese future rests on this.

Notes

1. Beverly Silver, *Forces of Labor: Workers' Movements and Globalization since 1870* (Cambridge: Cambridge University Press, 2003).

2. William W. Kelly, "Finding a Place in Metropolitan Japan: Ideologies, Institutions, and Everyday Life," in *Postwar Japan as History*, ed. Andrew Gordon (Berkeley: University of California Press, 1993), 189–238.

3. Kimiko Kimoto, "Kazoku, jendā, kaisō" [Family, gender, class], in *Koyō ryūdōka no naka no kazoku* [Family in the midst of the flexibilization of labor], ed. Keiko Funabashi and Michiko Miyamoto (Tokyo: Minerubua shoten, 2008), 65.

4. See James Robinson and Nobue Suzuki, introduction to *Men and Masculinities in Contemporary Japan: Dislocating the Salaryman Doxa*, ed. James Roberson and Nobue Suzuki (London: Routledge Curzon, 2003); Heidi Gottfried, "Japan: The Reproductive Bargain and the Making of Precarious Employment," in *Gender and the Contours of Precarious Employment*, ed. Leah F. Vosko, Martha MacDonald, and Iain Campbell (London: Routledge, 2009), 76–79.

5. Lee Edelman, *No Future: Queer Theory and Death Drive* (Durham, NC: Duke University Press, 2004), 12.

6. Ibid, 2.

7. Gottfried, "Japan."

8. Ibid.

9. Hiroko Takeda, "Structural Reform of the Family and the Neoliberalisation of Everyday Life in Japan," *New Political Economy* 13, no. 2 (2008): 162.

10. Ibid.

11. Tomiko Yoda, "The Rise and Fall of Maternal Society: Gender, Labor, and Capital in Contemporary Japan," in *Japan after Japan: Social and Cultural Life from the Recessionary 1990s to the Present*, ed. Tomiko Yoda and Harry Harootunian (Durham, NC: Duke University Press, 2006), 239–74.

12. Anne Allison, *Nightwork: Sexuality, Pleasure, and Corporate Masculinity in a Tokyo Hostess Club* (Chicago: University of Chicago Press, 1994).

13. Anne Allison, *Permitted and Prohibited Desires: Mothers, Comics, and Censorship in Japan* (Boulder, CO: Westview Press, 1996).

14. Chie Nakane, *Tate shakai no ningen kankei* [Vertical society] (Tokyo: Kodansha, 1967).

15. Francis Fukuyama, *Trust: The Social Virtues and the Creation of Prosperity* (New York: Free Press, 1995).

16. Takeo Doi, *"Amae" no kōzō* [The anatomy of dependence] (1971; repr., Tokyo: Kōbundō, 2001).

17. Takeda, "Structural Reform," 156.

18. Quoted in Hirokazu Miyazaki, "The Temporality of No Hope," in *Ethnographies of Neoliberalism*, ed. Carol Greenhouse (Philadelphia: University of Pennsylvania Press, 2010), 243.

19. Motoaki Takahara, *Fuan gata nashonarizumu no jidai* [The era of insecure nationalism] (Tokyo: Yōsensha, 2006).

20. David H. Slater, "The Making of Japan's New Working Class: 'Freeters' and the Progression from Middle School to the Labor Market," in *Social Class in Contemporary Japan: Structures, Socialization and Strategies*, ed. Ishida Hiroshi and David H. Slater (New York: Routledge, 2009).

21. Gottfried, "Japan."

22. Takeda, "Structural Reform."

23. Mark Driscoll, "Debt and Denunciation in Post-Bubble Japan: On the Two Freeters," *Cultural Critique* 65 (Winter 2007): 164–87. The term *parasite singles* was coined by Masahiro Yamada in Parasaito shinguru no jidai [The parasite single generation] (Tokyo: Chikuma Shobō, 1999) in reference to youngish adults who live even into their forties or fifties at home, eating their mother's cooking and spending whatever disposable income they make on a pampered lifestyle of boutique cafes, travel overseas, and indulgent hobbies.

24. Masahiro Yamada, *Kazoku to iu risuku* [Risk of the so-called family] (Tokyo: Keiso Shobō, 2001), 23.

25. Masahiro Yamada, "Keizai to kazoku" [From economics to family], in Funabashi and Miyamoto, *Koyō ryūdōka no naka no kazoku*, 12.

26. Yamada, *Kazoku to iu risuku*.

27. Makoto Yuasa, *Hanhinkon: "Suberidai shakai" kara no dasshutsu* [Reverse poverty: Escaping from the society that is sliding down] (Tokyo: Iwanami Shinsho, 2008), 84–86.

28. Yamada, "Keizai to kazoku."

29. Ayami Kamuro, "Danjo no hatarakikata ni miru gendai no hinkon" [Present-day poverty seen in the working styles of men and women], in *Kakusa to hinkon: 20 kō* [Difference and poverty: Twenty cases], ed. Tomio Makino and Eigo Murakami (Tokyo: Akashi Shoten, 2008), 20–31.

30. Toshiaki Tachibanaki, "Intorodakushon: Kakusa kara hinkon e" [Introduction: From difference to poverty], in Makino and Murakami, *Kakusa to hinkon*.

31. Kamuro, "Danjo no hatarakikata ni miru gendai no hinkon."

32. Ibid.

33. Laurent Berlant, "Nearly Utopian, Nearly Normal," *Public Culture* 19, no. 2 (2007): 273–301. For a longer discussion of these issues—of precarity as it registers in the realm of everyday life as well as longing for normativity and "home" in Japan today—see also Anne Allison, *Precarious Japan* (Durham, NC: Duke University Press, 2013).

34. Masahiro Yamada, *Kibō kakusa shakai:"Makegumi" no zetsubōkan ga niho no hikisaku* [Society of hope disparity: The despair of being a "loser" is tearing up Japan] (Tokyo: Chikuma Shobō, 2003).

35. NHK purojekuto, *Muen shakai* [The relationless society] (Tokyo: NHK shuppan sha, 2010).

36. *Asahi Shimbun*, "'Kozoku no kuni' shuzaihan" [Series on "Country of the empty tribe"], in *Kozoku no kuni: Hitoriga tsunagaru jidai e* [The country of the empty tribe: Toward an era of connections between people] (Tokyo: Asahi Shimbun Shuppan, 2012).

37. Karin Amamiya, *Ikisasero! Nanminka suru wamonotachi* [Let us live! Youth who have been made refugees] (Tokyo: Ōtashuppan, 2007).

38. Tomohiro Akagi, "Kibō wa sensō: Maruyama Masao o hippatakitai 31 sai furītā" [Hope is war: A thirty-one-year-old freeter who would like to slap Maruyama Masao], *Ronza* (January 2007): 53–59.

39. Hiroki Manabe, *3.11 kara kangaeru "kazoku"* [Thinking of "family" since 3.11] (Tokyo: Iwanami Shoten, 2012).

40. Kaori Sasaki, Tomoshi Okuda, Tōji Kamata, Susumu Shimazono, Masahiro Yamada, and Shinya Ichijō, *Muenshakai kara yūenshakai e* [From relationless society to relational society] (Tokyo: Zen nihon kankonsōsai gojo kyōkai, 2012).

41. Kōji Tsukino, *Ie no naka no hōmuresu* [Homeless inside home] (Niigata: Niigata nippō jigyōsha, 2004).

42. Sachiko Kaneko, "Japan's 'Socially Withdrawn Youths' and Time Constraints in Japanese Society," *Time and Society* 15, nos. 2/3 (2006): 233–49.

43. Tuuka Toivonen, "NEETs: The Strategy within the Category," in *A Sociology of Japanese Youth*, ed. Roger Goodman, Yuki Imoto, and Tuukka Toivonen (London: Routledge, 2012), 139–58.

44. Kaneko, "Japan's 'Socially Withdrawn Youths.'"

45. Yūji Genda, *Kibōgaku* [Hopology]. (Tokyo: Chuokoron shinsho, 2006).

46. Manabe, *3.11 kara kangaeru "kazoku."*

47. Ibid.

48. NHK purojekuto, *Muen shakai.*

49. Fiona Ross, *Raw Life, New Hope: Decency, Housing and Everyday Life in a Post-apartheid Community* (Cape Town: University of Cape Town Press, 2010), 198.

50. Over one million Japanese volunteered between March 11 and July 1, 2011. See "Borantia katsudō sha sū no suii" [Change in the number of volunteer activists], July 1, 2012, www.saigaivc.com/boranteakatsudōshasūsuii.

51. Manabe, *3.11 kara kangaeru "kazoku."*

52. Ibid.

53. Naoki Kimura, Shutaro Koyama, and Tomohiko Nara, "Community Design of the Temporary Housing Complex in Sumita," unpublished paper, 2012.

54. Nine hundred is the number typically cited for those who died lonely deaths following the Hanshin Earthquake. But according to one official report the number was actually 233 between 1995 and 1999 (*Asahi Shimbun*, July 10, 2012).

55. Manabe, *3.11 kara kangaeru "kazoku."*

56. Nihon kodomo sōsharu wāku kyōkai, *Kazoku ni shite hoshii koto shite hoshikunai koto* [The things we wish for and don't wish for regarding family] (Tokyo: Nihon kodomo sōshyaru wāku kyōkai, 2005).

57. Amamiya, *Ikisasero!*

58. Atsuko Nishikawa, *Otona no tame no shea hausu annai* [The share-house guide for adults]. (Tokyo: Daiyamondosha, 2012).

59. David Slater, Keiko Nishimura, and Love Kindstrand, "Social Media, Information and Political Activism in Japan's 3.11 Crisis," *Asia-Pacific Journal* 10, no. 24.1 (June 11, 2012), http://www.japanfocus.org/-nishimura-keiko/3762.

60. Anne Allison, *Millennial Monsters: Japanese Toys and the Global Imagination* (Berkeley: University of California Press, 2006).

CHAPTER THREE

Risk and Consequences: The Changing Japanese Employment Paradigm

Machiko Osawa and Jeff Kingston

The most significant trend in the Japanese labor market over the past two decades is the doubling of the percentage of the workforce hired as nonregular employees who do not enjoy job security or many other benefits routinely accorded regular full-time workers. Called the "precariat" (workers in precarious employment), they now constitute about 38 percent of the entire workforce, or roughly twenty million workers often employed under disadvantageous terms involving low pay, dead-end jobs, and easy termination. The spread of precarious work marks a tectonic change in Japan, a nation generally associated with job security and paternalistic employers. It correlates with a rise in poverty and inequality, and it carries implications for the solvency of pension and medical care systems, since contributions to social insurance are declining at a time when demands on these systems are increasing because of the graying of society.[1] The demographic time bomb also means that by 2030 there will be only two workers' taxes supporting each pensioner (down from four in 2000) while the population will shrink by 10 percent from 127 million in 2010 to 115 million. This stark context of an aging and declining population is a crucial factor in assessing the precaritization of employment. Our focus in this chapter is the causes and consequences of the precaritization of Japan's labor force and possible trajectories in the future.

The first question to ask here is: What has led to this radical shift in labor conditions in Japan today? As we see it, structural changes driven by globalization, corporate cost-cutting, and government deregulation of the labor market are the main factors behind the rise of the precariat.[2] These were the policy decisions made by industry and government amid the prolonged economic downturn known as the Lost Decade (caused by the implosion of land and stock prices that ensued when the bubble burst in the early 1990s). As Japanese firms confronted increased global competition, they responded by reducing the number of full-time jobs and progressively abandoning corporate paternalism in an effort to offset the cost disadvantages of an aging and more expensive workforce (receiving seniority-based wages). The government responded to the economic downturn by deregulating the labor market. Beginning in the late 1990s, during the Obuchi administration (1998–2000), the government revised employment laws to enable wider use of temporary, contract, and dispatched workers hired by firms through intermediary agencies. The 1999 Dispatched Manpower Business Act triggered a fairly rapid spread of contract work arrangements in many sectors of the economy.[3] In 2004, during the Koizumi administration (2001–6), the government further deregulated the labor market, allowing employment of contract workers in manufacturing, a critical sector where increased global competition led to fierce cost-cutting measures.

The Liberal Democratic Party (LDP) promoted labor deregulation in an effort to revitalize the Japanese economy, but in doing so it increased the vulnerability of many workers. As of 2012, more than two million Japanese were receiving welfare, the highest number since 1951 and double the level in 1999. Prime Minister Jun'ichirō Koizumi often invoked the slogan "self-responsibility" to rationalize deregulation and awaken the "animal spirits" of entrepreneurial competitiveness. Under Koizumi's mantra of "self-responsibility," employers and government shifted risk to workers, who came to understand the downside of flexible employment practices and business cycle adjustments firsthand.[4] And when a quarter of a million contract workers lost their jobs in the wake of the 2008 Lehman Shock (as Japanese call the wider crisis sparked by the subprime mortgage debacle), they discovered just how inadequate the safety net for displaced workers actually was.

Consequences

Changes starting in the Lost Decade have generated considerable pain for Japanese workers: an increasing number can find work only as contingent workers, and even regular workers face cuts in bonuses and paid overtime.[5] Moreover, the core workforce, shrinking as it is, finds that it needs to assume greater responsibilities and work longer hours. Now, in the third decade of what has been a very long Lost Decade of policy drift on many fronts, there is a growing malaise among Japanese as they cope with the consequences of economic stagnation. It is noteworthy that from 1995 to 2008 the number of regular workers decreased by 3.8 million, while the number of nonregular workers increased by 7.6 million.[6] This is a major new development in Japan's employment paradigm, as new graduates find it increasingly difficult to get a foothold on the career ladder as regular employees. Future career prospects hang in the balance because only about 20 percent of nonregular workers are able to switch over to regular jobs.[7] The concentration of job growth in nonregular jobs has also reinforced the marginalization of women in the workforce, as they are disproportionately represented among the precariat; 55 percent of women are employed as nonregular workers as of 2011, and only 7 percent of these succeed in moving to secure regular employment.[8]

Owing to the 2008 global economic crisis, Japanese manufacturers saw their orders dramatically drop, creating a domino effect throughout the economy. Employers cut their losses by sacking contract workers. And since many of these workers were on short-term contracts or indirectly employed through an intermediary, Japanese firms felt no obligation to keep them on the payroll and legally were not obliged to do so. It is noteworthy that public concern and media attention to the problem of the working poor heightened at this time. For example, the evening news and newspaper headlines often featured the plight of the precariat as suddenly unemployed workers protested outside factories and jammed the government employment offices known as "Hello Work." At the dawn of 2009 a coalition of nonprofit organizations (NPOs) established Toshikoshi Haken Mura (Village of Fired Contract Workers) across the street from the Ministry of Health, Labor and Welfare to pressure the government into providing assistance to Japan's disposable workers.[9] The strategy worked. In response to intense media coverage, the government relaxed eligibility criteria for receiving welfare and unemployment insurance benefits, enabling many fired nonregular employees to receive assistance.[10] This is an example of how a more vigorous civil society is raising awareness and advocating policy reforms, but the success has been limited to mitigating the consequences of deregulation. Nonregular employment and job insecurity remain stark realities for more than one-third of all workers. Employers are defending their turf resolutely against pressures from political parties and NPOs, maintaining that flexible employment arrangements (i.e., nonregular work) are essential for corporate survival in the face of recession at home and competition abroad.

The 2009 campaign for the Lower House of the Diet focused on "social disparity" (*kakusa shakai*) and the recognition that a "divided society" was not the Japan of egalitarian values that most Japanese identified with. The Democratic Party of Japan (DPJ) benefited from these anxieties because people held the LDP responsible for undermining accepted norms and for overseeing Japan's transition to a society of discernible "winners" and "losers." The victorious DPJ promised to help the precariat and the disadvantaged but did not deliver on these and other promises. There are many reasons why the DPJ failed, but in the end their fumbling governance discredited the social democratic alternative. Subsequently, the public mood shifted, as income disparities and the plight of the precariat were not an issue during the 2012 Lower House election campaign that the LDP won in a landslide. The planned consumption tax hike (supported by the LDP and DPJ), doubling in stages from 5 percent to 10 percent by 2015, is regressive and will have a greater adverse impact on lower-income households, welfare recipients, and retirees. In the battle over Japan's employment paradigm, the LDP is firmly in the employers' camp: "Abenomics" offers no improvement for the precariat and is likely to expand their numbers under the banner of promoting "flexibility" in the labor market.

Inequality and Poverty

During Japan's heady days of its so-called "economic miracle"—the decades of double-digit growth in the late 1950s and 1960s—income inequality was far less severe and was never a pressing political issue. Since the 1980s, however, disparities have increased, as have the number of working poor.[11] There is considerable debate about why this is so. Ōtake argues that inequality is rising in Japan because of an aging society and expansion of nonregular employment.[12] While the growing proportion of the population over sixty-five years old (23 percent in 2009) is certainly a factor, the Organisation for Economic Co-operation and Development (OECD) also attributes the growth in inequality and relative poverty rates in Japan to labor market dualism, that is, regular and nonregular employment.[13] The OECD concludes that the rising percentage of nonregular workers is a key factor in both these trends and asserts that there is a risk that this bifurcated employment system, along with inequality and poverty, will become entrenched. The spread of riskier employment has also led to a rise in divorce and the number of single-parent families, boosting Japan's child poverty rate to 16.3 percent as of 2012. The child poverty rate was the tenth highest among the thirty-five OECD countries in 2010.[14] In 2009 the government announced that the relative poverty rate in Japan had risen to 16 percent (or twenty-three million Japanese) from 15.3 percent in 2004 (for comparison, the rate in the United States is 17 percent) and only 8.1 percent in 1994. According to the government, this precipitous rise is due to three related factors: the expansion of nonregular employment, the growing number of single-parent households (more than one million on welfare), and the aging population. The relative poverty rate of those over sixty-five years of age is 20 percent.[15]

Growing socioeconomic disparity is a controversial reality in contemporary Japan. According to a 2008 OECD study, the average income of the top 10 percent of Japanese was ten times higher than that of the bottom 10 percent, up from eight times higher in 2001.[16] This finding shows just how sharp and abrupt the increase in inequality in Japan has been in the early twenty-first century. In 2008 the comparable ratio for the United States was 14:1, while in Germany it stood at 6:1. Tachibanaki reports a similar trend for Japan as the Gini coefficient (a measure of inequality) increased by 43 percent over two decades, from 0.349 in 1981 to 0.498 by 2002.[17] The OECD, using different data, calculates Japan's Gini coefficient at 0.314, only slightly lower than that of the United Kingdom (0.326) and the United States (0.337).[18]

The rise in relative poverty and the greater awareness of socioeconomic disparities also threaten the myth of social cohesion (and of a homogeneous one-class system) that postwar Japanese have been so attached to. One can see this in the way that the issues of poverty and precarious employment have entered public discourse.[19] A newspaper survey in 2005, for example, revealed that only 54 percent of Japanese saw themselves as middle class, while 37 percent self-identified as lower class. This is a radical shift from the latter half of the twentieth century, when 75 percent of the population consistently described itself as middle class.[20] Social anxieties are evident in the explosion in the number of publications on the subject of precarity, poverty, and a downwardly mobile population that started during the Koizumi era (2001–6), including, for example, Makoto Yuasa's *Anti-poverty* (2004), Atsushi Miura's *Downwardly Mobile Society* (2005), and Takuro Morinaga's *Getting By on Less than Three Million Yen* (2003).[21]

As Ayako Kano discusses in her chapter for this book, there is another disparity discrediting Japanese politics: a massive gender gap. In 2013, the World Economic Forum ranked Japan 105 out of 136 surveyed countries in its Global Gender Gap Report, just behind Cambodia and just ahead of Nigeria.[22] Since the forum began ranking countries, Japan has steadily slid downward from eightieth place in 2006, testimony to a disturbing pattern of women's marginalization in Japan and an inadequate policy response to this problem.

Marginalized Women

Given the limited alternatives, Japan has no choice but to tap its most under-utilized resource. It's hard to run a marathon with just one leg.
—Kathy Matsui, author of *Womenomics 3.0* (2010)

Women could actually save Japan.
—Christine Lagarde, director of the International Monetary Fund, October 2012

In terms of productivity, Japanese companies are undeniably losing out by not tapping the potential of their women workers.[23] A 2012 report by the consulting firm McKinsey & Company found that women are underrepresented in Japanese boardrooms, filling only 2 percent of such positions.[24] The percentage of women in managerial positions is similarly low (only 11 percent), despite a female labor force participation rate of 62 percent. Companies hurt themselves by not making use of the best talent available, as reflected in the positive correlation in Japan between greater representation of women in management and firms' earnings margins and returns on equity.[25] There is a growing if not belated consensus that if Japan seeks a better future (in terms of economic growth as well as social equity), it needs to ensure that women are given opportunities for leadership and better careers. Even social conservatives like Prime Minister Abe embrace womenomics, arguing that it is crucial to his growth strategy known as Abenomics. Abe gives strong rhetorical support for this agenda by urging firms to do more to bolster the role of women in the economy, calling on them to boost the percentage of women in leadership positions to 30 percent by 2020 and to appoint at least one woman to their board of directors. He is relying on PR and moral suasion rather than quota enforcement, prompting much skepticism about the possibility of achieving his lofty targets, but he is making an effort that has not been made in the past.

Gender diversity spurs innovation, more "thinking outside the box," and the opening up of new opportunities ranging from marketing and sales to design and improved brand reputation. According to Kaori Sasaki, president of ewomen Inc., a company that publishes a magazine for working women, "Postwar Japan made a strong economy by imposing a uniform ideology, but this no longer reflects reality in twenty-first-century Japan with more diverse lifestyles and expectations. The lack of gender diversity in Japanese firms is a major problem for the companies and society."[26] Sasaki expresses guarded optimism concerning prospects for improvement because diversity has become a political issue and many political and business leaders understand the need to tackle this problem.

As Kathy Matsui, chief Japan equity strategist for Goldman Sachs, told us, "The key is for top leaders to understand the logic of the importance of introducing diversity management into their company. Not just on the surface, but the real logic of it. I think that some of the Japanese companies that are globally expanding their business understand this logic. Without it [gender diversity], they cannot survive in the twenty-first century."[27] Toshifumi Suzuki, CEO of Seven & I Holdings, the largest convenience store chain in Japan, is one of those top executives who understand the importance of diversity. In his view, it is imperative that Japanese firms integrate women workers more effectively into the entire business operation. For one thing, they provide a different view of markets and services that can lead to the realization of new business opportunities. Still, he understands that integrating women more fully into corporate Japan will not happen overnight. He told us, "We have seven companies. I ordered all of them to have at least one female executive on their board of directors. In the future, I would like to increase this ratio to 30 percent. Recently we have created some stores that are staffed and managed entirely by women workers. I introduced this not so much to increase profits but to change the organizational culture. Having women-only stores helps promote communication among women workers so they can speak their opinions easily."[28]

In Japan, women often feel compelled to defer to their male colleagues and find it hard to express their opinions. In 2012 Risa S., twenty-four, a young Japanese woman who was educated overseas and hired in the management track in 2010 at one of Japan's leading finance companies, told us about finding the rigid male hierarchy unbearable.[29] Despite her intelligence, fluency in English and Japanese, excellent IT skills, and cosmopolitan poise, male colleagues only pointed out her deficiencies in formal Japanese language and ignored her input. She told us, "It's a real macho culture, and they can't deal with me being a woman who has spent so much time overseas. It's supposed to be an international company, but they are so backward. One guy kicked me out of his section because I disagreed with him, and now they give me assignments nobody else wants. I want to find another job." As of 2014, she had moved to an international company.

According to the 2012 McKinsey report, promoting gender diversity is not a priority in most Japanese companies. Only 32 percent of companies answered that they intended to actively implement such measures; this is less than half the rate reported by their Korean counterparts (66 percent) and below the Asian average of 38 percent. Anticipating that women will leave the company to give birth and raise children, and otherwise prioritize their families, senior male executives are reluctant to train and promote them. This imposes a glass ceiling that discourages women from aspiring to managerial careers.

Women who do get promoted face a major burden of balancing managerial and family responsibilities without sufficient support from the government, their employer, or their spouse. Despite a number of government-led reforms in recent years (see Ayako Kano's discussion in chapter 4 of this volume), women still experience difficulties achieving a viable work-life balance.[30] Besides inadequate support, women face uncertainties as they navigate the conflicting demands on their time. They also have few role models. Tadashi Yanai, president of Fast Retailing (Uniqlo), told us, "A real factor that prevents companies from utilizing women is that women still do not fully visualize their life combining motherhood and forming their own career. In our company, executives interview women workers and store managers and counsel them about their career path."[31] In his view, such mentoring is critical in helping women make adjustments as they juggle various responsibilities and pressures.

But mentoring is not the norm, and a stunning 74 percent of college-educated women quit their jobs voluntarily, more than double the rate in the United States (31 percent) and Germany (35 percent).[32] The percentage of women who drop out of the workforce in their thirties also remains high compared to the United States and Europe, where the rates of women's labor force participation remain relatively steady even during the child-rearing years.[33] While more than three-quarters (77 percent) of university-educated Japanese working women want to rejoin the workforce after leaving to tend to child rearing, only 43 percent of these are able to land any job, compared to 73 percent in the United States and 68 percent in Germany. Clearly, raising a family and pursuing a career is too much of an either/or choice in Japan. Overall, once children reach age four, Japanese women regardless of educational background demonstrate a strong desire to work, with increased preference for full-time jobs as the child grows older. After children reach age four, 72.3 percent of mothers with a child want to work, and 90.6 percent do after children reach age six, one-third on a full-time basis. When the child reaches age twelve, 95 percent wish to work, 54.4 percent full time.[34]

Government tax policies are also problematic, as they push married women into part-time work because households stand to lose deductions if the second income exceeds ¥1.03 million (about $12,000). In 2014 Abe proposed eliminating this tax break to encourage women to work more, but he could not convince members of his party to support this initiative and withdrew his proposal. In addition, child care waiting lists are long, and there are shortages of caregivers for the elderly. This means that many women who want to work full time are unable to do so because of their caregiving responsibilities. Abe proposed extending child care leave to three years but backtracked in the face of strong corporate opposition. He has moved, however, to expand child care by increasing the number of facilities and relying on private providers, addressing a long-standing shortage often cited as a major barrier to women's employment. Abe has also moved to relax immigration restrictions so that families can sponsor foreign maids to provide care services for children and the elderly, but the high cost of doing so makes this not an option for most working women.

As of 2012, women account for about 77 percent of Japan's nonregular workers and are disproportionately represented among poorly paid workers.[35] On average they earn about one-half of what male full-time workers do.[36] Furthermore, very few nonregular workers are given child care or family care leave, and in many cases employers don't contribute to their social insurance payments.[37] Overall, 40 percent of nonregular workers between the ages of twenty and thirty-four want a regular job, and 77 percent say the reason is that they want to earn more money.[38]

In some respects the 1986 Equal Employment Opportunity Law (EEOL) has improved gender equity in the labor force, but women remain significantly underrepresented in leadership positions. While the gender wage gap among full-time employees in Japan has improved from women earning 55 percent of male wages in 1980 to 66 percent in 2004 and 73 percent by 2011, it remains far larger than the OECD average of 84 percent in 2006.[39] Hence Japan's relatively large gender wage gap remains emblematic of a country lagging behind the times and the unfinished business of the EEOL.[40] As Yuko Abe concludes, "After the EEOL was enacted, neither married women's regular employment nor single women's regular employment advanced."[41] Although more women are graduating from junior colleges and universities, with the percentage of graduates increasing from 33.9 percent in 1980 to 55.9 percent in 2011, this has not translated into significant improvement in their job prospects, and the future does not look promising.[42] Gender disparity is still evident among new university graduates; in 2009 56.8 percent of women landed a full-time regular job compared to 79.3 percent of men.[43]

Discouraged Youth

Young workers are also having a hard time attaining regular employment. And for those who start out as nonregular workers, prospects for job training, skill development, and promotions up the career ladder are remote. As of 2007, 31 percent of Japanese aged fifteen to twenty-four (excluding students) worked in nonregular jobs.[44] Youth unemployment ranged from 4 to 5 percent in the 1990s but increased to 9.2 percent as of 2010.[45] Although Japan's youth unemployment rate is well below some of the more extreme cases in Europe (Spain's 46.4 percent in 2012, for example), the incidence of long-term youth unemployment in Japan is above the OECD average.

Typically, surveys report that over 90 percent of university graduates find a job, so the situation today is not quite the "ice age" that some describe.[46] Still, 20 percent of men and 43 percent of women settle for nonregular jobs.[47] And 15.5 percent of new graduates were NEETs (not in education, employment, or training).[48]

What, we might ask, do the young precariat want? Is it true, as the mass media suggest, that their desires for full-time work are on the wane? This is not what surveys suggest. Rather, among nonregular workers aged twenty to twenty-four, 57.3 percent want a regular job, while 42 percent of those aged twenty-five to thirty-four want to move to full-time work. Their reasons for preferring regular to nonregular work are straightforward: better pay and job security.[49] Nonetheless, it is striking that 58 percent of the twenty-five-to-thirty-four-year-old cohort today do not seek, or perhaps are discouraged about securing, full-time work. This development is hard to reconcile with the work-obsessed stereotype associated with their fathers' generation. Noritoshi Furuichi's 2011 best-selling book *Happy Youth in the Country of Despair* argues that young people no longer seek an identity in their work and don't aspire to the "empty affluence" of their parents.[50] Drawing on this finding and his experiences and acquaintances from a highly educated, privileged milieu, Furuichi reports that youth resist the rigors and limitations of corporate work culture. And, according to him, they are happier for it. He backs up this assertion by citing a 2010 government survey reporting that 65.9 percent of men and 75.2 percent of women in their twenties are satisfied. Although still in his twenties, Furuichi is an unlikely spokesman for marginalized youth because the vulnerable and less privileged are not on his radar screen. Yet there does seem to be a sea-change in the culture of work, as young people are less inclined to sacrifice private time and personal desires for their jobs and see little benefit in doing so.

But what is not captured in the above statistics, or in Furuichi's superficial assertions about "happiness," is the high level of anxiety among today's job seekers. Disquiet persists even among those who do get regular jobs, because everyone feels less secure about employment.[51] About one-third of recent university graduates leave their jobs within three years. This would seem to indicate that they are not adapting to the grind of mundane work, long hours, and transfers to remote branch offices that have long been a rite of passage for Japan's corporate warriors.[52] Morishima argues that youth are job-hopping because they are no longer willing to put up with the usual sacrifices expected by employers.[53] They are no longer certain that the company will survive, don't see the point of biding their time for slow-motion promotions in stodgy firms, and prefer familiar urban amenities close to friends and family.

It is not surprising that attitudes are changing among young Japanese given the unprecedented upheaval in a job market they are facing. Generally speaking, young people made a smooth and swift transition from education into stable jobs until the 1990s. They also experienced low rates of unemployment and job turnover. However, this system of relative job security declined under the wave of restructuring and deregulation during the Lost Decades. Abenomics is promoting further labor market deregulation that targets remaining job protections. The consequences for young workers are bleak in an era when mobility from nonregular jobs to regular jobs is limited. Whereas the transition from school to work used to be a ticket to a stable career and a middle-class life, for many young Japanese today this transition has turned into a one-way ticket to the employment periphery of precarious jobs and the working poor.[54] These "freeters" (young part-timers) were once romanticized as conscientious objectors and inspired dropouts. But, Furuichi aside, this image has not survived the grim realities facing young workers today.[55]

While young people in general are finding it increasingly difficult to grasp a rung on the career ladder and thus are getting trapped in low-level jobs, those with lower levels of educational attainment are most at risk. They have a harder time making the transition from school to work; they change jobs more often, and they also experience higher and longer periods of unemployment. Less educated youth have always fared more poorly in the job market than their better-educated counterparts, but one of the dire legacies of the Lost Decade is the much higher propensity of such outcomes. Today, those less educated are far more likely to end up as nonregular workers. And for those who remain nonregular workers, economic hardships will persist into retirement, because years of low wages mean they won't accumulate much in savings and will have to survive on a meager pension.

The Costs of Insecurity

The travails of young workers are a microcosm of the broader changes in a labor market marked by deregulation. Government deregulation of the labor market boosted incentives for employers to hire nonregular workers with low wages, no benefits, and no job security. This employment trend is common in other OECD economies, driven largely by intensified global competition, while Japanese employers have also adjusted to recession and low growth prospects at home. Japan's regulations and protections for nonregular workers are lax by OECD standards, but those for regular workers are very strict and backed up by social norms and court decisions. Japan's dual labor market, based on the gap between regular and nonregular workers, is a consequence of policy choices. These policy choices have facilitated the emergence of a precariat in which women and the young are overrepresented and have also increased the burden placed on the social safety net. For many workers shunted into nonregular jobs, the gap in job status, incomes, and prospects is likely to persist.

The growing gap embodied in the dual labor market creates a number of social problems and costs that pose serious challenges to policy makers. First, the precariat undermine the solvency of social insurance, as they contribute less.[56] Second, the precariat are much less likely to marry and procreate, exacerbating Japan's fertility woes. Lower fertility means fewer consumers and taxpayers in the future and a rising dependency ratio, with lower tax revenues (from fewer workers) supporting more and more retirees. Foreshadowed here is the eventual need for higher taxes accompanied by lower benefits. Third, a pauperized precariat contribute to deflation as they can't spend much. Fourth, this trend is also depressing productivity; there is little training for nonregular workers, and, because they are cheap labor, firms have little incentive to boost these workers' productivity. Fifth, there is a relatively high correlation between employment insecurity and suicide, another major social ill that the government is trying to reduce.[57] Since 1998 more than thirty thousand Japanese have committed suicide annually, and in recent years an increasing proportion are men in their twenties and thirties who are struggling to find work or suffering from financial distress. Thus the spread of nonregular employment comes at a high cost to society and to these expendable workers.

Greater job insecurity means that more people will need some kind of government safety net in the future, but there are not enough revenues to cover such outlays. Doubling the consumption tax to 10 percent by 2015, from 5 percent as of 2012, will be insufficient to pay for increased claims on social insurance by the growing ranks of the elderly and welfare recipients. Given that the government is awash in debt, with a 237 percent public debt to GDP ratio at the end of 2012, the trend toward lower tax revenues from an expanding precariat is bad news for everyone.

The profusion of low-paid nonregular employment is also depressing marriage rates and thus fertility. In 2011 the government found that ¥3 million ($30,000) income is a crucial dividing line; below that income level, only 8 to 10 percent of men in their twenties and thirties were married, while above ¥3 million, the proportion of married rose to 25 to 40 percent, rising with income.[58] By their early thirties, only 30 percent of nonregular workers married, compared to 56 percent of full-time corporate employees. Given that Japan's social welfare and elderly care systems rely heavily on family support mechanisms, the rising nonmarriage rate and lower fertility are exacerbating demographic problems and raise questions about who will care for these unmarried, childless poor in the future.

The growth of the precariat also affects national psychology, identity, and social cohesion. Widening income disparities and the emergence of a dual labor market are dividing people and relegating some to less appealing careers and a depressed standard of living.[59] For many of the "lost generation" who can't realize their ambitions, cannot find employment security, and can't marry and have children, the shared sense of purpose that motivated successive generations of post–World War II Japanese is waning, casting a cloud over Japan's possible futures.

Immigration

The issues of national identity and social cohesion, which have been of paramount importance to postwar Japanese, present another challenge with the doubling in the number of foreign residents between 1990 and 2008, from 1.1 million to 2.2 million. This influx has raised anxieties among some Japanese about an undesirable possible future of numerous unassimilated immigrants.[60] However, as of 2008, non-Japanese represent only 1.74 percent of Japan's population, a relatively small presence compared to foreign residents elsewhere (e.g., 5 percent in the United Kingdom, 8.2 percent in Germany). Japan as a mono-ethnic, homogeneous nation persists in the collective imagination even if there are some jarring signs of transformation evident in increasing numbers of international marriages and foreign enclaves.

In Japan, as in most countries around the world, immigration is a controversial topic. Current debate about labor migration to Japan focuses on what kind of workers should be allowed in—only skilled workers or also unskilled workers, how many and from where, for how long and under what terms.[61] This discourse is shaped by widespread perceptions that foreigners often resort to crime, although national crime statistics show, in fact, that foreigners do not commit crimes disproportionate to their numbers. Those who advocate a more open-door policy point to Japan's population decline, predicted labor shortages, and the need for more taxpayers to keep the national medical and pension schemes solvent.[62] Opponents insist on preserving the current degree of homogeneity and warn against the pitfalls of accommodating large resident foreign communities that have been evident in Europe.[63] The opponents are not only jingoists trying to haul up the drawbridges; there also is concern that until Japan can put in place laws and regulations that protect the human rights of migrant workers it should not extend them the welcome mat.[64]

Immigration could be a key policy option in addressing expected short-ages of both skilled and unskilled workers due to the demographic shrinking of the population, but there are no signs that the government will allow sufficient immigration to make much of a difference. To stabilize Japan's population and to avoid the consequences of a declining and aging population, the United Nations projects that Japan needs to raise immigration from a current level of about 50,000 a year to 650,000 a year, a level well beyond what anyone in a position of power is contemplating.[65] The aging of society means that more retirees are depending on a shrinking pool of workers to fund pensions and medical care; the dependency ratio was 2:11 in 1960, was 4:1 in 1999, and is projected to be 2:1 by 2030. This means there is an urgent need either to rapidly expand Japan's tax base by increasing the number of immigrants or to raise taxes and reduce benefits across the board.

Immigrants might also boost Japan's capacity to innovate and create new wealth, with their new ideas, language and cultural skills, global networks, and entrepreneurial spirit. The recent influx of Chinese since the 1990s demonstrates just how valuable immigrants can be as they have leveraged their transnational networks to facilitate and contribute to burgeoning trade and investment links.[66] Since 2007, Chinese have become Japan's largest foreign resident population (more than six hundred thousand), while an additional one hundred thousand have become Japanese citizens. Many come as students and stay on after securing jobs with Japanese firms.[67] Japan is the largest foreign investor in China, and China is Japan's largest trading partner, creating openings for transnational business entrepreneurs. One key factor giving Chinese advantages over other immigrants like ethnic Japanese born overseas, mostly from Brazil, is their greater degree of fluency in Japanese. Despite persistent Sino-Japanese diplomatic contretemps, economic relations remain vast and relatively buoyant, and there does not appear to be any significant impact on the Chinese community in Japan or on the influx of students.

In certain sectors of the economy, such as IT, that are currently facing a shortage of skilled workers, the government is allowing limited immigration. In 2012 the government initiated a new points system that targets foreigners with desired skills, achievements, and level of income. This fast track/permanent resident visa program targeted about two thousand people a year, but in 2013 only eight hundred applicants received the visa, an insignificant number that forced officials to ease eligibility criteria.[68] Even so, this program does not appear to offer a solution. Similarly, the elderly caregiver and nursing pilot programs, negotiated with Indonesia and the Philippines to mitigate severe shortages, are minuscule and doomed to failure and indicate reluctance to contemplate a significant non-Japanese population.[69] Given that Japan needs to recruit tens of thousands of caregivers to tend to its burgeoning ranks of elderly, a few hundred Filipinos and Indonesians a year are not making a difference. This is especially true given that most are unable to pass licensing exams and thus must return home with little to show for their efforts.[70]

The government justifies the strict limits on immigration in terms of public opinion, but in Japan there actually are few instances where the government defers to public opinion over important policy issues. As Daniel Aldrich has argued, "Japanese leaders and civil servants envision public opinion as malleable; in this approach, the people's perspective should be changed to match the perspective of the administration rather than elevated as a guide-star which should be followed."[71] There is reason, thus, to be skeptical when Ministry of Justice officials invoke anti-immigration public opinion to justify their desired policy goal. The prime minister's office conducted a survey in 2004 showing that the Japanese public is more ambivalent than xenophobic about immigration: only 29.1 percent unequivocally opposed immigration to mitigate labor shortages.[72] Moreover, even in remote rural Japan, foreigners are far more appreciated and welcome than one might imagine from government assertions about antiforeign public sentiments.[73] While prejudice against non-Japanese is common, and they are excluded from job opportunities, random acts of violence or hate crimes targeting foreigners are notable for their absence, and anti-immigration policies are not part of political campaigns. At the same time, however, the government is cracking down on undocumented migrants, and some detainees are subject to abuse.

While Japanese may be ambivalent about immigration, they nonetheless depend on the services (and labor) that foreign workers provide in various jobs ranging from convenience stores and restaurants to hot-spring resorts and manufacturing. Thus, given the country's dependence on unskilled foreign workers to take jobs that are unappealing to Japanese, the government will accommodate what is minimally needed in an ad hoc manner.[74] Immigration will persist but will remain limited and thus will not significantly boost consumption, fertility, or social insurance revenues. This minimalist approach to immigration may dim Japan's future prospects, but policy makers seem to consider it the lesser evil.

The Chimera of Reform

As we see it, policy makers face a daunting agenda: a rapidly aging population, job insecurity, income disparities, an inadequate safety net, underfunded social insurance programs, and the associated problems of low fertility and eroding social cohesion. If immigration is not a likely solution, Japan can ill afford to waste the potential of its women workers to the extent it does now, nor can it leave so many young people adrift. To improve its future prospects, the country needs to establish an employment system that facilitates a transition from nonregular work to regular work, improved work/life balance policies, more flexible working conditions, improved training programs for new employees and displaced workers, and a working environment that better taps into the diversity of life-cycle needs and aspirations in twenty-first-century Japan. Alas, this is a list of what is *not* happening, as reforms targeting the precariat, women, and youth are inadequate. PM Abe's resolute reputation notwithstanding, vacillating political leadership, coupled with bureaucratic complacency, suggests a muddling-through scenario of inadequate half-measures. The structural reform package unveiled by PM Abe in June 2014 shied away from transformative initiatives and instead opted for expedient compromise with the vested interests on various issues, including women, immigration, and the labor market.

Will there be a labor shortage in the future? The answer to this question is crucial because a labor shortage might help marginalized workers as firms compete to recruit and retain them. There is some encouraging news as the overall job offering-to-applicant ratio in 2014 rose to 1.09, the highest since 1992 and up significantly from 0.42 in 2009. However, the job offering-to-applicant ratio for full-time jobs in 2014 was 0.61, suggesting that that many new employees are joining the precariat because there is a shortage of full-time stable jobs. Back in 1988 the ratio of full-time job openings to applicants was 0.9, slipping to 0.82 in 2005 and 0.74 in 2013, indicating that there has been a significant structural shift in the labor market toward more nonregular jobs and less full-time employment, a trend with immense implications for young Japanese and women workers.[75]

Although the job market for regular jobs remains weak for young Japanese, demographic trends suggest a sharp drop in the working-age population, raising concerns about the possibility of labor shortages down the road. This can be seen, for example, in the fact that the number of eighteen-year-olds fell from 2 million to 1.2 million between 1991 and 2012. One projection suggests an overall shortage of 8.1 million workers by 2030 if GDP growth averages 2 percent. On the other hand, if GDP growth averages 1 percent, a more likely scenario, there will be 2.4 million excess workers.[76] (For reference, between 2001 and 2010, Japan's average GDP growth was 0.75 percent.)[77]

The welter of projections ranging from a labor shortage to surplus is confusing, and much depends on assumptions about economic growth. The prospect of a labor shortage is often invoked as a reason why conditions for nonregular workers will improve. But a 2012 government projection forecasts an overall loss of as many as 8.4 million jobs by 2030, representing a 13 percent decline in jobs from 2010.[78] If such a degree of job losses materializes, improvement in labor conditions for women, youth, and the precariat appears unlikely.

There are other discouraging signs. In the summer of 2012 there was a flurry of labor market reforms, but to what effect? There seems to be more window-dressing than substance to many of these reforms, driven by compromises between bureaucrats, politicians, unions, and business groups pushing different agendas. For example, the Diet passed legislation that revised conditions for mandatory enrollment in social insurance (providing pensions and medical care) that was aimed at boosting participation by precariat and requiring employer contributions. The new criteria, however, actually exclude most nonregular workers, demonstrating the difficulties of translating good intentions into meaningful reforms.[79]

In the same 2012 Diet session, the government also passed legislation requiring that firms continue to employ workers beyond the mandatory retirement age (sixty) until they are sixty-five years old if the employees wish to continue working.[80] This measure addresses a critical problem caused by increasing the age of pension eligibility to sixty-five beginning in 2013; those who retire at age sixty face a five-year gap before receiving pension payments. But this reform merely shifts the problem, because extending employment for older workers is not good news for new graduates looking for jobs.

The Diet also revised the labor contract law to improve employers' treatment of contract workers hired for fixed durations and to ban their unreasonable dismissal.[81] This revised law also stipulates that such contract workers should have the option of becoming permanent staff after five years' employment at the same workplace. The amendment prohibits employers from refusing to renew such contracts when it is deemed "reasonable" for workers to expect renewal of their contracts. In addition, the revised law bans "unreasonable" differences in the working conditions of contract and permanent employees.[82] As with other labor-related measures in Japan, there are no sanctions for noncompliance, and much will depend on voluntary compliance and judicial processes that can be ineffective, time-consuming, and expensive. It is worth recalling that a similar 1999 reform targeting improvement in temporary workers' situation had little positive impact and that the EEOL has also disappointed.[83]

There are thus good reasons to doubt whether the 2012 labor reforms will significantly affect employees, particularly those in irregular jobs. As one human resource manager commented to us, the revisions aimed at encouraging a shift in the labor force from nonregular to regular employment are unlikely to help irregular workers and may actually lead to an erosion of conditions for regular workers. In his view, cost cutting is the main reason why the precariat has expanded and why firms will subvert the reforms.

Possible Futures

The proliferation of poorly paid, insecure jobs in Japan is not unique among industrialized nations, just as the travails of its middle class and rising inequality have become a global phenomenon. The negative social repercussions of these trends are certainly evident in Japan, though not as much as in other industrialized economies. But will this situation persist?

Regarding Japan's possible futures, we anticipate further ad hoc, incremental adjustments that may partially mitigate the problems and manage the risks that workers in Japan are now confronting. Yet there will be a shrinking number of the stable, good jobs that the younger generation's relatively affluent parents took for granted along with the certainties and hopes these jobs provided. To some extent civil society organizations have successfully promoted improvements in the social safety net, but it is unlikely that they can overcome employers' vigorous embrace of the flexible employment policies that define Japan's new labor paradigm. The precaritization of employment in Japan is substantial (38 percent of jobs), and, for increasing numbers of workers and their families, the attendant risks are becoming the new normal. This unraveling of the implicit social contract of reciprocal obligations is also changing Japanese attitudes toward work as the rewards for loyalty and personal sacrifice decline.

The International Monetary Fund (IMF), focusing on the negative economic implications of an aging society in Japan, concludes that women can "save" the country, but only if the government and employers implement policies that reduce the gender gap in career positions and provide better support for working mothers.[84] But what is obvious to the IMF in 2012 is not happening on the ground, and there are few signs that key adjustments are being made that could significantly bolster gender diversity in the workplace. One of the stark possible futures for Japan is that women will remain a marginalized and squandered resource. Women's potential contributions to the economy and society will be diminished owing to the absence of sensible reforms that would enable them to balance career and family responsibilities. We believe that women will remain underrepresented in management and that glass ceilings and childbirth will continue to derail far too many careers because of rigidity in attitudes, employment policy, and employment practices.

Precaritization is disproportionately affecting women, and there are few signs that this trend will abate. An increasing proportion of Japanese are on the outside looking in, underscoring the precarious future of a Japan that fails to recognize, or take advantage of, the potential and vitality of all its population. In our opinion, as women fare, so fares Japan. Abenomics, however, shortchanges "womenomics," emphasizing expansion of day care facilities without addressing several other significant obstacles to promoting women's careers. Alas, the government and employers have not yet risen to the challenge facing the nation's precariat, and it is this dereliction and policy drift that casts a cloud over Japan's possible futures.

Notes

1. The working-age population (ages twenty to sixty-four) is projected to decline from 60.5 percent of the total population in 2006 to 47.7 percent by 2055, while the elderly population (sixty-five and over) will nearly double from 20.8 percent to 40.5 percent in the same period, and the total population will shrink from 127.77 million to 89.93 million. National Institute of Population and Social Security Research, *Population Statistics of Japan 2008*, 2008, www.ipss.go.jp/p-info/e/psj2008/PSJ2008.asp.

2. See Susan Houseman and Machiko Osawa, eds., *Nonstandard Work in Developed Economies: Causes and Consequences* (Kalamazoo, MI: Upjohn Institute, 2003); Machiko Osawa and Myoung Jung Kim, "Keizai no gurōbaruka nitomonau

rōdōryoku no hiseikika no yōin to seifu no taiō no Nikkan hikaku" [Globalization and increasing nonregular employment: A comparison of Japan and Korea], *Nihon Rōdō Kenkyū Zasshi* 595 (2010): 95–112; Hirokatsu Asano, Takahiro Ito, and Daiji Kawaguchi, "Why Has the Fraction of Contingent Workers Increased?," RIETI Discussion Paper Series 11-E-021, April 2011, Research Institute of Economy, Trade and Industry, www.rieti.go.jp/en/publications/summary/11030030.html; original Japanese, RIETI Discussion Paper Series 11-J-051, www.rieti.go.jp/en/publications/summary/11040019.html. In 1985, 16.4 percent of the workforce was employed on a nonregular basis, mostly part-time women workers.

3.   For an engaging analysis of this trend drawing on the author's fieldwork as a non-regular worker, see Huiyan Fu, *An Emerging Non-regular Labor Force in Japan* (Abingdon, UK: Routledge, 2011).

4.   See Jeff Kingston, *Contemporary Japan*, 2nd ed. (Oxford: Wiley-Blackwell, 2013), 77–92.

5.   For some of the positive consequences of the "Lost Decade," see Jeff Kingston, *Japan's Quiet Transformation* (Abingdon, UK: Routledge, 2004).

6.   Ministry of Health, Labor, and Welfare [hereafter MHLW], "Rōdōryoku chōsa shōsaishūkei" [Labor force survey—special tabulation], 2012, www.stat.go.jp/data/roudou/sokuhou/4hanki/dt/index.htm.

7.   Shin Arita, "Hikaku o tsujite miru higashiajia no shakaikaisōkōzō-shokugyō ga motarasu hōshukakusa to shakaiteki fubyōdō" [A comparative study of social stratification in East Asian societies: The reward differences between occupation and social inequality], *Shakaigaku Hyōron* 59, no. 4 (2009): 663–81. His findings are based on 2005 Social Stratification and Mobility Survey data collected by the University of Tokyo. This 20 percent figure tallies with the findings of MHLW, *Rōdō hakusho* [Labor employment white paper] (Tokyo, 2006), while similar findings are reported in Yūji Genda, "Zenshoku ga hiseishain datta rishokusha no seishain e no ikō ni tsuite" [Change from nonregular to regular employee status], *Nihon Rōdō Kenkyū Zasshi* 580 (2008): 61–77. He reports that mobility differs by educational attainment, with an overall mobility rate of 21.9 percent and a rate for high school graduates of 10.4 percent. The rate of mobility for nonregular workers declines as the duration of such employment increases, dropping to 6 percent after ten years.

8.   Arita, "Hikaku," 663–81.

9.   For in-depth analysis, see Toru Shinoda, "Which Side Are You On? Hakenmura and the Working Poor as a Tipping Point in Japanese Labor Politics," *Asia-Pacific Journal*, April 4, 2009, http://japanfocus.org/-Toru-SHINODA/3113.

10. Prior to mid-2010, nonregular employees who were working at least twenty hours a week and were expected to work for more than one year were eligible for unemployment insurance, and employers had to contribute. However, since most nonregular workers did not get such long contracts they were in effect excluded. As of 2010, anyone working more than twenty hours a week and expected to be hired for more than thirty-one days must enroll in the unemployment insurance program, and employers are required to contribute. MHLW, "Koyō hoken seido" [Employment insurance system], 2010, 2014, www.mhlw.go.jp/bunya/koyou/koyouhoken/osirase.html. Following the Lehman Shock and reports that many nonregular workers were ineligible for unemployment insurance or welfare, the government created a new program that provided rent, living expenses, and training to anyone who lost his or her job. Whereas welfare had been restricted in practice to those who were physically incapable of working, the new guidelines relaxed eligibility criteria. MHLW, "Daini no seifutīnetto shien gaido" [Guide to the second safety-net], n.d., www.mhlw.go.jp/bunya/koyou/employ/dl/taisaku2b.pdf (accessed December 23, 2012).

11. Machiko Osawa, *Nihongata wākingu pua no honshitsu* [Japan's working poor] (Tokyo: Iwanami Shoten, 2010).

12. Fumio Ōtake, "Aging Society and Inequality," *Japan Labor Bulletin* 38, no. 7 (1999): 5–11; Fumio Ōtake, *Nihon no fubyōdō* [Inequality in Japan] (Tokyo: Nihon Keizai Shimbunsha, 2005).

13. OECD, *Economic Survey of Japan 2006: Income Inequality, Poverty and Social Spending* (Paris: OECD, 2006).

14. Nihon keizai shinbun, "Kodomono hinkonritsu saiaku no 16.3%" [Child poverty 16.3%, the worst figure], July 16, 2014, www.nikkei.com/article/DGXNASDG15H15_V10C14A7CR8000/.

15. Relative poverty is defined by the government as the number of people whose annual income is less than half the national disposable income. In 2009 the average national disposable income was ¥2.24 million, meaning that 16 percent of the population was living on less than ¥1.12 million. See "Poverty in Japan," *Japan Times*, editorial, January 25, 2010, www.japantimes.co.jp/text/ed20100125a2.html. Also see Toshiaki Tachibanaki, "Inequality and Poverty in Japan," *Japanese Economic Review*, 57, no. 1 (March 2006): 16; Dustin Dye, "Japan Poverty Rate at a Record High," *Foreign Policy Blogs*, July 14, 2011, http://foreignpolicyblogs.com/2011/07/14/japan-poverty-rate-record-high/.

16. OECD, *Divided We Stand: Why Inequality Keeps Rising* (Paris: OECD, 2011), and OECD, *Growing Unequal?* (Paris: OECD, 2008).

17. Tachibanaki, "Inequality," 3.

18. R. S. Jones, "Income Inequality, Poverty and Social Spending in Japan," OECD Economics Department, Working Paper No. 556, 2007, http://dx.doi.org/10.1787/177754708811.

19. Hiroshi Ishida and David Slater, eds., *Social Class in Contemporary Japan* (Abingdon, UK: Routledge, 2009), and Yūji Genda, *A Nagging Sense of Insecurity* (Tokyo: I-House Press, 2005).

20. David Pilling, "Land of the Rising Inequality Coefficient," *Financial Times*, March 14, 2006.

21. Makoto Yuasa, *Han hinkon-suberidai shakai kara no dasshutsu* [Anti-poverty: Escaping a nosediving society] (Tokyo: Iwanami Shinsho, 2004); Atsushi Miura, *Karyū shakai* [Downwardly mobile society] (Tokyo: Kōbunsha Shinsho, 2005); Takuro Morinaga, *Nenshū 300 manen jidai o ikinuku keizaigaku* [Getting by on less than three million yen] (Tokyo: Kobunsha, 2003).

22. World Economic Forum, *The Global Gender Gap Report 2011*, 2011, http://www3.weforum.org/docs/WEF_GenderGap_Report_2011.pdf .

23. This section's first epigraph is from Kathy Matsui's *Womenomics 3.0* (New York: Goldman Sachs, 2010), www.goldmansachs.com/japan/ideas/demographic-change/womenomics-2011/womenomics3.pdf. The second epigraph quoting Lagarde is from comments at a press conference in Tokyo regarding Japan's graying society and stagnant economy; Agence France Press, October 13, 2012.

24. McKinsey & Company, *Women Matter: An Asian Perspective. Harnessing Female Talent to Raise Corporate Performance*, June 2012, www.google.com/url?sa=t&rct=j&q=&esrc=s&source=web&cd=1&ved=0CCAQFjAA&url=http%3A%2F%2Fwww.mckinsey.com%2F~%2Fmedia%2FMcKinsey%2520Offices%2FJapan%2FPDF%2FWomen_Matter_An_Asian_perspective.ashx&ei=G6q-VOzsBISfyQTD1IGgBg&usg=AFQjCNERLztjWW9oopYmigCHoydhoCfUJA&bvm=bv.83829542,d.aWw.

25. On the correlation between women employees and profits, see Naomi Kodama, Kazuhiko Odaki, and Yoko Takahashi, "Why Does Employing More Females Increase Corporate Profits? Evidence from Japanese Panel Data," *Japan Labor Review*, 6, no. 1 (2009): 51–71.

26. Kaori Sasaki, president of eWomen, interview by Machiko Osawa, Tokyo, September 13, 2012.

27. Kathy Matsui, chief Japan equity strategist for Goldman Sachs (Japan), interview by Machiko Osawa, Tokyo, September 12, 2012.

28. Toshifumi Suzuki, chief executive officer of Seven & I Holdings, interview by Machiko Osawa, Tokyo, June 15, 2012.

29. Risa S., interview by Jeff Kingston, Tokyo, July 12, 2012.

30. Machiko Osawa, "Japan's Changing Economy and Women Workers," *Japanese Economy* 32, no. 4 (2004–5): 96–108, and Helen McNaughton, "From 'Postwar' to 'Post-Bubble': Contemporary Issues for Japanese Working Women," in *Perspectives on Work, Employment and Society in Japan*, ed. Peter Matanle and Wim Lunsing (London: Palgrave Macmillan, 2006), 31–57.

31. Tadashi Yanai, president of Fast Retailing (Uniqlo), interview by Machiko Osawa, Tokyo, September 20, 2012.

32. Sylvia Ann Hewlet and Laura Sherbin, *Off Ramps and On Ramps Japan: Keeping Talented Women on the Road to Success* (New York: Center for Work-Life Policy, 2011).

33. For an international comparison of the age-specific labor force participation of women, see Prime Minister's Office, "The Gender Equality White Paper (2011)," 2011, www.gender.go.jp/whitepaper/h22/zentai/html/zuhyo/index.html.

34. Cabinet Office, "Josei no Life Planning-shien ni kansuru chōsa" [Women's life planning support survey], 2007, www.gender.go.jp/kaigi/senmon/wlb/siryo/pdf/wlb02-4-2.pdf.

35. For an assessment of the disadvantages of nonregular employment for women, see Heidi Gottfried, "Pathways to Economic Security: Gender and Non-standard Employment in Contemporary Japan," *Social Indicators Research* 88 (2008): 179–96.

36. For the proportion of nonregular workers who are women, see MHLW, *Rōdōryoku chōsa* [Labor force survey], January–March 2012, www.mhlw.go.jp/stf/houdou/2r9852000002ea8h-att/2r9852000002eac3.pdf. On the percentage of women engaged as nonregular workers, see MHLW, *Rōdōryoku chōsa-syōsai shūkei* [Labor force survey, 2014], 2014, www.stat.go.jp/data/roudou/sokuhou/4hanki/dt/pdf/05500.pdf. For wage gap details, see Prime Minister's Office, "Gender Equality White Paper (2011)."

37. Since 2005, fixed-term contract workers who are hired for more than one year are eligible for child care leave if it is expected that they will be employed at the time of the child's birth. These criteria effectively exclude almost all women contract workers. MHLW, "Ikuji-Kaigō kyūgyohō ni okeru seido no gaiyō" [Outline of child care and elder care leave law], 2005, http://www2.mhlw.go.jp/topics/seido/josei/hourei/20000401-38.htm.

38. MHLW, *Rōdōryoku chōsa-syōsai shūkei*.

39. For details on the gender wage gap, see MHLW, "Hataraku josei no jitsujō" [White paper on working women], 2011, www.mhlw.go.jp/stf/houdou/2r9852000002ea8h.html. For OECD average, see OECD Social Policy Division, *Gender Brief*, March 2010, www.oecd.org/els/social.

40. For analysis of the gender wage gap, see "The Gender Gap in the Japanese Labor Market," special issue, *Japan Labor Review* 6, no. 1 (2009), www.jil.go.jp/english/JLR/documents/2009/JLR21_all.pdf. On the EEOL, see Charles Weathers, "Changing White Collar Workplaces and Female Temporary Workers in Japan," *Social Science Japan Journal* 4, no. 2 (2001): 201–18.

41. Yuko Abe, "The Equal Employment Opportunity Law and Labor Force Behavior of Women in Japan," *Journal of the Japanese and International Economies* 25 (2011): 39–55.

42. The percentage of female high school graduates entering four-year universities (24.6 percent) exceeded those entering junior college (23.7 percent) for the first time in 1996. As of 2008 the percentage of high school graduates attending a four-year university increased to 42.6 percent, while the figure for those enrolling in junior colleges fell to 11.5 percent. On higher education enrollment by women, see Ministry of Education, Culture, Sports, Science, and Technology, "Gakkō kihon chōsa" [Basic survey on education], 2013, www.mext.go.jp/b_menu/toukei/chousa01/kihon/kekka/1268046.htm. For an overall assessment of women, education, and employment, see Toshiaki Tachibanaki, *The New Paradox for Japanese Women: Greater Choice, Greater Inequality* (Tokyo: I-House Press, 2010).

43. MHLW, "Jakunensya koyō jittai chōsa" [Survey on youth employment], 2010, www.garbagenews.net/archives/1521689.html.

44. OECD, *Jobs for Youth—Japan* (Paris: OECD, 2009). Including students, the figure for youth nonregular employment is 46 percent.

45. "Left Behind: The Jobless Young," *Economist*, September 11, 2011, www.economist.com/node/21528614.

46. David Pilling, "Youth of the Ice Age," *Financial Times*, July 6, 2012. These figures are somewhat inflated because they are based on surveys of university job placement offices and do not include students classified as not actively seeking a job.

47. On the employment rate of university graduates, see *Shūshoku (naitei)* [Employment rates of university graduates], Honkawa Yutaka, March 23, 2015, http://www2.ttcn.ne.jp/honkawa/3160.html. For gender differences, see MHLW, "Jakunensya koyō jittai chōsa" [Survey on youth employment], 2015 and 2013.

48. Ministry of Education, Culture, Sports, Science, and Technology, "Gakkō kihon chōsa" [Basic survey on education], 2012, www.mext.go.jp/component/b_menu/houdou/__icsFiles/afieldfile/2012/08/30/1324976_01.pdf.

49. MHLW, "Paato-taimu rōdōsha sōgō jittai chōsa" [Survey on status of part-time workers], 2011, www.mhlw.go.jp/toukei/list/132-23e.html#03.

50. Noritoshi Furuichi, *Zetsubō no kuni no kōfuku na wakamonotachi* [Happy youth in the country of despair] (Tokyo: Kodansha, 2011).

51. "University Degree and Full-Employee-Status No Protection against Joblessness in Japan," *Mainichi*, January 8, 2012; Martin Fackler, "In Japan, Young Face Generational Roadblocks," *New York Times*, January 27, 2011.

52. MHLW, "Shinki gakusotsusha no rishoku jōkyo ni kansuru shiryō" [Survey materials regarding separation of newly hired workers], 2010, www.mhlw.go.jp/topics/2010/01/tp0127-2/24.html, news.mynavi.jp/news/2014/11/11/035.

53. Motohiro Morishima, "Tenshoku dekiru kaisha ka dōka ni nayamu shūkatsu gakusei no kyōchū" [Anxious students hunt for jobs], *President*, June 2012, http://president.jp/articles/-/6231.

54. Mary Brinton, "Social Class and Economic Life Chances in Post-industrial Japan: The 'Lost Generation,'" in Ishida and Slater, *Social Class*, 114–34, and Ayako Kondo, "Does the First Job Really Matter? State Dependency in Employment Analysis," *Journal of Japanese and International Economies* 21 (2007): 379–402.

55. On freeters, see Yuki Honda, "Freeters: Young Atypical Workers in Japan," in Matanle and Lunsing, *Perspectives on Work*, 143–68. For a wide-ranging assessment of youth problems in contemporary Japan, see Roger Goodman, Yuki Imoto, and Tuukka Toivonen, eds., *A Sociology of Japanese Youth* (Abingdon, UK: Routledge, 2012).

56. For an overview of proposed social security reforms, see MHLW, "The Comprehensive Reform of Social Security and Tax," 2011, www.mhlw.go.jp/english/social_security/kaikaku.html.

57. On suicides among people under age thirty due to their failure to land jobs, see "Dismal Job Opportunities for Under 30s Caused 150 Suicides in 2011," *Mainichi*, May 14, 2012. For the strong correlation of unemployment and suicide in Japan, see W. Michael Coz and Jahyeong Koo, "Miracle to Malaise: What's Next for Japan," *Economic Letter-Insights from the Federal Reserve Bank of Dallas* 1, no. 1 (2006), www.dallasfed.org/research/eclett/index.cfm.

58. "Rise in Single-Member Households Reflects Concerns about Income," *Japan Times*, July 31, 2011.

59. "Rising Poverty in Japan," *Japan Times*, editorial, May 19, 2009.

60. Gabriele Vogt, "Foreign Workers in Japan," in *The Sage Handbook of Japanese Studies*, ed. James Babb (London: Sage Publications, 2015), 567–82.

61. For a comprehensive and insightful assessment of immigration policy and discourse in Japan, see Glenda Roberts, "Voicing the 'I' Word: Proposals and Initiatives on Immigration to Japan from the LDP and Beyond," *ASIEN* 124 (July 2012): 48–68.

62. "Gaikokujin katsuyō ni 'kokka 100nen no keio" [Immigration policy requires a century-long perspective], Nihon Keizai Shimbun, April 21, 2104.

63. "Fukyō demo motemote gaikokujin rōdōsha ukeiresaku ni igi!" [Objections to accepting foreign workers], *Wedge*, June 2009, 28–36.

64. Hidenori Sakanaka, *Towards a Japanese-Style Immigration Nation* (Tokyo: Japan Immigration Policy Institute, 2009).

65. John Haffner, "Immigration as a Source of Renewal in Japan," *Policy Innovations*, January 19, 2010, www.policyinnovations.org/ideas/commentary/data/000161.

66. Gracia Liu-Farrer, "Making Careers in the Occupational Niche: Chinese Students in Corporate Japan's Transnational Business," *Journal of Ethnic and Migration Studies* 37, no. 5 (2011): 785–803.

67. The unpredictable outcomes of immigration policy regarding Chinese in Japan are explored by Gracia Liu-Farrer, "Ambiguous Concepts and Unintended Consequences: Rethinking Skilled Migration in View of Chinese Migrants Economic Outcomes in Japan," *ASIEN* 124 (July 2012): 159–79. Also see Nana Oishi, "The Limits of Immigration Policies: The Challenges of Highly Skilled Migration in Japan," *American Behavioral Scientist*, April 2012, http://abs.sagepub.com/content/early/2012/04/12/0002764212441787.

68. "Few Biting So Far on Special Visa for Workers," *Japan Times, July 20, 2014*.

69. Gabriele Vogt, "Caregiver Migration to Greying Japan," in *Demographic Aspects of Migration*, ed. Thomas Salzman, Barry Edmonston, and James Raymer (Wiesbaden: Springer, 2010), 327–48.

70. Kingston, *Contemporary Japan*, 146–49. On discouragement among caregivers and their departure from Japan, see "Foreign Caregiver Exits Put Program in Doubt," *Japan Times*, June 20, 2012.

71. Daniel Aldrich, "Networks of Power," in *Natural Disaster and Nuclear Crisis in Japan*, ed. Jeff Kingston (Abingdon, UK: Routledge, 2012), 131.

72. Cabinet Office, "Gaikokujin ukeire ni kansuru yoron chōsa" [Japanese attitudes toward foreign workers], 2004, http://survey.gov-online.go.jp/h16/h16-foreigner-worker/index.html.

73. Lieba Faier, *Intimate Encounters: Filipina Women and the Remaking of Rural Japan* (Berkeley: University of California Press, 2009).

74. Gabriele Vogt, "Closed Doors, Open Doors, Doors Wide Shut? Migration Politics in Japan," *Journal of Current Japanese Affairs* 5 (2007): 3–30.

75. MHLW, "Rōdō shijō bunseki Report No. 29" [Labor market analysis report no. 29], February 28, 2014 www.mhlw.go.jp/seisakunitsuite/bunya/koyou_roudou/koyou/roudou_report/dl/20140228_02.pdf.

76. Shinichirō Kobayashi, "Shōshi kōreika ga susumuto rōdōryoku wa hontōni fusoku suru no ka" [Will there really be a labor shortage in an aging society?], *Keizai no Prism*, no. 66 (March 2009): 1–22.

77. "Average Annual GDP in Japan, 1980–2009," *Social Democracy for the Twenty-First Century: A Post-Keynesian Perspective*, May 22, 2012, http://socialdemocracy21st-century.blogspot.jp/2012/05/average-annual-gdp-in-japan-1980-2009.html.

78. *Koyō seisaku kenkyūkai hōkoku* [Report on employment policy] (Tokyo: MHLW, 2012), www.mhlw.go.jp/stf/houdou/2r9852000002gqwx.html.

79. The new criteria require enrollment in social insurance for anyone working at least twenty hours a week and earning more than ¥88,000 a month in firms with at least five hundred employees, and employers must contribute, but most nonregular workers don't qualify. For reform details, see MHLW, "Nenkin seido no kaisei ni tsuite" [About social security reform], 2012, www.mhlw.go.jp/seisakunitsuite/bunya/nenkin/nenkin/topics/2012/tp0829-01.html. The Japan Institute of Labor and Policy Training conducted a survey of part-time workers in 2010, finding that 48.8 percent of part-timers earned less than ¥1.1 million in 2009; Japan Institute of Labor and Policy Training, "Tanjikan rōdōsya jittai chōsa kekka" [Results of survey on part-time workers], press release, December 27, 2010, www.jil.go.jp/press/documents/20101227.pdf. The reform will not obligate employers to make contributions for most nonregular employees, as many are employed at smaller firms and as the legislation exempts poorly paid employees from paying social insurance. In considering the monthly wage criteria it is important to bear in mind that the minimum hourly wage in Japan averages ¥737 while the new income threshhold is based on a minimum ¥1,100 per hour, 50 percent above minimum wage. It is also relatively easy for firms and nonregular workers to evade what amounts to an unwelcome tax; "Pāto shufu ga kieru? Pāto rōdōsha e no shakaihōken tekiyōkakudai no zehi" [Are housewives leaving the part-time labor force? The case for expanding social security benefits for part-time workers], April 24, 2012, www.toyokeizai.net/articles/-/9004.

80. On extending employment for retirees, see "Mandatory Retirement Takes a Leap Forward," *Japan Times*, March 24, 2013. Also see MHLW, "Konenreisha kōyō antei hō no kaisei" [Revised elderly workers' employment stability law], 2012, www.mhlw.go.jp/seisakunitsuite/bunya/koyou_roudou/koyou/koureisha/topics/tp120903-1.html.

81. The law was implemented in August 2013; see MHLW, "Rōdōsha hakenhō kaiseihō" [Revised law of dispatched workers], 2012, www.mhlw.go.jp/bunya/koyou/dl/roudou_haken0329.pdf.

82.   Violators are subject to being publicly named by the government. For more details, see "Ihō kōi niyoru bassoku gyōsei shobun oyobi Kankoku kōhyō" [Penalty, administrative measures, recommendations and public announcements of firms violating the law], 2012, www.mhlw.go.jp/general/seido/anteikyoku/jukyu/haken/youryou/dl/13.pdf.

83.   Charles Weathers, "Women in Japan's Temporary Services Industry," JPRI Working Paper No. 85, March 2002, Japan Policy Research Institute, www.jpri.org/publications/workingpapers/wp85.html.

84.   Chad Steinberg and Masato Nakane, "Can Women Save Japan?" IMF Working Paper 12/248, October 2012, International Monetary Fund, 26, www.imf.org/external/pubs/ft/wp/2012/wp12248.pdf.

CHAPTER FOUR

The Future of Gender in Japan: Work/Life Balance and Relations between the Sexes

Ayako Kano

Fighting men and nurturing women. In the days and weeks immediately following the disaster of 2011, certain images of Japan became highly visible while others receded from view. In the short term, hegemonic gender norms seemed to return, such as the strong muscular male—Self-Defense Forces soldiers carrying survivors on their backs—and nurturing females—Fukushima mothers expressing anxiety about their children's safety. News reports also told of women in their thirties—the demographic group that had been enjoying a single lifestyle—who were now eager to find marriage partners.[1] In the immediate wake of the triple disaster, gender roles seemed to revert to older models—sturdy protective men and vulnerable childbearing women. Yet it soon became clear that these images, prominent in the early aftermath of 3/11, were selective. Other realities did not make it so readily into the press: women, along with men, in the rescue and reconstruction efforts, and fathers joining mothers in demonstrations and public actions around nuclear safety.[2]

In Japan's response to crisis—to the disaster of 2011 as well as the earlier global financial crisis of 2008—are we likely to see a retreat to earlier sociological patterns, persistence of recent patterns, or the onset of genuine change? In focusing on the gendered dimensions of this recovery, I would contend that these are all likely possibilities. In this chapter I will first examine the scholarly, social, and political attention placed on gender as a category, noting the rise of a "weak male" discourse at a time when advocacy for gender equality seems to be competing for attention with concern over economic disparity. Turning from popular discourse to policy, I will describe recent governmental gender policies and the controversy surrounding their implementation. The conservative backlash suggests a lack of social consensus about the state's goals and means of achieving gender equality. Finally, turning from policies to possibilities, I will present several future scenarios, both pessimistic and optimistic, for gender in Japan.

Gender as a Category

Gender was a topic of intense academic and political conversation from the 1990s into the early 2000s. Now, however, its prominence seems to have decreased and attention has shifted elsewhere, to economic disparity and the aging population, for example. Is the focus on gender at a turning point? Eiji Oguma wonders whether the era when gender was heatedly discussed might have been as short as from the late 1960s to the mid-1980s, when class was of less concern—because Japanese saw themselves overwhelmingly as middle class[3]—and thus more attention was paid to other sociological distinctions like gender. But as economic and generational disparities begin to pull apart the putative homogeneity of Japanese society today, are we at the threshold of a period when it might take unusual effort to keep gender in the foreground of intellectual concern?[4] One answer to this question is suggested by the discourses of the "weak male" and "herbivorous male" that have circulated in the media since about 2006.

As Machiko Osawa and Jeff Kingston's "Risk and Consequences" (chapter 3 of this volume) describes, socioeconomic conditions have significantly worsened since the 2000s for a particular segment of the Japanese population: men in their thirties and forties. While the precarious labor force has been overwhelmingly female, many men were also unable to find full-time employment during the 1990s—the "Lost Decade"—and have found themselves trapped in a succession of unstable and low-wage jobs. They were called "freeters"—a contraction of *freelance* and the German *Arbeiters* (workers)—initially a word connoting freedom from the constraints of full-time employment but, by the late 2000s, suggesting a predicament with no escape. Not having regular full-time employment status (even though many worked more hours as irregular employees) meant that freeters lacked a number of fringe benefits and also found it more difficult to marry, because of the perception that they were not capable of financially supporting wives and children. The intense resentment and despair of this demographic group found expression in several spectacular acts of violence. A twenty-five-year-old former contract worker killed seven people with a hunting knife in a busy intersection in the middle of Tokyo's Akihabara district in 2008. And a former contract worker at a Mazda automobile plant killed one worker and injured eleven by driving a Mazda station wagon into a crowd in the company parking lot.

These gruesome events, sensationalized by media coverage, brought renewed attention to a debate that started in 2007 with the publication of an essay by Tomohiro Akagi, a thirty-one-year-old self-described freeter, in the liberal journal *Ronza*. Akagi claimed that the outbreak of a war was the only hope for men in his situation, since war alone could shake up the economic and social status quo. Soon Akagi became the unofficial spokesperson for his demographic group, and he provoked feminists and other progressives by claiming that the plight of the "weak man" was worse than that of any other group, including women and ethnic minorities, in Japan. He asserted that women and minorities received financial assistance and legal protection from the government, while "weak men" received no such support. Akagi insisted, rather comically but stridently, that the only other way out was for a strong woman to marry and support him.[5]

Another discourse, concerning the "herbivorous male," became associated with "weak men" trapped in irregular labor, though it originated in a different context. First coined by freelance writer Maki Fukasawa in 2006, the term was soon popularized as a label for the growing number of young Japanese men who did not fit traditional macho stereotypes. They were modest, sensitive types, a contrast with the brash and bossy "carnivores" chasing after money and women during the economic bubble of the 1980s.[6] Some observers, such as profeminist sociologist Masahiro Morioka, welcomed this trend as a progressive masculinity.[7] But soon the image of the herbivorous male became conflated with that of the weak male as the tenuous economic recovery was stalled by the global financial crisis of 2008. This also coincided with the nationalist panic about a vulnerable Japanese state surrounded by threateningly muscular entities like China and North Korea. As I will discuss below, this resurgence of nationalism and the crisis of masculinity fueled a backlash against government gender policy, which was often represented as benefiting strong women over weak men.

The focus on "weak men" may be part of a general shift in political, social, and academic attention from gender equality as a problem for women to economic disparity as a problem for men. As a scholar I am particularly interested in this shift, but I also find it troubling. For example, the shift in focus from gender to class obscures how the two categories overlap. In policy and media discussions, freeters are usually assumed to be male, and the discourse of weak men assumes that there is no issue of weak women. Because marriage (dependence on one man) and sex work (dependence on multiple men) are two of the alternatives putatively open to any woman, there is little discussion of the actual problem of weak women, such as divorced women and single mothers.[8] The shift in academic attention from gender to class thus masks feminized poverty.[9]

The reason economic disparity is receiving attention now is that the model worker, that is, the adult male aged twenties to fifties, is being threatened. He was the full-time male employee of Japan Inc., the dismantling of which has been the cause of much social disruption, as described in Anne Allison's "Precarity and Hope" (chapter 2 of this volume). He was the "Nihonjin" (Japanese) in the famous and infamous "Nihonjinron" discourse from the 1980s extolling the unique characteristics of Japanese society; changes in his profile are thus big news in academic discussion of Japan.[10] He is also the most "productive" member of society that Japanese social policy was designed to protect.[11] Now his status is in jeopardy, but women have not, in fact, taken his position. Instead, a more structural shift has occurred.[12]

Government Gender Policy

Why was Akagi so angry about the plight of the weak man? What part of society looked hospitable to strong women? The decade from 1995 to 2005 may go down in history as the time when "gender" became one of the most visible and hotly contested terms in Japanese political discourse. In the mid-1990s the Japanese government embarked upon a set of remarkably broad initiatives to promote gender equality that appeared to approximate a form of "state feminism"; this also entailed an unprecedented level of feminist involvement in policy making.[13] What followed was a similarly unprecedented backlash, culminating in 2005, when the attack on government gender policy was spearheaded by Shinzō Abe, who would be named prime minister shortly thereafter. Feminists fought back, and by 2006 half a dozen publications had appeared, rallying academics and activists in a remarkable flurry of networking and alliance building.[14]

This surge of activity differed from the debates in the 1980s that led to the Equal Employment Opportunity Law (EEOL) of 1986. Many feminist activists had seen the EEOL as a demoralizing defeat in which measures serving as "protection" for women were eliminated without guarantees of "equality."[15] Perhaps because of its gradualist nature the EEOL had not aroused a backlash.

Something happened, however, in the following decades. After the real estate bubble burst, the Japanese economy was in recession for a decade. But for women it was a boom time, for various reasons as will be discussed later. The 1992 Child Care Leave Law guaranteed up to a year of partially paid child care leave for either the mother or the father. The 1997 Nursing Care Insurance Law socialized the cost of caring for the elderly, reducing the symbolic and practical burdens of daughters and daughters-in-law. The 1998 Law to Promote Specified Nonprofit Activities (also known as the NPO Law) made it easier for women's groups to gain legal status. The 2000 Anti-stalking Law and the 2001 Law for the Prevention of Spousal Violence and the Protection of Victims (known as the DV Law) criminalized behavior that had previously been dismissed as personal domestic disputes. The passage of these laws seemed to signal that the Japanese state was embracing feminist ideals, or that feminist ideals had become part of state policy.

Government initiatives that started around 1995 led to the 1999 Basic Law for a Gender-Equal Society and the subsequent drafting of the Basic Plan for a Gender-Equal Society. The Basic Plan is updated every five years, with the Third Basic Plan announced in December 2010.[16] What these initiatives have meant in terms of concrete results for women, however, is vague. A centralized Gender Equality Bureau was created within the Cabinet Office, and administrative divisions charged with carrying out the goals of the initiative were set up within each state ministry and agency. At local levels as well, prefectures and cities were asked to draw up ordinances and concrete plans to promote a "gender-equal society." Although skeptics see this as not much more than pie-in-the-sky rhetoric, the mainstreaming of gender equality as a matter of state policy is itself noteworthy.

How did the government arrive at policies promoting a "gender-equal society"? There were fortuitous circumstances, including the fact that the generally conservative Liberal Democratic Party (LDP) was forced into coalition with two progressive parties, both led by women, in the years 1996–98.[17] The right people were at the right places at the right time, including politicians, bureaucrats, and scholars serving on a key advisory council.[18] Larger historical forces and global trends were also at play, including the rise of international and domestic grassroots feminism.

The significant impact of internationalism on Japanese gender policy has been well documented.[19] As in many other countries, the United Nations International Decade for Women, 1975–85, was the catalyst for the creation of a national machinery in Japan to address women's issues. The series of World Conferences on Women punctuating the decade (Mexico City 1975, Copenhagen 1980, Nairobi 1985) spurred both international and domestic feminism. The International Women's Year Liaison Group founded in 1975 in Japan operated as an umbrella organization for domestic women's groups. The government established regular channels of communication with this group, thus maintaining an efficient and manageable way to incorporate women's voices into policy making.[20] International feminism has thus affected Japanese women's issues and policy making for four decades.

Without domestic feminism, however, external initiatives and pressure would not have found traction. These domestic trends are epitomized by the phrase "age of women" (*onna no jidai*), which became a slogan for activists as well as a buzzword for advertisers in the mid- to late 1980s as women's purchasing power increased. Women also became more active in the political arena, and female candidates were elected to office, often supported by activist housewives.[21] An intellectual discourse of feminism bloomed in this climate, and books with *feminizumu* in the title multiplied on bookstore shelves.[22] Many scholars were recruited as experts by national and local government advisory councils addressing issues of concern to women.[23] These domestic trends in the late 1980s and 1990s compounded international trends.[24] As domestic women's groups increasingly participated in electoral politics and policy making at various levels, international pressures also led the government to create a national machinery to deal with women's issues.

The demographic crisis—low birthrate, rapidly aging population—arguably affected gender policy the most. The causes of the declining birthrate, discussed in Sawako Shirahase's "Demography as Destiny" (chapter 1 of this volume), include delayed marriage, more individuals staying single, and continued stigma against childbirth outside marriage. In the early 1990s, public discourse tended to blame the declining birthrate on the increasing numbers of women with higher education and pursuing careers outside the home. In a striking departure from this rhetoric, current government policy makes a direct link between the objectives of creating a gender-equal society and boosting the birthrate.[25] This is reflected in the preamble to the Basic Law: "To respond to the rapid changes occurring in Japan's socioeconomic situations, such as the trend toward fewer children, the aging of the population, and the maturation of domestic economic activities, it has become a matter of urgent importance to realize [a] Gender Equal Society in which men and women respect each other's human rights and share responsibilities, and every citizen is able to fully display their individuality and ability regardless of gender."[26] The government is wagering that a more gender-equal society will boost the birthrate and the economy. But when these initiatives begin to appear counterproductive—as I believe they might, given the difficulty of reversing the birthrate decline—what will the government's response be? Gender equality should be pursued, in my opinion, because it is the right thing to do, not because it might raise the birthrate, help the economy, or save the nation. I will return to the question of how to boost the birthrate later in this chapter.

Responses to Gender Policy

From about 2000 to 2006, the state feminist initiatives outlined above met fierce resistance. One of the engines behind the backlash to these policy changes was the resurgence of Japanese nationalism. For example, the popular base for the backlash had much in common with the Japanese Society for History Textbook Reform: a controversial group that from the mid-1990s sought to create overtly nationalistic textbooks. Indeed, the resurgence of a nationalist discourse occurred at the same time that the Basic Law for a Gender-Equal Society was being discussed and implemented. Especially contentious was the inclusion of the so-called "military comfort women" issue in the state-approved middle school history textbooks.[27] Once this controversy began to die down, the nationalists turned to gender as the next target.[28]

This turn was prompted by another contentious issue, that of the surnames of married couples.[29] In 1996, the government's advisory council on legal systems proposed that the civil code be revised to introduce the option of married spouses keeping their respective surnames. Although this revision was proposed during a feminist upswing, it faced severe political opposition from conservatives who argued that separate surnames would lead to the collapse of the family. In 1997 the forces against the proposal formed the Japan Conference; this soon grew into the largest coalition of conservative groups in Japan.[30] As scholars have pointed out, several disparate sets of activists, including advocates for nationalist textbooks and opponents of separate surnames, were brought together in opposition to the government's gender policies.[31] There is also evidence that the backlash was orchestrated at a higher level and that the conservative Sankei media network played a significant role.[32] By the end of the spin cycle, the initial musings of a few pundits had been transformed into what were taken to be newsworthy facts. Government officials sensitive to actual or potential criticism from politicians and the mass media began to censor themselves, and eventually this self-censorship began to replicate itself throughout society in a vicious pattern.[33]

Politically, the backlash gained traction within conservative and neonationalist circles. Eriko Yamatani, a former journalist and editor for the Sankei media network, won a seat in the Lower House in 2000 and later headed the LDP's Project Team for Investigating the Status of Radical Sex Education and Gender Free Education. She was joined on the Project Team by Shinzō Abe, who became prime minister in 2006. The project team attacked what it saw as overly explicit and permissive sex education and opposed "gender-free" educational reforms that had sought to correct decades of subtle sexual discrimination, such as putting the class roster of boys before the roster of girls.[34] By the end of 2005, *gender-free* was singled out in the government's Second Basic Plan for Gender Equality as a term to be avoided because it might lead to confusion.[35] The backlash had reached the highest levels of government.

While the nationalist undertones of the backlash suggested the continuing influence of conservatives in Japan, other dynamics were concurrently at work. The backlash seems to have tapped into a widespread sense of anxiety and resentment around gender, especially among young men alienated from society.[36] This crisis in masculinity was fueled by the bleak outlook for the economy and the disturbing prospect of Japan's decline in international status as China became more dominant. The backlash found traction precisely because Japan had been mired in these conditions for at least a decade by 2005, and in times of economic stagnation or decline cultural politics tends to become conservative.[37]

The most visible critical response to this ideological turn came from academic feminists in the form of an unprecedented level of networking and alliance building among scholars. Even those who were initially cautious about terms like *gender-equal society* and *gender free* came to realize that the backlash threatened the entire range of ideas and practices associated with feminism, women's rights, and gender equality. The Women's Studies Association of Japan published a book with detailed information refuting the arguments of the backlash,[38] and a number of other edited volumes appeared, constituting a feminist counterattack dubbed the "fight back."[39]

However, certain differences in position and emphasis have emerged among those fighting back. Some see the defense of government policy for gender equality as primary, while others want to maintain a critical distance. For example, Yoshiko Kanai is one among several feminists who have pointed out the increasingly elitist leanings of Japanese gender equality policy. Implementation is centered on how to keep elite women such as researchers, doctors, and upper-grade civil servants in the workforce through the childbearing and child-rearing years. Kanai notes that by removing barriers for these elite groups of women the policy promotes the neoliberal idea that women who fail to rise to these levels are held back only by their own lack of ability, resolve, and discipline.[40]

A historical perspective is instructive here. The close collaboration of prominent feminists with colonialist and militarist elements in the political structure of pre-1945 Japan is a negative legacy.[41] In the prewar period, women's lack of formal political powers meant that many women's groups found it useful to ally themselves with state bureaucrats in order to accomplish their goals, while autonomous women's groups were likely to be persecuted and resistance to the state was punished.[42] Cooperation between state and women's groups continued in the postwar period for various reasons. Keiko Kaizuma has pointed out that women have tended to look to the state to achieve their goals because autonomous citizens' groups have been masculinist and unwelcoming to women's efforts.[43] Miriam Murase has shown that the government has constrained the autonomy of the women's movement through official women's groups and women's centers.[44] This has created a division between mainstream women's groups close to the state and radical feminist groups opposed to the state. The emergence of state feminism in the 1990s did little to alter this basic picture. Though more scholars and activists identifying themselves as feminist have been drawn into the various state-sponsored projects for a gender-equal society, many remain fundamentally skeptical of the goals and methods of government policies.

Some aspects of state feminism in Japan are found in other advanced industrialized nations as well. In countries with the most effective forms of state feminism, such as Australia, Denmark, the Netherlands, and Norway, the offices in charge of feminist issues were set up under social democratic governments that prioritized gender equity.[45]

In the case of Japan, the state feminist machinery was put in place under a relatively progressive coalition government. With the collapse of the coalition and the return to a more conservative regime in 1998, the backlash was able to gain momentum and eventually reach the highest levels of government. The generally more liberal Democratic Party of Japan (DPJ) came to power in September 2009, but political paralysis at top prevented it from pushing strongly in the direction of gender equality.

On December 17, 2010, during the brief DPJ rule, the Third Basic Plan for a Gender-Equal Society was announced. Because this plan was initially prepared under the leadership of Mizuho Fukushima, a well-known profeminist leader of the Social Democratic Party then in coalition with the DPJ, there was some hope that it would be more progressive than the Second Basic Plan, which had embodied the government's backpedaling under conservative LDP leadership. Indeed, when the interim report for the Third Plan was released in April 2010, the conservative Sankei newspaper reported with alarm that the plan aimed to destroy the family, pointing in particular to its advocacy of selective surnames and the deletion of language critiquing the term *gender free*, which had been in the Second Plan.[46] The final version of the plan retreated on the selective surname issue from "reform is needed" to a promise to "continue examining the issue."[47]

Other newspapers noted that the most noteworthy feature of the Third Plan was the emphasis on men. This included boosting male participation in child care and housework. Only 1.72 percent of men take advantage of child care leave; the plan aims to boost this to 13 percent by 2020. Currently the average father of a child under the age of six spends sixty minutes per day on child care and housework; the plan aims to raise this to 2.5 hours per day.[48]

On the one hand, increased emphasis on male participation in reproductive labor is certainly welcome. As the Third Basic Plan itself notes, one of the reasons why the earlier plans did not receive much popular support was that they were regarded as plans to push women into the workforce. This was problematic because it allowed gender equality to be portrayed as an issue primarily affecting elite women competing with men in the workplace. The Third Basic Plan brought the issue back to families and to men's roles.

On the other hand, this shift in emphasis to men is part and parcel of a kind of backpedaling, in which the model of work/life balance replaces a model of gender equality in the workplace. As a case in point, one of the most prominent neologisms associated in the media with the Third Basic Plan was *ikumen*: men who engage in *ikuji*, or child care.[49] When a few male mayors and governors declared they would take a few hours off from work for a few weeks to care for their young children, a heated debate ensued about the practice. A shift thus occurred in public discussions about gender, from equality for women in society to the participation of men in child care.[50] This, too, seems to have had the effect of displacing the focus from gender to something else, as it becomes obvious that the ability of men to take time off from work to participate in child care depends a great deal on the structure of labor. Nonetheless, it is also important to insist that it is a gender issue, because an increase in *ikumen* also depends on men's ability to move beyond the image of masculinity that is tied up with a 24/7 focus on their job.[51]

In December 2012, the LDP ousted the DPJ and returned to power, led by Shinzō Abe, who had spearheaded the backlash against state feminism. This time, his message on gender has been less blatant, combining the promotion of traditional motherly roles with the utilization of women in the workforce in order to recharge the economy and to refortify the nation. Meanwhile, emphasis on male participation in housework and child care has become less prominent, presumably because this would divert male labor power needed for economic recovery. Instead, an alternative source of household help was beginning to be discussed by spring 2014: importing domestic helpers from other nations.[52]

The Future of Gender

What do these debates about government policies and their engagement (or not) with a gender-equal society tell us about the possible future of gender in Japan? The most plausible scenario is that, because of political inertia and a focus on other issues in the next several years, gender policy will continue along the same general parameters set in the 1990s. No major advances or reversals are likely, though small adjustments are to be expected. This means continued policy emphasis on gender equality for the sake of boosting the birthrate, but also possible shifts in tactics and emphasis—such as the one described above, from women's equality in the workplace to work/life balance and male participation in child care. Yet this scenario is subject to pressure from several directions.

The backlash points to the enduring nostalgia for the "traditional" family consisting of a male breadwinner, full-time housewife, and multiple children. Such a notion of family is an ideology fed by biological essentialism: the belief that biological differences between men and women dictate different social roles for men and women.[53] Proponents claim that promoting the continued employment of women during the childbearing years destroys the "traditional Japanese family." Ironically, such a family was never a statistical majority in Japan, even during the period of rapid economic growth when the social system was designed around such a model family.[54] Yet such a conservative discourse has found receptive ears in the segment of the Japanese population that identifies with this elusive and fading ideal. While this ideal is simply not a practical reality for the majority of Japanese households today (because of the decline in regular employment, the disappearance of the family wage, women's desires for varied life-course choices, and the perceived and actual cost of having many children), we need to pay attention to the underlying desires, fears, and frustrations embodied by those who still cling to it and who are thus fueling the backlash to policies of gender equality like the Basic Plan. The government policy has had the effect of angering both men—who are told they are not fully men unless they also engage in housework and child care—and women—who are told housework and child care are not sufficient to make them fully women.[55] At the same time, the social norms surrounding the male breadwinner and the full-time housewife are such that the father who takes time off for child care is always seen as not caring enough about his job, and the mother who also works outside the home is always seen as not caring enough about her children. Attention to these kinds of dilemmas and anxieties is needed if the policy is to succeed.

If a reversion to the traditional family model is difficult to imagine as a possible future, so is a short-term radical acceleration of the trend toward gender equality. A factor that might stimulate change in gendered relations is large-scale immigration—something that is discussed in relation to the problems posed by the declining birthrate and aging population. There are multiple reasons why large-scale immigration has not been a politically viable option for Japan,[56] and some of these reasons are discussed in Osawa and Kingston's "Risk and Consequences" chapter in this volume. Here, in keeping with a focus on the gendered aspects of the issue, I would like to briefly note that immigration in the form of short-term workers to address the labor shortage would bring about different (good, bad, or uncomfortable) consequences for gender relations in Japan. An increase in migrant care workers and domestic helpers could substantially lessen the burdens and help the careers of Japanese women, but it would also drain care resources from the global South, commodify care, and alter family relations.[57] Indeed, even in the 1980s Japanese feminists were almost unanimously opposed to the idea of using domestic helpers, especially from the global South. And while the government has cautiously opened the door for nurses from Indonesia and the Philippines, the hurdles are still very high as of the writing of this chapter, requiring the mastery of Japanese written language and the passing of a written exam.

Nonetheless, it is possible to argue that both the hopes and the challenges of the future lie in the direction of immigration and globalization, rather than in a return to the past and a turn to isolationism, in a Japan that curls back and in on itself. For example, international marriage accounted for 4.3 percent of new marriages (i.e., a little less than one in twenty-three marriages) in 2010, and 3.9 percent (a little less than one in twenty-five new marriages) in 2011.[58] The network of globalized households became intermittently visible in the aftermath of 3/11, as families had to make decisions about evacuation and relocation. Additional globalization of families is likely to come from the increase in Japanese youth seeking education and employment opportunities abroad. In 2014, the Abe administration began moving cautiously in the direction of increasing short-term immigrant labor in order to deal with the anticipated building boom for the Tokyo Olympics of 2020, but this will not come about without friction.

The century-long history of Japanese debates about motherhood, labor, and the role of the housewife suggests that possible future scenarios will mainly divide over whether society should be designed for singles or for families.[59] Among advocates of the latter, there is a division between those who favor traditional forms of family grounded in the sexual division of labor and those who favor various alternative forms of family. Herein lies the difficulty of the government's current position on gender-equal society: It is too conservative for prosingle feminists and pro-alternative family feminists who question the state's advocacy of a heterosexual reproductive family, yet too radical for traditionalists who see the state as dismantling such families by targeting the sexual division of labor.

The most hopeful scenario for Japan, from the perspective of gender equality, would be a society that supports both traditional and alternative forms of families as well as single living, cares for the elderly and invests in the young, addresses the challenges of globalization and a multicultural society, and pushes for women's increased participation in the labor force and decision making, as well as for male participation in housework and child care. This may or may not boost the birthrate, but it will come closer to the ideal society envisioned by women's liberation activists in the 1970s: "a society in which we can give birth, a society in which we want to give birth."[60] Women's full participation in all aspects of social, economic, political, and academic activities is a worthy objective even if it does not lead to a higher birthrate. Gender policy and hope for Japan's future must be linked thoughtfully and deliberately, not instrumentally.

Concretely, above and beyond the measures associated with the Basic Plans for a Gender-Equal Society, some of the following measures would be needed to bring about both gender equality and hope for the future, if that hope is to be linked to "more children":

1. *Everyone working shorter hours.* More day care facilities need to be available, with more flexible hours, sick-child care and so on, but if laborers are expected to work until late evening no amount of day care will solve the child care conundrum.

2. *A radical shifting of resources from the elderly to children.* This cannot happen in the current political model in which the interests of the elderly drive electoral politics. One might thus consider "giving children the vote" through proxy voting by parents.[61]

3. *Help for parents.* One of the radical innovations of the Nursing Care Insurance Law was to create a system in which the elderly could receive care within their homes but from professional care providers rather than family members. Japan needs an equivalent for families with children, namely subsidized housework and child care help within the home.

4. *Lowering the bar of social expectations for motherhood.* Child care after school and during school vacation needs to be provided as a matter of routine, without making mothers feel that they are somehow failing. Furthermore, day cares and schools need to consider full-time employed mothers the norm: no expectations for elaborate boxed lunches, hand-sewn floor-wipes, individual labeling of hundreds of items used in class, etc.

Of course, financing such expanded child care services will be impossible without reconsidering how tax dollars are currently being spent. Furthermore, making it materially easier to have and raise children is only part of the solution; one would have to ask, What would make Japanese people *want* to have more children? Or at least *not mind* having more children? The answer is more hope, less fear. The alternative—to do nothing and let demography become destiny—is rather bleak to contemplate. If current trends continue, Japan's population of 128 million will shrink by one-third, and seniors will account for 40 percent of people by 2060.[62] Another alarmist estimate released in 2012 shows that if current trends continue and there is no influx of population from the outside, Japan will have no children by 3011.[63] Even in the short term, a laissez-faire scenario of letting current demographic trends persist without forcefully addressing the negative consequences would probably lead to increased problems of isolation, precarity, and loss of hope, especially among the young. When one thinks of the planet rather than the nation, then promoting reproduction becomes hard to justify. But this philosophical conundrum should not distract us from the need in front of our eyes: more hope for the children and youth who are alive now.[64]

Feminist scholar Chizuko Ueno has written that the disasters of 2011 potentially fulfilled an ominous desire on the part of some Japanese to "reset" a Japan mired in stagnation and decline, to return to zero and start over.[65] She was referring to people like Tomohiro Akagi, cited earlier, for whom the only prospect for hope was war. The wish for some catastrophic event to shake up the status quo, the sense that only such an event would have the power to alter the current setup—these are the sentiments recalled with horror after 3/11. "But behold," said Ueno, "society cannot be reset," because entropy would protect the status quo. She also noted the rise of populist heroes like Osaka mayor Tōru Hashimoto, whose call for radical reform tapped into some people's desire for change. Change must happen, Ueno reminded us, but not through a resetting of society, a suspension of critical thought, or the granting of carte blanche to heroes—only by individuals deciding their own fates day after day will change happen and a different future be built.[66] This is a call both for a different kind of thought and action in daily life and for a different kind of politics.

In writing this chapter, I have been acutely aware of what has been called the trap of aerial distance in feminist scholarship.[67] As a transnational scholar, born in Japan, educated in Germany, Japan, and the United States, holding a Japanese passport but also a US permanent resident card, institutionally located on the Atlantic coast of the United States, raising children with dual

Japanese and American citizenship, my perspective is that of someone who is neither wholly outside nor wholly inside Japan. I have a visceral memory of what it is like to live as a young girl and a young woman in Japan, and more recently of what it is like to live there as a mother and a professional.[68] I also have a more aerial academic view, of long-term historical trends as well as more recent policy challenges.

My view is partial, in both senses of the term: limited and partisan. It is the view of someone who has chosen to live elsewhere and yet keeps an eye on Japan. In such a view, the future of gender in Japan is cloudy, but the forecast contains the possibility of hope.

Notes

1. "Jishin ni genpatsu 'tayoreru hito hoshii' kekkon shitai onnatachi zōkachū" [Earthquake and nuclear incident increase the number of women who wish to marry and "find someone dependable"], *J-Cast News*, April 17, 2011, www.j-cast.com/2011/04/17093282.html?p=all.

2. Ulrike Woehr, "'Datsu genpatsu no tayōsei to seijisei o kashika suru: Jendā, sekushuariti, esunishiti no kanten kara" [Making the diversity and politics of "anti-nuclear power" visible: From the perspectives of gender, sexuality, ethnicity], in *"Daishinsai" to watashi* [The Great Earthquake and I], ed. Hiroshima Joseigaku Kenkyūjo (Hiroshima: Hiroshima Joseigaku Kenkyūjo, 2012). Gender analysis of the aftermath of Hurricane Katrina is also instructive. See Emmanuel David and Elaine Enarson, eds., *The Women of Katrina: How Gender, Race, and Class Matter in an American Disaster* (Nashville, TN: Vanderbilt University Press, 2012), as well as the articles on the Social Science Research Council's website "Understanding Katrina: Perspectives from the Social Sciences," various dates, http://understandingkatrina.ssrc.org/ (accessed May 25, 2012).

3. This is in an interview with prominent feminist sociologist Chizuko Ueno in a special journal issue devoted to her. Chizuko Ueno, "Ueno Chizuko o fuwake suru: 'Tsui gensōron kara *Kea no shakaigaku* made" [Dissecting Ueno Chizuko: From the "couple illusion" to the sociology of care], interview by Eiji Oguma, *Gendai Shisō* 39, no. 17 (2011): 8–56. In the interview Ueno suggests that gender comes to the foreground of scholarly attention only when class recedes into the background. But elsewhere she strongly implies that gender continues to be the most important category for her. See Chizuko Ueno, "Sekushuariti wa ika ni katarieru/enai no ka" [How sexuality can or cannot be discussed], interview by Naoko Miyaji, *Gendai Shisō* 39, no. 17 (2011): 152–73.

4. For further discussion of the historicity of the category of gender, see Ayako Kano, *Acting Like a Woman in Modern Japan: Theater, Gender, and Nationalism* (New York: Palgrave, 2001).

5. The *Ronza* essay is collected in Tomohiro Akagi, *Wakamono o migoroshi ni suru kuni: Watashi o sensō ni mukawaseru mono wa nani ka* [A nation that lets its youth die: What makes me turn toward war] (Tokyo: Sōfūsha, 2007).

6. Maki Fukasawa coined the term in her online serialized column for *Nikkei Business Online*. These columns are collected in Maki Fukasawa, *Sōshoku danshi sedai: Heisei danshi zukan* [The herbivorous male generation: An illustrated guide to Heisei men] (Tokyo: Kōbunsha, 2009).

7. Masahiro Morioka, *Sōshoku kei danshi no renai gaku* [Romantic love studies for the herbivorous male] (Tokyo: Media Factory, 2008).

8. On women NEET (not in employment, education, or training), see "Josei NEET 'kaji tetsudai' ima wa mukashi shinkoku na mondai kakaeru rei mo" [Women NEET: "Housework helper" is a thing of the past, and some harbor serious problems], *47 News*, May 1, 2012, www.47news.jp/feature/woman/womaneye/2012/05/post_20120416141639.html. For a historical analysis of sex work as a financial "last resort" for poor families, see Holly Sanders, "Prostitution in Postwar Japan: Debt and Labor," PhD diss., Princeton University, 2005. More recently, sociologist Hiroshi Kainuma has published a series of articles describing the lives of women and men at the margins of contemporary society, including women engaged in precarious/entrepreneurial forms of sex work. See Hiroshi Kainuma, Hyōhaku sareru shakai [Bleached society] (Tokyo: Daiyamondosha, 2013).

9. Feminized poverty is certainly not a new phenomenon, though existing discussions have tended to focus on single mothers rather than on the poverty of women per se. See "Boshi katei heikin nenshū 291 man en: kosodate setai shotoku no 44% domari" [Single mother households' average annual income is ¥2,910,000: Only 44 percent of the average income of households with children], *Sankei Shimbun*, September 16, 2012, http://headlines.yahoo.co.jp/hl?a=20120916-00000090-san-soci.

10. For example, see Harumi Befu, *Hegemony of Homogeneity: An Anthropological Analysis of Nihonjinron* (Melbourne: Trans Pacific Press, 2001).

11. Rodger Goodman, "Anthropology, Policy and the Study of Japan," in *Family and Social Policy in Japan: Anthropological Approaches*, ed. Roger Goodman (Cambridge: Cambridge University Press, 2002), 1–28.

12. Labor lawyer Mami Nakano disputes the idea that the current crisis of the working poor is merely the consequence of the globalization of labor. Globalization exacerbates the existing distortions of the labor market, and in Japan these have

included the disparities between regular and irregular employees, large and small corporations, and male and female workers. Mami Nakano, *Rōdō danpingu: Koyō no tayōka no hate ni* [Labor dumping: At the end of the diversification of employment] (Tokyo: Iwanami Shoten, 2006).

13.   For a definition of *state feminism*, see Dorothy McBride Stetson and Ann Mazur, eds., *Comparative State Feminism* (London: Sage Publications, 1995).

14.   For an extended discussion of the formulation of Japanese government gender policy and the varied responses to it, see Ayako Kano, "Backlash, Fight Back, and Back-Pedaling: Responses to State Feminism in Contemporary Japan," *International Journal of Asian Studies* 8, no. 1 (2011): 41–62.

15.   Kiyoko Kamio Knapp, "Don't Awaken the Sleeping Child: Japan's Gender Equality Law and the Rhetoric of Gradualism," *Columbia Journal of Gender and Law* 8, no. 2 (1999): 143–95; Keiko Higuchi, "Josei seisaku no tōtatsuten to kore kara no josei sentā" [The point reached by women's policy and the future of women's centers], *Josei Shisetsu Jānaru*, no. 8 (2003): 66–105. See also Joyce Gelb, "The Equal Employment Opportunity Law: A Decade of Change for Japanese Women?" *Law and Policy* 22, nos. 3–4 (October 2000): 385–407.

16.   Although "gender-equal" is the official English translation given for *danjo kyōdō sankaku*, the Japanese phrase actually means "male-female joint participation." It is an intentionally vague phrase that avoids the Japanese word *byōdō*, meaning "equality." The terms *equality* (*byōdō*) and *gender* (*jendā*) both have a complicated history within Japanese political discourse.

17.   The New Party Sakigake led by Akiko Dōmoto, and the Social Democratic Party led by Takako Doi. For further analysis, see Mari Ōsawa, Teruko Ōno, Kiyomi Kawano, and Kazuko Takemura, "Danjo sankaku no kōbō" [The struggle for male-female participation], in *"Posuto" Feminizumu* ["Post" feminism], ed. Kazuko Takemura (Tokyo: Sakuhinsha, 2003), 143–44.

18.   For more on the role of feminist scholar Mari Ōsawa on the advisory council that formulated this policy, see Kano, "Backlash," 47–48.

19.   See Joyce Gelb, *Gender Policies in Japan and the United States: Comparing Women's Movements, Rights and Politics* (New York: Palgrave Macmillan, 2003), and Jennifer Chan-Tiberghien, *Gender and Human Rights Politics in Japan: Global Norms and Domestic Networks* (Stanford, CA: Stanford University Press, 2004).

20.   See Mitsuko Yamaguchi, "Josei shodantai no josei seisaku ni taisuru gōi keisei katei: Zenkoku soshiki 50 dantai no rentai to kōdō" [The process of consensus formation among women's groups on women's policy: The alliance and actions of fifty national groups], *Joseigaku kenkyū*, no. 2 (1992): 53–70, and Miriam Murase,

Cooperation over Conflict: The Women's Movement and the State in Postwar Japan (New York: Routledge, 2006), 109. Murase also points out that this access by the International Women's Year Liaison Group came at the expense of grassroots groups, which were excluded from the policy-making process.

21. Robin M. LeBlanc, *Bicycle Citizens: The Political World of the Japanese Housewife* (Berkeley: University of California Press, 1999).

22. Ayako Kano, "Nihon no 1970 nendai-90 nendai feminizumu" [Japan's feminism of the 1970s–1990s], in *Feminizumu no meicho 50* [50 classics of feminism], ed. Yumiko Ehara and Yoshiko Kanai (Tokyo: Heibonsha, 2002), 501–18, and Ayako Kano, "Towards a Critique of Transhistorical Femininity," in *Gendering Modern Japanese History*, ed. Barbara Molony and Kathleen Uno (Cambridge, MA: Harvard University Press, 2005), 520–54.

23. Michiko Kanda, Sumiko Yazawa, Yoriko Meguro, and Hiroko Hara, "Joseigaku kenkyūsha to seiji jissen" [Women's studies and political practice], *Joseigaku Kenkyū* no. 2 (1992): 71–96.

24. For an overview of feminism as a social movement, see Vera Mackie, *Feminism in Modern Japan: Citizenship, Embodiment and Sexuality* (Cambridge: Cambridge University Press, 2003).

25. Manabu Akagawa, *Kodomo ga hette nani ga warui ka!* [What's wrong with fewer children!] (Tokyo: Chikuma Shobō, 2004).

26. Gender Equality Bureau, "Basic Act for Gender Equal Society (Act Number 78 of 1999)," 1999, www.gender.go.jp/english_contents/about_danjo/lbp/index.html.

27. See Chizuko Ueno, *Nashonarizumu to jendā* [Nationalism and gender] (Tokyo: Seidosha, 1998). For a translation, see *Nationalism and Gender*, trans. Beverly Yamamoto (Melbourne: Trans Pacific Press, 2004).

28. Yoshiko Kanai, "Jendā bakkurasshu no kōzō to naimen" [The structure and interiority of gender backlash], *Ajia Taiheiyō ni Okeru Jendā to Heiwagaku* [Gender and peace studies in the Asia-Pacific] no. 4 (2005): 159–76.

29. Fumie Asano, "'Bakkurasshu no jidai" [The Backlash Era], in *Jendā gainen ga hiraku shikai: Bakkurasshu o koete* [Gendered perspective: Overcoming the backlash], ed. Yuibutsuron Kenkyū Kyōkai (Tokyo: Aoki Shoten, 2006), 266–86.

30. For more on the Japan Conference (Nippon Kaigi), see their webpage at www.nipponkaigi.org (accessed September 18, 2012).

31. Makoto Hosoya, "Danjo byōdōka ni taisuru kin'nen no handō wa naze okiru no ka?" [Why is there a reaction against the movement for gender equality in recent years?], *Sekai* 738 (April 2005): 96–105.

32. Mieko Takenobu, "Yappari kowai? Jendā furī basshingu" [Scary as expected? Bashing "gender free"]," in *Jendā furī toraburu: Basshingu genshō o kenshō suru* ["Gender

free" trouble: Examining the attack], ed. Ryōko Kimura (Tokyo: Hakutakusha; Gendai Shokan, 2005), 22–23.

33. Fumika Satō, "Feminizumu ni iradatsu 'anata' e: 'Ikari' wa doko e mukau beki nano ka" [For "you" frustrated by feminism: Where your "anger" should be directed], *Ronza*, April 2006, 213.

34. Kimura, *Jendā furī toraburu*.

35. The Second Basic Plan, "Danjo kyōdō sankaku kihon keikaku (dainiji)," 2005, can be downloaded from www.gender.go.jp/kihon-keikaku/2nd/honbun.html.

36. Shinji Miyadai, "Nejireta shakai no genjō to mezasu beki daisan no michi: Bakkurasshu to dō mukiaeba ii no ka" [The present condition of a distorted society and the third way for which we must strive: How we should face the backlash], in *Bakkurasshu! Naze jendā furī wa tatakareta no ka?* [Backlash! Why "gender free" was attacked], ed. Chizuko Ueno et al. (Tokyo: Sōfūsha, 2006), 10–99.

37. Susan Faludi describes a similar dynamic in the Reagan era in *Backlash: The Undeclared War against American Women* (New York: Crown, 1991).

38. Nihon Josei Gakkai Jendā Kenkyūkai, ed., *Q&A danjo kyōdō sankaku/jendā furī basshingu: Bakkurasshu e no tettei hanron* [The controversy over male-female co-participation and "gender free" bashing: Counterarguments to the backlash] (Tokyo: Akashi Shoten, 2006).

39. See Haruo Asai, Kunio Kitamura, Noriko Hashimoto, and Yukihiro Murase, eds., *Jendā furī/sei kyōiku basshingu: Koko ga shiritai 50 no Q&A* [The attack on gender free and sex education: Fifty questions and answers] (Tokyo: Ōtsuki Shoten, 2003); Kimura, *Jendā furī toraburu*; Ueno et al., *Bakkurasshu!*; Midori Wakakuwa, Shūichi Katō, Masumi Minagawa, and Chieko Akaishi, eds., *"Jendā" no kiki o koeru! Tettei tōron! Bakkurasshu* [Overcoming the crisis of gender!] (Tokyo: Seikyūsha, 2006), and Yuibutsuron Kenkyū Kyōkai, *Jendā gainen ga hiraku shikai*.

40. Yoshiko Kanai, *Kotonatte irareru shakai o: Joseigaku/jendā kenkyū no shiza* [Toward a society in which we can be different: The perspective of women's studies and gender scholarship] (Tokyo: Akashi Shoten, 2008), 244. For a more recent analysis and elaboration of the ethics of care as a response to the excesses of neoliberalism and libertarianism in contemporary Japan, see Yoshiko Kanai, *Izon to jiritsu no rinri: "Onna/haha" (watashi) no shintaisei kara* [The ethics of dependence and independence: From the corporeality of "woman/mother" (myself)] (Tokyo: Nakanishiya Shuppan, 2011).

41. For an overview of the debate surrounding the scholarly discourse on women as collaborators versus women as victims of the militarist regime, see Ueno, *Nashonarizumu to jendā*.

42. Sheldon Garon, *Molding Japanese Minds: The State in Everyday Life* (Princeton, NJ: Princeton University Press, 1997). See also Barbara Molony, "Equality versus Difference: The Japanese Debate over 'Motherhood Protection,' 1915–50," in *Japanese Women Working*, ed. Janet Hunter (London: Routledge, 1993), 122–48. Mikiso Hane, *Reflections on the Way to the Gallows: Voices of Japanese Rebel Women* (New York: Pantheon, 1988), reminds us of the fate of women who rebelled against the state.

43. Keiko Kaizuma, "'Otoko dewanai mono' no haijo to teikō: Dansei shi ga 'undō' ni toikakeru mono" [Exclusion and resistance of "nonmales": Men's history and "movements"], *Jōkyō*, 3rd ser., no. 45 (November 2004): 156–57.

44. Murase, *Cooperation over Conflict.*

45. Stetson and Mazur, *Comparative State Feminism*, 287–91.

46. "Danjo kyōdō keikaku: Kazoku no kizuna o kowasu tsumori ka" [Male-female co-participation plans: Will they destroy family ties], *Sankei Shimbun*, April 16, 2010, http://sankei.jp.msn.com/politics/policy/100415/plc1004152054010-n1.htm.

47. The Third Basic Plan, "Danjo kyōdō sankaku kihon keikaku (daisanji)," 2010, can be downloaded from the website of the Gender Equality Bureau Cabinet Office, www.gender.go.jp/kihon-keikaku/3rd/index.html. The plan also called for "positive action" including quotas and incentives, to increase the participation of women in leadership positions, such as members of the Upper and Lower House, advisory council members, corporate managers, and researchers in science, technology, engineering and mathematics (STEM). For many of these positions, the goal of 30 percent female representation by the year 2020 was proposed.

48. "Dansei no ikukyū shutoku 13% mokuhyō: 2020 nen made Kan seiken ga kihon keikaku" [The Kan administration's plan for men's child care leave], *Asahi Shimbun*, December 17, 2010, www.asahi.com/national/update/1217/TKY201012170145.html.

49. By late 2012 a new term had been coined: *ikujii*, or grandfathers who help care for their grandchildren. See Ikujii purojekuto [Child-caring grandfathers project], 2013, www.fathering.jp/ikujii/.

50. "'Ikumen' shien ni jūten: Danjo kyōdō keikaku kettei" [Male-female co-participation plans approved], *Tokyo Shimbun*, December 17, 2010, evening ed., www.tokyo-np.co.jp/article/politics/news/CK2010121702000203.html.

51. Maria Mies has identified a global trend of "housewifization" of labor. This is labor that is interrupted by reproduction, that is, care for self and family, and is therefore underpaid. Maria Mies, *Patriarchy and Capital Accumulation on a World Scale: Women in the International Division of Labor* (London: Zed Books, 1986).

52. "Gaikokujin rōdōsha kaigo, kaji ni kakudai; shushō 'josei katsuyaku e kitai" [Foreign laborers to be expanded for care work and housework: Prime minister says,

"Utilize them for women's active participation"], *Sankei shimbun*, April 5, 2014, http://headlines.yahoo.co.jp/hl?a=20140405-00000074-san-bus_all.

53. For more detail, see Emi Koyama and Chiki Ogiue, "Koko ga yoku deru! Nanatsu no ronten" [These are often on exams! Seven points of contention] in Ueno, *Bakkurasshu!*, 371–75.

54. Mari Ōsawa, *Danjo kyōdō sankaku shakai o tsukuru* [Building a male-female co-participation society] (Tokyo: NHK Books, 2002), 57.

55. For a summary of how wage labor is tied up with masculinity but has been often seen as antithetical to femininity, see Robin Leidner, "Identity and Work," in *Social Theory at Work*, ed. Marek Korczynski, Randy Hodson, and Paul K. Edwards (Oxford: Oxford University Press, 2006), 424–63.

56. For one summary, see Hidenori Sakanaka, "The Future of Japan's Immigration Policy: A Battle Diary," trans. Andrew J. I. Taylor, *Asia-Pacific Journal: Japan Focus*, www.japanfocus.org/-sakanaka-hidenori/2396. For a more recent opinion, see Hidenori Sakanaka, "An Immigration Stimulus for Japan: Allowing in More Foreign Workers Would Boost Growth, Especially in Quake-Ravaged Areas," *Wall Street Journal*, June 15, 2011, http://online.wsj.com/article/SB10001424052702303714704576384841676111236.html.

57. V. Spike Peterson, "Global Householding: The Good, the Bad, and the Uncomfortable," *e- International Relations*, March 30, 2010, www.e-ir.info/?p=3653.

58. According to Ministry of Health, Labor, and Welfare statistics available at "Kōsei rōdōshō jinkō dōtai chōsa" [Ministry of Health, Labor, and Welfare demographic survey], 2013, www.mhlw.go.jp/toukei/list/81-1a.html.

59. On the debates, see Ayako Kano, "Nihon feminizumu ronsōshi 1: Bosei to sekushuariti" [A history of Japanese feminist debates: Motherhood and sexuality], in *Wādomappu feminizumu* [A lexicon of feminism], ed. Yumiko Ehara and Yoshiko Kanai (Tokyo: Shinyōsha, 1997), 196–221. For more information on the singles/families divide at the policy level, see Fumino Yokoyama, *Sengo Nihon no josei seisaku* [Postwar Japanese women's policy] (Tokyo: Keisō Shobō, 2002).

60. For a discussion of Japanese women's liberation philosophy, see Setsu Shigematsu, *Scream from the Shadows: The Women's Liberation Movement in Japan* (Minneapolis: University of Minnesota Press, 2012).

61. Demeny voting, named after a proposal by demographer Paul Demeny, would be one such possibility. See Paul Demeny, "Pronatalist Policies in Low-Fertility Countries: Patterns, Performance and Prospects," *Population and Development Review* 12 (suppl.): 335–58.

62. Mari Yamaguchi, "Japan Population to Shrink by One-Third by 2060," Associated Press, January 30, 2012, http://news.yahoo.com/japan-population-shrink-one-third-2060-112432967.html.

63. See "Web Clock of Child Population in Japan," http://mega.econ.tohoku.ac.jp/Children/index_en.jsp (accessed May 31, 2012). The Tōhoku University press release in English, "No Children on the Children's Day after 1,000 Years Due to Birthrate Declining," May 10, 2012, can be found at www.tohoku.ac.jp/english/2012/05/press20120510-01.html. This is based on government population figures released by the Ministry of Internal Affairs and Communications, Statistics Bureau on May 5, 2012, "Sōmushō tōkeikyoku," www.stat.go.jp/data/jinsui/topics/topi590.htm.

64. A statistic released in May 2012 notes the increase in suicide rates among the young. "Shūkatsu shippai shi jisatsu suru wakamono kyūzo: 4 nen de 2.5 bai ni" [The rapid rise in youth who commit suicide after failing to find a job: An increase of 2.5 times over the past four years], *Yomiuri Shimbun*, May 8, 2012, http://headlines.yahoo.co.jp/hl?a=20120508-00000690-yom-soci.

65. Chizuko Ueno, "'Shakai o risetto shitai' to iu fuon na ganbō?" [An alarming desire to reset society?], published in various newspapers, January 2012, http://wan.or.jp/ueno/?p=1362.

66. This is also in line with Ueno's advocacy of feminism "for the weak." See Chizuko Ueno, *Ikinobiru tame no shisō: Jendā byōdō no wana* [Philosophy for survival: The trap of gender equality] (Tokyo: Iwanami Shoten, 2006).

67. Jane Roland Martin, "Aerial Distance, Esotericism, and Other Closely Related Traps," *Signs: Journal of Women in Culture and Society* 21, no. 3 (1996): 584–614.

68. I lived in Kyoto from July 2009 to June 2010 with my husband and two sons, ages six and four.

CHAPTER FIVE

After Fukushima: Veto Players and Japanese Nuclear Policy

Jacques E. C. Hymans

The major goal of this chapter is to explain Japan's failure to adopt a coherent and credible long-term nuclear policy for at least three years after the March 2011 disaster at the Fukushima Daiichi nuclear power plant.[1] Studying this political failure is important for three main reasons. First, the persistent uncertainty surrounding Japan's nuclear future has been costly economically and psychologically. Second, few expert observers anticipated that Japan's nuclear policy crisis would last so long. Third, by identifying the causes of Japan's nuclear policy gridlock, we can better map out possible future scenarios for significant policy change.

The chapter is organized as follows. In the next section, I present a brief description of Japan's long post-Fukushima nuclear policy disarray. After that, I highlight the contrast between Japan's continuing disorientation and the clearer decisions that many other states made about their reliance on nuclear energy in response to the Fukushima disaster. I then argue that Japan's inability to coalesce around a new nuclear policy consensus was due not merely to the unanticipated disaster but also to well-known political problems that had racked the Japanese nuclear policy-making arena for decades prior to the accident. In particular, I stress the high number of institutionalized "veto players" in the Japanese nuclear policy-making arena as a key cause of the country's nuclear policy gridlock. The chapter's penultimate section assesses the potential for the end of gridlock and the enactment of significant nuclear policy change in the future, especially in light of the bankruptcy and government takeover of the Tokyo Electric Power Company (TEPCO). The final paragraphs summarize and conclude.

My point in highlighting Japan's political failure since Fukushima is not to demand that the country's policy makers adopt this or that alternative nuclear policy mix. Rather, the point is to better understand the sources of Japan's indecision. The goal is analytical, not prescriptive.

Japan's Nuclear Policy Disarray

Social scientists often note that external shocks and natural disasters provide unparalleled opportunities for major policy change.[2] Scholars of postwar Japanese politics have placed particular stress on the importance of shocks as stimuli for new policies.[3] Accordingly, many observers expected that the Fukushima nuclear disaster of March 2011 would swiftly catalyze a major nuclear policy overhaul.[4] After all, even before the disaster, Japan's nuclear energy ambitions were considerably out of step with those of most of its developed-country peers. For instance, the rest of the developed world had long since abandoned the idea of extracting plutonium from the waste products of spent uranium fuel and using it to power plutonium-based nuclear reactors—the so-called "plutonium economy." Yet Japan had clung to that plan for fifty years despite poor technical results, soaring costs, and diplomatic frictions.[5] Japan was already long overdue for a course correction.

At first glance, a major Japanese nuclear policy change might appear to have occurred right after Fukushima. Japan had fifty-four operative nuclear power reactors at the time of the multiple explosions that damaged four reactors at Fukushima Daiichi in March 2011. After the accident, one by one the fifty remaining reactors in the country were taken offline. By May 2012, for the first time since 1966 no nuclear power reactors were operating in the country.[6] This was certainly a dramatic change in Japan's nuclear *behavior*, but it was not the result of a dramatic change in Japanese national *policy*. Instead, Japan's descent to nuclear zero between 2011 and 2012 was the unintended consequence of a regulatory snafu.

The Fukushima accident had revealed, in tragic fashion, that the existing nuclear safety standards were woefully inadequate. For example, the off-site emergency command posts were not equipped with air filters to keep out radioactive particles, so when the accident happened the emergency response personnel themselves had to evacuate the premises.[7] This and thousands of other safety items had to be reviewed in the aftermath of March 2011. In principle, new safety rules could have been developed without shutting down the undamaged reactors. But Japan's antiquated safety regulations featured a standard technical requirement to shut down each reactor after thirteen months in operation for an intensive top-to-bottom safety check and recertification.[8] With the safety rules in turmoil, after a reactor was taken offline as scheduled, the government simply could not legally certify its fitness for a restart.[9]

The result was the gradual shutdown of Japan's entire nuclear reactor fleet, which had previously been providing more than a quarter of the nation's electricity. Attempting to reverse the trend, the government hurriedly declared the safety of two reactors at the Ōi power plant in Fukui Prefecture and approved their restart in July 2012.[10] But it had to use fancy legal footwork to do this because the new nuclear safety rules were still not yet in place. The action caused a storm of protest—including tough criticism from the head of the Nuclear Safety Commission himself, and the largest street demonstrations that the country had seen in decades.[11] As a result, the government hesitated to repeat its questionable maneuvers. When the two Ōi reactors finished their thirteen-month operating period in September 2013, the country returned once again to nuclear zero.[12] At the time of this writing, July 2014, all of Japan's nuclear power reactors were still idle, and no restarts were expected until at least after the summer.[13]

In short, the total collapse of Japanese nuclear power production over the three years from 2011 to 2014 was not the product of a clear new national nuclear policy. Instead, the technological accident at Fukushima led to the subsequent political accident of an unintended, open-ended, nationwide nuclear shutdown.

The unplanned shutdown of the nuclear fleet was hardly the only policy failure in the aftermath of Fukushima. Longer-term nuclear policy questions also became bogged down in political wrangling and remained unresolved more than three years after the accident. Below I briefly describe the inconclusive debates that took place in three key policy areas: nuclear safety standards, the long-term energy mix, and fuel cycle technologies.

First, as noted above, Japan's nuclear safety standards took much longer to overhaul than most experts had anticipated. Soon after the accident, the Democratic Party of Japan (DPJ)-led government announced its intention to create a new Nuclear Regulation Authority (NRA) modeled on the well-respected US Nuclear Regulatory Commission. Practically everyone agreed that this was a good idea. The NRA law was widely expected to sail through the Diet. Not even the powerful Ministry of Economy, Trade, and Industry (METI), which had previously been in charge of nuclear safety regulation, opposed the creation of a new nuclear safety czar outside its jurisdiction.[14] But at the last minute the opposition Liberal Democratic Party (LDP) attacked the government's proposal on the grounds that the NRA needed to be an "Article 3 organization"—a special status providing absolute independence. The LDP was seeking political advantage by tacking to the "left" of the DPJ on nuclear safety. The LDP ended up blocking the NRA law's passage through the Diet for months until the DPJ finally gave in to its demands.[15] Because of this political struggle, it was not until September 2012 that the new agency could finally begin the hard work of crafting new Japanese nuclear safety regulations.[16] The NRA finally produced its new safety regulations for commercial power plants in July 2013, more than two years after the accident. Only then did it begin assessing the reactors' readiness one at a time—a process that could take several years to complete. The Diet's failure to quickly pass the NRA law was a key reason why Japan's entire nuclear reactor fleet went dark and stayed that way for such a long time.

As of July 2014 the NRA was up and running, and the power companies had spent over ¥2.2 trillion to fulfill its new safety requirements.[17] Yet there remained considerable institutional uncertainty about the staying power of the new nuclear safety regime. After returning to power in December 2012, the LDP and its allies conveniently forgot their prior insistence on the NRA's absolute independence and started lambasting it for not moving more swiftly to approve reactor restarts. Even more problematically, the politicians sought to curtail the regulator's independence by aggressively trying to pack its top ranks with pronuclear advocates who had received significant sums of money for research projects or consulting jobs from the electrical power companies (EPCOs) over the years.[18] The LDP's goal was obviously to speed up the restarts, but in so doing it was also inviting more political conflict and thereby hurting the chances for public acceptance of any restarts. It was also inviting intervention by the courts. The Fukui District Court ruled in May 2014 that the 2012 Ōi nuclear power plant restart had been illegal, and it even called into question the very possibility of certifying a nuclear plant's safety in earthquake-prone Japan.[19] If the NRA's legal status of absolute independence became compromised, the courts could weigh in even more strongly against any renewed operation of Japan's nuclear estate.

Another area of persistent policy confusion and uncertainty was Japan's future energy mix. To supply its short-term energy needs in the face of the shutdown of the entire nuclear fleet in 2012, Japan turned to strict conservation and imports of vast amounts of old-school fossil fuels.[20] These emergency measures kept the lights on. But the imports sent Japan's trade balance into deficit, and no one thought that a massive increase in the country's fossil fuel dependence was a good idea. Japan therefore needed to decide on a rational long-term energy plan, and notably on the role of fossil fuels, renewables, and nuclear. But as of July 2014 there still was no plan.

The government did recognize that its 2010 plan to raise the nuclear portion in Japan's electricity mix to 50 percent by 2030 had become impossible.[21] But what percentage of the total would be possible and desirable for nuclear? And what other energies would make up the difference?

Many voices argued that Japan needed to increase its reliance on renewable energies such as solar and wind power, which had represented only 2 percent of Japan's electricity production prior to the disaster (10 percent if one includes large-scale hydropower).[22] Although the electrical power companies and heavy industry were skeptical of these technologies, in September 2011 DPJ prime minister Naoto Kan coerced the Diet to pass a new feed-in tariff subsidy system for renewables. He was able to achieve this reform by making the feed-in tariff a condition for his stepping down from power.[23] The new system came into effect in July 2012, and soon thereafter solar panels and wind turbines were popping up all over the country.

With the creation of the feed-in-tariff system, Kan certainly made his mark on Japanese energy policy. But the key question of whether the increased future reliance on renewables would come at the expense of nuclear power or fossil fuels remained unresolved. This persistent lack of clarity can be seen in the vapid new "Strategic Energy Plan" released by METI in April 2014, which broke precedent by failing to assign numerical targets for the country's future level of reliance on different energy sources. The document stated that the future use of nuclear energy would be "lowered to the extent possible," but what that statement might mean in practice was anybody's guess.[24] At one extreme, it could mean that the government would be actively discouraging continued reliance on nuclear power; at the other, it could mean that the government intended nuclear to take an even more prominent position than it had held before Fukushima, albeit less than the government's pre-2011 projections had anticipated.

Such waffling as late as mid-2014 reflected the fact that the political class had become deeply divided over the long-term future of nuclear power. Kan produced the first major breach in the elite consensus in July 2011 when he called on Japan to plan its complete exit from nuclear power. The prime minister's statement was reported by worldwide media as the inevitable denouement of the Fukushima accident.[25] But domestically Kan was pilloried for his stance, not only by the LDP and heavy industry but even within his own party, and he ended up weakly declaring a few days later that it was merely his "personal view."[26]

The idea of a nuclear phaseout did not die when Kan was replaced as prime minister by the DPJ politician Yoshihiko Noda, however. On September 14, 2012, Noda's Energy and Environment Council—composed of the most powerful ministers in the government—embraced the nuclear phaseout option in a decision that it presented as definitive. The council pledged that Japan should plan for zero nuclear power generation by the year 2040. But it also declared that, in the meantime, Japan should operate existing reactors at full power, resume building the planned reactors whose construction had been approved prior to the disaster, and continue to strive for commercial reprocessing of spent reactor fuel to extract plutonium for more energy production.[27] In other words, the Noda plan was for Japan's nuclear operations to return to their prior path, but with the understanding that everything would once again come to a screeching halt in about twenty-five years' time. This plan was attacked from all sides as self-contradictory and unrealistic. Then, remarkably, less than a week after the council's decision had been unveiled, the full cabinet failed to endorse its own top ministers' stance.[28] Noda continued to insist that nuclear zero by 2040 was the government's policy, but his credibility was in tatters.

The return to power of the LDP and Shinzō Abe after the December 2012 national elections was widely believed to herald the return of old-time nuclear boosterism, even though the party was vague about its nuclear plans during the campaign. After returning to power, however, Abe and his government continued to avoid getting specific about its nuclear intentions.[29] As noted above, the government did not even dare to put a number on the country's future level of reliance on nuclear power in its April 2014 "Strategic Energy Plan."

Why did the LDP—and above all *this* LDP, under Abe's bull-in-a-china-closet style of leadership—tread so gingerly around the nuclear issue? The LDP's cautiousness was due in part to the continuing massive unpopularity of nuclear power in public opinion. For instance, in exit polls at the time of the December 2012 national Diet elections, 79 percent of respondents favored either a gradual or an immediate complete nuclear phaseout, whereas only 15 percent opposed a phaseout.[30] The LDP found it very hard to change this dynamic in the face of a steady stream of reports of the haplessness of TEPCO in its attempts to deal with contaminated water and other mishaps at the Fukushima Daiichi nuclear site. Abe's implausible claim that Fukushima Daiichi was "under control" in his speech to the International Olympic Committee in October 2013 greatly undermined his personal credibility on the nuclear issue.[31]

But the Abe government's lack of clarity about Japan's nuclear future was not just due to its fear of coming clean about its intentions in the face of hostile public opinion. There were also major fissures over Japan's nuclear direction within the upper ranks of the LDP. Most strikingly, Abe's former mentor, ex-prime minister Jun'ichirō Koizumi, developed an increasingly hard-line antinuclear position and went public with his views beginning in August 2013. Taking his campaign a step further, in 2014 he drafted former prime minister Morihiro Hosokawa to run for governor of Tokyo on an antinuclear platform against the LDP-backed independent Yōichi Masuzoe, who had tried to stake out a moderate position on the issue.[32] Hosokawa lost, but his and Koizumi's highly publicized stance destroyed the Abe team's attempt to claim that the antinuclear camp was composed merely of irresponsible leftists and the untutored masses.

As of July 2014, it appeared that the Abe government was content to continue supporting nuclear in a wink-wink nudge-nudge way, without detailing specific plans for Japan's future energy mix. That might be good electoral politics, but the Japanese bureaucracy and big business do not appreciate such a high level of uncertainty.

The question of investments in the nuclear fuel cycle was yet another area of surprising lack of decisive policy change after Fukushima. When you burn uranium for energy in a nuclear breeder reactor, as a by-product you get plutonium containing even more energy than the uranium you started with. The awareness of this strange and wonderful physical property led many states over the years to try to bring about a "nuclear fuel cycle" of cheap and inexhaustible energy. But the fuel cycle theory proved difficult to put in practice, and it was delicate diplomatically, since plutonium is a key ingredient for nuclear weapons. So, one by one, most states dropped out of the game.[33] Apart from Japan, the states that stuck with big fuel reprocessing and/

or plutonium fast-breeder reactor plans after the 1980s were either nuclear weapon states (though not the United States) or states that were warming up to join the nuclear weapon club, notably India and North Korea.

Japan maintained its commitment to building a purely civilian plutonium economy despite major technical problems and cost overruns.[34] The Rokkasho reprocessing plant was still not fully operational in 2011, two decades after the original estimated start date. Similarly, the Monju fast breeder reactor was almost never in operation because of a serious 1995 sodium leak and then various other technical problems and accidents over the years.[35] And the sorry saga of Japan's uranium enrichment work was almost as unedifying. Yet the flow of state funding for these sensitive technologies was unending. The largely unsuccessful effort to complete the nuclear fuel cycle from the 1960s up to 2011 may have cost almost $250 billion.[36]

In the aftermath of Fukushima, many observers believed that Japan would shut down its white elephant fuel cycle projects. Those projects were not only extravagant but also even more prone to serious, life-threatening accidents than conventional power plants such as Fukushima Daiichi. But the fuel cycle policy remained in place. Indeed, remarkably, at the same time that Japan's reactors were being shut down one by one with little prospect of a quick restart—and with a decent chance that they would never return to service— in January 2012 Japan Nuclear Fuels, Ltd. (JNFL) actually moved to start up the Rokkasho reprocessing plant for a test run.[37] The Princeton physicist and nuclear policy expert Frank von Hippel described Japan's attempt to launch its reprocessing plant while not having any operating power reactors as being simply "crazy."[38] Yet even the DPJ government's nuclear phaseout policy proposal of September 2012 actually doubled down and explicitly endorsed this "crazy" policy course. Later, in April 2014, the LDP government reaffirmed Japan's commitment to creating a complete fuel cycle, while also declaring that the Monju reactor would be modified to burn more plutonium than it produced.[39] Such modifications would be no easy task, especially given that the reactor had never worked properly in the first place. Moreover, shortly after the government's decision, the NRA revealed additional data falsification issues by Monju's operator, the Japan Atomic Energy Agency, and cast doubt on that agency's fitness to run any kind of nuclear facility.[40] As of July 2014, the fate of Monju remained unclear.

In sum, this section of the chapter has shown that, on the four topics of reactor restarts, nuclear safety standards, long-term energy mix, and fuel cycle technologies, the severe shock of March 2011 did not produce a decisive nuclear policy shift during the three years after the accident. With the partial exception of the creation of the NRA to oversee nuclear safety, the traditional lines of Japanese nuclear policy had neither been significantly changed nor clearly reaffirmed. Instead, the policy had simply become more blurry and disconnected from the reality on the ground.

As of July 2014, it appeared that Japanese reactor operations would probably rebound somewhat over the subsequent months and years. But without a coherent long-term policy, future nuclear restarts and re-stops could be expected to be highly inconsistent and politicized and to routinely violate economic and technical rationality. Since Japan had been unable to arrive at a new nuclear policy equilibrium after three years of debate, it was reasonable to ask if it ever could.

Japan's Nuclear Policy in International Comparison

It is often helpful to use international comparisons to gauge how surprising or unsurprising a country's policy choices may be. In the previous section of this chapter, I documented a very high level of nuclear policy confusion and uncertainty since 2011 in Japan. By contrast, this section of the chapter will show that other countries reacted much more decisively to Fukushima. Below, I compare Japan's nuclear policies before and after Fukushima with those of eleven other rich democracies with significant nuclear operations. This is the right comparison group from a social-scientific perspective because of their similar political, social, and economic contexts. For our purposes here, how China or North Korea responded to Fukushima is much less relevant than how France or South Korea responded.

In the 2000s, as the world was faced with high oil prices and the reality of hydrocarbon-caused climate change, many rich democracies began gingerly to return to the option of nuclear power after the long pause following the 1986 Chernobyl nuclear disaster in the Soviet Union.[41] Like an old necktie sitting at the bottom of the closet, Japan's long-standing commitment to increasing its reliance on nuclear power was so out of date that it had come back in fashion. But then Fukushima came along and ruined the party.[42]

As shown in table 5.1, Fukushima had a major impact on the nuclear plans of Japan's peer comparison group: rich democracies with a significant nuclear establishment. Twelve countries including Japan fall into this category. I define "rich democracies" as states with membership in the Organisation for Economic Co-operation and Development, and I define a "significant nuclear establishment" as states that were operating at least five nuclear power reactors as of December 31, 2012. Table 5.1 (pp. 120–21) shows the evolution between March 2011 and July 2014 of these twelve countries' long-term (i.e., fifteen-to-twenty-five-year) projected reliance on nuclear power production as a proportion of their overall electricity needs. The table sorts the countries' policies into three broad categories: "planned increase," "planned neutral," or "planned decrease or phaseout." I define a "neutral" stance as an expected change of no more than 3 percent in the projected role of nuclear in the country's future electricity mix compared to the pre-2011 number. Note that in some cases countries that are coded as "neutral" planned to build new reactors as of July 2014, mostly in order to replace the power lost from older units that were slated for decommissioning.

Table 5.1 provides clear evidence of a major shift away from nuclear among Japan's peer group countries in the wake of Fukushima. Putting aside the case of Japan, six of the eleven relevant comparison countries made clear decisions to rely much less on nuclear in the future than they had been planning to do prior to the accident, whereas five decided to persist with their prior expected levels. Of the six that decided to downshift their planned reliance, three decided for a complete nuclear phaseout, one decided to shift from a small reduction to a big reduction, and two decided to scrap planned increases. These were major policy shifts.[43] The overall post-Fukushima drop in the nuclear expectations among Japan's peer group was even more striking in light of the strong pre-2011 expectations of a coming nuclear "renaissance." Of course, Fukushima was not the only driver of the changed nuclear plans of Japan's peer group, and in many cases the changes were controversial and not irreversible. But Fukushima was clearly a very strong force for change in all of these places, as it affected both the politics and the economics of nuclear power. If we put this global reaction together with the fact that Fukushima happened in Japan, Japan's failure to clarify its nuclear plans in the aftermath of the accident is all the more surprising.

Veto Players and Japan's Nuclear Policy Rudderlessness

Why did Japanese decision makers fail to coalesce around a clear and credible long-term nuclear policy for at least three years after the accident?

TABLE 5.1   Rich and Nuclearized Democracies' Long-Term Plans for Nuclear Energy as a Proportion of Their Total Electricity Needs, before and after Fukushima

	Planned Decrease or Phaseout	Planned Neutral (±3%)	Planned Increase
Before Fukushima (March 2011)	France (small decrease)[1] Germany (decrease)[2]	Belgium[3] Canada[4] Spain[5] Sweden[6] Switzerland[7] United Kingdom[8] United States[9]	Czech Republic[10] Japan[11] South Korea[12]
After Fukushima (July 2014)	*Belgium* (phaseout by 2025) *France* (major decrease) *Germany* (phaseout by 2022) *Japan?* *Switzerland* (phaseout by 2034)	Canada *Czech Republic* *Japan?* *South Korea* Spain Sweden United Kingdom United States	

N.B. Italicized country name indicates a significant post-Fukushima policy shift.
Source: Compiled by the author.

Notes to Table:

1. France now plans to decrease its reliance on nuclear from 75 percent of electricity to 50 percent by 2025. For the pre-Fukushima policy, see International Energy Agency, *Energy Policies of IEA Countries: France, 2009 Review* (Paris: IEA, 2009); for the post-Fukushima policy, see Pierre Le Hir, "Une transition énergétique encore très fragile," Le Monde, July 2, 2014, www.lemonde.fr/planete/article/2014/07/02/la-transition-energetique-ne-fait-toujours-pas-consensus_4449692_3244.html.

2. Germany's post-Fukushima policy shift is well described in International Energy Agency, *Energiepolitik der IEA-Länder, Deutschland, Prüfung 2013* (Paris: IEA, 2013).

3. For the pre-Fukushima policy, see International Energy Agency, *Energy Policies of IEA Countries: Belgium, 2009 Review* (Paris: IEA, 2009); for the post-Fukushima policy, see "Le gouvernement 'bétonne' la sortie du nucléaire," LeVif.be, November 13, 2013, www.levif.be/info/actualite/belgique/le-gouvernement-betonne-la-sortie-du-nucleaire/article-4000449254356.htm.

4. For the pre-Fukushima policy, see International Energy Agency, *Energy Policies of IEA Countries: Canada, 2009 Review* (Paris: IEA, 2009); for the post-Fukushima policy, see National Energy Board of Canada, "Canada's Energy Future 2013: Energy Supply and Demand Projections to 2035," November 2013, www.neb-one.gc.ca/clf-nsi/rnrgynfmtn/nrgyrprt/nrgyftr/2013/nrgftr2013-eng.pdf.

5. For the pre-Fukushima policy, see International Energy Agency, *Energy Policies of IEA Countries: Spain, 2009 Review* (Paris: IEA, 2009); for the post-Fukushima policy, see Elena G. Sevillano, "La Central de Garoña ya tiene una ley a medida para reabrir," El País, February 22, 2014, http://sociedad.elpais.com/sociedad/2014/02/21/actualidad/1392990332_049345.html.

Perhaps the most commonly offered hypothesis to explain Japan's post-Fukushima policy disarray was that the country suddenly found itself with no good energy options. Oil and gas come from unstable parts of the world, have high price volatility, and produce climate change; solar, wind, and other renewables are generally expensive and largely unproven as large-scale power sources; and nuclear energy is now perceived as being highly dangerous. Therefore, the government simply did not know what to do. As a government source explained to the *Asahi Shimbun* in late August 2012, "I think the politicians are having trouble making up their minds."[44]

Yet there was no shortage of people who leaped in with bright ideas about how to build a new energy policy framework in Japan. And politicians are used to being blindsided by unexpected events and impossible policy dilemmas. In fact, it is almost definitional to their profession to make difficult choices quickly and to take responsibility for the results—or at least to appear to be doing so.[45] But this time, they simply waffled. Why?

---

6. The pre- and post-Fukushima policies are well described in International Energy Agency, *Energy Policies of IEA Countries: Sweden, 2013 Review* (Paris: IEA, 2013).

7. The pre- and post-Fukushima policies are well described in International Energy Agency, *Energy Policies of IEA Countries: Switzerland, 2012 Review* (Paris: IEA, 2012).

8. There is rather more uncertainty about UK plans than about those of most other countries because of a heavily market-driven approach to the energy sector. The current government has reduced the uncertainty by offering a large indirect subsidy for new nuclear building to replace older reactors that have been or will be decommissioned. The pre- and post-Fukushima policies are well described in Paul Bolton, "UK Energy Statistics," House of Commons Library, September 9, 2013, www.parliament.uk/briefing-papers/sn03631.pdf.

9. There is rather more uncertainty about US plans than about those of most other countries because of a heavily market-driven approach to the energy sector. The pre- and post-Fukushima policies are well described in US Energy Information Administration, "Long-Term Outlook for Nuclear Generation Depends on Lifetime of Existing Capacity," April 25, 2013, www.eia.gov/todayinenergy/detail.cfm?id=10991.

10. For the pre-Fukushima policy, see International Energy Agency, *Energy Policies of IEA Countries: Czech Republic, 2010 Review* (Paris: IEA, 2010); for the post-Fukushima policy, see Ian Willoughby, "Czech Republic to Cease Being Major Energy Exporter and Import Instead, HN Reports," Radio Praha, June 24, 2014, www.radio.cz/en/section/business/czech-republic-to-cease-being-major-energy-exporter-and-import-instead-hn-reports.

11. For the pre-Fukushima policy, see Ministry of Economy, Trade and Industry, "Strategic Energy Plan of Japan," June 2010, www.meti.go.jp/english/press/data/pdf/20100618_08a.pdf; for the post-Fukushima policy, see METI, "Strategic Energy Plan," April 2014.

12. For the pre-Fukushima policy, see International Energy Agency, *Energy Policies of IEA Countries: The Republic of Korea, 2012 Review* (Paris: IEA, 2012); for the post-Fukushima policy, see Jane Chung, "South Korea Cuts Future Reliance on Nuclear Power, but New Plants Likely," Reuters, January 14, 2014, http://uk.reuters.com/article/2014/01/14/uk-nuclear-korea-idUKBREA0D05K20140114.

Japanese politicians were hamstrung less by a lack of good *policy* options than by a lack of good *political* options—and by their limited power to reshuffle the political deck. One major political problem caused by Fukushima was the serious difference of opinion about the value of nuclear energy that divided the majority of the Japanese power elite from the majority of ordinary citizens.[46] The power elite, and notably the so-called "nuclear village" of big business, the electrical utilities, and key government ministries, wanted to return to business as usual. They thought that abandoning nuclear power would kill Japan's manufacturing economy. But the mass public became increasingly antinuclear, not least because of its serious doubts about the competence and honesty of the "nuclear village." By March 2012, 79.6 percent of the public moderately or strongly endorsed the idea of an eventual complete phaseout from nuclear power, and its antinuclear spirit remained solid thereafter.[47] Antinuclear masses even went into the streets by the tens of thousands to protest reactor restarts during the summer of 2012—the first time in decades that Japan had seen such an outpouring of public sentiment on any issue.[48] In a democracy, the public's strongly held views could not be ignored even if they were considered unrealistic by many elites.

But the elite-mass nuclear policy standoff was by no means the only cause of Japan's nuclear policy disarray. It was merely one additional layer of difficulty for a policy-making process that even insiders had long found to be incredibly frustrating. In an interview I conducted before the Fukushima accident, one influential figure in the nuclear establishment told me that the major nuclear players had responded to increasing problems in the sector since the 1990s with "a lack of willingness to collaborate, and even occasionally forming a kind of circular firing squad."[49] And the lack of elite harmony before March 2011 became a vicious blame game after it. Indeed, it may be precisely because the elites were already deeply divided that public opinion was able to have such a big impact on the post-Fukushima policy debate. The prime minister and his cabinet were not capable of leading this squabbling group of actors; they were part of the squabble.

The conventional wisdom is mistaken in suggesting that the "nuclear village" was a cohesive community that knew what policies it wanted and how to push them through. Actually Japanese nuclear policy was gridlocked long before Fukushima, largely because the "nuclear village" included many distinctive, legally empowered actors—"veto players," in the language of contemporary political science—with different viewpoints and mutual suspicions.[50]

Veto players are individual or collective actors that have de facto institutionalized authority to unilaterally block major policy change. Many recent comparative politics studies agree that, to quote Andrew MacIntyre, "the wider the dispersal of veto authority, the greater the risk of policy rigidity."[51] Veto authority typically comes about through gradual processes of historical institutionalization. In Japan, veto authority over fundamental aspects of nuclear policy had gradually dispersed very widely over the decades—and not just to different parts of the state but also to the private, regional monopoly electrical utilities and the heavy manufacturers.[52] This dispersion of power over nuclear policy was much more extensive in Japan than in most other countries. Moreover, because veto power on this issue began to disperse very early in Japan in comparison with other states, it became harder to reverse. Once the key actors became established as veto players, they were able to spread their tentacles far and wide across the entire policy sector. The gradual entrenchment of the nuclear veto players over time is a good example of the "increasing returns" process of historical institutionalization.[53] Meanwhile, the increasing complexity of the Japanese nuclear arena led the veto players to perceive an ever-greater potential for severe "negative externalities" as a result of any major policy reform.[54]

We can count at least seven institutional actors that have traditionally been deeply embedded in the policy-making process to the extent of holding de facto veto power over major nuclear policy changes in Japan. Table 5.2 identifies the seven traditional veto players, the source of their veto power, the amount of time since they definitively rose to veto player status in the nuclear policy-making arena, and their generic nuclear policy preferences.

In addition to the seven veto players listed in table 5.2, note that the new nuclear safety agency, the NRA, acted as a major block on the government's nuclear restart intention after its birth in 2012. I have not included the NRA in the table because of the importance of historical institutionalization processes. In other words, however powerful it may seem on paper, a new organizational actor inevitably requires time to put down roots and become strong enough to consistently stop others from undermining its interests. Therefore, although as of July 2014 the NRA seemed to have all the legal characteristics of a veto player, it was necessary to wait and see whether those characteristics would persist.

In addition, as noted previously, after the accident the courts started to make sporadic rulings on the nuclear issue. The courts certainly had the ability to become yet another veto player if they chose to exercise their full constitutional powers. But, as of July 2014, whether the judiciary would become fully engaged remained to be seen.[55]

The final asterisk to table 5.2 is that the AEC's long-standing veto power was ended by new legislation in 2014. The AEC still existed, but it was a shadow of its former self.[56] This is an extraordinary event from the perspective of veto players theory, and careful study will be required to determine how this fate could have befallen an institution that had wielded tremendous power in earlier decades. My off-the-record interviews indicate that the AEC was a willing participant in its own demise. In the aftermath of 2011, the AEC commissioners found themselves unable to fulfill their mandate to bring the various nuclear players together, especially because of the expansion of the circle of active players and the hot glare of the media and elected politicians. As a result, they were more relieved than angered to watch the government take over their statutory role of setting long-term nuclear policy.

As shown by the fate of the AEC, the mere existence of many veto players does not make change impossible. If all the players agree on a policy change, then it can happen. But the greater the number of veto players, the more unlikely such agreement becomes. The difficulty of major change in a context of multiple veto players is clearly borne out by the history of Japanese nuclear policy. Not only recently but also in the distant past, serious initiatives to change Japan's nuclear direction by one or another of these powerful actors have been consistently blocked or dramatically watered down by others, in line with the expectations of historical institutionalist veto players theory. The result has been many decades of nuclear policy stasis. For instance:

- *Nuclear weapons.* Numerous high-ranking Japanese politicians over the years have been tempted to seek the bomb. Political pressures in this direction were strongest in the 1950s and 1960s, prior to Japan's accession to the Nuclear Nonproliferation Treaty. But as Hiromi Arisawa, an original member of the AEC who served for seventeen years, told the *Asahi* newspaper upon his retirement in 1972, "We were pressed repeatedly for permission to do basic research on how to make an atomic bomb. They tried to persuade us to do so by saying that such research was permissible under the Constitution. Naturally, I always refused."[57] It would be hard to find a clearer indication of the old AEC's veto power than this.

TABLE 5.2   Japan's Traditional Nuclear Policy Veto Players

Actor	Source of Veto Power	Age of Veto Power	Policy Preferences
Prime minister/governing party coalition	Constitutional authority to pass legislation	1950s–	Achieve popular and sustainable policies in line with political views
Upper House majority when divided government	Constitutional authority to pass legislation	Sporadic; most recently, 2010–13	Achieve popular and sustainable policies in line with political views
Regional monopoly electrical power companies (EPCOs)	Traditionally, legal monopoly on electricity generation, transmission, and distribution; own and operate most of Japan's nuclear facilities, including fuel cycle facilities	1950s–	Maximize power production with existing nuclear reactors; minimize own investment costs
Atomic Energy Commission (AEC)	Authority under Atomic Energy Basic Law to set long-term nuclear policy	1950s–2014	Promote peaceful use of nuclear power; achieve nuclear policy consensus
Ministry of Economy, Trade, and Industry (METI)	Authority under Energy Policy Basic Law to draft long-term energy policy and set retail electricity rates, pass out funds to localities, etc.	1970s–	Increase domestic energy production; build the "plutonium economy"; increase nuclear exports
Prefectural governors	Quasi-legal requirement to approve Nuclear Safety Agreement with plant operator	1970s–	Achieve sustainable and popular policies; get subsidies from national government and EPCOs
Nuclear plant makers (e.g., Hitachi, Mitsubishi, Toshiba), backed by Keidanren	Makers of most of Japan's reactors; would also be key for reactor decommissioning	1990s– (previously were in coalition with the EPCOs)	Increase nuclear construction at home and abroad

Source: Compiled by the author.

- *Reprocessing.* In the early 2000s, the nine EPCOs, along with neoliberal forces inside METI and the Koizumi government, pushed for a retreat from the costly and fruitless fuel cycle policy. The EPCOs were already skeptical of the plan for spent fuel reprocessing in the 1970s, but they had bowed to the wishes of the government, Mitsubishi Chemical, Sumitomo Chemical, and other heavy manufacturers to create the JNFL consortium that would build the Rokkasho reprocessing plant.[58] By the 2000s, the EPCOs had turned clearly against making any more investments in that money pit. To fend off their attack, METI first quashed its internal neoliberal dissenters who agreed with the EPCOs. Then it pushed the Diet to create a special "reprocessing fund" worth ¥12.7 trillion in May 2005. In this act, the government agreed to pay all existing debts and future costs associated with the Rokkasho facility, using special surcharges on electricity transmission and household consumption.[59] The EPCOs ended up accepting this as a partial win and, against their better judgment, agreed to keep working on the project.

- *Nuclear power production.* As noted above, Kan's July 2011 attempted peremptory announcement of a nuclear power phaseout was overwhelmingly rejected by the other veto players, and he had to backtrack. Noda's more carefully deliberated phaseout plan met with the same ignominious fate. It failed even to gain the endorsement of Noda's own cabinet.

It was fundamentally because of the fractionalized nature of the Japanese nuclear policy-making arena that these serious attempts to overturn the existing order did not succeed.

It is also important to note that such serious attempts at major nuclear policy reform have historically been rare. Why was the traditional nuclear policy not under more pressure, more often? This brings us to the second key historical institutionalist insight: the effects of the intertwining of different strands of nuclear policy over time. In other words, Japan's nuclear policy rigidity has been a function not only of the large number of veto players but also of the legacies of the deals that the veto players struck with each other in the past.

The difficulty of bringing about change in the context of intertwined policy strands can be seen in the case of the white elephant Rokkasho reprocessing plant. Prior to 2011, a METI bureaucrat informed me that even though

METI had historically been strongly in favor of Rokkasho for energy security reasons, at some point most METI bureaucrats realized that the plutonium economy was never going to materialize. But they nevertheless kept funding the Rokkasho project, mainly because of Japan's continuing inability to find a site to build a permanent nuclear waste storage facility.[60] The existence of the Rokkasho facility, even in its unfinished condition, had become necessary to justify the national government's promises to local and prefectural governments that the large quantity of spent fuel in above-ground storage sites under their jurisdiction was merely there "temporarily" and would be taken off their hands once Rokkasho could be brought into operation. Otherwise those governments would no longer agree to host nuclear power reactors. Moreover, a large quantity of spent fuel is already present at Rokkasho itself, and it would be next to impossible to convince the local and prefectural governments to take it back. Thus Japan arrived at the ridiculous situation of endless massive spending on a still-inoperative fuel-reprocessing plant that was not going to solve the problem of long-term waste disposal even if it did enter into service. Rokkasho's importance for central-local relations was such that not even the shock of Fukushima could change the national government's determination to keep the dream alive, even at a time when it was seriously contemplating a complete nuclear phaseout.

The question then arises, why has Japan faced so much trouble finding a permanent nuclear waste site? Despite generous state and corporate offers of payments to localities over the years, as of July 2014 no amount of money had been sufficient to convince any of them to become the permanent dumping ground for Japan's nuclear waste.[61] Of course the waste siting issue is a headache in many countries, but some have found solutions. One important reason why the waste siting issue has proven so difficult in Japan and other places is that antinuclear activists have effectively mobilized the public's instinctive "nuclear fear."[62]

Ironically, then, the actions of the antinuclear activists may be said to be partially responsible for the persistence of METI's commitment to building the plutonium economy. After all, if there were a permanent waste site, the genuine reason METI has had for keeping Rokkasho on life support would disappear overnight.

One of the leading antinuclear activists, Hideyuki Ban of the Citizens' Nuclear Information Center, explained to me that although he has tried to convince fellow activists to be "more flexible" on the waste issue and other issues, the antinuclear movement itself is riven with internal divisions that keep it locked into a fundamentalist antinuclear position.[63] This point brings up the third historical institutionalist insight. The nuclear village's veto player–driven gridlock is matched by an equally high level of fractionalization among its antinuclear opponents, with the result that neither side can compromise with the other. The bad blood created by this polarized situation leads to even more gridlock. And if this conflict spiral was already intense before Fukushima, it became even more intense after it.

The Fall of TEPCO and Japan's Possible Nuclear Futures

In the previous section of the chapter, I argued that if we want to understand why Japan failed to come up with a coherent set of policy reforms during the three years and counting *after* Fukushima, then we need first to understand why it was unable to reform its traditional nuclear policy for so many years *before* the accident. The answer, in short, is the large number and complex relationships of Japan's entrenched nuclear veto players. This insight can also help us to better understand the kinds of potential structural changes that could finally open the door to major nuclear policy reform in the future.

Before Fukushima, no institutionalized veto player had ever been disestablished from the nuclear policy-making arena. Once a veto player, always a veto player. If this tradition were to hold firm, then there would be little reason to imagine any other possible nuclear future for Japan than an unlimited extension of the post-Fukushima policy disarray. The potential addition of the NRA to the lineup of veto players seemed to foretell even more fractionalization and gridlock in the future. But Fukushima did change the traditional veto players lineup to some extent. First, the AEC's veto power was ended. Second, and potentially much more significant, in 2012 the government took over TEPCO, the giant utility that had been the operator of Fukushima Dai-ichi. The post-Fukushima political and economic weakness of TEPCO and its sister EPCOs raises the possibility that their veto power could be ended as well. And if that were to happen, radical changes in Japanese nuclear policy would certainly become imaginable.

TEPCO was by far the largest of the nine EPCOs—private, vertically integrated, regional electrical utility monopolies—and it was their unquestioned leader in their many political battles with the Japanese state.[64] Under TEPCO's leadership, the EPCOs had notably succeeded in preventing the implementation of retail electricity liberalization, thus bucking the strong liberalizing trend across most of the rest of the industrialized world during the 2000s.[65] However, the Fukushima accident caused the company to descend into virtual bankruptcy, and the government gained a majority stake of voting shares in the company.[66] Bankrupt TEPCO was still providing electricity, but it was certainly not in a position to fight one-on-one with the government anymore. The other EPCOs were not nationalized, and they continued to fight for their interests. But without the giant TEPCO to lead them, the EPCOs' veto power was in peril. In January 2013, a METI panel came out in favor of definitively breaking up the power generation, transmission, and distribution functions of the utilities and introducing true competition into the retail electricity market.[67]

The prospect of neoliberal electricity market reform was a dagger pointed at the heart of the EPCOs. It also provided a glimmer of hope for those who wanted to see Japan exit from nuclear power.[68] In a truly market-based energy sector, power companies would probably be unwilling and even unable to take on the enormous risk of new nuclear plant construction, with its very long lead times before any profits appear. And the government would no longer have its thumb on the scales to encourage such investments. Therefore, Japan's nuclear estate would become obsolescent. It might linger on for a while, but as the reactors aged they would not be replaced. This is essentially the story of the United States nuclear power industry since the 1980s.

The nationalization of TEPCO made electricity market liberalization and, as a consequence, major nuclear policy change more possible; but it also undermined the desire of the politicians and bureaucrats to pursue that objective. When the government became the majority shareholder in TEPCO, all of the company's gigantic and upward-spiraling financial liabilities became the government's responsibility. Anticipating these costs, the Ministry of Finance had weighed in strongly against METI's drive to achieve control of the company in the spring of 2012.[69] But METI won, so the question then became how its "prize" would be paid for. The two basic options were to raise taxes or to return TEPCO to profitability. Anyone would prefer the latter option. But TEPCO's business model has always depended heavily on its monopoly status and on its cash-cow nuclear reactor fleet.[70] The same is also true of most of the other EPCOs, whose own financial situations went from rosy to critical in just a few months because of the nationwide nuclear shutdown.[71] Therefore, the nationalization of TEPCO greatly complicated the government's calculations, paradoxically dimming its enthusiasm for liberalizing reforms at the very moment when its power to achieve them was at its height. Table 5.3 summarizes how the government perceived its main policy dilemmas.

Because of the government's newly complicated policy calculations, after the nationalization there was a marked slowdown in the momentum toward a big-bang change in Japan's electricity market. The December 2012 return to power of the LDP, historically a close ally of the EPCOs, made the road to liberalization even more challenging. A step in that direction was taken in November 2013 with the passage of a law foreseeing the creation of a genuine national grid.[72] But the hard work still lay ahead. To bring a genuine free market into existence, over forty laws would have to be amended or written anew, over the determined objections of the EPCOs and their many allies within the LDP and METI.[73] Such a massive reform would be a tall order for any prime minister, let alone one who was also determined to revive the nuclear estate from its dormancy. As of July 2014, it appeared that the government would most likely opt for a partial, or even superficial, reform that would leave the EPCOs in a strong position to continue to control the lion's share of the market, while maintaining the flow of subsidies to the nuclear industry.

In the wake of the Fukushima shock, most expert observers expected that Japanese nuclear policy would quickly find a new equilibrium. Some believed that resource-poor Japan would swiftly reaffirm the centrality of nuclear energy in its economy; others expected a definitive decision to move stepwise toward nuclear zero. On two occasions during 2012, the international press confidently reported that such a definitive national decision for nuclear zero had in fact been made, just as in Germany, Switzerland, and Belgium. But in fact, Japan abjectly failed to settle on a new nuclear policy for more than three years after the accident. There was neither a grand nuclear policy turnaround nor a strong reaffirmation of the traditional nuclear policy. There had been a nationwide nuclear shutdown, but it was unintentional. There was a new nuclear safety regulator, but its independence was fragile. The relative portion of nuclear in the country's future energy mix was entirely unknown. The continued support for fuel cycle facilities in this context was simply crazy.

Why did this policy failure happen? In this chapter, I have noted the rise of antinuclear public opinion after Fukushima, but I have also stressed that

TABLE 5.3   How Nationalizing TEPCO Complicated the Government's Policy Calculations

Issue	Interest as the Government Only	Interest as TEPCO's Largest Shareholder
Reactivation of reactors	Prior to reactivation, requiring greatly increased safety and consent of localities and prefectures	Reactivating at least seven reactors as soon as possible to put balance sheet back in the black
Further electricity rate hikes	Implementing lower rates to encourage economic growth	Implementing big rate hikes to avert bankruptcy
Electricity system reform	Separating power generation and distribution businesses to encourage competition and limit EPCO power	Going slow on deregulation. If competition intensifies and TEPCO loses customers, rate hikes become impossible and it goes bankrupt
Paying for nuclear decommissioning and decontamination	Making TEPCO pay for everything	The more TEPCO is made to pay, the closer it comes to bankruptcy, especially if its reactors remain offline

Source: Adapted by permission from Chiaki Toyoda and Takeyo Miyazaki, "Govt, 'New TEPCO' Face Thorny Path," *Daily Yomiuri*, August 2, 2012, 7.

this was an additional complication for an already highly gridlocked policy-making arena. There were three interlocking structural obstacles to building a credible and comprehensive nuclear policy in Japan both before and after the devastating Fukushima nuclear accident:

- First, the difficulty of gaining agreement among a large number of well-entrenched and mutually distrustful veto players

- Second, the difficulty of changing course in light of the complex legacy of past policy compromises among the veto players

- Third, the existence of a similarly fractionalized situation in the antinuclear camp, leading to extremism and rigidity on that side as well, and ultimately a polarized pro- versus antinuclear debate that further undermined momentum for policy reform

The fact that Japanese policy makers achieved so little in the nuclear policy arena between 2011 and 2014 did not mean that significant nuclear policy change was impossible, however. The most likely potential pathway to major nuclear policy change would run through electricity market liberalization. The nationalization of TEPCO made it much more feasible for the government to pursue liberalization if it cared to. However, the nationalization of TEPCO also made the government less eager to enact such reforms.

Japan's nuclear future remains deeply uncertain. But what can be said with certainty is that future political debates will carry deep scars from the long post-Fukushima period of political confusion, indecision, and recrimination. Japan's nuclear policy meltdown has dealt a severe blow not merely to Japan's economy and environment but also, and most troubling of all, to the credibility of the country's fundamental political institutions.

Notes

1. Thanks to Anne Allison, Joonhong Ahn, Frank Baldwin, Christina Davis, Toshihiro Higuchi, Kohta Juraku, Rieko Kage, Naoaki Kashiwabara, Bill Keller, Ellis Krauss, John Mueller, Gregory Noble, Atsushi Sadamatsu, Paul Scalise, Masa Takubo, Frank von Hippel, Masaru Yarime, and participants at the Possible Futures Japan conference for their close readings of earlier drafts of this chapter. Thanks also to participants at seminars at Temple University Japan, the University of Tokyo, and the Association for Asian Studies annual conference in Toronto for their comments and questions. Special thanks to Professor Satoru Tanaka for hosting me at the University of Tokyo while I was conducting this research. Funding was provided by the Mellon Foundation New Directions fellowship program and the Japan Foundation Center for Global Partnership.

2. See, e.g., Thomas A. Birkland, *Lessons of Disaster: Policy Change after Catastrophic Events* (Washington, DC: Georgetown University Press, 2007); Bryan D. Jones and Frank R. Baumgartner, *The Politics of Attention: How Government Prioritizes Problems* (Chicago: University of Chicago Press, 2005); Frank R. Baumgartner, "Taking Advantage of 'Crisis,'" paper presented at the workshop "Politics in Times of Crisis," Heidelberg, Germany, December 2009, www.unc.edu/~fbaum/papers/Baumgartner_Crisis_Dec_2009.pdf; Jeffrey W. Legro, "The Transformation of

Policy Ideas," *American Journal of Political Science* 44, no. 3 (July 2000): 419–32; David A. Welch, *Painful Choices: A Theory of Foreign Policy Change* (Princeton, NJ: Princeton University Press, 2005).

3. See esp. Kent E. Calder, "Japanese Foreign Economic Policy Formation: Explaining the Reactive State," *World Politics* 40, no. 4 (1988): 517–41; Kent E. Calder, *Crisis and Compensation: Public Policy and Political Stability in Japan* (Princeton, NJ: Princeton University Press, 1991); Richard J. Samuels, *3.11: Disaster and Change in Japan* (Ithaca, NY: Cornell University Press, 2013).

4. In his recent book, the American Japanese politics specialist Richard Samuels bravely fesses up to his own "outsized expectations and claims" about the likely effect of Fukushima on Japanese policies in the aftermath of the disaster. At the time, Samuels believed that Japanese politics would undergo a dramatic transformation on a par with what occurred in the United States after September 11, 2001. Samuels, *3.11*, xii–xiii.

5. Masafumi Takubo, "Wake Up, Stop Dreaming: Reassessing Japan's Plutonium Reprocessing Program," *Nonproliferation Review* 15, no. 1 (2008).

6. Chico Harlan, "Japan to Shut Off Its Last Reactor," *Washington Post*, May 4, 2012, A9.

7. Phred Dvorak and Mitsuru Obe, "Panel Finds Japan Was Unprepared for Nuclear Disaster," *Wall Street Journal*, December 27, 2011, http://online.wsj.com/article/SB10001424052970203391104577121872005287232.html.

8. Legislation from 2009 had allowed operators to apply to increase this to eighteen months, but as of March 2011 most reactors were still on the thirteen-month schedule. See "Nuclear Power in Japan," World Nuclear Association fact sheet, updated September 2012, www.world-nuclear.org/info/inf79.html.

9. Nuclear Regulation Authority, "Enforcement of the New Regulatory Requirements for Commercial Nuclear Power Reactors," July 8, 2013, www.nsr.go.jp/english/e_news/data/13/0912.pdf.

10. "Irresponsible Reactor Startup," *Japan Times*, July 6, 2012.

11. Kazuaki Nagata, "Oi Reactors Pass Stress Tests, Safety Panel Says," *Japan Times*, March 24, 2012.

12. Mari Iwata, "Japan Court Blocks Reactor Restarts," *Wall Street Journal*, May 21, 2014.

13. "Japan to Experience Nuclear-Free Summer," *Asahi Shimbun*, June 25, 2014, http://ajw.asahi.com/article/0311disaster/fukushima/AJ201406250047.

14. METI official, interview by author, February 8, 2012.

15. "Opposition's N-Safety Plan to Be OK'd by Govt, DPJ," *Yomiuri Shimbun*, May 13, 2012, www.yomiuri.co.jp/dy/national/T120512002930.htm.

16. James Conca, "Fukushima Slugfest—Japan's New Nuclear Regulation Authority," *Forbes*, October 9, 2012, www.forbes.com/sites/jamesconca/2012/10/09/fukushima-slugfest-japans-new-nuclear-regulation-authority/.

17. "Nuclear Safety Expenditures Top ¥2 Trillion," *Japan Times*, July 5, 2014, www.japantimes.co.jp/news/2014/07/05/national/nuclear-safety-expenditures-top-%C2%A52-trillion/#.U8oqDxDzmmw.

18. Mari Saito and Kentaro Hamata, "Independence of Japan's Nuclear Regulator Questioned after Shakeup," Reuters, June 10, 2014, http://uk.reuters.com/article/2014/06/10/japan-nuclear-regulator-idUKL4N0OR16X20140610.

19. Iwata, "Japan Court."

20. "Japan's 2012 LNG Imports at Record High on Nuclear Woes," Reuters, January 23, 2013, www.reuters.com/article/2013/01/24/energy-japan-mof-idUSL4N0AT00Y20130124.

21. "METI Decides on Basic Energy Plan through 2030: Raise Energy Self-Sufficiency to 70%," *Atoms in Japan*, June 14, 2010, www.jaif.or.jp/english/aij/member/2010/2010-06-14b.pdf.

22. International Energy Agency, *Energy Policies of the IEA Countries: Japan 2008 Review* (Paris: International Energy Agency, 2008), 150.

23. "Feed-in Tariff Scheme for Renewable Energy," paper presented to the Ministry of Economy, Trade and Industry, July 17, 2012, www.meti.go.jp/english/policy/energy_environment/renewable/pdf/summary201207.pdf.

24. METI, "Strategic Energy Plan," April 2014, www.enecho.meti.go.jp/en/category/others/basic_plan/pdf/4th_strategic_energy_plan.pdf.

25. Chico Harlan, "Japanese Prime Minister Naoto Kan Calls for Phase-Out of Nuclear Power," *Washington Post*, July 13, 2011, www.washingtonpost.com/world/japans-prime-minister-calls-for-phase-out-of-nuclear-power/2011/07/13/gIQA-XxUJCI_story.html.

26. "Kan: Nuclear Phaseout Comments 'Personal,'" *Nikkei Weekly*, July 18, 2012, 1.

27. Hiroko Tabuchi, "Japan Sets End of 2030s to Phase Out Atom Power; Plan Would Let Industry Recoup Investments, but Tokyo Hints at Flexibility," *International Herald Tribune*, September 15, 2012, 5; Hiroko Tabuchi, "Japan Says It Will Keep Working on Reactors," *International Herald Tribune*, September 17, 2012, 19.

28. "The Endorsement That Wasn't," *Japan Times*, September 23, 2012.

29. "LDP's Vague Nuclear Energy Policy," *Japan Times*, December 26, 2012.

30. "Exit Poll: Anti-nuclear Votes Spread across the Board," *Asahi Shimbun*, December 17, 2012, http://ajw.asahi.com/article/0311disaster/fukushima/AJ201212170097. Thanks to Ellis Krauss for bringing this article to my attention.

31. "Survey: 76% Don't Believe Fukushima Situation 'under Control'; Abe Support at 56%," *Asahi Shimbun*, October 7, 2013, http://ajw.asahi.com/article/behind_news/politics/AJ201310070064.

32. Takao Yamada, "Former PM Koizumi's Anti-nuclear Case Makes Sense," *Mainichi Shimbun*, August 26, 2013, http://mainichi.jp/english/english/perspectives/news/20130826p2a00m0na008000c.html.

33. Herbert Kitschelt, "Four Theories of Public Policy Making and Fast Breeder Reactor Development," *International Organization* 40, no. 1 (1986): 98.

34. Frans Berkhout, Tatsujiro Suzuki, and William Walker, "The Approaching Plutonium Surplus: A Japanese/European Predicament," *International Affairs* 66, no. 3 (1990): 523–43.

35. Hiroko Tabuchi, "Japan Strains to Fix a Reactor Damaged before Quake," *New York Times*, June 17, 2011.

36. Samuels, *3.11*, 112.

37. "Furnace Fault Delays Tests at Spent Fuel Nuclear Plant," *Daily Yomiuri*, February 5, 2012, 2.

38. Eric Talmadge and Mari Yamaguchi, "Japan to Make More Plutonium Despite Big Stockpile," Associated Press online, June 1, 2012, http://bigstory.ap.org/content/japan-make-more-plutonium-despite-big-stockpile.

39. METI, "Strategic Energy Plan," April 2014, esp. 54, www.meti.go.jp/english/press/2014/0411_02.html.

40. "Falsified Inspections Suspected at Monju Fast-Breeder Reactor," *Japan Times*, April 11, 2014, www.japantimes.co.jp/news/2014/04/11/national/falsified-inspections-suspected-at-monju-fast-breeder-reactor/#.U82xURDzmmw.

41. Sharon Squassoni, *Nuclear Energy: Rebirth or Resuscitation?* (Washington, DC: Carnegie Endowment for International Peace, 2009), http://carnegieendowment.org/files/nuclear_energy_rebirth_resuscitation.pdf.

42. See Charles D. Ferguson, "Nuclear Power's Uncertain Future," *National Interest*, March 15, 2012, http://nationalinterest.org/commentary/nuclear%27s-uncertain-future-6643; Frank Uekoetter, "Fukushima, Europe, and the Authoritarian Nature of Nuclear Technology," *Environmental History* 17, no. 2 (2012): 277–84.

43. It should be mentioned that Finland has continued to plan an increase in its nuclear reliance. Finland does not appear in table 5.1 because it did not meet the threshold of five operating reactors as of 2012.

44. "Noda Gives No Quarter in Meeting with Anti-nuke Activists," *Asahi Shimbun*, August 22, 2012, http://ajw.asahi.com/article/behind_news/politics/AJ201208220079.

45. Max Weber, "Politics as a Vocation," in *From Max Weber: Essays in Sociology*, ed. H. H. Gerth and C. Wright Mills, new ed. with preface by Bryan S. Turner (Abingdon, UK: Routledge, 1991), 77–128.

46. See, e.g., Daniel P. Aldrich, "Post-crisis Japanese Nuclear Policy: From Top-Down Directives to Bottom-Up Activism," *Asia-Pacific Issues*, no. 103 (January 2012), www.eastwestcenter.org/sites/default/files/private/api103.pdf.

47. "Japan's Majority Favor Phasing Out Nuclear Power: Poll," Reuters, March 18, 2012, www.reuters.com/article/2012/03/18/us-japan-nuclear-poll-idUSBRE82H0I20120318.

48. Hiroko Tabuchi, "Tokyo Rally Is Biggest Yet to Oppose Nuclear Plan," *New York Times*, July 16, 2012.

49. Akira Omoto, member of the Atomic Energy Commission, interview by author, quotation confirmed in e-mail, May 31, 2012.

50. Jacques E. C. Hymans, "Veto Players, Nuclear Energy, and Nonproliferation: Domestic Institutional Barriers to a Japanese Nuclear Bomb," *International Security* 36, no. 2 (2011): 154–89.

51. Andrew MacIntyre, "Institutions and Investors: The Politics of the Economic Crisis in Southeast Asia," *International Organization* 55, no. 1 (2001): 81.

52. For a similar take on veto players analysis as applied to Asian developmental states, see Joseph J. St. Marie, Kenneth N. Hansen, and John P. Tuman, "The Asian Economic Crisis and Bureaucratic Development: A Veto Player Analysis," *International Relations of the Asia-Pacific* 7, no. 1 (January 2007): 1–22.

53. Paul Pierson, *Politics in Time: History, Institutions, and Social Analysis* (Princeton, NJ: Princeton University Press, 2004).

54. Scott E. Page, "Path Dependence," *Quarterly Journal of Political Science* 1 (2006): 87–115. The relevance of negative externalities for historical institutional analysis of Japanese politics is underscored by Ellis Krauss and Robert Pekkanen, *The Rise and Fall of Japan's LDP: Political Party Organizations and Historical Institutions* (Ithaca, NY: Cornell University Press, 2010), 27–28. Thanks to Ellis Krauss for bringing this to my attention.

55. The Ministry of Foreign Affairs could also be noted as a veto player with respect to Japan's obligations under the Nuclear Nonproliferation Treaty, but not with respect to the civilian nuclear issues that are the focus of this chapter.

56. "Law Enacted to Scale Down Functions of Atomic Energy Commission," *Kyodo News*, June 20, 2014, https://english.kyodonews.jp/news/2014/06/297188.html.

57. Arisawa quoted in Selig S. Harrison, "Japan and Nuclear Weapons," in *Japan's Nuclear Future: The Plutonium Debate and East Asian Security*, ed. Selig Harrison (Washington, DC: Brookings Institution Press, 1993), 12.

58. Kazuhisa Mori, former head of the Japan Atomic Industrial Forum who brokered the deal, interview by author, February 24, 2009.

59. Tadahiro Katsuta and Tatsujiro Suzuki, "Japan's Spent Fuel and Plutonium Management Challenges," Research Report of the International Panel on Fissile Materials, September 2006, http://cybercemetery.unt.edu/archive/brc/20120621073056/, http://brc.gov/sites/default/files/documents/katsuta_suzuki_report.pdf.

60. METI official, interview by author, July 28, 2010. Ministry of Foreign Affairs official Kumao Kaneko also labeled the negotiations with governors as the "real reason" for the government's continuing support for Rokkasho in "Rokkasho saishori kōjō wa kakubusō no tame dewa nai" [The Rokkasho reprocessing plant is not for nuclear armament], *Enerugī* [*Energy*], November 2005, 13, quoted in Takubo, "Wake Up," 77–78.

61. Daniel P. Aldrich, *Site Fights: Divisive Facilities and Civil Society in Japan and the West* (Ithaca, NY: Cornell University Press, 2008).

62. Spencer R. Weart, *The Rise of Nuclear Fear* (Cambridge, MA: Harvard University Press, 2012), esp. 245–47.

63. Hideyuki Ban, Citizens' Nuclear Information Center, interview by author, February 17, 2012.

64. See Richard J. Samuels, *The Business of the Japanese State: Energy Markets in Comparative and Historical Perspective* (Ithaca, NY: Cornell University Press, 1987).

65. Paul J. Scalise, "The Politics of Restructuring: Agendas and Uncertainty in Japan's Electricity Deregulation," PhD diss., Oxford University, 2009.

66. "TEPCO to Be Nationalized July 25, Gov't to Acquire Up to 75% Stake," *Japan Economic Newswire*, May 21, 2012.

67. "METI Panel Wants Utilities Monopolies to End by 2020," *Japan Times*, February 10, 2013.

68. See, e.g., Andrew DeWit, "Japan's Remarkable Renewable Energy Drive—After Fukushima," *Asia-Pacific Journal* 10, no. 11 (2012), www.japanfocus.org/-Andrew-DeWit/3721.

69. "If TEPCO Wants Bailout, It Must Accept Reality," *Asahi Shimbun*, February 13, 2012, http://ajw.asahi.com/article/views/AJ201202130063.

70. Scalise, "Politics of Restructuring," esp. 213–14.

71. Mia Stubbs, "Lights Dim for Japan's Nuclear Utilities," Reuters, April 4, 2012, www.reuters.com/article/2012/04/04/refile-japan-idUSL6E8F4AF120120404.

72. Aaron Sheldrick and Osamu Tsukimori, "Japan Passes Law to Launch Reform of Electricity Sector," Reuters, November 13, 2013, www.reuters.com/article/2013/11/13/us-japan-power-deregulation-idUSBRE9AC08N20131113.

73. "Japan Girding for Battle Royal over Power Market Deregulation," *Nikkei Asian Review*, February 19, 2014, http://asia.nikkei.com/Politics-Economy/Policy-Politics/Japan-girding-for-battle-royal-over-power-market-deregulation.

CHAPTER SIX

Japan's Megadisaster Challenges: Crisis Management in the Modern Era

William J. Siembieda and Haruo Hayashi

Japan is a hazard-prone country,[1] and for nearly a century it has made incremental reductions to its hazard risk status.[2] The twenty-first century, however, presents larger threats from megadisasters, of which the Great East Japan Earthquake on March 11, 2011, is an example. The government and societal responses to the 3/11 disaster event, as well as responses to the 1995 Great Hanshin-Awaji (Kobe) Earthquake, demonstrate that disaster management in Japan is still evolving. The administrative reforms begun in 2001 by Prime Minister Jun'ichirō Koizumi are still being refined and reexamined in terms of fit and function.[3]

In fact, for the first time since the Meiji Restoration (1868–1912) we see a new approach to disaster management emerging: a shift from natural science and engineering to a more holistic view that embraces the actions of people and business in achieving societal safety. Built on the principle of partnerships with both the business sector and civil society as well as flexibility within the central government, this approach is an adaptation to the present realities— the demographic and economic transitions of the last twenty years—that combine to place more emphasis on constructing a disaster-resilient society. A key element of Japan's future disaster management will be the concept of operational continuity (the ability to continue activities under conditions of hardship) in all sectors of society. The continuance and swift renewal of household socioeconomic status, for example, reduces the hardships inherent in recovery. Through an overall reduction of uncertainty, collective actions establish a positive direction for reconstruction.

When a large-scale disaster event occurs, two types of "management" are needed. The first is crisis management, where big decisions are made quickly in an effort to prevent further damage and injury to the people, the economy, and the environment. The second is recovery management, a process that focuses on the hardship period and leads to the reconstruction of people's lives, the economic activities of the area, and the places and spaces damaged by the disaster. The latter type is complex, as it addresses both the physical and the social disruption caused by the event. While it may seem that these types of management occur concomitantly after an event, crisis and recovery management can occur separately, as the following examples demonstrate.

A positive example of crisis management occurred in Chile in March 2010. Sebastián Piñera, the newly inaugurated president, entered office facing the aftereffects of the country's largest compound disaster event (the February 27 earthquake and subsequent tsunami and soils deformation). This billionaire businessman-turned-politician rapidly set up emergency and reconstruction committees. The former addressed the immediate needs of stability and assistance, while the latter was for the longer period ahead. Piñera appointed a national ministry member to implement reconstruction, and the president's role after that was to ensure that fiscal resources were available and to make executive decisions on an as-needed basis.[4] The president was consulted on major policy issues and allowed the institutional ministerial apparatus to carry out disaster management.

Chile's reconstruction from the February 2010 disaster event represents an effective example of crisis management, but nonpresidents can apply crisis management skills as well. Mayor Katsunobu Sakurai of Minamisoma (a city in Fukushima Prefecture) showed leadership in the crisis and recovery periods of the 3/11 nuclear accident, for example. As a result of the disaster, the government partitioned Minamisoma into three sections by access—restricted, limited, and unrestricted—thus creating different recovery conditions for the town's people. In the restricted area, evacuation was mandatory; limited restriction meant residents might be able to return soon. While the government wanted to treat people differently by area, the mayor said everyone in his town was a member of one community. All had been affected by the nuclear accident, and all needed to be treated as equals. This clear sense of purpose and equity carried over into recovery activities and will continue to be a key factor in the town's reconstruction and eventual reunification. In essence, Sakurai's vision for the town was holistic and inclusive, not procedural. He provided the needed focus for the reconstruction carried out by others.

This chapter further explores how Japan's current disaster and recovery system emerged from the Kobe Earthquake and was tested by 3/11. These events provide lessons that can be applied to even larger threats such as a high-probability Tōkai-Tōnankai-Nankai (TTN) earthquake or Tokyo Near Field (TNF) earthquake. Those threats, as well as other potential threats, encompass millions of people, local governments in many prefectures, and large economic impacts and will be far more costly and disruptive than previous events. These will be compound, complex disasters involving more than one hazard and creating damages beyond single-hazard estimates. This is a form of "precarity" for the country (see chapter 2 of this volume by Anne Allison for discussion of this condition), and these highly probable disaster events, which are estimated to occur in less than a twenty-year horizon, mean Japan must be "smarter" than in the past and focus on countermeasures that result in modest, not extreme, levels of economic and social disruption.

In the last 150 years, Japan has shown a remarkable capacity to reinvent itself.[5] During the Meiji Restoration the country embraced modernization using the Western model. Advancements in industry and technology built an industrialized country with a growing population that acted collectively in supporting the national vision. Aside from the Great Kanto Earthquake in 1923, where fire caused most of the deaths, there were few large earthquakes, and disasters were not considered a major threat to the country. Then, after World War II and the Allied Occupation (1945–52), Japan again looked to the West and used technology, collective purpose, and close ties between government and industry to become a leading economy. In 2014, the country finds itself again with an imperative to embrace technology in order to lessen the costs of disasters (natural and manmade), attenuate disruption to society from disasters, and utilize business and civil society in new ways.

1995: The Tipping-Point Year

In the 1960s and 1970s Japan was expanding in terms of productivity, population, and wealth. Around 1995, however, a mix of changes occurred that influenced the future of Japan's disaster management. First, the number of productive people (ages fifteen to sixty-four) markedly declined to about eighty-five million, and there were more individuals aged sixty-five and older than zero-to-fourteen-year olds, which meant that as the years progressed the country would have fewer people available to work, to pay into the national welfare system, and to attend to the needs of an expanding elderly population (see Sawako Shirahase's discussion of these issues in chapter 1 of this volume). Demographic and economic transitions are shown in figure 6.1 along with disaster loss data demonstrating the relatively low losses until 1995.

In addition to a decline in the productive population, the growth in gross domestic product (GDP) leveled off in 1995, signaling that the country was entering a steady economic period, which would have implications for its possible futures. While Japan experienced rapid economic growth from 1960 to 1980, in 1995 the growth rate in per capita income leveled off and has since remained stable (or flat), and level GDP growth resulted in a decline in tax revenue. In fact, beginning in 2011, the government has issued bonds to pay for expenditures that the shortfall in tax revenues cannot cover (financial issues are discussed in chapter 7, by Saori Katada and Gene Park). In the years ahead, then, even fewer resources will be available to meet expanding social welfare needs and service the public debt.[6] The combination of a decrease in tax income with an increase in government expenditures reduces Japan's capacity to handle major disasters and places the present disaster management policy framework in question.

Reconstruction management after previous large-scale events was based on the assumption that population and economic growth would be sufficient to meet the fiscal and human resource needs of the next compound disaster event. That assumption no longer holds true. Since the 2011 earthquake and tsunami particularly, new questions are being asked in the Tōhoku region. For example, is it necessary to replace schools if there are no children to attend them, or should higher levees be built in villages where fewer people will live in the future? The current thinking for recovery is focused on helping the remaining residents and those who return to build good human relationships.[7] Stemming the flight of younger families is also an underlying policy objective, encouraging people to remain in the region and promoting community ties as a highly valued asset. This can be achieved in part by actions both to lessen the impact of future large events and to reduce societal discontinuity. For example, increasing the replacement target rates for older homes vulnerable to seismic and fire damages would decrease the need for temporary housing, enable more people to return to work, and be less stressful at the household level. In all, the future goal will be to lower the projected hardship with limited resources.

While new questions continue to be asked with each large-scale event, in essence it was the 1995 Kobe Earthquake that heightened awareness of

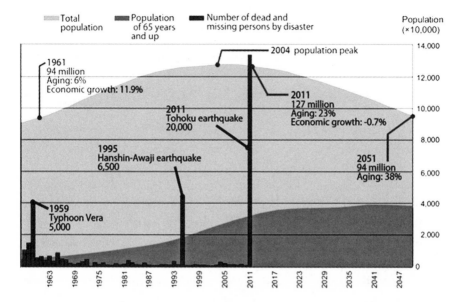

Total population / Population of 65 years and up / Number of dead and missing persons by disaster / Population (×10,000)

- 2004 population peak
- 1961 94 million Aging: 6% Economic growth: 11.9%
- 2011 127 million Aging: 23% Economic growth: -0.7%
- 2011 Tohoku earthquake 20,000
- 1995 Hanshin-Awaji earthquake 6,500
- 2051 94 million Aging: 38%
- 1959 Typhoon Vera 5,000

FIGURE 6.1   Major population, economic, and disaster trends over time. (Adapted from Government of Japan, "Bōsai ni kanshite totta no gaikyō Heisei 24 nendo no bōsai ni kansuru keikaku" [A summary of measures taken for disaster management and plans for disaster management for fiscal year 2012, white paper on disaster management], www. bousai.go.jp/kaigirep/hakusho/pdf/H24_honbun_1-4bu.pdf.)

the destructive power of major earthquakes and led to reorganization of the disaster management apparatus at the cabinet level.

Japan's Disaster Management System

The impact of large-scale hazard events is partly derived from the socioeconomic and political contexts, which also shape recovery from such events.[8] From 1947 to the 1970s the approach was simple emergency management, generally centered on fire and flood protection. If a new type of natural hazard disaster event occurred, then a law was passed outlining how the government would react the next time. The 1947 Disaster Relief Act, for example, was based on losses in the 1946 Nankai Earthquake, and the 1949 Flood Control Act was a response to the typhoons in 1945 and 1948. As cities grew, the mixture of old wooden houses and new buildings of mixed materials created many fire risks; an important hazard, fire was covered in the 1948 Fire

Services Act,[9] and the Fire Agency, whose name became the Fire and Disaster Management Agency (FDMA) after the 1995 Kobe Earthquake, was created as an independent agency and placed under the Ministry of Home Affairs.[10] The agency does not direct local fire brigades but helps train them and supplies fire science information. A small agency in terms of staff size, it continues to have national influence.

In 1961, two years after the Ise Bay Typhoon that caused tremendous destruction in the Nagoya area and the loss of more than five thousand lives, the Disaster Countermeasures Basic Act (DCBA) was enacted. The DCBA defined "protection of national land as well as citizens' lives, livelihoods, and property from natural disasters" as a national priority and established an operative hierarchy through disaster management councils at three levels: national, prefectural, and municipal. Authority and responsibilities stem from this structure, at least in concept. There are plans at each level that follow similar guidelines; yet most address emergencies, not disaster management. In 1963 the Basic Disaster Management Plan (updated several times) was issued. Working out roles in practice, however, is an ongoing process, as we saw in the 1995 Kobe event as well as the 3/11 events. The DCBA is a half century old, and with even larger threats on the horizon it needs to be revisited and continually updated.[11]

From the 1970s to 1995 the government adopted a hazard-by-hazard countermeasure approach to disaster management that diffused expertise and control. Many different ministries implemented legislation for earthquakes, volcanic eruptions, and other hazards. Among the most important was the revision in 1981 of the 1950 Building Standards Act, which is the paradigm for all modern seismic design and construction practices.[12] The value of the act was demonstrated in the 3/11 quake by the very low damage to buildings constructed after 1981 in the Tōhoku and Tokyo metropolitan regions. The management of nuclear energy safety was also part of this framework, but it wasn't until 1999 that the Special Measures Act for Nuclear Emergency Preparedness established detailed procedures.[13] With each law, national ministries expanded their in-house capabilities, but they were not required to share their specialized expertise. Indeed, separation of function, not integration of function, is characteristic of Japan's governance system.

Rather than being controlled by one central body, Japan's disaster management system is decentralized and spread out among ministries and agencies. For example, the Meteorological Agency is under the Ministry of Land,

Infrastructure Transport, and Tourism; the new Nuclear Regulation Authority is under the Environment Ministry; and the FDMA is under the Ministry of Internal Affairs and Communication (see figure 6.2). On the one hand, such decentralization creates problems of cooperation and coordination during large complex disaster events. On the other, this decentralized system enables more government agencies to be involved in disaster management, as will become evident in the section below on the projected TTN earthquake.

The absence of a single operational disaster management agency was an important factor in the decision to allow Kobe and Hyogo Prefecture to conduct recovery and reconstruction with substantial multiyear financial support from the central government. After the 1995 Kobe disaster event, however, there was an intense internal debate on the need for a separate national agency along the lines of the US Federal Emergency Management Agency (FEMA).[14] Despite some advocates of the move, the single-agency concept was not carried forward, as no decision could be reached on its specific powers: that is, what powers the ministries would relinquish and how the agency would be funded. Nevertheless, the need for an authority to conduct recovery and reconstruction remained. Then, in 1998, a subtle move toward a national agency occurred. The 1998 Comprehensive National Development Act indicates that if Japan is to be a safe and comfortable place to live the damage caused by disasters must be minimized. The act specifies a series of actions including encouraging earthquake-resilient buildings, supporting research into disasters and their prevention, promoting disaster management manuals, and providing assistance to people affected by a disaster. This act reflected a consensus after the Kobe Earthquake that large-scale disaster events are of national concern and should be managed through directed central government action.

In 2001, under the leadership of Prime Minister Koizumi, the operational ministries made some progress towards a multihazard and multiple-defense approach to disaster management, and they continue to do so. Establishment of a minister of state for disaster management in the Cabinet Office in 2001, for example, reflects an effort at new partnerships between government, industry, and technical experts. This unit functions as a government-wide planning office (see figure 6.2), though not all ministries are part of it (for instance, those tied to special industrial sectors such as nuclear energy are less likely to participate). To advise both the prime minister and the Cabinet Office, the 2001 administrative reforms

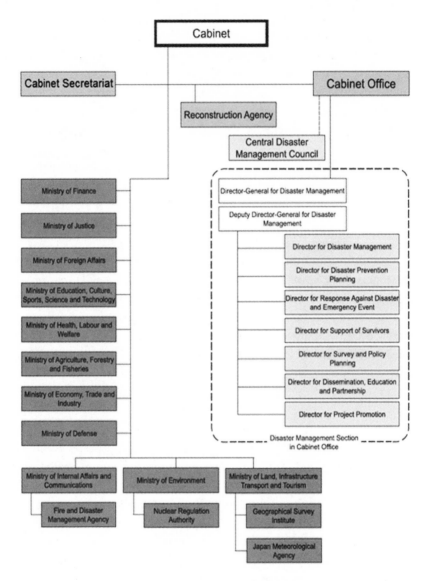

FIGURE 6.2 Japan's disaster management organization in 2012. (Adapted from the Government of Japan [2011] Cabinet Office, "Naikaku no ichitsuke/naikakufu no soshiki no gaikyō" [The Cabinet Office's role in the cabinet/structure], 2011, www.cao.jp/en/pmf_index-e.html.)

clustered councils together, such as the Central Disaster Management Council (CDMC).[15] The CDMC is an important vehicle for developing major disaster risk and damage scenarios and has offered opinions and revised scenarios upon request. The council enables a range of stakeholders to voice input and deliberate on disaster management policy issues. That is, the CDMC can create expert panels whose findings are reported to the council and may be forwarded to the cabinet and beyond. In general, the CDMC describes itself as "a place of wisdom that helps the cabinet and the prime minister." A key aspect of Prime Minister Koizumi's administrative reforms was the separation of functions and reliance on political leadership: bureaucratic practices of creating new organizations for each issue and focusing on products, such as levees, rather than processes certainly affect how disaster management works in Japan.

Since 2001, the CDMC has developed policy frameworks for the major areas at risk, including Tokyo, Tōkai-Tōnankai-Nankai, and the Chishima trench. This has raised the levels of hazard and risk knowledge while allowing programmatic action to start within these areas. Trust building between ministries and open systems of information flow, such as the CDMC mechanism, should lead to more systematic dissemination of information. We believe, however, that the lack of a functional multihazard approach contributed to the Fukushima accident because nuclear safety was not part of the council's work. While the council commissioned reports and studies on floods, volcanoes, and earthquakes, no work had been done on nuclear disaster: nuclear safety was assigned to the Nuclear Safety Commission established in 1978 under the Atomic Energy Basic Act.[16] The compartmentalized Japanese system is generally driven by rules and procedures, which is clearly not well suited to disaster management. Disaster management systems work best under a framework of flexibility and adaptation.

Still, the Japanese system does show flexibility in that it allows for exceptions to rules and extends time limits. For example, support for disaster-related temporary housing is limited to two years, but the limit was relaxed in the Tōhoku region for up to five years in some areas. A formal procedural structure established through ministry policy drives the disaster management process, including exceptions and extensions, but this is not a linear process. Japan's current disaster management process is an iterative one where needs, projects, budgets, and priorities are vetted from the ministries to the Cabinet Office and back again until agreements are reached.

There are two different concepts in Japanese for "recovery": *fukkyū* (復旧) and *fukkō* (復興). The former means "return to status quo ex ante," while the latter means "adapt to the status quo ex post." In the current disaster management system, *fukkyū* is the objective around which to organize recovery and reconstruction, but that system was designed primarily to cope with flooding and typhoons. As a result of the unprecedented 1995 Kobe Earthquake devastation, stakeholders had to adapt to a new status quo ex post; *fukkō* is a very ambitious and new kind of operational process in Japanese disaster management.[17] Unlike *fukkyū*, in *fukkō*-minded recovery there is neither a clear objective nor a consensus about how to develop one. The focus is on the "new conditions" created by the event and the actions needed to address these conditions. The basic principles of reconstruction planning set down in the Reconstruction Design Council's 2011 report to the prime minister reflect the *fukkō* way of thinking.[18]

The Kobe Earthquake

The Hanshin-Awaji Earthquake of 1995 was the largest earthquake since World War II, with 6,434 people killed, 250,000 buildings destroyed, and a reconstruction cost of ¥10 trillion (see table 6.1). The event inspired wide-scale volunteerism by youth and spurred creation of nongovernmental organizations.[19] The earthquake also raised official recognition of disasters to the cabinet level, encouraged stronger regional governmental associations, and increased municipal disaster preparedness and recovery projects throughout the country. In fact, until the 3/11 disaster event, Kobe was the reference point for disaster management lessons, although the 2004 Chūetsu Earthquake (M6.8) and the 2007 Chūetsu Offshore Earthquake (M6.9), both in Niigata Prefecture, added further information.[20] Many lessons learned from Kobe related to long-term economic recovery, the impact of demographic change (an aging population), and livelihood as a central concept in recovery. After the event, authorities found that Kobe could not regain the port business and related jobs it had, even after large investments in improved facilities: many small manufacturing businesses and shops never returned, as they lost competitive advantage over time and their local client base changed in composition and tastes. Such findings demonstrate that shortening the disruption time and supporting operational continuity are important parts of both the preparedness and the reconstruction strategies for Japan's disaster

TABLE 6.1 Comparative Earthquake Damages, Actual and Estimated

Earthquake	Tōkai- Tōnankai-Nankai	Near Field Tokyo	East Japan (Tōhoku) 2011	Hanshin-Awaji (Kobe) 1995
Magnitude	M 8 each or more	M 7.3+	M 9.0	M 7.3
Killed/missing	27,000[a]	11,000	19,294	6,434
Injured	300,000	240,000	6,100	44,000
Buildings–collapsed	450,000	200,000	126,500	105,000
Building–heavy damage	——	——	227,600	144,400
Buildings–burned	90,000	650,000	—	7,400
Evacuees (max.)	6,000,000	7,500,000	480,000	320,000
Reconstruction cost (¥ trillion)[b]	60	65	25	10

a. This is the 2003 estimate. The 2012 estimate gives figures of up to 320,000 deaths and ¥100 trillion in damage ("Nankai Quake Projected Toll Radically Raised," *Japan Times*, August 30, 2012).
b. ¥79 = $US1.

Source: Adapted by permission from Itsuki Nakabayashi, "How to Optimize the Urban Recovery after Earthquake Disaster: Preparedness for Recovery from the Next Tokyo Earthquake," *Journal of Disaster Research* 7, no. 2 (2012): 227–38.

management system.[21] On the administrative side, Kobe gave rise to the Cabinet Office of Disaster Management, which set in motion a broader perspective on countermeasures that has moved in less than two decades from hardware, as in the building of higher levees, to inclusion of local people, as in the provision of training for forty-three Tokyo neighborhoods, disaster manuals in many wards, and evacuation plans and training related to victim identification. The private sector is accordingly more involved through business continuity and assistance efforts.[22]

Tōhoku Earthquake

Apart from the Kobe Earthquake of 1995, the 3/11 event is the deadliest and costliest disaster in Japanese history, with 19,294 killed/missing, 320,000 evacuees, and a cost of ¥16.9 trillion. The impact was felt nationally, with the GDP falling 6.8 percent in the first quarter of 2011 and remaining negative until the last quarter of the year, which was significantly less than the four-quarter-long GDP decline of 14.8 percent during the 2008 financial crisis (known in Japan as the Lehman Shock).[23] While ten prefectures were affected by the event, damage was mostly concentrated in three: Iwate, Miyagi, and Fukushima. The country's first compound multilocation disaster was made more difficult by the nuclear accident at the Tokyo Electric Power Company (TEPCO) Fukushima Daiichi plant and the explosion and ventilation of radioactive materials into the air, land, and sea one day later.

The nuclear accident made 3/11 a national threat that revealed unsuspected vulnerabilities in the inspection and response systems and also called into question the relationship between industry as producer, distributor, and owner of energy and the government as regulator. Power from the two multiple reactor nuclear plants in Fukushima (Daiichi #1 and Daiichi #2) was sent to the Tokyo area, whereas the Tōhoku region obtained power from fossil fuel plants that were not damaged. Consequently, Fukushima will bring change to Japan's energy program at the regional level because Fukushima Prefecture no longer wants nuclear energy facilities and proposes instead to develop alternative energy plants. Solar and wind renewable plants (sponsored by Toshiba) in Minamisoma, for instance, would help achieve the prefecture's objective. A loose coalition of citizen and environmental interests have formed a national movement against the use of nuclear power and are seeking a change in the government's nuclear policy in terms of energy production and safety (see chapter 5 on nuclear power by Jacques Hymans).

The 3/11 recovery experience also signals the emergence of strengthened regional governance practices and a healthy tension between decentralization and centralized policy.[24] Japan's powerful ministries are hence under pressure to form different types of partnerships with regional areas. The 2012 White Paper on Disaster Management called for local government involvement in mitigation measures, but how this would take place has yet to be articulated.[25] As well, the Building Communities Resilient to Tsunamis Act (December 2011) established multiple lines of defense that can be applied to risk area categories formulated by the Ministry of Land Infrastructure, Transport, and Tourism.[26] Such practices are further evidence of the shift toward a holistic view of disaster management brought about as a result of the 3/11 disaster event.

The recovery and reconstruction strategy for 3/11 is indeed new to Japan. In fact, because of multilocational damages, a special economic development zone was immediately established for a group of prefectures in which municipalities and prefectures prepare project proposals (with some autonomy) and the ministries approve or disapprove them. Nine months after 3/11, a Reconstruction Agency was established under the cabinet (not inside a ministry), whose charge it was to coordinate project applications, administer activities in the Special Reconstruction Zone, and award grant funds to the local governments. The first-year performance of this agency was not exemplary, and its operations were reorganized under the Abe government.

The Reconstruction Agency is an intermediate authority that facilitates program and project requests from lower levels of government to the ministries that approve funding of projects that meet their guidelines. The agency has no direct authority; it negotiates between and among the major players. This administrative model has the benefit of reflecting local desires at the cost of not being a gatekeeper to ensure that funds are given to the most needed projects. Still, with such large sums of funding available, perfect allocation is an ideal though not a real outcome, and the Japanese media has reported cases of misused funds. Nevertheless, the overall objective of such systems is to keep projects flowing into the affected areas, as doing so results in economic stimulus and reconstruction of place. The Reconstruction Agency after 3/11 exemplifies the Japanese bureaucratic tendency to create an organization when a new task appears rather than to assign the mission to an existing organization.[27]

The Japanese way of recovery contrasts with how the New Zealand Canterbury Earthquake Recovery Authority (CERA) operates. CERA is a direct agent of the national government with legislative authority to develop and implement a recovery program, make land use decisions, and enter into fiscal arrangements. CERA established new zoning categories for Christchurch, acquired over seven thousand residential parcels it determined to be on dangerous soils, and replanned the entire central business district into a tightly compact area composed of specified land use areas called precincts (i.e., sports, medical, government). In addition, CERA supported a new alliance between local government units and large construction companies to improve and make resilient the underground water and wastewater systems. This alliance established a management board to oversee both finance and construction of the improved infrastructure investments.

China's response to disaster is also very different from Japan's. Whereas in Japan it took nine months to establish a Reconstruction Agency, in China one month after the 2008 Wenchuan Earthquake the central authority enacted legislation, issued regulations, and mobilized national resources.[28] Then a Wenchuan recovery plan was issued in four months, and provincial governments were charged with organizing the implementation of recovery plans at the municipal level with extensive assistance from the central government and from other municipal and provincial governments outside the damage zone. Such non-central government support is known as the counterpart assistance mechanism, in which the helping provinces are required to provide some resources from their own funds (at least 1 percent of the annual budget), and this lowers the central government's burden. This mechanism has resulted in twenty-four provinces receiving help from twenty provinces outside the region.

Despite differences in approach to recovery, it is clear that the 3/11 experiences provide enough field evidence to develop new local land use policy that lowers risk for residential uses and gives industry more flexibility in a crisis. Building standards for seismic resilience demonstrated their effectiveness, with 81 percent of the post-1981 buildings having no extensive earthquake damage, for example, but the tsunami wave and the debris it carried inland were what destroyed houses and buildings in Tōhoku. Such an experience has led to a regional discussion on the height and extent of levees and sea walls, which at its best will be resolved through local partnership-driven decisions. Of course, there are more lessons to be learned from the 3/11 disaster event.

Lessons from 3/11

The Internet, technology, and support from the private sector were important factors in 3/11. The main source of information about the Kobe Earthquake was the Emergency Management Agency, which collected, filtered, and distributed it, mostly in traditional ways: from the top down and one-sidedly. The 3/11 event, in contrast, was globalized when nongovernmental organizations (NGOs) placed conversations with disaster victims on the Web.[29] The Internet was used for the first time in simple ways, in ways beyond what the Emergency Management Agency could provide. Social media offered a means of communications for a wide range of people; the disaster affected hundreds of towns with great variation in topography and access. The government's position changed from the sole source of information in 1995 to one of many sources in 2011. The challenge was to relay credible information about the disaster; official spokespersons were not always deemed trustworthy. The handling of information about the nuclear accident and radiation exposure is a case in point.

Indeed, technology saved many lives in 3/11. For instance, the sensors on Shinkansen high-speed trains slowed or halted them when the earthquake occurred, and no lives were lost due to train crashes; sensors on trucks and vehicles sent data to satellites that provided routing data about which roads were open and how to navigate travel. As well, in Fukushima Prefecture evacuees were linked through the Internet via computer tablets given to families in dispersed locations so they could find out if relatives and loved ones were safe and if their homes were still standing. After 3/11, some new "community-ware" applications emerged that combined video, instant phone messaging, emergency local radio stations, and logistic information that enabled emergency services to rescue people in need of assistance. Reconstruction will continue to test how "smart" technologies can be integrated into a strategy for improved safety in the home and the community from natural hazard risks.

Alongside the Internet and technology, private companies stepped up quickly with funds to support NGOs and emergency radio stations and to purchase equipment for community wares. Corporations surely have an interest in recovery and have thus begun to think more about their roles in the community in response to a disaster event.

Since 3/11, the central government's coordination of relief activities has been widely criticized. Various ministries were involved, some of them with conflicting portfolios, and it took nine months to launch the Reconstruction Agency, although the basic guidelines for recovery were in place by June 2011. The prefectures took four to nine months to complete recovery plans, as did most of the coastal municipalities. And overall, only 65 of the 241 municipalities eligible for disaster relief met the target date for plans. Funds for reconstruction flowed to prefectures and municipalities in one year, though not all the funds available were dispersed. Some requests did not meet ministry guidelines, and there was a capacity constraint as to how much funding could be converted into actual project work in any given year. Major disruption in the electronics sector took only three to four months to resolve, thanks to strong support from corporate headquarters outside the region providing direct assistance to local manufacturing sites. Such assistance got the supply chain working and put people back to work, lessening personal hardships.

To be sure, the nuclear accident was the most important part of the 3/11 compound disaster. The Nuclear and Industrial Safety Agency (NISA) in the Ministry of Economy, Trade, and Industry, the ministry responsible for regulating nuclear power, was the lead agency in Fukushima Prefecture, and its actions influenced the initial recovery efforts of other ministries. For example, defining the zones for restricted and limited occupancy outlined the work effort for relief actions, decontamination, and temporary housing. After thirty-six months, however, it is not clear how all the decisions related to stabilization and cleanup of the TEPCO Fukushima Daiichi plant will be made. This protracted delay supports Nakamura and Kikuchi's observation that Japan's tradition of collective and consensual decision making is not practical in a crisis.[30] In an emergency, the leadership of the country must demonstrate fortitude and determination regardless of the political consequences. Prime Minister Kan's attempts to resolve the nuclear accident quickly were skeptically seen by the bureaucracy and the nuclear industry as interference with the efforts of NISA, in effect interfering with the established chain of command. His actions were used as a partial rationale for TEPCO's mistakes, although TEPCO later admitted its staff was not adequately trained in crisis management.[31]

How the government handled relief activities was widely criticized, but the NGOs and business communities performed well, using lessons learned in the Kobe Earthquake.[32] NGOs/nonprofit organizations (NPOs) were given a seat at the table in the field headquarters of the Disaster Management Agency and Social Welfare Councils. One researcher dubbed this collaborative effort an expression of the "New Public Commons" called for in a Reconstruction Design Council report to the prime minister.[33] This experience supports the growing acceptance by some parts of government that collective efforts by the whole society are required in large-scale disaster events. One day after 3/11 a volunteer coordinating office was established in the Cabinet Secretariat, and an Internet portal for information on volunteering and donation was soon set up for worldwide use.

On the private sector side, corporations quickly provided support in different ways. Yamato Holdings donated ¥14.3 billion to municipalities to help businesses replace lost and damaged equipment and repair facilities. Mitsubishi Corporation headquarters gave ¥2 billion to NGOs and volunteer groups, and Softbank donated three hundred cell phones and call plans to the Nippon Foundation and the Japan Platform. Many companies established employee leave programs, and tour and bus companies scheduled special "volunteer" runs to the devastated areas. Civil society and private business joined to provide national support to the affected people. In all, civic organizations were a logistical umbrella for assistance. The Japan Civil Network for Disaster Relief in East Japan had 581 member organizations; Rescue Stock Yard and the Japan NPO Center were most prominent. Since 3/11, this effort has become "a potent national asset" with the capacity to match goodwill to actual needs in the field.[34]

From a policy perspective, the actions of civil society and the government must be in balance during the recovery phase of any disaster. This balance, however, is more a function of actual needs during the calamity than a predetermined set of procedures to be rigidly followed. As Thoku demonstrates, large-scale disasters are messy experiences.

Tōkai-Tōnankai-Nankai Earthquakes

Moving forward over the next twenty years, earthquakes in the Tōkai region pose dangers far greater than 3/11 and are the most important threat to Japan's future. These potential earthquakes could affect eight major prefectures and forty-seven million people and could cause damages ten times higher than 3/11. The historical record of earthquakes dating back to the 1700s clearly indicates a high probability of events in these areas (see figure 6.3). The Suruga and Nankai troughs are a ditch area in the Pacific Ocean off Tōkai and Shikoku, and strain on the earth's crust along the Suruga trough has been building for approximately 160 years, ever since the Ansei-Tōkai Earthquake in 1854. These areas have been designated for intensified measures against earthquakes, and work on risk reduction has begun. Suffice it to say, a TTN quake would be a compound disaster event with a prolonged impact.[35] Some estimates predict casualties of between 120,000 (daytime) and up to 320,000 (nighttime).[36] These figures are at least five to fifteen times the 2003 government casualty estimate. A full-force event in the Nankai trough could, according to Kawata, create damages worth between ¥100 and 150 trillion. Nearly seven hundred municipalities and up to thirty prefectures could need disaster relief assistance.[37]

To prepare for TTN earthquakes, several prefectures have jointly developed plans that complement those of the central government. The flexibility of a disaster prevention council could be enhanced by adding NPO or volunteer groups, but at the time of this writing Japan does not wish to engage in such pluralism.[38] But active participation in the International Organization

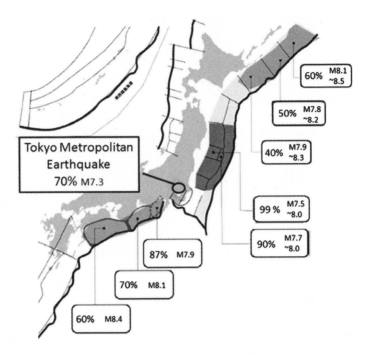

Within the figure:

60% M8.1 ~8.5

50% M7.8 ~8.2

40% M7.9 ~8.3

Tokyo Metropolitan Earthquake 70% M7.3

99% M7.5 ~8.0

90% M7.7 ~8.0

87% M7.9

70% M8.1

60% M8.4

FIGURE 6.3   Major earthquake threat areas in Japan to 2040. (Based on National Earthquake Research Council, "Jishin chōsa kenkyū suishin honbu zenkoku jishin yosoku chizu 2010 nendoban tebiki, kaisetsuhen" [Headquarters for Earthquake Research Promotion, national seismic hazard assessment maps 2010: Commentary section], 2010, www.jishin.go.jp/main/chousa/10_yosokuchizu/index.htm.)

for Standardization's Business Continuity Management scheme (ISO 22301) makes business sense because a TTN earthquake event will disrupt key manufacturing and commercial activities,[39] and global purchasers of parts and services are likely to seek other suppliers.

Tokyo Near Field Earthquake

In addition to a projected TTN earthquake, there is a 70 percent chance that the Tokyo metropolitan area will be jolted by a devastating earthquake (M7.3+) in the next thirty years, with an estimated eleven thousand casualties, two hundred thousand collapsed buildings, and 650,000 burned buildings (see figure 6.3). With a Tokyo Near Field (TNF) earthquake, the region faces a possible economic loss of up to ¥112 trillion, about 1.5 times the national budget.[40] Depending on the extent of damage to transport facilities, some 6,500,000 people may be stranded in the central business district, unable to return to their homes in the suburban residential zones.[41] If countermeasures are not taken, widespread damage will disrupt business for an extended period of time. Such large estimated losses are why business continuity plans have emerged in recent years.

Preparation for TNF began in 1997, and then in 2003 an extensive effort at local training and visioning in forty metropolitan area communities began. The concentration of over thirty-six million people as well as the hub of socioeconomic activity in the Tokyo metropolitan area puts the country's well-being in jeopardy. The existence of over four hundred thousand wooden structures in the region must be addressed both as a safety concern and to lower recovery costs. In fact, damage to houses is projected in four prefectures: Tokyo, Kanagawa, Chiba, and Saitama. In particular, after a TNF earthquake, at issue is the continuity of the region as the nation's economic and financial center. The construction industry's capacity to rebuild is another concern. In 2008, there were about 157,000 housing starts in the metropolitan area, a figure less than 20 percent of the estimated 850,000-unit replacement need. For office buildings, too, the potential damage is massive. Tokyo is the world's largest commercial building market. As much as 41 percent of the buildings' square footage was built under the pre-1981 standards and thus would constitute a large share of the estimated ¥55 trillion in damage to buildings.[42] In this type of event, the construction industry's supply capacity would be strained, and options such as inviting foreign firms (and labor) to enter the market warrant consideration.

A TNF earthquake is but one of the many predicted events in the region. The emphasis on preparing people for eminent disasters, rather than emphasizing hardening facilities, is wise because a disaster on this scale would probably overwhelm the national government in the short term. The Tokyo government, instead, would probably be placed in charge of recovery and reconstruction, which would be in line with the Kobe experience as well as that of New York City after 9/11. After 9/11, the US federal government provided $20 billion in initial base funding and allowed the local authorities to manage recovery (unlike the situation in New Orleans after Katrina). This unique New York–based response ultimately involved finance, multistate quasi-public agencies, public works improvements (expanded subway stations, for example), public health, and cultural activities.[43] It is important to note that damage in the 9/11 event was concentrated in one small area of Lower Manhattan, whereas a Tokyo Near Field earthquake would be spread out through at least four prefectures, and Japan must be prepared.

Technology can help in Tokyo if and when a TNF quake occurs. Getting information to the large number of people involved may be bolstered through extended-life cell phone batteries (multiday types), for example, and special applications included in cell phones sold in the region could provide information, provide lower power consumption on the phone, and allow messaging to be grouped together so that families can know where their members are and first responders can assess needs. While technology can surely help after a disaster hits, reliance upon technology would require reinforcement of cell towers. Increasing the numbers of emergency supply storage centers would lessen the reliance on debris-cleared streets and operating transit systems and also could improve early response actions. Geographical Information System (GIS) tagging of centers and cell phones would allow people to find assistance and human contact. Proposed municipal business continuity plans with data storage and sharing among a system of cities outside the region would be a good technology application that would address concern over having enough public employees available for data management after a large event like a TNF earthquake.

Alternative Models for Disaster Management

Public safety and the environmental consequences of mistakes made in the 3/11 event raise questions about Japan's tradition of centralized, collective decision making and its suitability for large-scale compound disasters, particularly when nuclear power is involved. The Reconstruction Agency's general recovery strategy reflects a problem faced by Japan in redefining its global place and economic future. We expect, however, that the lessons learned from 3/11 will be applied to make incremental but not structural adjustments in the near-term future. This is the Japanese way and probably will not change overnight. But is there an alternative model that might fit Japanese governance protocol? We think so.

In Japan, disaster management is an "issue" to be addressed, not a "core" element of government services such as the ministries of finance, economy, public works, and education that attract the best and the brightest of university graduates. While we do not expect disaster prevention or recovery management to be the first choice of ambitious young bureaucrats, through a cabinet-supported campaign for cross-training such posts can become their top choice for rotation to other ministries. We believe those newly hired government workers should serve in disaster management sections such as prevention planning, education, and project promotion. The Cabinet Office can endorse this pattern of career development and improve the quality of disaster management staffing and cross-ministry understanding. Officials with this background can facilitate coordination and intergovernmental actions that define progress during the recovery and reconstruction periods.[44] Revisiting the 1998 national development plan and its call for minimizing damage from disasters can be the basis for an updated dialogue on disaster management policy.

Consensus Decisions

Japan's central government works on a ministry-driven consensus-building model founded on consultation and agreement among the key groups within a legal framework. A group leadership model as opposed to an individual leader model and the political resistance to vesting too much power in a single person or a position fit Japan's collectivist culture. The Japanese form of checks and balances, by reaching a consensus, has strengths and weaknesses for disaster management. On the positive side, because reconstruction occurs over many years there is a greater operational need for continued cooperation among many ministries than for a single strong leader. The radioactive contamination of land in Fukushima Prefecture is a case in point because several ministries will be involved there for a decade or more (among them Environment; Land, Infrastructure, Transport, and Tourism; and Economy, Trade, and Industry). Given the short tenure of Japanese prime ministers (see Ellis S. Krauss and Robert J. Pekkanen's discussion of political leadership in chapter 12 of this volume), success at the collective level will rest with the ministries. By contrast, Australia and New Zealand view strong, singular leadership as essential to "get the job done."[45] To that extent, upgrading from a pass-through and coordinating agency for funds to an implementation body that directs consensus building among ministries could improve the Japanese Reconstruction Agency.

To be sure, a reconstruction agency will be needed when TTN earthquakes hit, and the 3/11 experience provides lessons for what such an agency needs to do, with the core strategy focusing on a principle of operational continuity that minimizes the loss of everyday relationships among people (which supports self-efficacy), with businesses transactions, and with society at large (which supports collective efficacy). The objective is to prevent isolation as long as possible for all sectors of society and in this way to reduce the hardship costs (including loss of family, unstable daily life activities, isolation, and prolonged dislocation) of the event. To be effective in reaching their objective, ministries need to be flexible and adaptive and able to improvise solutions that are outside the in-place programs and rules.[46] Fortunately, Prime Minister Shinzō Abe's government, which is regarded as powerful, stable, and nuclear supportive, has committed to the improvement of disaster resilience as one of its core goals by "mainstreaming disaster risk reduction" in every government policy domain. The implementation of this goal provides a real chance to promote national disaster preparedness for the anticipated large-scale disasters facing Japan, such as TTN and TNF quakes.

In a large-scale event, even a nuclear accident, entities such as the Union of Kansai Governments could, with assistance from the central government, implement recovery on their own terms. The Union of Kansai Governments was established in 2010 by seven prefectures—Shiga, Kyoto, Osaka, Hyogo, Wakayama, Tottori, and Tokushima—as a special local public entity with a twenty-member assembly and administrative commissions. One of its major purposes is regionwide disaster preparedness including training and planning. With some adjustments this type of entity could be established in other areas of Japan and could engage in multihazard planning and capacity building for recovery. For example, the Union of Kansai Governments could adopt a model close to the one used in the recovery from floods in Queensland, Australia, if the financial issues can be resolved.[47] A new governmental alliance to prepare for Tōkai-Tōnankai-Nankai earthquakes might function in a similar way, and Japan could benefit by supporting this type of recovery management option.

Japan is aware of and preparing for disasters of all types. For many decades the government has supported the development of the natural science and engineering needed to understand hazards and has begun to combine physical countermeasures with roles for the citizenry and business community.

In 3/11, the pre-event estimation models for an earthquake and tsunami used assumptions about the ocean fault condition that underestimated the actual event. Although it is difficult to gauge in advance the impact of a once-in-a-thousand-year event, it can be a teaching moment for the future. The present thinking set down by the Committee for Policy Planning on Disaster Management is that there should be no unexpected disaster, even if it cannot be predicated perfectly.[48] This would result in more risk transparency and a balancing of optimistic as well as pessimistic projections. As of September 2012, adjustments are being made in the nuclear science and engineering community, the CDMC, and the management section of the Disaster Ministry, and a new Nuclear Regulation Authority (NRA) is in place. The CDMC invests in the science and understanding of the location, extent, and timing of disasters and has direct access to the cabinet. An expanded council could help clarify the benefits of a new people-centered approach to disaster management. This would satisfy two conditions of Japanese governance: being incremental and practical.

To be an effective participant in Japan's disaster management system, the newly formed NRA must demonstrate the independence to conduct proper oversight of the nuclear power industry. Many observers are skeptical of its ability to do that because 80 percent of the NRA staff are holdovers from its less-than-effective predecessor. Much progress is possible in disaster management if the NRA and the Disaster Ministry Management Section of the cabinet coordinate their efforts and adopt the CDMC practice of special panels and discussions of hazards and risks within the cabinet structure.

The shift under way now from "hardware" to inclusion of "people ware" will contribute to a less vulnerable future. The 3/11 experience of a weak reconstruction agency points out the need for stronger reconstruction models for earthquakes such as those predicted for the Tokyo Near Field and the Tōkai-Tōnankai-Nankai areas. We think some type of regional association, possibly modeled after the Union of Kansai Governments, should be established, begin to conduct risk reduction work now, and become a regional link to the central government when large-scale disasters occur. Acceptance of the new socioeconomic conditions (*fukkō*) construct supports "open versus closed" solutions.[49] Expanded use of household-level distributed technology (cell phones, iPads, and reverse messaging) will help because more people are willing to adopt it. Investment in risk reduction technology such as messaging-linked smoke detectors will result in better safety and probably new Japanese products to sell to a worldwide market.

With a stable and possibly declining economic future, the burden of recovery from a major disaster will be greater than in the past. The triple whammy for the future—age group transition, stable or lower per capita income, and less tax revenue—means less fiscal capacity for disaster management. The country cannot afford it. Thus in the next twenty years Japan will benefit from working through what a holistic disaster risk reduction model can accomplish as a replacement paradigm for the current threat-by-threat and agency-by-agency approach. Experiments in risk reduction such as accelerating the replacement rate of high-risk housing in the Tokyo metropolitan region would test this new thinking. A long-term strategy for deconcentration of activities in the Tokyo region makes sense from the standpoint of recovery and human safety.

Operational continuity is a useful strategy for compound disasters because it applies to people, employment, the environment, civil society, and government, and it supports making the community more resilient through regionally and locally derived solutions.[50] Mayor Sakurai exemplified this approach in Minamisoma. The sooner people can resume their lives after a large-scale disaster, the fewer governmental and societal resources will be needed. Flexible and adaptive approaches must be valued as much as rule-based sets of actions. Japan's future rests on holistic prevention investments that lessen loss of life and recovery investments that speed up the return of a healthy society working in safe places. A strong policy of disaster impact reduction balanced with that of rapid recovery of the whole affected society would make Japan a less precarious country.

Acknowledgments

The authors wish to thank Ying Ying Sun, Zhou Yu, Tomoko Ukai, and Sidra Jocelyn Scharff for their translating, graphics, and editing contributions, respectively.

Notes

1. Japan's location, geographical features, meteorological profile, and mode of production make it susceptible to earthquakes, typhoons, torrential rains, volcanic eruptions, and industrial and nuclear accidents.

2. These adjustments include safer buildings, tsunami countermeasures, warning system engineering techniques, hazard event preparation, and natural science knowledge about the physical environment.

3. Akira Nakamura and Masao Kikuchi, "What We Know, and What We Have Not Yet Learned: Triple Disasters and the Fukushima Nuclear Fiasco in Japan," *Public Administration Review* 71 (November–December 2011): 893–99.

4. William Siembieda, Guillermo Franco, and Laurie Johnson, "Rebuild Fast but Rebuild Better: Chile's Initial Recovery Following the 27F Earthquake and Tsunami," *Earthquake Spectra* 28, no. S1 (2012): 621–41.

5. The Tokugawa Shogunate responded to disasters through adaptation. The 1657 Meireki Fire, for example, led to the mandating of ceramic roof shingles rather than wooden ones in urban areas. See Peter Duus, "Dealing with Disaster," in *Natural Disaster and Nuclear Crisis in Japan: Response and Recovery after Japan's 3/11*, ed. Jeff Kingston (London: Routledge, 2012). 175–87.

6. Japan holds substantial foreign assets that could be sold to finance recovery.

7. Yoshiaki Kawata, "Downfall of Tokyo Due to Devastating Compound Disaster," *Journal of Disaster Research* 6, no. 2 (2011): 176–84.

8. See Ben Wisner, J. C. Gaillard, and Ilan Kelman, eds., *The Routledge Handbook of Hazards and Disaster Research Reduction* (Abingdon, UK: Routledge, 2012).

9. In the 1923 Great Kanto Earthquake, 447,128 houses were lost to fire.

10. After 1995 the Fire Agency was called the Fire and Disaster Management Agency, reflecting the agency's enhanced role and focus under Toshifumi Akimoto.

11. Some parts of the act pertaining to Tokyo New Field and the Tōkai-Tōnankai-Nankai earthquake and tsunami threats were updated in June 2012.

12. The 1981 code introduced a two-phase design system. Phase 1 is a structure able to withstand a moderate seismic event with almost no damage several times over the life of a building, and phase 2 is a design for a structure that will not collapse under one severe seismic event.

13. Government of Japan, Nuclear Emergencies Preparedness Act (1999), 3, www.oecd-nea.org/law/legislation/japan.pdf.

14. President Jimmy Carter created FEMA in 1979, but the agency had a lackluster performance record until President William Clinton appointed James Lee Witt, a national emergency management leader, as its director in 1993. President George W. Bush removed the agency's cabinet status, however. In 2003, FEMA was absorbed into the Department of Homeland Security (DHS), and in 2006 it was reestablished as a named entity within the DHS.

15. The four councils created in 2001 were Economy and Fiscal Policy, Science and Technology, Gender Equality, and Disaster Management.

16. The Nuclear Safety Commission operated until 2012, when its functions were given to the Nuclear Regulation Authority. Elena Shadira, "Fukushima Fallout: Gauging

the Change in Japanese Energy Policy," *International Journal of Disaster Risk Science* 3, no. 2 (2012): 69–84.

17. Haruo Hayashi, "Some Thoughts Triggered by Dr. Johnson's Paper," discussion paper presented at the Public Entity Risk Institute (PERI) Disaster Theory Workshop, Washington, DC, November 2010.

18. Japan Reconstruction Design Council, *Towards Reconstruction: Hope beyond the Disaster* (Tokyo: Cabinet Secretariat, June 25, 2011).

19. Mayumi Sakamoto, "The Rise of NGOs/NPOs in Emergency Relief in the Great East Japan Earthquake," *Japan Social Innovation Journal* 2, no. 1 (2012): 26–35.

20. Kashiwazaki-Kariwa Nuclear Power Plant #2007 in Niigata, for example, was tested for several years before reopening after it was shut down in 2007 because of the release of a small amount of radioactive iodine from an exhaust pipe.

21. Robert B. Olshansky and Stephanie E. Chang, "Planning for Disaster Recovery: Emerging Research Needs and Challenges," *Progress in Planning* 72 (2009): 200–209.

22. Shinichi Okabe, "3.11 Japan Earthquake and Business Continuity Management," paper presented at the Proceedings of the International Emergency Management Society Workshop on the 2011 East Japan Earthquake Disaster, Tokyo, May 22–23, 2012, 5–10.

23. Government of Japan, *Road to Recovery*, March 2012, 9, http://japan.kantei.go.jp/policy/documents/2012/__icsFiles/afieldfile/2012/03/07/road_to_recovery.pdf.

24. Siembieda, Franco, and Johnson, "Rebuild Fast," 621–41.

25. Government of Japan, "Bōsai ni kanshite totta no gaikyō Heisei 24 nendo no bōsai ni kansuru keikaku" [A summary of measures taken for disaster management and plans for disaster management for fiscal year 2012, white paper on disaster management], www.bousai.go.jp/kaigirep/hakusho/pdf/H24_honbun_1-4bu.pdf.

26. There are red, yellow, and orange risk zones with different countermeasures for each. See the Knowledge Notes publication by Japan in collaboration with the Global Facility for Disaster Reduction and Recovery and the World Bank, October 2012, particularly "Urban Planning, Land Use Regulation and Relocation," in Cluster 2, 8–9, http://wbi.worldbank.org/wbi/Data/wbi/wbicms/files/drupal-acquia/wbi/drm_kn4-2.pdf.

27. Neil R. Britton, "National Planning and Response: National Systems," in *Handbook of Disaster Research*, edited by Havidán Rodríguez, E. L. Quarantelli, and Russell Rowe Dynes (New York: Springer, 2007), 347–67.

28. Richard Hu, "Planning Large Scale Post-disaster Recovery after the Wenchuan Earthquake in China," in *Managing Urban Disaster Recovery: Policy, Planning,*

Concepts and Cases, ed. Edward J. Blakely, Eugenie L. Birch, Roland V. Anglin, and Haruo Hayashi (Berkshire, UK: Crisis Response Publications, 2011), 43–45.

29. Voices from the Field, an NGO, translated conversations with victims from Japanese into other languages and posted them on the Web. A closed panel of moderators provided commentary as needed.

30. Nakamura and Kikuchi, "What We Know," 893–99.

31. "Tepco Finally Admits Nuke Crisis Avoidable," *Japan Times Online*, October 13, 2012.

32. Simon Avenell, "From Kobe to Tohoku: The Potential and the Peril of a Volunteer Infrastructure," in Kingston, *Natural Disaster*, 53–77.

33. The Reconstruction Design Council, made up of nongovernmental members, was appointed by the prime minister to provide "expert" views on a strategy for recovery. Mayumi Sakamoto, "The Rise of NGOs/NPOs in Emergency Relief in the Great East Japan Earthquake," *Japan Social Innovation Journal* 2, no. 1 (2012): 26–35.

34. Britton, "National Planning," 347–67.

35. Kawata, "Downfall of Tokyo," 176–84.

36. For daytime casualties, see "Triple Quake Toll Put at 400,000," *Daily Yomiuri*, June 11, 2012. For nighttime casualties, see "Nankai Quake Projected Toll Radically Changed," *Japan Times*, August 30, 2012.

37. Kawata, "Downfall of Tokyo," 176–84.

38. Shingo Nagamatsu, Haruo Hayashi, and Yoshiaki Kawata, "The Problem of Disaster Management Policy and Local Plan for Disaster Prevention," *Institute of Social Safety Science* 7 (2005): 395–404.

39. ISO 22301:2012 specifies the requirements for a documented management system to protect against and recover from disruptive incidents. ISO 22301, the first international standard for business continuity management, was developed to help organizations minimize the risk of such disruptions.

40. Shingo Nagamatsu and Haruo Hayashi, "Economic Recovery Scenario Planning for a Tokyo Inland Earthquake," *Journal of Disaster Research* 7, no. 2 (2012): 203–14.

41. Itsuki Nakabayashi, "How to Optimize the Urban Recovery after Earthquake Disaster: Preparedness for Recovery from the Next Tokyo Earthquake," *Journal of Disaster Research* 7, no. 2 (2012): 227–38.

42. Nagamatsu and Hayashi, "Economic Recovery," 203–14.

43. David Mammen, *Creating Recovery: Values and Approaches in New York after 9.11* (Tokyo: Fuji Press, 2011).

44. See Blakely et al., *Managing Urban Disaster Recovery*.

45. Australia and New Zealand have had major disasters in the recent past. Australia had fires (Victoria, 2009) and floods (Queensland, 2011–12), and New Zealand had

earthquakes (Canterbury, 2010–11). In each case a special recovery authority was established. In the Queensland floods and Christchurch earthquakes, the recovery authorities received special powers to conduct the recovery. Queensland provided the major part of the funding and received a large grant from the central government. A special board oversaw the recovery, and a high-level professional managed the implementation. Victoria also paid a large share of the recovery from its own budget; a single manager reported to the president of Victoria. The special authority had budgetary and coordination authority but no power to change existing laws. In New Zealand, CERA had broad powers over land use decisions, finance, infrastructure, and demolition. CERA reported directly to a national minister, as New Zealand is a unitary government with no state level units, only municipalities and districts. See James Smart, "The Role of Post-disaster Institutions in Recovery and Resilience: a Comparative Study of Three Recent Disasters—Victorian Bushfires (2009), Queensland Floods (2010–11), and Canterbury Earthquakes (2010–12)," working paper, Institute for Governance and Policy Studies, Victoria University, Wellington, 2012.

46. In 3/11, ministries used their "exception" and "extension" authority in many ways. For example, the two-year limit on temporary housing was extended to five years in many areas because of the inability to find appropriate land parcels to build permanent housing. In response to TTN earthquakes, the two-year limit could be replaced with a more flexible standard.

47. See Smart, " Role of Post-disaster Institutions."

48. Atsushi Koresawa, "Government's Response to the Great East Japan Earthquake and Tsunami," *Journal of Disaster Research* 7 (August 2012): 517–27.

49. Daniel Alesch and William Siembieda, "The Role of the Built Environment in the Reconstruction of Cities and Communities from Extreme Events," *International Journal of Mass Emergencies and Disasters* 32, no. 2 (August 2012): 197–211.

50. Douglas Paton and David Johnson, eds., *Disaster Resilience: An Integrated Approach* (Springfield, IL: Charles C. Thomas, 2006).

CHAPTER SEVEN

Fiscal Survival and Financial Revival: Possible Futures for the Japanese Economy

Saori N. Katada and Gene Park

Japan's fiscal situation is grim. Once a model of fiscal discipline, Japan now has the most indebted government among the industrialized democracies. In 2011 the accumulated public debt totaled over 230 percent of the gross domestic product (GDP), which is much higher than Greece's debt of 165.6 percent and those of Italy and Spain at 121.1 percent and 67.4 percent, respectively.[1] In 2011, Japan's budget deficit was 10 percent of GDP; since 1994 the government has run deficits ranging from just under 4 percent to over 11 percent.[2] The question is not if but when Japan will be forced to reckon with its looming fiscal crisis.

Seemingly arcane and technical, how governments spend money and how they pay for this spending is intensely political, touching on nearly every aspect of the state and society, including many of the themes explored in this book. These choices are ultimately decisions about what kind of society Japan will be and how it will address future challenges. With one of the most rapidly aging societies in history, Japan confronts enormous demands on its social security system. As the population ages (see Sawako Shirahase on Japan's demography in chapter 1 of this volume), will the government be able to uphold the basic social pact with its citizens? In the context of a rapidly changing regional and security environment, including a rising China, can Japan maintain its foreign policy and defense goals? More immediately, will Japan dodge a sovereign debt crisis such as that racking Europe? The sustainability of Japan's public finances has very significant consequences for its future.

Despite the dire fiscal circumstances, Japan remains a major financial power. Collectively, the nation controls immense financial assets accumulated from the historically high savings of its households, its overseas investments, and its well-known exporting prowess. Moreover, Japan's private financial institutions have fared relatively well during the global financial crisis of 2008, after rebuilding from a prolonged banking crisis. Japan's financial resources have helped fund the government's large and persistent budget deficits. Indeed, Japanese institutions and investors hold over 90 percent of the government's debt, which is why many commentators argue that Japan will not go the way of Greece.

In recent years private financial institutions have played a growing role in financing the public sector, particularly in the wake of the triple disaster—earthquake (M9.0), massive tsunami, and nuclear meltdown—that Japan experienced in March 2011 (hereafter 3/11), which led to even larger budget deficits. As a consequence, the fates of private finance and public finance have become even more intertwined through the private sector's purchase of large amounts of Japanese government bonds (JGBs).

Understanding this mutually dependent relationship between public and private finance is vital to comprehending Japan's future economic prospects. Are the private and public financial spheres a delicate house of cards that will come down in the coming years? Or can Japan avoid such a fate? Our answer is that over the medium term—three to five years—we expect Japan to muddle through despite the hazards. If we look at the longer term, however, the picture is less sanguine, as structural and demographic factors will reduce the government's range of options.

This chapter is divided into three parts. We first discuss the development of Japan's fiscal crisis and its current fiscal position. Next we focus on the link between private and public finance, assessing the midterm risks that the private sector faces from its large holdings of government debt. Finally we look at medium- and longer-term prospects—Japan's possible futures.

The Public Sphere: The Making of Japan's Fiscal Crisis

Japan's fiscal woes essentially come down to one problem: the inability to close the gap between spending and revenue. The predicament first emerged at the end of the 1960s. Until then, the government maintained a very high degree of fiscal discipline, keeping budget spending low and budgets balanced. Indeed, Japan's fiscal performance was outstanding compared with that of other developed democracies. Japan was able to maintain a small and balanced budget because of rapid growth but also through the creative use of an off-budget public finance system that relied on funds from the postal savings system, public pension reserves, and other funds known as the Fiscal Investment Loan Program (FILP).[3] Japan regained sovereignty with the end of the US Occupation in February 1952, and the government did not rely on bonds to close a budget deficit until 1965, when revenue growth slowed.[4] The real turning point was the start of the 1970s, when Prime Minister Kakuei Tanaka abandoned the policy of balanced budgets to finance greater redistributive spending. Tanaka increased spending on public works and enhanced Japan's relatively modest welfare state, while at the same time delivering large tax cuts.

During the second half of the 1970s and through the 1980s, the government gradually shifted to a period of fiscal consolidation. Corporate taxes were hiked and a variety of excise taxes imposed. The government also began to consider a value-added tax (VAT), a significant shift, since the Liberal Democratic Party (LDP) and the Ministry of Finance (MOF) both had been opposed to a regressive tax on consumption.[5] Prime Minister Masayoshi Ōhira attempted to introduce the VAT but met widespread opposition, including from his own party. Despite backtracking on the proposal, the LDP was punished in the next general election, lost its majority for the first time, and had to form a coalition with a minor splinter party. Prime Minister Yasuhiro Nakasone (1982–87) also unsuccessfully pushed for a VAT. In 1989 Prime Minister Noboru Takeshita finally introduced a 3 percent consumption tax, only to be rewarded with the loss of his party's majority in the Upper House.

The government was moderately successful in reining in expenditures, particularly under Nakasone, who called for a policy of "fiscal reconstruction without tax hikes." Zero-growth ceilings capped budgets from 1983 to 1987, although in practice the limits were often exceeded by passage of mid-year supplementary budgets. The Nakasone administration sought savings through administrative reform and sold government assets, including stock in Nippon Telegraph and Telephone Corporation and the Japanese National Railways. It checked welfare spending by eliminating free medical care for the elderly in 1982 and consolidating public pension programs in 1985 (later, in 1994, the pension eligibility age would be raised from sixty to sixty-five).

The government also limited budget expenditures for public works, although the LDP tried to avoid the political cost of reducing pork barrel spending by shifting it onto the off-budget FILP.[6] Even after the official period of fiscal consolidation, government finances continued to improve, largely because of the economic bubble, which generated large natural increases in revenue as income and asset prices grew rapidly. From 1988 to 1991, Japan ran a primary balance budget surplus (a surplus on expenditures excluding debt servicing).

In the 1990s public finances took a dramatic turn for the worse (figure 7.1). To combat the postbubble stagnation, the government embraced a fiscal stimulus that combined tax cuts and higher spending. Some tax cuts were made permanent, further reducing the government's extractive capacity, which, combined with slower growth, led to a decline in general account tax revenue of 30 percent from 1990 to 2011.[7] At the same time, the government increased public works spending to stimulate the economy. Other factors further eroded Japan's fiscal position: the rapid aging of the population increased social security outlays, and a banking crisis required a costly bailout.

For a brief moment during the 1990s, as the economy was recovering, Prime Minister Ryūtarō Hashimoto again attempted fiscal consolidation by passing the Fiscal Structure Reform Law (FSRL), which committed the government to keeping budget deficits below 3 percent of GDP and to eliminating the issuance of deficit financing bonds by 2003. Soon after the FSRL came into effect, however, the onset of the Asian financial crisis, combined with the contractionary impact of a rise in the consumption tax from 3 percent to 5 percent, pushed the economy back into recession, resulting again in the use of fiscal stimulus and eventual termination of the FSRL.[8]

As the economy regained its footing in the new century, the government once again turned to fiscal consolidation under Prime Minister Jun'ichirō Koizumi (2001–6), who revived the old political slogan of "fiscal reconstruction without tax hikes." Koizumi combined administrative reform, including privatization of the postal system (later suspended), budget cuts, and caps on the issuance of bonds. Unlike Nakasone, Koizumi also set his sights on the FILP, shrinking the system and making cuts in politically sensitive areas such as public works.

Before leaving office, Koizumi attempted to lock in reforms by finally addressing the revenue problem, which he had studiously avoided. Koizumi's multiyear fiscal consolidation plan—the Integrated Revenue and Expenditure Reform (IRER)—aimed to restore a primary balance by 2011. The

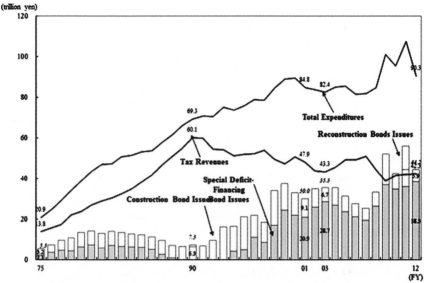

FIGURE 7.1   Japan's fiscal balance, 1975–2012.

Notes: The Ministry of Finance used settlement data for FY1975–2012, the fourth supplementary budget for FY2011, and a draft budget for FY2012 for the original graph on which this figure is based.

Ad hoc deficit financing bonds (approximately ¥1 trillion) were issued in FY1990 as a source of funds to support peace and reconstruction efforts in the Persian Gulf region. Reconstruction bonds (approximately ¥11.6 trillion) were issued in FY2011, which were used as a temporary measure until the financial resources would be secured by revenues, including the special tax for reconstruction. Measures and projects for reconstruction from the Great East Japan Earthquake, expected to be implemented within the first five years (FY2011–FY2015), would be financed by issue of reconstruction bonds. General Account Primary Balance is calculated on the easy-to-use method of National Debt Service minus Government Bond Issues, and is different from the Central Government Primary Balance on an SNA analysis.

Source: Adapted from the Ministry of Finance, FY2012 Budget, "Japan's Fiscal Condition," December 2011, 2, www.mof.go.jp/english/budget/budget/index.html.

IRER called for a combination of cuts between ¥11.4 and ¥14.3 trillion and tax increases. While in some ways the IRER was a departure from the policy of administrations in the 1990s, objections within the LDP prevented a clear revenue-side strategy, in essence kicking the can down the road.

The IRER was soon overtaken by events. Following the onset of the global financial crisis in fall 2008, Prime Minister Tarō Asō passed in April 2009 the largest fiscal stimulus package in Japan's history, totaling 3 percent of GDP, effectively abandoning the IRER and Koizumi's ceilings on bond issuance. In September 2009, the Democratic Party of Japan (DPJ) came to power after a landslide election victory. The new administration initially avoided discussion of a tax hike. Like Koizumi, Prime Minister Yukio Hatoyama promised not to raise the consumption tax for four years and to limit the issuance of new bonds. After Hatoyama's brief tenure, Prime Minister Naoto Kan took a more aggressive approach to fiscal consolidation and publicly supported raising the consumption tax, a move that contributed to the loss of the DPJ majority in the House of Councillors. Under Kan, the government set the target of halving the primary balance deficit by 2015 and achieving a primary balance surplus by 2020. The devastation of 3/11, however, led to temporary abandonment of fiscal consolidation.

Subsequently, the Noda administration recommitted to fiscal consolidation, staking its future on a controversial hike in the consumption tax from 5 percent to 8 percent in April 2014 and then to 10 percent in October 2015 (the Abe administration suspended the latter raise in November 2014). Noda achieved a major goal with passage of the legislation in August 2012.

The tax hike still falls short of closing the fiscal gap, however. Since 2009, around half of Japan's general revenue has come from government bonds. The Organisation for Economic Cooperation and Development (OECD) estimates that the consumption tax would have to rise to 20 percent to reach government targets.[9] Furthermore, government officials recognize that they will have to increase revenue from other sources as well, including income and inheritance taxes. The government is also running out of targets for expenditure cuts, which have been central to previous attempts at fiscal consolidation. Discretionary spending has been shrinking, while demographic changes are driving increased expenditures. Spending for social security is growing by ¥1 trillion per year.

The Private Sphere: Financial Crisis and Reform

Japan's public debt has not led to a Greece-like sovereign debt crisis because the debt is financed within Japan without reliance on foreign investors. Currently 93 to 95 percent of Japan's debt is held domestically, while more than 70 percent of Greek public debt is held by nonresident investors. Such "domestic absorption" is sustained by Japan's financial resources. Despite an apparent decline from its heyday of the late 1980s when Japan's financial power seemed insurmountable, the country is still a major financial power with large financial assets held domestically ($18 trillion in 2010) and internationally ($7.3

trillion in 2011). These amounts make Japan the largest external creditor in the world and the second-largest holder of domestic assets after the United States. Not only the size of Japan's financial assets but also the particular structure of the financial sector and its relations with the domestic market have helped sustain budget deficits and high public debt.

Japan's economic system since World War II has depended heavily on the close relationship between Japanese financial institutions, particularly banks, and the MOF. The main banks presided over related *keiretsu* (affiliated business groups such as Mitsubishi and Mitsui) through stock holding, credit distribution, and financial expertise,[10] and the MOF protected these banks from failure under the so-called convoy system, whereby banks moved together slowly and conservatively under the tight oversight of regulators. The MOF in turn controlled many aspects of credit allocation through regulations and administrative guidance to promote rapid industrialization and economic growth from the 1950s through 1980s.[11] The government also relied heavily on these banks to finance its public debt. The banks formed an underwriting syndicate group to allocate the new issues. After the Bank of Japan (BOJ) decreased its repurchases of JGBs in the mid-1970s for fear of inflation, private banks absorbed a larger share.[12] The purchase of JGBs has continued to be an important part of business of Japanese financial institutions, in effect increasing their dependence on the government.[13]

The close relationship between banks and the government persisted even as the government liberalized finance in the 1980s. The old way of banks relying on business from large corporations gradually eroded, however. As Japan's large corporations became globally competitive, they began to produce, operate, and raise funds abroad, thus decreasing their reliance on Japanese banks. This deprived the banks of their best customers.[14] The bursting of the bubble economy in the early 1990s revealed the vulnerability of Japanese banks that were exposed to real estate investments and bad loans. The government intervened to save them from bankruptcy and propped up stock prices to support their balance sheets. Through the first half of the 1990s, the government implemented a Price-Keeping Operation whereby MOF annually bought up 2 percent of Japan's quoted stock shares by tapping into the state-controlled funds invested in the national pension, postal saving, and postal life insurance schemes.[15] The ministry also buttressed its estimated $65 billion per year open-market stock buying through restricting the supply of new stocks (thus supporting prices of existing stocks) by vastly altering regulatory and tax laws.

The convoy system ended in the aftermath of a government bailout of a failed mortgage lending company in 1995 and the collapse of major financial institutions in 1997. Politicians attributed these crises to collusion between the banks and the MOF, which they argued weakened Japan's financial system and led to corruption.[16] Starting with the Hashimoto administration, the LDP took several major steps to put distance between the MOF and the financial system, including the separation of the MOF's financial and fiscal functions by creating the Financial Supervisory Agency, later renamed the Financial Services Agency. The Hashimoto administration also implemented the Bank of Japan Law in 1998, which gave the BOJ more independence from the MOF and launched the Big Bang financial reform in autumn 1996. The Big Bang was implemented from 1998 through 2005 on the basis of the FSRL, which revised existing laws pertaining to the finance industry, including the Banking Law, the Securities and Exchange Law, and the Insurance Business Law. These changes were to make Japan's financial markets "free (liberalizing entry, financial product innovation, and prices, etc.), fair (codifying and making transparent the financial rules and increase investor protection), and global (introducing 'global standards' to Japan's legal and accounting systems as well as strengthening financial supervision)."[17] The goal was to revitalize the financial market by allowing new entrants, innovation, and business conducted under transparent rules and accounting standards.[18]

By 2006, the financial system seemed to have entered a new era of greater independence from the government. First, the financial players were bigger and healthier. Helped by the Big Bang legislative changes, which allowed the establishment of holding companies, major banks merged with others to enhance their competitive edge. In 2000 the Industrial Bank of Japan, Fuji Bank, and Daiichi Kangyō Bank merged to establish Mizuho Holdings (later Financial Group). Two years later the Sumitomo Mitsui Financial Group was formed, and the merger of the UFJ Group with the Tokyo-Mitsubishi Financial Group was completed in January 2006. As a result, Japan now houses three megabanks whose asset sizes are among the top twenty-five in the world.

Second, the financial system became much more transparent. The FSRL not only enabled the massive public bailout of Japanese banks but also revealed the full scope of the bad debt problem.[19] Adherence to the global financial standards was a crucial component of the Big Bang in order to make Tokyo an attractive site for financial businesses. For instance, the Financial

Services Agency completed implementation of the Basel II agreement prior to the onset of the global financial crisis, much earlier than any other advanced country.[20]

Finally, the Bank of Japan replaced the MOF as the central force in the fight against deflation (Japan's GDP deflator declined annually from 1998 through 2006). The BOJ's "super-expansionary" policy kept the interest rate near 0 percent with additional quantitative easing measures, including the purchase of government bonds and bank-owned stocks.[21] The expansion of the monetary base during this period, however, did not fend off deflation because the funds pumped in by the BOJ were quickly absorbed by the banks themselves, which were liquidating their nonperforming loans, and never reached the real economy.[22]

By the final month of Koizumi's tenure in September 2006, the banks appeared to have shaken off the heavy hand of the government. The decade-long problem of nonperforming loans was behind them, and the Big Bang liberalization was expected to reinvigorate Tokyo as a financial center. Japanese financial institutions, particularly banks that were not affected by the toxic financial assets of the subprime mortgage crisis, looked ready to expand.[23] Curiously, however, a financial revival did not take place. In fact, while liberalization created distance between the government and the financial sector, financial institutions purchased massive amounts of JGBs, increasing the mutual dependence between private and public finance.

The Fiscal-Financial Connection

Seemingly separate challenges, Japan's fiscal crisis and financial stagnation, are two sides of the same coin. The government's ability to issue large amounts of bonds largely depends on the willingness of Japanese financial institutions to absorb them. As discussed above, the government has for the last twenty years run persistent deficits and turned to the financial market for funds. This gap between income and expenditures is unlikely to be filled anytime soon;[24] thus the private financial sector's willingness to purchase government bonds is crucial. With deregulation, dissolution of the convoy system, and the formation of the Financial Services Agency, the Finance Ministry's ability to pressure institutions to purchase JGBs is now very limited. The government also abandoned use of the JGB-purchasing syndicate group in 2006. Nevertheless, these institutions seem quite willing to sustain

JGB purchases. By the end of 2011, of almost US$10 trillion in Japanese debt, 9 percent was held by the BOJ, 9.2 percent by public pensions, and 6.7 percent by foreign investors. The remaining three-quarters of outstanding JGBs was held by Japan's private sector, including banks (41.5 percent), insurance companies (22.4 percent), and, directly, households (3.8 percent).[25] A significant portion of the holdings of private financial institutions is in JGBs: 35 percent of total assets of pension and insurance funds and 7 percent of assets of deposit-taking institutions.[26] Most striking, as of 2011 the holdings of JGBs by Japan Post (Japan's postal system, which includes a large postal bank and postal insurance operation) were 72 percent of its assets. The amount of JGBs held by megabanks has increased too. In December 2011, the volume of JGBs in the balance sheet of Bank of Tokyo-Mitsubishi UFJ was larger than the amount of its corporate and consumer loans combined.[27]

Why are financial institutions so eager to buy JGBs? First, Japan has a savings-investment imbalance. As seen in figure 7.2, the economy has excess savings in the household and nonfinancial private sectors. In addition to the high though declining savings rate, the deflationary economy puts even a very low interest rate on savings deposits in positive territory. The corporate sector is not borrowing because companies are not expanding productive capacity. Many firms are drawing down their debts by repaying outstanding loans. The two sectors that absorb the excess savings are the government and overseas investors.

Second, Japanese savers and financial institutions remain conservative and highly risk averse. Even after the Big Bang, more than half of Japan's vast household financial assets are held as bank deposits and cash (56.5 percent in 2011). Only a very limited amount is invested in stocks (5.8 percent) compared to 14.4 percent (cash and deposits) and 31.5 percent (stocks), respectively, in the United States.[28] After Japan's banking crisis of the 1990s and first part of the new century, Japan's financial institutions have also been extremely risk averse,[29] slow to adopt new financial instruments such as collateralized debt obligations, and cautious about high-risk investment when the depositors do not demand high returns.[30] Japan's regulations also create incentives for investors to remain conservative. The equivalent of US$1 trillion in the Public Pension Reserve Funds has to be, by law, invested in bonds whose credit rating is BBB or above.

Finally, global regulations motivate banks to hold more JGBs than otherwise. In spring 1993 Japanese banks implemented the BIS capital adequacy

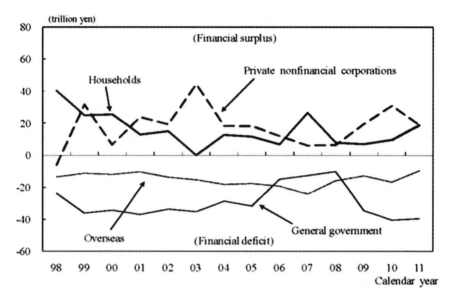

FIGURE 7.2   Japan's financial balance, 1998–2011

Notes: The financial surplus and deficit of the general government sector are adjusted as follows. The effects of debt assumption of the JNR Settlement Corporation and of the Special Account for the National Forest Service by the general government are removed for FY1998. The effects of reclassification of the Japan Expressway Holding and Debt Repayment Agency into the central government are removed for FY2005. See Bank of Japan, "Treatment of Expressway Companies Etc. in the Flow of Funds Accounts and Revision of the Flow of Funds Accounts," September 15, 2006, www.boj.or.jp/en/statistics/outline/notice_2006/ntsj20.htm. The transfer of reserves in the FILP Special Account to the central government is removed by ¥12.0 trillion for FY2006, ¥11.3 trillion for FY2008, ¥7.3 trillion for FY2009, ¥4.8 trillion for FY2010, and ¥1.1 trillion for FY2011. The effects of investment in equities to Japan Post holdings by the central government are removed for FY2007. See Bank of Japan, "Treatment of the Japan Post Bank, Etc. in the Flow of Funds Accounts and Revision of the Flow of Funds Accounts," March 21, 2008, www.boj.or.jp/en/statistics/outline/notice_2008/ntsj25.htm.

Source: Bank of Japan, "Basic Figures of the Flow of Funds: Second Quarter of 2012," September 25, 2012, 13, www.boj.or.jp/en/statistics/sj/index.htm.

standard (Basel I) that mandates major banks to maintain an equity-to-asset ratio above 8 percent. The principle is that the higher the ratio of equity (common stock and other owners' equity) to bank assets (cash and bonds, loans and investment), the more prudent the bank's asset management will be. In calculating assets, the rules allow banks to apply risk weight to their assets from very secure (zero risk weight) to full risk (100 percent). Government bonds from the OECD countries carry zero risk weight.[31] Although the rule was revised in Japan in 2007 (Basel II), the zero risk weight on the JGB remained in place. Consequently, Japanese banks carrying a huge amount of JGBs do not have to count them as part of their assets in complying with the BIS standard.[32] This zero risk weight has further encouraged the banks to hold JGBs.[33]

In summary, the complementary interests of the government and financial institutions have led to stable demand for JGBs at the cost of developing a more vibrant financial system in Japan. Moreover, the government's chronic deficits and debt and the exposure of the financial sector to this debt are troubling. We now turn to Japan's fiscal and financial trajectory and offer a baseline prediction for Japan's mid- to long-term future.

The Sustainability of Japan's Fiscal and Financial Position

Japan's public and private financial spheres have become increasingly entwined. On the one hand, private financial institutions have supported the government's revenue needs, allowing it to raise funds at very low cost. On the other hand, the private sector's significant purchase of government debt has exposed it to the risks in the public sector. A decline in the price of JGBs held by financial institutions would erode their capital base, which could have serious ramifications for the financial sector and the economy at large, as a recent IMF report cautioned.[34] Moreover, Japanese holdings of JGBs are expected to increase from 24 percent of assets in 2011 to 30 percent in 2017.[35] Financial institutions have become increasingly aware of the risk posed by heavy exposure to JGBs. If the banks' appetite for JGBs were to decline, the government would find it more difficult to finance its deficits, which would exacerbate Japan's fiscal situation and, in the worst case, could spark a sovereign debt crisis. Is this grim scenario likely? What does the future hold? For the medium term—three to five years—Japan should be able to muddle through. The conditions that will allow this, however, are not likely to persist over the longer term. We turn to them now: economic growth and trade, the financial market, and demography.

Economic Growth and Trade

Better economic growth would generate more revenue, but growth alone will not solve Japan's fiscal problems. Since the early 1990s, the country has run a "structural deficit"—the deficit that exists even if the economy is running at full capacity. In 2011, Japan's cyclically adjusted deficit was -7.3 percent of

GDP, higher than any other country in the OECD.[36] The government can attempt to increase the economic growth rate through supply-side ("structural" reforms), including deregulation and liberalization. Even if successful, however, such steps are unlikely to have an effect in the next three to five years. Pushing them through parliament would be a drawn-out process, and the outcome would not necessarily deliver growth. Moreover, even if supply-side measures boosted growth by 1 percent per year, the ratio viewed as the probable maximum for a technologically developed country, such growth would be far from closing Japan's deficit.[37]

Japan could boost growth through exports as well. Manufacturing exports, the cornerstone of Japan's post–World War II economic recovery and expansion, helped push growth under Koizumi. The prospects for trade-led growth, however, are limited. After the collapse of Lehman Brothers in September 2008, the US export market contracted; the ensuing financial crisis also triggered an appreciation of the yen that hurt exports. Then the devastation of 3/11 disrupted supply chains, leading to a large contraction in exports, and increased oil imports as closures of nuclear power plants brought more reliance on thermal power generation. As a result, Japan accrued a net trade deficit in 2011 for the first time in thirty-one years. This trade deficit may be, not an ephemeral event, but a harbinger of things to come. In the last twenty years, increasing domestic production costs and a strong yen spurred the Japanese private sector to invest and produce abroad. About 20 percent of Japan's manufacturing is currently located overseas, and the rate is much higher for mainstay industries such as automobiles (51 percent) and home electronics (30 percent).

The indicators for regional export-led growth are not favorable. China, Japan's largest export market, is experiencing an economic slowdown. Japan faces tough competition from countries like South Korea, which excels in similar industrial sectors and benefits from a policy that keeps its exchange rate low. The current economic instability, including the ongoing euro crisis, puts upward pressure on the yen. The environment is not favorable for a weak yen policy to enhance Japanese manufacturing competitiveness. The Japanese government has also tried to promote exports through free trade agreements. The DPJ government appeared interested in expanding such agreements, including the ambitious Trans-Pacific Partnership, but powerful domestic constituencies like agriculture were opposed. Despite Japan's manufacturing prowess (discussed by Takahiro Fujimoto in chapter 8 of this volume), the old model of domestic manufacturing and exports as the foundation of Japan's economic growth is not promising.

Trade is only one component of the current account. Japan also generates income from investments abroad (nearly US$116 billion in 2011 alone),[38] which is why the current account remains in surplus. Japan's trade deficit would have to be four to five times larger than in 2011 for its current account balance to turn negative, according to one estimate.[39] Middle-of-the-road forecasts predict that Japan may run a current account deficit by the 2020s.[40]

In the long run, the day will come when Japan must supplement its current account deficit with foreign funding. That does not portend disaster; indeed, some experts argue that Japan will be able to finance its deficits abroad. One consequence on the fiscal side, though, is that the government will be exposed to greater market pressures and more susceptible to contagion effects. A drop in the price of JGBs could also trigger a financial crisis given the large holdings by private financial institutions. On the finance side, Japan will have to compete internationally to attract financial inflows.

Financial Market Factors

Despite the relatively muted prospects for economic growth over the medium term, Japan should be able to finance its deficits without any major problems. The corporate and household sector in Japan had combined assets of ¥2,275 trillion at the end of 2010 and liabilities of ¥840 trillion.[41] Japan's net debt is 130.6 percent of GDP, which is high but much lower than the headline-making gross public debt figure often cited.[42] Ironically, financial turmoil created by the global financial crisis and the European sovereign debt crisis in the early 2010s has produced some positive effects on medium-term prospects for Japan's fiscal sustainability and financial revival. The Tokyo market looks comparatively better, leading to a significant inflow of funds as investors search for safety.[43] This has been good news for the Japanese government, since such inflows help keep down its borrowing costs.

The sustainability of JGBs depends on two factors: interest rates and the bond markets. Japan's interest rates are likely to remain low for the medium term. Unlike Greece, Spain, or Portugal, debt and deficits have not led to higher interest rates in Japan. In fact, interest rates on ten-year government bonds have been remarkably stable, ranging from 1.0 to 1.2 percent since 3/11,[44] and the government's net interest payments have remained modest despite its high level of debt.[45] Given ongoing deflation, the possibility of interest rates rising significantly is low. The government also benefits from the fact that the national debt is denominated in yen and Japan has its own central bank, a situation very different from Greece. The BOJ could choose to purchase more JGBs, in effect allowing the government to finance its own debt.

How sustainable are bond markets? Private actors have been large holders of JGBs, and they have done well with their investments. Nonetheless, their appetite for JGBs in the future depends on the bonds' security. The JGB credit rating suffered significant downgrading in the early 2000s and then recovered from 2007. But with the accumulation of large fiscal debts, the rating by the major credit rating agencies began to decline in 2011. Financial institutions are increasingly sensitive to the risk, since a decline in the price of their JGB holdings would erode their capital base.[46] For example, Fitch downgraded Japan's three megabanks from A to A– two months after downgrading the JGB in 2012, citing concerns over their high JGB exposure.[47] A change in risk perception could reduce the banks' willingness to finance the government sector, adversely affecting Japan's fiscal situation.

As the aging society set in, the country's net household saving rate, which used to exceed 20 percent during the mid-1970s, dropped below 3 percent in the late 2000s.[48] The trend will continue. In the long run, therefore, large, sustained trade deficits, combined with a deteriorating current account balance and a declining savings rate, could force Japan to finance its deficit abroad, which would require a revitalized financial market.

As discussed above, the government has attempted to make Japan's financial market globally attractive.[49] Foreign ownership of stocks traded on the Tokyo Stock Exchange increased from 13 percent in 1998 to 28 percent in 2007. Yet Tokyo is still far from becoming a global financial center. The exchange, a modern, highly computerized bourse, has in the past attracted foreign companies, but the number of non-Japanese corporate listings has dramatically declined since the high point of 127 in 1991 to 60 in 1998 and a mere 11 in 2011.[50] The lack of investors in stocks has been a problem. The crowding-out effect by the public sector continues to stunt the growth of the securities market in Japan. Moreover, because of the nation's debt servicing burden, the BOJ is under tremendous political pressure to keep its interest rate low even when the economy recovers from deflation. Tokyo has been losing ground to other Asian financial centers such as Hong Kong and Singapore.

Demography
In the not-so-distant future, Japan's fiscal situation will worsen because of the demographic challenge. Of the industrialized democracies, Japan has

one of the most unfavorable demographic profiles. The population has been shrinking since 2005 and is already one of the oldest, with 23 percent over age sixty-five. The comparable figure for the United States is 13 percent.[51] Japan's fertility rate is about 1.3 children per couple, far below the replacement rate. These demographic trends can be alleviated by increasing fertility, but according to Shirahase, the prospects for doing so are not bright. A modest child care subsidy introduced by the DPJ to increase the birthrate was halted because of fiscal constraints and opposition by the LDP.

Immigration could stem population decline and increase the labor force. To keep the population constant, however, Japan would need to admit four hundred thousand immigrants per year until 2050, which is highly unlikely.[52] Neither the government nor the public appears willing to allow immigration on this scale. As Japan's population ages, spending on welfare for pensions and health care will rise and the smaller workforce will shrivel the tax base and squeeze public finances. The aging population may also reduce the government's ability to finance deficits domestically. As the elderly draw down savings, the pool of household savings, which has financed more than half of the government's stock of JGBs, will diminish, and by 2021 gross public debt will exceed all household financial assets.[53]

Possible Futures for the Japanese Economy

Just over the horizon is a huge fiscal problem for Japan. Large deficits and high public debt have consumed a growing share of the country's financial resources. Economic growth alone will not save Japan. For the time being, however, with a current account surplus, the household and corporate sectors are more than able to cover the government's financing needs. Longer term is an entirely different story, and Japan faces a transition from a creditor nation to a net borrower. That will require Japan to finance its deficits abroad, exposing the government to the pressures of international financial markets. Not only might foreign investors demand a higher interest rate, but reliance on foreign financing would be likely to add to the uncertainty and volatility in bond markets. Barring a change in attitudes and policy toward immigration, the demographic vise will tighten.

Can Japan revitalize its financial market? Despite more than a decade of liberalization and innovation, corporations and financial firms have largely avoided investing in non-JGB securities, both causing and reflecting the lack of dynamism in Japan's financial markets. Although financial institutions have not been affected by the financial crises in the United States and Europe, the Tokyo market has not cultivated effective financial players or become an attractive international market.

We do not expect any sudden change in the mutually dependent interests of the government and the country's financial sector over the medium term. But there is some tension between Japan's financial industry and the government sector. A robust financial market in Tokyo could make it harder for the government to finance deficits. As securities recover, funds may shift away from financing the government sector, and a greater appetite for risk may lead to greater overseas investment. To tackle the twin challenges in private and public finance, Japan has to couple credible medium-term fiscal consolidation (but only after economic recovery) with development of a strong financial industry. Fiscal survival and financial revival are intricately linked; carefully disentangling the ties between the public and private financial spheres by reducing the government's need for deficit financing and revitalizing the financial market will be a step toward building a brighter economic future for Japan.

Epilogue

Upon coming to power in December 2012, LDP prime minister Shinzō Abe embarked on an economic policy dubbed "Abenomics." It is a three-pronged strategy (or "three arrows" as Abe and the media call it): expansionary monetary policy, fiscal stimulus, and structural reforms to improve productivity. The first and arguably the boldest move is a monetary stimulus through an unprecedented increase in quantitative easing. The government is set to increase the balance sheet of the BOJ by 30 percent of GDP by the end of 2014, twice the increase of US monetary expansion. The Abe administration also passed a relatively large fiscal stimulus in the form of a ¥5 trillion supplementary budget. The goal of both the monetary and the fiscal stimulus is to overcome persistent deflation and achieve an annual target inflation rate of 2 percent. Structural reform targets an array of areas intended to improve growth, from increased labor participation (especially of women) to electricity deregulation. The market thus far (July 2013) has responded positively to Abenomics, with 4.1 percent annualized real GDP growth in the first quarter of 2013.[54]

Abenomics matters in two critical ways to the interdependency of the fiscal and financial sectors. First, monetary and fiscal stimulus will contribute to even higher public debt. Second, the attempt to increase inflation, if success-ful, would increase interest rates and drive down bond prices. Given the large holdings of JGBs by Japanese banks, this could in turn significantly erode their capital base and make them reluctant to hold JGBs. At the same time, a spike in interest rates would also increase the government's debt repayment burden as new JGBs are issued. In the most optimistic scenario, the gov-ernment could engineer a soft landing through economic growth generating higher tax revenues to alleviate budget deficits and allow banks to shift out of JGBs. Of course, sustained economic growth would require reforms resisted by politically strong sectors such as agriculture and small and medium-sized enterprises. Which scenario will unfold is not yet clear. In any case, the gov-ernment will need to reduce carefully the exposure of the financial sector to JGB risk.

Notes

1. International Monetary Fund [IMF], *Fiscal Monitor: Addressing Fiscal Challenges to Reduce Economic Risks* (Washington, DC: IMF, 2011), statistical table 7, 70–71, www.imf.org/external/pubs/ft/fm/2011/02/pdf/fm1102.pdf.

2. Organisation for Economic Cooperation and Development [OECD], General Assessment of the Macroeconomic Situation, *OECD Economic Outlook* 2011, no. 2 (2011), 249. The government has significant assets including foreign reserve assets and stock in public companies. When these assets are taken into consideration, Japan's net debt is 130.6 percent of GDP, which is still very high but much lower than the headline-making gross public debt figure often cited. See IMF, "Fiscal Monitor," 71, and William W. Grimes, "Japan's Fiscal Challenge: The Political Economy of Reform," in *Japan in Crisis: What Will It Take for Japan to Rise Again?* ed. T. J. Pempel and Yongshik Bong (Seoul: Asian Institute for Policy Studies, forthcoming).

3. Gene Park, *Spending without Taxation: FILP and the Politics of Public Finance in Japan*, Studies of the Walter H. Shorenstein Asia-Pacific Research Center (Stan-ford, CA: Stanford University Press, 2011).

4. These government bonds were, more precisely, "construction bonds" to cover pub-lic investment; the government had previously issued bonds for various public and quasi-public corporations. For details, see Park, *Spending without Taxation*.

5. Masaru Mizuno, *Zeisei kaisei gojūnen: Kaiko to tenbō* [Revising the tax system over fifty years: Future prospects] (Tōkyō: Ōkura Zaimu Kyōkai, 2006), 113.

6. Park, *Spending without Taxation*.

7. Grimes, "Japan's Fiscal Challenge."

8. Gene Park, "The Politics of Scarcity: Fixing Japan's Public Finances," in *The Routledge Handbook of Japanese Politics*, ed. Alisa Gaunder (New York: Routledge, 2011), 273–83.

9. OECD, *OECD Economic Surveys: Japan 2011* (Paris: OECD Publishing, 2011), 64.

10. Masahiko Aoki, Hugh Patrick, and Paul Sheard, "The Japanese Main Bank System: An Introductory Overview," in *The Japanese Main Bank System: Its Relevance for Developing and Transforming Economies*, ed. Masahiko Aoki and Hugh Patrick (New York: Oxford University Press, 1994), 1–50.

11. See Kent E. Calder, *Strategic Capitalism: Private Business and Public Purpose in Japanese Industrial Finance* (Princeton, NJ: Princeton University Press, 1993), and Frances McCall Rosenbluth, *Financial Politics in Contemporary Japan* (Ithaca, NY: Cornell University Press, 1989).

12. Henry Laurence, *Money Rules: The New Politics of Finance in Britain and Japan* (Ithaca, NY: Cornell University Press, 2001), 118.

13. For example, Laurence explains that in 1978 the MOF had to respond to demand and loosened the conditions of Article 65 of the Securities and Exchange Law (the Glass-Steagall–like separation of security and banking businesses) to allow banks to sell government bonds on the open market. Laurence, *Money Rules*, 117.

14. As early as 1982, big business's reliance on bank loans declined to 17.5 percent of its total funds (1978–82 average) from 30.2 percent only five years before (1973–77 average). Koichi Hamada and Akiyoshi Horiuchi, "The Political Economy of the Financial Market," in *The Political Economy of Japan*, vol. 1, *The Domestic Transformation*, ed. Kozo Yamamura and Yasukichi Yasuba (Stanford, CA: Stanford University Press, 1987), 249.

15. David Asher, "What Became of the Japanese 'Miracle,'" *Orbis* 40, no. 2 (1996): 215.

16. Jennifer A. Amyx, *Japan's Financial Crisis: Institutional Rigidity and Reluctant Change* (Princeton, NJ: Princeton University Press, 2004). Several MOF officials in charge of bank inspections were arrested for accepting excessive gifts in exchange for confidential information.

17. Ministry of Finance, *Kinyū sisutemu kaikaku no gaiyō* [Outline of the financial system reform], 1997, www.fsa.go.jp/p_mof/big-bang/bb30.htm.

18. Tetsuo Toya, *Kinyū bigu ban no seiji keizaigaku: Kinyū to kōkyō seisaku sakutei ni okeru seidohenka* [The political economy of the Japanese financial Big Bang: Institutional change in finance and public policy making] (Tokyo: RIETI, 2006), 144–45.

19. Mark Metzler, "Review Essay: Toward a Financial History of Japan's Long Stagnation, 1990–2003," *Journal of Asian Studies* 67 (May 2008): 663.

20. Official of the Financial Service Agency, interview by Saori N. Katada, July 2009.

21. Yoichi Arai and Takeo Hoshi, "Monetary Policy in Great Stagnation," in *Japan's Great Stagnation: Financial and Monetary Policy Lessons for Advanced Economies*, ed. Michael Hutchison and Frank Westermann (Cambridge, MA: MIT Press, 2006), 157.

22. Arai, Hoshi, and Shimizu blame the government's continued protection of bank deposits for the liquidity trap. Depositors felt safe with their money in a bank protected by the government guarantee and did not spend or use it for other investment purposes. See Arai and Hoshi, "Monetary Policy," 157; Katsutoshi Shimizu, *Kokusai kiki to kinyū shijō* [The JGB crisis and Japan's financial market] (Tokyo: Nihon Keizai Shimbun Shuppansha, 2011), chap. 4.

23. In September 2008 Japan's large financial institutions launched a financial offensive and purchased a large stake in Morgan Stanley (Tokyo Mitsubishi UFJ Financial Group) and the Asian branch of bankrupt Lehman Brothers (Nomura).

24. In March 2010, the analyst calculated that the BOJ would hit its JGB purchase limit within three to four years if the BOJ followed its announced policy. Shin Takayama, "Nihon kokusai no kokunai shōka kōzō wa itsumade iji dekiruka" [How long can the "domestic absorption" of Japanese government bonds be sustained?], Tokyo-Mitsubishi UFJ Bank, *Keizai Review*, no. 2010-8 (April 28, 2010).

25. Ministry of Finance, *Quarterly Newsletter on Japanese Government Bonds*, April 2012, 7.

26. Data from Kiichi Tokuoka, "The Outlook for Financing Japan's Public Debt," IMF Working Paper WP/10/19 (2010), https://www.imf.org/external/pubs/ft/wp/2010/wp1019.pdf, 16. Three megabanks hold more than this average, ranging from 14 to 17 percent of their respective total assets in 2009.

27. Gillian Tett, "Ties between Sovereigns and Banks Set to Deepen," *Financial Times*, December 22, 2011.

28. BOJ, "Flow of Funds: Overview of Japan, US, and the Euro Area," Bank of Japan Research and Statistics Department, Tokyo, 2012, www.boj.or.jp/en/statistics/sj/sjhiq.pdf, 13.

29. Two bankers and an official in the Japan Bankers' Association, interview by Saori N. Katada, Tokyo, June 2012.

30. Japanese economist, interview by Saori N. Katada, Tokyo, July 2012.

31. Ryozo Himino, *BIS kisoku to Nippon* [BIS Rules and Japan], 2nd ed. (Tokyo: Kinyū Zaisei Jijō Kenkyū kai, 2007), 50–54.

32. Shimizu, *Kokusai kiki to kinyū shijō*, 144–45.

33. Official of the Japan Bankers' Association, interview by Saori N. Katada, Tokyo, June 2012.

34. IMF, *Global Financial Stability Report: Restoring Confidence and Progression on Reforms, October 2012* (Washington, DC: IMF, 2012).

35. Ibid., 53.

36. OECD, "OECD Economic Outlook No. 90," *OECD Economic Outlook: Statistics and Projections (2011)*, database, annex table 25 (2011), 250.

37. Grimes, "Japan's Fiscal Challenge."

38. Japan External Trade Organization, Japanese Trade and Investment Statistics, Japan's Outward and Inward Foreign Direct Investment, www.jetro.go.jp/en/reports/statistics/ (accessed October 29, 2012).

39. Richard Katz, "Game Changer: The 2011 Trade Deficit and Risks of JGB Crisis," *Oriental Economist* 80, no. 2 (2012): 2.

40. Ibid.

41. Lam R. Waikei and Kiichi Tokuoka, "Assessing the Risks to the Japanese Government Bond (JGB) Market," IMF Working Paper WP/11/292, 2011, https://www.imf.org/external/pubs/ft/wp/2011/wp11292.pdf, 5.

42. IMF, *Fiscal Monitor*, 71.

43. IMF, *Global Financial Stability Report: The Quest for Lasting Stability* (Washington, DC: IMF, 2012), 52–55.

44. IMF, *Japan: 2011 Article IV Consultation*, IMF Country Report No. 11/181 (Washington, DC: 2011), 4.

45. Takeo Hoshi and Takatoshi Ito, "Defying Gravity: How Long Will Japanese Government Bond Prices Remain High?," mimeo, 2012, Tokyo.

46. Yasuhiro Matsumoto, "Hōgin 4 gurupu no kokusaihoyu" [JGB holdings of the four Japanese financial groups], *Ekonomisuto*, September 27, 2011, 34–35.

47. "Ōte ginkō o kakusage" [Downgrading Japanese megabanks], *Asahi Shimbun*, July 21, 2012, morning ed., 8.

48. Japan's saving rate is now lower than that of the United States or Italy. See *OECD Economic Outlook*, various issues.

49. In 2004, the Financial Services Agency published its initiative "Program for Further Financial Reform: Japan's Challenge: Moving toward a Financial Services Nation," December 2004, www.fsa.go.jp/news/newse/e20041224-2.pdf. In 2008, it also introduced the "Plan for Strengthening the Competitiveness of Japan's Financial and Capital Markets," December 21, 2007, www.fsa.go.jp/en/news/2007/20071221/01.pdf.

50. Such decline has been attributed to high listing costs and alternative Internet listing opportunities. Sayuri Shirai, "Evaluating the Present State of Japan as an International Financial Center," mimeo, 2009, MPRA: Munich Personal RePEc Archive, 8–9 (graph).

51. Robert Dekle, "Remember Japan?," *Milken Institute Review*, spring 2012, 8.

52. Ibid.

53. Waikei and Tsuruoka, "Assessing the Risks," 8.

54. Cabinet Office, Quarterly Estimates of GDP, 2013, www.esri.cao.go.jp/en/sna/data/sokuhou/files/2013/qe131_2/gdemenuea.html.

CHAPTER EIGHT

Manufacturing in Japan: Factories and National Policy

Takahiro Fujimoto with Frank Baldwin

Japan's economy has been in deep trouble, and the causes are clear: the global recession triggered by the 2008 financial crisis, appreciation of the yen, the rise of China, and the triple disaster in eastern Japan on March 11, 2011.[1] These Four Horsemen of an economic apocalypse have an outrider: pessimism, a pervasive lack of confidence that manufacturing can survive in Japan. "We have to move production overseas or we'll go bankrupt," say frightened managers. They are panicky and shortsighted, in our view. A strategy for recovery and a return to growth must include retention of the best manufacturing sites, or *genba*, in Japan.[2]

Japan's national economy is an array of manufacturing sites—a productive core that supports the standard of living—and includes first-rate factories and product design centers as well as retail and service hubs.[3] From the perspective of manufacturing management, the head offices of Japanese corporations (especially the large multinationals) are abetting deindustrialization.

The art of making things (*monozukuri*) is much more than assembly work that turns out automobiles or machining operations that build their engines.[4] Products—tradable artifacts—emerge from a creative union of design information and materials, what Aristotle called a combination of form and matter. The added value essentially inheres in the former (think of Steve Jobs and Apple or slick Japanese consumer electronic gadgets). Making things begins with the creation of good designs that please customers at home and abroad and generate revenue. A production site is the wellspring—the space and organization—where the designs and material meet. Turning them into products is at the heart of Japanese-style manu-facturing technology.

On the eve of World War II the manufacturing sector accounted for about 24 percent of Japan's total employment. After the war, for historical and geopolitical reasons including a chronic labor shortage throughout the rapid-growth era, long-term employment and business relationships were the rational choice for Japanese industry because the costs of replacing work-ers and switching suppliers were relatively high. A division of labor was suppressed within companies and facilitated among them. Manufacturers depended on a cross-trained regular workforce that stayed at the same fac-tories for decades and was supplemented by temporary or seasonal employ-ees during peak production periods. Adaptability based on the teamwork of multiskilled employees became the norm, as distinct from the emphasis in the United States on specialization and narrow job classifications defined by work rules. Although unevenly distributed in Japan during the second half of the twentieth century, this teamwork-oriented organizational capability is still a source of industrial competitiveness for certain products that require intensive coordination.[5]

The Tōhoku Disaster

The toll from the 3/11 earthquake and tsunami was 15,869 dead, 6,109 injured, and 2,847 missing, with property damage estimated at ¥16.9 trillion.[6] The regional infrastructure—roads, bridges, seaports, and railways—was badly damaged by flooding and landslides. Sendai Airport was knocked out of ser-vice. Japan has not suffered such a loss of life and devastation over so large an area since World War II. The impact on business overseas was enor-mous when global supply chains were disrupted; the digitalization of prod-ucts compounded the problems of industrial recovery compared to the Kobe Earthquake in 1995. Suppliers and supply routes for electronic machinery control panels, application-specific integrated circuits, and flat panel dis-plays are concentrated in Tōhoku. Toyota alone had more than one hundred parts suppliers there, mostly second tier or lower. Renesas Electronics' Naka plant, Hitachinaka, Miyagi Prefecture, maker of semiconductors for micro-controllers with a 30 percent share of the world market, was badly damaged, and production was off for about three months.[7] Japanese plants overseas had to suspend operations because the global supply network of electronic parts is rooted in Japan. Overall, the assembly lines of domestic automotive manufacturers were shut down for about a month, although some plants were stopped for only a few days, thanks to rapid personnel transfers and procurement of alternative supply sources. The Nissan Motor Company, for example, assigned three senior executives to recovery and "brought all of its supply chain management teams from overseas plants to Japan for real-time assessments and to facilitate communication."[8] The infrastructure proved resilient: the Tōhoku Expressway and other roads were reopened, and limited bullet train service was restored in six weeks.

Postdisaster soul-searching included consideration of moving production to western Japan or overseas. Seismic activity is widespread in Japan; manufacturers can run but they cannot hide, and other countries have earthquakes, too, not to mention floods, riots, and terrorism. Risk has no boundaries, but the greatest risk is of losing competitiveness. There has been no dearth of suggestions to mitigate future natural disasters: reduce just-in-time delivery and stockpile parts, maintain dual tooling, duplicate entire production lines, and institute dual sourcing. The catch-22 is that these changes would raise costs; Japanese manufacturers must remain competitive.[9] An earthquake is over in seconds, while global rivalry continues around the clock.

Work Style

Many foreign observers were amazed at the reaction of people in the devastated region. Public order did not break down, emergency services responded, and local authorities soon set up evacuation centers, even though many lacked electricity and water for a time. The swift cooperative response at the community level stood in stark contrast to the sluggishness of central government officials, some corporate leaders, and the heads of certain electric power companies, for example. There was remarkable coordination between headquarters and production sites at most of the large companies affected, disproving the oft-heard criticism of "strong factories, weak headquarters."

Until 3/11 many Japanese were resigned to having been forgotten by a world bedazzled by China, an impression now dispelled. The goodwill toward Japan demonstrated by more than 130 countries and millions of people went beyond sympathy. It was a collateral dividend of our national work style, from the warm hospitality (*omotenashi*) shown to tourists at retail outlets in Tokyo to the cooperative adaptability of Japanese foreign aid teams overseas.[10]

That distinctive work style—flexible teamwork—helped Japan's good manufacturing sites maintain most of their competitive strength after 3/11. For instance, the Sagamihara plant of the Toyota Group's Central Motor Company used to produce about one hundred thousand vehicles per year at peak times. After the 2008 financial crisis, sales plummeted by 70 percent. Temporary workers, about a fifth of the total, were released to cut costs; regular employees found ways to raise productivity. Redundant workers were assigned to non–assembly line tasks such as improving operating procedures and making tools and equipment in house. Some were sent to other companies in the Toyota group such as Hino, a subsidiary that makes trucks. Despite a 70 percent reduction in volume, the company was in the black again by 2010. The attitude of the president and employees made the difference: "The company is in trouble, but it's a chance for us to show what we can do."

A small textile company in Ishikawa Prefecture is another case study in survival against low-wage competition. The plant has several hundred very efficient looms. One operator can handle sixty machines; about 80 percent are in operation at any time. The firm makes a relatively integral product—high-performance uniforms—for a niche market. Outstanding productivity brought labor savings, a dilemma for President Watanabe (not his real name). This is a little business, he said, but a big employer in this community: "If we fired several dozen employees, I wouldn't be able to walk down the main street." Innovation was the answer. Through research and experimentation, the firm found advanced applications for carbon-fiber fabrics that led to a new line of products. In manufacturing terminology, process innovation created effective demand. I have seen many similarly tenacious plants since 3/11. Profits and stock prices do not tell the whole story of an industry or factory.

Pessimism

For many years the media have kept up an uninformed drumbeat about the end of manufacturing in Japan. Commentators lament the decline of industrial communities, politicians decry the imminent collapse of small- and medium-sized companies, and editorials urge the relocation of factories overseas (while bemoaning the hollowing out of Japanese industry!). The Tōhoku region aside, is the picture so unremittingly grim? I visit factories, development centers, or service units around Japan at least once a week and know from personal observation that the situation varies greatly by area and firm. I suspect that others who have actually been inside plants have the same opinion. As with reports of Mark Twain's death, the demise of manufacturing in Japan is greatly exaggerated.

Of course, the recession has taken a heavy toll. One of the authors lives in Tokyo, but many of his relatives reside elsewhere, some in a rural town in Tōhoku with a population of less than thirty thousand where many businesses in the shopping arcade are closed. Once-bustling shops are shuttered permanently. Some of the shutters have come off; the street looks like a mouth with teeth missing. A few of his relatives still run businesses there, but the situation has been very difficult since the collapse of Lehman Brothers in March 2008.

Nevertheless, the picture is mixed. Even at the lowest point in 2009–10, quite a few companies had record sales and profits, and others, though hard hit, kept their factories going and steadily improved operations. For example, the heads of small- and medium-sized companies in the northern Kanto area, including diemakers and second-tier automobile subcontractors, got together socially one night, and the author joined them. A senior leader from a struggling diemaker said, "It's no longer possible to manufacture in Japan," and the others agreed. I took this to be a common attitude. Later I talked with one of the younger managers in the restroom. "Despite my remarks earlier," he said, "we actually had our highest profits ever last year, but don't tell anyone that." If a subcontractor were to say, "We are doing great," customers would immediately demand a lower unit price and the tax office would pay closer attention to his return. Companies with a good bottom line are generally close-mouthed, while those struggling complain loudly about tight margins. Visits to firms in the Tōkai area, such as Hamamatsu, the birthplace of Honda and Suzuki, yielded the same impression. Some of the bearish managers today were rapidly expanding exports of high-precision machine tools just before the global financial crash. The higher they had climbed, the harder they fell. The motorcycle parts industry, which relied too much on exports to the US market, is a case in point. Silent in boom times, they are now upset and outspoken.

On the other hand, consider the case of Nihon Seiki, a machine-tool maker in Hamamatsu, Shizuoka Prefecture, with forty-three employees (as of 2010) that has been about the same size for forty years. The company weathered the economic downturn with aplomb. In 2009 they received zero orders, but they had quite a backlog to work on. Having anticipated a slump,

Nihon Seiki next dismantled and rebuilt a large stock of used machines they had accepted as trade-ins and sold them at discounted prices to maintain a cash flow. Typically, veteran lathe operators switched to dismantling and rebuilding the used machines. Small- and medium-sized companies have ultraversatile workers who function much like utility players in baseball and willingly fill in where needed. Nihon Seiki hired high school graduates who were taught technical skills by experienced employees, Baby Boomers now fostering a new generation. Orders from China picked up, and the company suddenly had a healthy backlog. "We survived again," said the president, a technology development specialist. The point is, there are winner and losers, and the winners (and potential winners) have to be kept in Japan.

China surpassing Japan in gross domestic product was a hot topic in early 2011 that faded into the larger pessimistic background after 3/11. Japan's fall to third place below the United States and China may be meaningful in international politics, but in economic terms China has reached a level of per capita productivity only one-tenth that of Japan. That the Chinese people are getting wealthier is good in itself and also benefits Japan in two ways: Japanese companies can sell more products to them, and it is easier to compete against Chinese factories where wages are rapidly increasing. Japan has no hegemonic agenda for East Asia. The purpose of economic growth is to attain high levels of per capita gross domestic product (GDP) and income that enrich the lives of the maximum number of Japanese (everybody if possible). To maintain those levels, we need (nearly) full employment and higher productivity in the agricultural and service sectors too. After all, manufacturing accounts for only about 20 percent of Japan's GDP. But in the long term Japan cannot prosper unless our factories are productive. Whether our GDP is third or fourth in the world is irrelevant.

Where the demand comes from, domestic or foreign, is of secondary importance. What matter are consumers willing to spend money on Japanese products. Incidentally, exports as a percentage of GDP stood at 13.5 percent in 2009, even after the financial crisis, the same as in 1985, when the yen was at 240 per US dollar. Those exports, despite the yen's appreciation, show the overall strength of Japanese industry. In 2013, even with the exchange rate below ¥80 = $US1, plants around Japan exported manufactured goods and equipment worth about ¥60 billion, although the trade surplus has gone, largely because of the sharp rise in fossil fuel imports.[11]

Some economists contend that Japan does not have to make things because a trade balance is less important than the balance of payments. Just because

Great Britain and the United States have strong financial sectors does not mean Japan can too. For the foreseeable future Japan will have to be a manufacturer, not a banker (see chapter 7 by Saori Katada and Gene Park in this volume).

Today gloom and doom is in fashion. The media sell information and exaggerate both good and bad news. Television presenters and guest commentators go on and on about "communities in trouble" and "small businesses facing bankruptcy." A contrarian who said, "Some industrial communities are doing well" would be deluged with angry phone calls: "Don't you know what's happening out here?" An empathetic message is good for ratings. The politicians' standard sound bite—"Everyone is suffering and we will help you"—goes down easily with the public.

The Hollowing Out of Japanese Industry

The vague, emotive Japanese term for "hollowing out," *kūdōka* (空洞化), means the vital center is gone.[12] The word debuted in an academic journal in January 1987, following the 1985 Plaza Accord that devalued the US dollar against the yen. At that time, unlike today, *kūdōka* had a nuanced meaning—to clear the way for new industries. Politicians and economists began to speak of *kūdōka* in the mid-1990s, when the exchange rate reached $1 = ¥80. Prime Minister Ryūtarō Hashimoto mentioned *kūdōka* in a cautionary way in a 1994 policy speech; in a government report the next year the word implied a reduction in domestic manufacturing, but it was not pejorative or alarmist. Mainstream economists used it to describe a change in the national economy and industrial structure such as the shift by stages from textiles to heavy industry to a service economy. These transitions were inevitable and not to be thwarted; the government's role was to smooth the process.

In the 1995 *Economic White Paper*, *kūdōka* meant the maturation and decline of an industry and was consistent with Kaname Akamatsu's "flying geese" pattern of economic development and Raymond Vernon's theory of product life cycles. Predictable, an aspect of technology transfer, and an investment opportunity for Japan, *kūdōka* was an evolutionary process. To proponents of free trade who opposed protectionism, the decline of an industry and its replacement by another was the outcome of free economic competition, as natural as the sun rising in the east and setting in the west. Economists coined "sunset industries" to describe sectors that were no longer competitive. Other industries dawned and took up the slack in the balance of payments, though dislocated workers were caught in the crosshairs of technological change. Many governments, Japan's included, try to ameliorate such a situation through worker retraining and the designation of "savior" fields to lead the next wave of economic growth, but it is usually very difficult to identify a high-growth industry before it starts to grow. Bureaucrats are not very good at picking winners; few of these would-be stars have panned out. Rapid growth usually comes from within an established industry. These policies were not perceived as an attempt to halt industrial transformation.

At the industry level, there was no objective standard to measure when the sun was setting, including the increase in overseas production sites, and to conclude that hollowing out was under way. It was in the eye of the beholder. If the pace of change exceeded the "normal" speed of decline and was the result of management errors, the loss of an industry's core elements could have been attributed to human action.

In the wake of 3/11, however, some industrialists and commentators have conflated evolutionary restructuring with hollowing out and the oft-heard "loss of Japan's manufacturing sector." Divorced from economic logic, empirical observation, or statistical analysis and influenced by demographic trends—aging of the population—and uncertain times, the term has morphed from a technical synonym for diversification to suggest an apocalyptic vision of abandoned factories, mass unemployment, and a beleaguered future.

For example, an article entitled "Hollowing Out and the Japanese Economy" in the *Nihon Keizai Shimbun* in December 2011 advocated shifting production facilities overseas as part of a package of changes to revitalize the economy.[13] An editorial in the same newspaper in January 2012 called for investment and manufacturing abroad not only to serve markets there but to export to Japan as well.[14] A commentator in *Forbes* called it "quite remarkable" that Japan's leading economic journal was "not only accepting, but plainly encouraging, the much-feared 'hollowing out' of manufacturing, or at least declaring relocation of much of Japan's manufacturing capacity abroad."[15] Many major publications have endorsed this abandonment of factories in Japan, often in the name of avoiding *kūdōka!*[16] Superficial and uninformed, these views have often ignored the reality of continuous capability building, failed to understand comparative advantage theory, which denies the possibility of overall hollowing out of entire industries, overlooked the decreasing international wage differential, and dogmatically assumed that manufacturing industries always relocate to lower-wage countries.

If managers lose the will to fight or the mood in the boardroom clouds decision making, domestic production can slip away faster than market conditions dictate. By contrast, there is no fatalistic resignation at the factory level. We have never heard a worker or supervisor say, "Oh, the yen went up again. We're finished." They do not passively accept that when the yen reaches ¥75 = US$1 they will have to turn out the lights and leave. Production staff thinks, "Let's improve efficiency or find a different product to make." They have coped with the yen's appreciation for forty years and survived. Hollowing out is a possible outcome, not a first cause. This mind-set has not wavered even when, as in 2013, Abenomics depreciated the yen somewhat. Manufacturing professionals know that a favorable trend may change at any time.

The worst-case scenario is that corporate managers, swayed by the fallacy of inevitable deindustrialization, succumb to short-term thinking and the herd mentality and close even very productive domestic factories. Because of stagnant demand and productivity increases, employment in the manufacturing sector has already fallen from 16.02 million in 1992 to 9.98 million in 2012.

Off to China

This chorus of negativity has created the impression that small- and medium-sized enterprises are a vanishing breed. Statements by senior executives in large corporations have a similar tone and reinforce the business community's pessimism, creating a vicious cycle of doubt about the future. American friends who socialize with the boardroom elite say that certain Japanese corporations suffer from organizational depression. According to a survey by the Japan Bank of International Cooperation released in December 2011, "87.2 percent of Japanese manufacturers plan to strengthen or expand their business overseas in the next three years."[17] In 2012, the evacuation reached Dunkirk proportions.

Paradoxically, while the managers and directors are frightened, supervisors and designers in the frontline factories are focused on the great game of international competition. The situation reminds me of a soccer match: the good factories are like veteran players who have gotten yellow warning cards for decades—the high value of the yen, the recession, and Asian competition—but are still on the pitch unbowed. Only the team owner can give them a red penalty card and take them off the field. Production workers and supervisors are playing hard and keeping the game within reach, but senior management has forgotten that it is a long contest. Swayed by the ubiquitous pessimism and short-term shareholder expectations, they make a decision: We're moving to China. Game over.

Wages in China and other industrializing countries started to rise rapidly from the turn of the century and have doubled about every five years. Consider this tale of two typical companies in the office machine industry. Company C retained efficient operations in Japan and opened a factory in China, transferred capability to the plant, and doubled its productivity. Company D closed its factories in Japan and opened new ones in China to export globally. Company D's Chinese factory could not improve productivity as fast as Company C because there was no support from a "mother factory" in Japan. D eventually had to abandon most of its production lines in China and moved to low-wage countries—Vietnam, Indonesia, Burma, and Cambodia. New products lagged behind, partially because of the physical separation from the development center in Japan. A company engineer said, "Without a factory where I can have hands-on contact with the molds and designs, talk to colleagues about function and architecture, and see the products take shape, I am hamstrung." Skype calls and occasional visits are not enough.

Our position here stems from neither nationalism nor neomercantilism. We are simply saying that in this era of globalization multilateral companies should follow two principles when they set up offshore operations: proximity to the market and long-term competitive advantage. When an industry is losing its competitive edge because of costs, the fear that management may relocate production overseas may invigorate domestic plants to improve productivity.[18] The decision should not be based just on wage comparisons or short-term cost calculations. Global business is constantly affected by long-term changes in wages, productivity, exchange rates, and organizational learning.

Most plants in Japan have an advantage in productivity over the same firm's factories overseas, but many are handicapped by exchange rates and wages. Yet over the long haul manufacturing sites in Japan may give a firm a sustainable global strategy.[19] Among the reasons are that the R&D center and a "mother factory" can create easy-to-build product designs and can transfer productivity breakthroughs to the overseas operations. This plant can also be responsive to the domestic market and can operate with short lead times.[20]

With the enormous uncertainty in the world economy and public finances—from Eurozone foreign debt to Japan's national debt—a crash of the US dollar or the yen cannot be ruled out. The yen could rise to ¥60 per $1 or fall to ¥150 per $1. In a span of three to five years the wages in emerging industrial economies and the comparative productivity between Japan and abroad may swing by 100 percent or more. Putting all your manufacturing eggs in overseas baskets is not a wise policy. Who will be accountable if Japan's manufacturing base is moved abroad and then debt-ridden national finances and the currency collapse? That happened to some countries during the 1997 Asian financial crisis. Saori Katada and Gene Park discuss potential potholes down the road in chapter 7 of this volume.

Comparative Advantage: Theory and Practice

The classic trade theory of comparative advantage advanced by David Ricardo in the early nineteenth century, a simple conception based on the difference in the cost of production of cloth and wine in England and Portugal, still provides a framework for understanding trade phenomena in the twenty-first century.[21] The standard two-country, two-good model ($N = 2$) with refinements is extendable to international competition where many goods are produced and traded. Conventional trade theory has a macro perspective, the standpoint of policy makers and economists who look at a nation, a region, or the global market. Yoshinori Shiozawa and Fujimoto started from the micro viewpoint of managers and factory heads in interfirm competition within the same industry and intrafirm competition within the same multinational corporation and then integrated these two approaches into a macro-micro loop perspective. The real-world puzzle for Japanese firms and factories is how to compete with rivals in China and other low-wage countries. As noted, the heart of the matter is often whether a Japanese firm should shift production to China, Thailand, Vietnam, or India. That decision is where theory meets the bottom line.

Generally speaking, the wage ratio is a macro variable beyond the reach of individual firms, which are affected by the aggregated result. But management and factory leaders know that physical labor productivity—what economists call labor-input coefficients—is not a given (although the standard Ricardian model assumes it is), and every day managers strive to improve it with an eye on such factors as wages, exchange rates, and competitors' prices.

In aggregate these firm-level activities dynamically change the average and variance of labor input costs in each country/industry. If even herculean efforts fall short, a company may not survive.

A factory manager in Japan cannot affect exchange rates in London or wage levels in China. He can try to overcome the cost disadvantage quickly by doubling or tripling his plant's physical productivity and replicating it in the firm's overseas plants. There are often conversations on the production line in Japan to the effect that "if Chinese wages are a tenth of ours, then we have to achieve productivity ten times that of China." Attaining labor productivity even five times that of a factory in China is no mean feat. In the case of standard bulk products in the petrochemical industry, where production tends to be embodied in the equipment and it is difficult to differentiate organizational capabilities, offsetting the advantage of a low-wage competitor may be difficult. Likewise, in fields where technological knowledge is encapsulated in the production equipment or the components have standardized interfaces, such as memory semiconductors and many digital products, industrial latecomers can bypass the time-consuming stage of building coordinative capabilities and catch up with advanced countries by making what are called modular products.

Japanese manufacturers, however, have tended to overcome the high-wage handicap with fuel-efficient cars, precision industrial machinery, functional chemicals, and specialty steel, products with an integral architecture in which intensive coordination between modules, components, and production processes matters. Many complex integral products require subtle coordination in design and tacit knowledge that is difficult to imitate. Low-wage countries, particularly those with volatile labor markets and high turnover ratios, will not readily overtake Japan in these fields.

The notion of design-based comparative advantage tries to apply the Ricardian theory on production to design activities, costs, and locations. If Japan sustains its rich endowment of coordinative capabilities at domestic sites, the country will tend to export relatively complex integral products, giving up production of many simpler modular products, whether they are high-tech or not. In other words, manufacturing sites for product and process development, as well as for initial production at least of relatively integral goods, have a good chance to survive in Japan.

The trick is to reduce non-value-added time (*muda* in Japanese) like waiting and walking as a fraction of labor time. We know from experience that a factory's productivity can usually be raised by 20 percent by making minute reciprocal adjustments in existing resources: for example, modifying machine tools to one-touch operation, adding flow-control limit switches to automated equipment, and retraining workers to perform multiple tasks. We have witnessed many of Japan's coordination-intensive factories double labor productivity in a year, triple it in three years, and raise the bar 500 percent over five years.

Japanese company managers and economic journalists often say domestic wage levels should be lowered or the yen should be devalued (or a competitor's currency should be adjusted) if the nation is to remain competitive. It is true that if the average wage rate is lowered, in the short run the unit cost of a factory will go down and its cost competitiveness will temporarily improve. But if productivity is not also improved, the company will soon have to slash wages again because factories in another low-wage country will enter the global labor market, and socioeconomic problems follow. Raising the ratio of temporary workers will result in deflation and social unrest due to income inequality. In the interest of the next generation's living standards, lower wages cannot be a long-term remedy.

The global race to the bottom on wages is already problematic. The protests at Foxconn Technology Group, a manufacturing partner of Apple in China, and the violence and wildcat strikes at the Nissan Motor Company's subsidiary in Manesai, India, and at Mulit-Suzuki's Gurgaon factory in India show how a disaffected workforce can cripple a manufacturing subsidiary abroad.[22] In the end, the organizational strength of a factory rests on teamwork, which if undermined hurts productivity. A Japanese industry that can remain competitive only by cutting wages will soon disappear, and the same fate will befall industries in the emerging economies.

Exchange rates are beyond the scope of this paper. Suffice it to say that governments often try to force devaluation of another country's currency—the US campaign against the yuan—but in the long term exchange rate fluctuations are caused by many economic and noneconomic factors such as the growth and savings rates, capital investment, interest, and inflation. Japan mostly ran a trade surplus for more than thirty years with unfavorable exchange rates; stronger productivity is more important than a weaker yen.

As noted, policy makers and their guru economists have a macroeconomic perspective, whereas manufacturing engineers put themselves in the shoes of a factory manager, a microeconomic perspective. A dynamic, design-based reinterpretation of classical Ricardian trade theory helps to explain contemporary trade phenomena and shows that relentless capability improvement sustains comparative advantage in manufacturing. That is Japan's ace in the hole.

Tax Policy

Cursory and shortsighted, in recent years discussions about keeping manufacturing in Japan have produced few sustained policies or significant government funding for human resource development and shop-floor productivity improvements. It is time to get serious about a factory-first approach.

The effective corporate tax rate in Japan has been 41 percent, on a par with the US rate but higher than in the Eurozone and other countries in Asia. Keidanren, the big-business federation, has long campaigned against the "high" taxes in Japan and warned that unless they were cut, domestic manufacturing would be hollowed out. The government's plan to lower the effective corporate ratio was delayed by 3/11 but came into effect in April 2012 and is now 38.01 percent, lower than the US rate of 39.2 percent.[23]

Will Japanese multinational corporations now keep their factories in Japan because of a tax cut? Unfortunately the answer is "no." There is little evidence of a link between production sites and the business tax rate, though rates do affect where corporate headquarters are based, particularly whether a foreign company has a subsidiary or its Asian headquarters in Japan. Only a handful of Japanese companies have set up headquarters overseas; no exodus is under way or in the offing, according to surveys of business plans. Managements transfer manufacturing offshore in search of lax regulatory frameworks, cheap wages, lower material costs, and exchange rate advantages.

Lowering taxes for managements that have lost faith in manufacturing here may just allow them to retain more earnings and pay higher dividends. What a perverse irony if corporate leadership uses a tax break to build new factories abroad while closing domestic plants! Lower rates should be applied only to companies that keep production and jobs in Japan and rely mainly on a stable workforce, regardless of whether the ownership is Japanese or foreign. The amount of income tax withheld from employees could be the basic criterion for selective corporate tax reduction.[24]

Many Japanese companies are part of global networks and contribute little to industry at home. Corporations that benefit industry and employment overseas should get tax benefits from those national and local governments.

The US states of Tennessee and Indiana offered tax concessions and other advantages to attract Japanese automakers.

A revenue-neutral reduction in corporate taxes can be crafted on the basis of a corporation's total value-added contribution to government finances such as the income, corporate, and consumption taxes that stem from production sites. Companies with factories in Japan that provide stable employment, pay good wages, have above-average productivity, and sell top-of-the-line products deserve preferential treatment. Those with a quick-fix mentality that rely on temporary employees and pay relatively low wages and no benefits should get tax relief commensurate with their contribution to the national economy. Konosuke Matsushita, the pioneer industrialist and founder of Panasonic, described a corporation's objective as "the progress and development of society and the well-being of people." The first principle of his management philosophy was a "contribution to society." Matsushita's paternal management style included lifetime employment and assurance against layoffs. Of course, the world has changed, yet his core principles are still valid, and special consideration for companies that benefit Japan is sound public policy.[25]

Some people may say, "These matters should be left up to the market." Not being protectionists, we basically agree. For the government, however, leaving price competition to the market and encouraging capability building by firms and industries are two very different things. The latter is not protectionism.

Empirical research in evolutionary economics shows that the market is more tolerant than the analogy with natural selection suggests and puts companies on probation for a long time. General Motors had a thirty-year grace period to rebuild itself; despite a falling market share, the automaker survived. The tax system should facilitate comeback efforts; otherwise myopic managers will indiscriminately pull up good plants with the weeds.

Factories and Global Warming

Plants in Japan and abroad can help counter global warming if they are integral to mitigation.[26] Reduction of CO_2 on a global scale will come from global collaboration by consumers, equipment designers, and producers of manufactured products such as fuel-efficient cars, advanced power stations, smart cities, and reusable containers. To ignore the worldwide matrix in which domestic factories are embedded and impose a uniform domestic emission standard will just blur the goals and deteriorate into a fruitless international political game where countries claim compliance but evade real action. A better approach would be to set multiple goals that include the domestic industry's contribution to lowering greenhouse gas emissions in other countries through the design and production of equipment and systems.

In March 2010 the Hatoyama cabinet submitted to the Diet a Basic Act on Global Warming Countermeasures that sets a reduction target for greenhouse emissions of 25 percent below the 1990 level by 2020. Reviewed after 3/11 and still under consideration, the bill calls for a single domestic accrual format that is unlikely to motivate enterprises and a Domestic Transmissions Trading Scheme that would just complicate matters. We suggest two concomitant categories of domestic production, as mentioned above—the export of equipment and of designs that reduce CO_2 emissions regardless of where the products are made.

Inclusion of technological contributions would be a game changer, giving managers an incentive to keep operations (jobs) in Japan and giving local communities a second lease on life. The design and manufacture of goods that ameliorate environmental degradation could easily become complex products with integral architecture that would give Japan a competitive advantage.

Confronted with difficult but straightforward goals, good Japanese factories have a "can do" attitude. Everyone rolls up their sleeves and pitches in. That is why we need, in addition to the 25 percent reduction goal, domestic standards that are meaningful at the working level. So what if other countries scoff that this is a self-serving ploy to promote exports? Self-interest is the norm in international negotiations. The objective is to involve Japanese factories in the campaign against global warming and ease the concerns of manufacturers. Superior manufacturing is wholly compatible with CO_2 reduction. In Japan's great factories improvements to shave costs go hand in hand with those to lower the consumption of materials and energy. That is the Toyota method, emblematic of Japanese manufacturing philosophy since World War II.

Pitting the interests of business and consumers against each other will not stimulate progress on global warming. If the pledge of a 25 percent reduction in greenhouse gases raises costs, some multinational corporations may escape overseas, and consumers cannot be expected to embrace an increase in the cost of living. Adding production sites to the mix would help balance the effort much as a third wheel stabilizes a tricycle. By remaining in Japan, manufacturers provide employment and a sense of purpose to workers/consumers. All have a mutual interest in a prosperous, stable society. Helping to reduce CO_2 emissions here can also increase competitiveness in factories in other countries by the transfer of know-how. Conversely, if desperate managers shut down operations in Japan, there will be an irreversible decline in living standards here and no abatement in global warming.

The UN cap-and-trade initiative is not the only answer. The Clean Development Mechanism combines domestic emission allocations to countries, industries, and companies (caps) with a reward point system for international contributions and bartering emission rights (trade). Although it is an economically ingenious mechanism born out of intensive bargaining, compliance with international agreements is never assured. More fundamentally, as advocates of solutions rooted in production sites, we think letting parties off when they fail to meet CO_2 emission targets is wrong in principle and sends a flawed message. Estimating emissions by the CO_2 coefficient for each type of fuel yields only a rough figure and makes it difficult to set emission targets for an individual company. Even with arbitrary caps on precise trades, as long as it is impossible to verify who has reduced CO_2 emissions, manufacturers will not act. On the other hand, contributing to the worldwide reduction of CO_2 emissions as a way to compensate for excessive domestic CO_2 emissions is easy to understand, and manufacturers can go along.

Other countries applauded the 25 percent reduction goal and are waiting to see what happens next. Japan can amend that policy and take the lead on this issue. As the proverb goes, "He that is first in his own cause seemeth just." Bargaining over dual-track targets might move each country a step further toward setting its own standard, which would be much better than a stalemate over a single index.

A one-size-fits-all reduction rate for the whole world is dubious. For countries to commit to an attainable numerical target they are comfortable with would be modest but meaningful progress. China and India could set reduction targets tied to their GDP. Partnerships are feasible: for instance, Japan could assist China, the world leader in emissions, with technology, and the reduction would count for both. If a highly efficient power plant designed and made in Japan was exported to China and CO_2 emissions there were reduced, both countries would earn credit. The activist slogan "Think globally, act locally" captures the value of a positive engagement by factories in environmental protection.

Blue-Collar Workers as Mentors

That senior production employees are a valuable asset is widely recognized in Japan. As Sawako Shirahase discusses in chapter 1 of this volume, a low birthrate is shrinking the workforce and eventually will lead to a labor shortage. Human resource development in manufacturing should tap the pool of retirees. In many factories in Japan, for instance, the value-adding time ratio to productive working hours is less than 10 percent. Taiichi Ohno, founder of the Toyota production system, stressed this ratio as a critical performance variable on the shop floor that few organizations properly measure. Manufacturing consultants recognize that an enormous amount of time is wasted that can never be recovered![27] Productivity could be increased threefold if the ratio was raised from 10 percent to 30 percent. At Fuji-Xerox's Kashiwazaki factory, Niigata Prefecture, for example, the productivity of the main assembly line was raised by roughly 2.8 times between 2010 and 2012. During that time the value-added time ratio increased threefold.

This kind of productivity does not require large capital investment or advanced production technologies. What is needed are mentors who can teach the manufacturing process, people who spent many years improving productivity and understand lead time, quality control, flexibility, and capability. These blue-collar savants—former group and section leaders and managers—worked in a particular factory and are unfamiliar with practices in other firms and industries, but they can learn how to create flows of good design information elsewhere. Japan needs schools all around the country where retirees who want to keep working can be trained as instructors.

In 2004 the Manufacturing Management Research Center at the University of Tokyo established a Manufacturing Instructors School (MIS), a pilot project to build capability at small and midsized companies all over Japan, including in nonmanufacturing industries. The media coined the term *2007 Problem* to describe the loss of thousands of skilled technicians when the Baby Boomer generation reached sixty and began to retire that year. The MIS concept was to train retired leaders and managers from blue-chip companies to transfer their experience and knowledge. Some large corporations retain retirees to teach their own younger technicians, which helps those firms but not the manufacturing sector as a whole. Having worked at the same company for thirty years, many retirees think their knowledge is not applicable elsewhere or that an artisan's skills cannot be explained to neophytes. They have to be trained how to impart their experience not only to other companies but across industries. MIS developed a curriculum, verification procedures, and partnerships with local governments. More than eighty MIS graduates are mentoring the next generation of blue-collar workers around Japan.

Industrial policy in Japan to spur innovation at the grassroots level has resulted in many small- and medium-sized enterprises with a specific technology that lack general manufacturing know-how. That is where a trained instructor comes in. Senior lathe operators and supervisors usually know far more than just their trade. They understand the value flow of production, the processes before and after their own, and how to connect specific technologies. Most importantly, they spent their careers in a work environment of productivity and quality improvement or *kaizen*.[28] These clusters of tacit knowledge imbue the spirit and methods at the heart of great manufacturing, the nexus that creates value added at the factory level.

In 2009 MIS began to partner with local authorities and universities to diffuse manufacturing know-how. Personnel come to MIS to learn the pedagogy of instruction; Gunma Prefecture and a city in Shiga Prefecture set up programs run by trained instructors, and the Engineering Department at Yamagata University started one in 2012. A tool and die company in Gunma Prefecture enrolled about one hundred employees in the course.

These programs could underpin a national policy for small and medium-sized enterprises that includes a regional industrial component. Regrettably, national spending for training in manufacturing has been deeply cut since 2010; less than ¥1 million is currently allocated. South Korea now spends much more on such training than Japan. In 2011 Seoul started to fund similar retraining of selected retirees as instructors in manufacturing know-how.[29]

Although there have been some signs in Japan that government funding may be restored, the policy has been inconsistent, and support tends to be short term and quantitative to promote investment and employment rather than qualitative to enhance manufacturing capability and productivity. The bureaucracy is affected by frequent changes of direction imposed by the administration in power and the ruling party. Japan needs long-range supply-side policies to promote manufacturing and human resource development at the regional level across industries. MIS graduates could help transfer productivity know-how from factories to farms and stores.

The decline of US manufacturing in the period 2000–2010 is a cautionary tale for Japan: 5.7 million jobs lost, two-thirds of the manufacturing sectors making less than a decade earlier, and an overall 11 percent drop in output. Many American economists and politicians were not alarmed, attributing the decline to "productivity-driven restructuring" and a supposed inevitable fall in factory jobs everywhere.[30] Others cited offshoring of production facilities, especially to China, currency manipulation, and China's targeting of US industry since 2001 when Beijing joined the World Trade Organization.[31] US (and Japanese) manufacturers must contend with these factors in the macroeconomic background.

Apple Corporation, an American icon, once made its products in the United States but now produces them overseas. Instead of "Made in the USA," they are labeled "Designed by Apple in California." Company executives pragmatically explain that favorable conditions prompted the decision to manufacture in China: flexible labor, abundant engineering resources, and rapid production adjustments.[32]

Broadly considered, however, Apple's corporate success is a loss for US manufacturing. "We are not able to capture the fruits of innovation," said Michael Porter, Harvard University. "Too much of the innovation activity generates manufacturing activity outside of the United States. Apple is a great example. Apple until recently [was] not going to make anything in the States despite the fact that they're a tremendous juggernaut of innovation."[33]

A theme of this chapter, the link between innovation and manufacturing, has played out in the United States over decades. It is not just jobs that are lost when products are made offshore. Peter Morici, University of Maryland, noted the cost of exporting innovation. "Years ago Kodak decided to specialize in film and send camera-making to the Far East. Then their labs developed the digital camera and they forgot how to make them in the sense they lost the ability to manufacture shutters, lenses. And they missed out on the revolution in cameras. Now Kodak is virtually out of business."[34]

Morici added that "the movement for manufacturing abroad has taken design and engineering abroad with it" and pointed to the cell phone industry. "Korea . . . is starting to get dominance in cell phones because first they start manufacturing. And then they develop the engineering that supports the manufacturing [and the] product development and before you know it you've lost your industry."[35] Manufacturing abroad spreads from one part to another, according to Morici, from hybrid cars to batteries and cells. "There is a reason those things don't happen in the United States," he said.

Some US manufacturing sectors may get a second chance. New hydraulic fracturing technology has opened up enormous natural gas reserves in North America at prices far cheaper than those in Europe or those of imported liquefied natural gas (LNG) in Japan. Japan, however, faces, not an energy windfall, but a shortfall: higher fossil fuel costs and electricity rates. Perhaps a technological kamikaze lies ahead for Japan, but trade statistics allow for no wishful thinking: a trade deficit in 2011, the first in three decades, was followed by a record trade gap in 2012 of ¥6.93 trillion ($78.2 billion).[36] The outlook for 2014 is still worse, with a $50 billion current account deficit for the half-year term as exports dropped from the previous year.[37]

A steady decline in manufacturing akin to the US experience through off-shoring and uncompetitive policies will blight Japan's future. The best manufacturing sites and industrial design facilities should be retained, not only because they provide jobs and meaningful lives at home, but because they make products that raise living standards and delight consumers around the world.

Notes

1. The authors wish to acknowledge the assistance of Maki Yoshida, Takuya Ozaki, and Jean-Francois Roof. Takahiro Fujimoto did the fieldwork for this chapter; his observations are stated in the first-person singular.

2. In popular usage a *genba* (現場) is where work takes place, a worksite, i.e., the space where people produce goods and services. In manufacturing management, the *genba* is an intraorganizational mechanism nearly at the bottom of the hierarchy. *Genba* have economic and social roles: they generate profit and provide stable employment, the cornerstone of a quality life.

3. The retail and agricultural sectors are beyond the scope of this chapter, but the philosophy and techniques of manufacturing are applicable. See Takahiro Fujimoto, *Monozukuri kara no fukkatsu* [Manufacturing and economic growth] (Tokyo: Nihon Keizai Shimbunsha, 2012), 371–400.

4. *Monozukuri* is the duplication of design data into material, or the art, science, and craft of making things.

5. Takahiro Fujimoto, *Monozukuri no genbahatsu no kokka senryakunin kansuru nōto* [A factory-based strategy for manufacturing] (Tokyo: Manufacturing Management Research Center, 2012), 353.

6. Casualty figures are from National Police Agency of Japan, "Damage Situation and Police Countermeasures Associated with 2011 Tohoku District—off the Pacific

Ocean Earthquake," August 29, 2012, https://www.npa.go.jp/archive/keibi/biki/
higaijokyo_e.pdf. Damage estimates are from the Cabinet Office, *Higashi Nihon
Daishinsai ni okeru higaigaku no suikei* [Estimated damages in the Great East Japan
Earthquake], June 24, 2011.

7. Fujimoto, *Monozukuri kara no fukkatsu*, 201–9. See also Tadahiko Abe, "A Suggestion for Japanese Industry after the Great Tohoku Earthquake," Fujitsu
Research Institute, November 2011, http://jp.fujitsu.com/group/fri/en/column/
message/2011/2011-11-17.html.

8. Dan Reynolds, "Lessons from Tohoku," *Wharton Magazine*, January 26, 2012,
http://whartonmagazine.com/issues/winter-2012/lessons-from-tohoku.

9. *The Global Competitiveness Report, 2012–2013* (Geneva: World Economic Forum,
2012), 12–13. Japan ranks tenth in competitiveness, and China is twenty-ninth.

10. According to Shisedo executive Yasuharu Kawazoe: "In Japanese we say 'omotenashi'
which means hospitality. This is how we differentiate ourselves on the retail level. For
example, when a customer purchases a product from our counter, then turns to leave,
our beauty consultants are instructed to go to the front of the counter and say goodbye.
The more memorable we make our counter experience . . . the greater the chances are of
our customers returning." *Japan Times*, March 26, 2007. In hopes of learning Japanese
work styles, in 1984 General Motors formed a joint venture with Toyota, the New United
Motor Manufacturing plant, in Fremont, California. Once dubbed "the worst workforce
in the automobile industry in the United States," American employees absorbed the ethic
of industrial teamwork and improved quality. "Episode 403 NUMMI," *This American
Life*, March 26, 2010, www.thisamericanlife.org/radio-archives/episode/403/nummi.

11. Ministry of Finance of Japan, Trade Statistics of Japan (accessed February 12, 2015).

12. Fujimoto, *Monozukuri kara no fukkatsu*, 34–40.

13. "Hollowing Out and the Japanese Economy," *Nihon Keizai Shimbun*, December 19,
2011.

14. "Yushutsu ni tayarazu tōshi de kasegu kōzō ni tenkan o" [Shift from exports to
manufacturing overseas], *Nihon Keizai Shimbun*, January 26, 2012.

15. Stephen Harner, "The Nikkei to Japan's Manufacturers: To Survive, Invest
Abroad," *Forbes*, January 29, 2012.

16. For typical coverage of hollowing out, see *Asahi Shimbun*, January 27 and March 20,
2012; *Sankei Shimbun*, January 25, 2012; and *Nikkei Shimbun*, June 7, 21, and 26 and
July 25, 2012.

17. "Looking Abroad," *Daily Yomiuri*, December 6, 2011. It was the highest ratio since
the survey started in 1989. Only one-quarter of manufacturers intended to expand
operations in Japan.

18. See Amano Tomofumi, *Higashi Ajia no kokusaibungyō to Nihon kigyō isshin tana seichō e no tenbō* [The international division of labor in East Asia and renewed growth for Japanese multinational corporations] (Tokyo: Yuikaku, 2005).

19. Takahiro Fujimoto and Yoshinori Shiozawa, "Inter and Intra Company Competition in the Age of Global Competition: A Micro and Macro Interpretation of Ricardian Trade Theory," *Evolutionary and Institutional Economics Review* 8, no. 2 (2012): 212–16, 223–29.

20. See Yamaguchi Takahide, *Takokuseki kigyō no soshiki nōryoku-Nihon no mazā kōjō shisutemu* [Japan's "mother factory" system and the organizational capability of multinational corporations] (Tokyo: Hakuto Shobo, 2006).

21. Fujimoto, *Monozukuri kara no fukkatsu*, 93–124; Takahiro Fujimoto, "Architecture-Based Comparative Advantage: A Design Information View of Manufacturing." *Evolutionary and Institutional Economics Review* 4, no. 1 (2007): 55–112.

22. Chi-Chi Zhang, "Apple Manufacturing Plant Workers Complain of Long Hours, Militant Culture," CNN, February 6, 2012, http://edition,cnn.com/2012/02/06/world/asia/china-apple-foxconn-worker/index.html; "1 Dead, over 90 Injured in Clashes at Maruti Suzuki's Manesar Plant; Stock Down 8.2%," *Economic Times*, July 19, 2012, http://articles.economictimes.india-times.com/2012-07-19/news/32730966_1_maruti-suzuki-s-manesar-manesar-plant-mswu; "Riot-Stricken Suzuki Plant to Reopen Soon," *Daily Yomiuri*, August 13, 2012; "DNA Maruti to Restore Full Production in Manesar in 15–30 Days," *Economic Times*, August 24, 2012, www.dnaindia.com/india/1732398/report-maruti-to-restore-full-production-in-manesar-in-15-30-days.

23. Fujimoto, *Monozukuri kara no fukkatsu*, 344–62. See also Scott A. Hodge, "What Is Japan's New Tax Rate?," Tax Foundation, March 30, 2012, http://taxfoundation.org/blog/what-japans-new-tax-rate; Grant Thornton, "Reduction in Corporation Tax Rates," *Japan Tax Bulletin*, January 2012, 1–2.

24. Fujimoto, *Monozukuri kara no fukkatsu*, 360–61.

25. Ibid., 361. See also Vadim Kotelnikov, "Konosuke Matsushita (1894–1989): Founder of Panasonic Corporation," 1000 Ventures, n.d., www.1000ventures.com.business_guides/cs_biz_leaders_matsushita.html (accessed January 24, 2013).

26. Fujimoto, *Monozukuri kara no fukkatsu*, 362–70. See also Ministry of Foreign Affairs, "Fact Sheet: G8 Action on Energy and Climate Change," May 19, 2012, http://mofa.go.jp/policy/economy/summit/2012/energy_climate.html. For a skeptical assessment, see Generation Green, "What Does 'Cap-and-Trade' Mean?," n.d., www.generationgreen.org.cap-and-trade.htm (accessed January 24, 2013). In 2013 the Abe administration retreated from a numerical target for cutting greenhouse emissions.

27. Bovino Consulting Group, "Employee Productivity . . . Stop the Non-Value Added Time/Activities," July 2009, www.bovino-consulting.com/articles/wp-content/uploads/2013/06/Issue-1303-1_Stop-Non-Value-Added-Time.pdf.

28. Takahiro Fujimoto, *The Evolution of a Manufacturing System* (New York: Oxford University Press, 1999). See sections on *kaizen* (continuous improvement).

29. Fujimoto, *Monozukuri kara no fukkatsu*, 445–57; and Takahiro Fujimoto and Tetsuo Yoshimoto, "Sharing Manufacturing Knowledge among Industries: A Challenge for the Instructor School at University of Tokyo," in *The Dynamics of Regional Innovation: Policy Challenges in Europe and Japan*, ed. Yveline Lecler, Tetsuo Yoshimoto, and Takahiro Fujimoto (Singapore: World Scientific Publishing, 2012), 393–418.

30. Robert D. Atkinson, Luke A. Stewart, Scott M. Andes, and Stephen J. Ezell, "Worse Than the Great Depression: What Experts Are Missing about American Manufacturing Decline," Executive Summary, report, Information Technology and Innovation Foundation, Washington, DC, March 2012, www2.itif.org/2012-american-manufacturing-decline-exec-sum.pdf, 1–5.

31. Michael Dolga, "Offshoring, Onshoring, and the Rebirth of American Manufacturing," special report, TD Economics, October 15, 2012, www.td.com/economics, 1–7; Loren Thompson, "Intelligence Community Fears U.S. Manufacturing Decline," *Forbes*, February 14, 2011, www.forbes.com/sites/beltway/2011/02/14/intelligence-community-fears-u-s-manufacturing-decline/. During the decade China reportedly targeted US "producers of steel, chemical, glass, paper, drugs and any number of other items with prices they cannot match. . . . The United States has lost an average of 50,000 manufacturing jobs *every* month during the same period."

32. Charles Duhigg and Keith Bradsher, "How the U.S. Lost Out on iPhone Work," *New York Times*, January 21, 2012, www.nytimes.com/2012/01/22/business/apple-america-and-a-squeezed-middle-class.html?pagewanted=all&_r=0.

33. Michael Porter, interview, *National Business Report*, January 21, 2013. Porter is co-leader of the Harvard Business School's US Competitiveness Project.

34. Peter Morici, interview, *National Business Report*, January 21, 2013. Morici teaches at the University of Maryland and was chief economist at the US International Trade Commission.

35. Ibid.

36. Kaori Kaneko and Tetsushi Kajimoto, "Japan Logs Record Trade Gap in 2012 as Exports Struggle," Reuters, January 23, 2013, www.nbr.com/news/story/id=tag%3Areuters.com%2C0000%3Anewsml_BRE90No16.

37. Eleanor Warnock, "Japan's Current Account Falls into Deficit," *Wall Street Journal*, August 7, 2014.

CHAPTER NINE

Integrated Solutions to Complex Problems: Transforming Japanese Science and Technology

Masaru Yarime

Japan's isolation from the outside world ended in the mid-nineteenth century, and the Meiji Restoration brought to power a modernizing elite that introduced Western science and technology to serve national goals.[1] The new government invested domestic resources to transform the country and created a military-industrial complex that brought victory in the Russo-Japanese War and challenged the Allied Powers in World War II. Defeat in 1945 ended support of research and development for military purposes, and economic growth became the national priority. The oil supply crises in the 1970s induced a shift from an industrial structure based on heavy industries to one that emphasized resource-efficient sectors. Many government-led projects developed energy- and resource-saving technologies such as photovoltaic cells that could be commercialized by private firms.

When the real estate and stock market bubble collapsed in the early 1990s and globalization accelerated, the national objective became achieving economic recovery by strengthening industrial competitiveness. The government created a Basic Science and Technology Plan and implemented policy and regulatory changes to promote university-industry collaboration. Today Japan faces serious societal challenges such as climate change, an aging population, and natural disasters. The Great East Japan Earthquake in March 2011 shook public trust in scientists and engineers, reminding the nation that scientific knowledge must address urgent problems but has its limits.

After a brief overview of science and technology from the Meiji Restoration to the years of recovery from World War II, I will look at three periods:

the 1970s–1980s, the 1990s–2000s, and the time since the Tōhoku disaster. Finally, I will consider possible futures for Japanese science and technology in an increasingly globalizing and uncertain world and will argue that intellectual exchange and collaboration across disciplinary and geographical boundaries to produce knowledge and human resources will be a crucial challenge for Japan.

Modernization, War, and Recovery

Science and technology were critical components of Japan's modernization, symbolized by the slogan "Fukoku Kyōhei" (Rich nation, strong army), as the government sought to create new industries and a powerful military force. Those twin objectives required a sound scientific and technological base with well-developed human, financial, and institutional resources.[2] The government imported superior technology, hired engineers from abroad, encouraged entrepreneurs to assimilate foreign technologies for the new factories, and created an educational system to train the populace.[3] Science and technology policy functioned effectively, helping to establish a human as well as a physical capital base for a modern nation. Newly created heavy industries such as steel, machinery, and chemicals grew at an annual rate of more than 10 percent in the first four decades of the twentieth century.[4]

Adding to government efforts, the private sector took entrepreneurial initiatives in acquiring technology and investing in unfamiliar and uncertain sectors like heavy industry, which still lagged far behind the West. Japan inherited absorptive capacities from indigenous technologies and fostered cumulative capacity at the firm level.[5] Scientific and technological knowledge was transferred to Japan through various channels. Private firms hired experts to get the latest know-how, and many Japanese studied in Western universities and research institutes. Knowledge was also obtained by reverse engineering of imported machinery and equipment. Technology spilled over from direct investment by foreign companies to domestic suppliers and employees in subsidiaries. Japanese manufacturers started to build world-class production facilities and develop advanced products, notably in such industries as steel, shipbuilding, and chemicals.[6] However, these industries were to a significant extent dependent on Western technologies even in the late 1930s; the outbreak of World War II stopped the inflow of critical scientific knowledge, which contributed to Japan's defeat.

Although science and technology policy largely succeeded in establishing a basic industrial infrastructure, it did not lead to military victory. After defeat in 1945 and demilitarization steps by the Allied Occupation that dismantled the military-industrial complex, successive Japanese governments focused first on swift recovery from wartime destruction and then on pursuit of economic development. This postwar shift transferred R&D resources previously devoted to the military to the development of civilian technologies. The government directed the flow of advanced technology by allocating scarce foreign currency to fields of strategic importance. Imports and direct investment were restricted, prompting foreign companies to sell their technologies to Japanese firms rather than to try to penetrate the Japanese market or start production in Japan. The technological and human infrastructure established before the war absorbed, assimilated, and improved the technologies introduced from abroad.

Japanese firms conducted R&D activities and entered the international market as serious competitors. Indigenous innovation became increasingly important; R&D expenditures by the private sector more than tripled in the latter half of the 1960s.[7] Government support, on the other hand, remained modest and decreased significantly in the 1960s. Financial incentives provided through tax breaks, subsidies, and low-interest loans accounted for less than 3 percent of industrial R&D expenditures at the time, much smaller than the proportion in the United States and other industrialized countries.

Oil Crises and Industrial Transformation

The oil supply crises in the 1970s prompted the government and industry to accelerate scientific research to conserve energy and create new energy sources. The manufacturing sector made remarkable improvements in resource and energy efficiency in production processes. Total energy consumption per unit of gross domestic product (GDP) declined by almost 20 percent from 1970 to the end of the 1980s.[8] A high level of investment in R&D as well as in plants and equipment was maintained throughout those decades. In the period from 1973 to 1987, R&D expenditures rose more than four times, which corresponded to an increase in their proportion of the gross national product (GNP) from 2.0 to 2.8 percent.[9] The two oil crises, coupled with the sharp appreciation of the yen in the 1970s and 1980s, induced a transition in Japan's industrial structure from a relatively strong reliance on energy- and resource-intensive heavy industries to reliance on high-value-added, knowledge-intensive fields.

Science and technology policy gradually shifted from promoting technological capacity in well-established sectors to encouraging basic research that was expected to create radically new innovations in emerging fields such as electrical and communication equipment and the electronics industry. Enactment in 1961 of the Law on Mining and Manufacturing Industry Technology Research Associations is often credited with encouraging technological development through close collaboration between the public and private sectors.[10] From the 1960s to the 1980s, ninety-four research associations were established to solve specific technological problems, and they received substantial funding from the government.[11] In 1983, for example, the associations received more than half of all R&D subsidies.[12]

Government-initiated R&D projects also addressed long-term energy security. The Sunshine Project (1974) developed alternative energy technologies, with a particular focus on photovoltaic technologies, and the Moonlight Project (1978) encouraged energy-saving technologies. These programs funded renewable energy and energy efficiency R&D for more than twenty years, and at least 120 private firms participated. The programs were managed by the New Energy and Industrial Technology Development Organization, a subsidiary organization of the Ministry of Economy, Trade and Industry (formerly the Ministry of International Trade and Industry [MITI]). National research institutions and universities also joined in. Most of the funding went to renewable energy technologies, especially solar cells, and to alternative fuels such as coal liquefaction.[13] These programs focused on improving energy efficiency on the supply side through technology without behavioral change on the demand side.[14]

Public R&D programs made a significant contribution to technological development, particularly in the field of energy saving. In the case of research associations such as the Very Large Scale Integration Association, complementarity of resources from different companies was very important, and the establishment of a temporary research institute with personnel sent from the private sector was an effective way to deal with the limited mobility of researchers in the Japanese labor market.[15] Most importantly, these projects fostered the spillover of created knowledge. On the other hand, public R&D investments have a high risk of failure, and significant lead time is required before new technologies are brought to the market. In addition to long-term government R&D support, a marketing strategy to respond to and influence market demand and a deployment policy are essential. Public R&D programs often functioned as a way for MITI to distribute subsidies to private companies that were developing the technologies it considered important. By supporting research associations, the government was able to avoid favoring specific firms in an industry at a minimum cost for oversight of the subsidies.[16]

Science and Technology in Knowledge-Based Economies

The 1980s saw the emergence of industries that critically depend on advanced research, notably biotechnology and information and communication technology. Since then, the emphasis has increasingly been placed on discoveries that enhance economic growth and international competitiveness.[17] Rapid knowledge creation and easy access to sources came to be regarded as the key components of innovation.[18] Collaboration across organizational boundaries has become commonplace. In rapidly developing fields where sources of knowledge are widely distributed, no single organization can monitor breakthroughs and produce significant innovation. Many recent studies suggest that interorganizational networks play a crucial role in influencing the direction of technological development.[19] The new paradigm of science and technology encourages cooperation by governments, universities, and industry to stimulate economic growth through innovation.

The United States was the first to move in this direction by establishing explicit institutional conditions to strengthen the economy by strategic utilization of science and technology.[20] A major milestone was the passage of the Bayh-Dole Act (1980), which allowed universities to apply for patents based on the results of scientific research activities funded by the federal government.[21] Similar legislation was enacted in other industrialized countries as well. Japan adopted in the 1990s a series of public policies aimed at facilitating innovation, including the Science and Technology Basic Law (1995) and the First Science and Technology Basic Plan (1996). The Plan was a comprehensive and systematic design to promote science and technology over the next five years. University-industry collaboration was considered an effective way to do this, and the Law for Promoting Technology Transfer from Universities (1998) established the legal framework. Institutional reforms were subsequently implemented in many areas of science and technology.

Having mostly caught up with other industrialized countries in science and technology by the 1980s, Japan intensified R&D to spur innovation.

Total R&D expenditures measured as a percentage of GDP increased from a little more than 2 percent at the beginning of the 1980s to 3 percent in the late 2000s and have remained at the highest level among the major industrialized countries. A characteristic of Japanese science and technology is that the government provides a relatively small amount of financial assistance for R&D activities. The ratio has been at its lowest since the beginning of the 1980s, fluctuating between 20 and 30 percent (figure 9.1). On the other hand, while the ratio for most of the other countries has been declining, Japan's has been relatively stable. The business sector accounts for approximately 70 percent of total R&D spending in Japan, although the figure dipped in the most recent year for which data are available.

Government-funded R&D by sector breaks down into universities, business enterprises, public institutes, and nonprofit organizations. Since the 1980s, the picture has changed very little: the academic sector receives almost half of government funding, the public sector approximately 40 percent, and the rest goes to the private and nonprofit sectors. Industry in Japan receives a very small percentage in comparison with other countries, in many of which the private sector accounts for 20 to 30 percent of official outlays. That is partly because Japan conducts little R&D on military and space technologies, which tend to be developed by the public sector in other countries, especially the United States.

Financial and Human Resources for R&D

In Japan corporations generally use their own money for research. The ratio of R&D expenditure to GDP in the private sector has increased since the 1980s, reaching approximately 2.5 percent in 2008, just before a sharp decline in the following year.[22] The manufacturing sector accounts for approximately 90 percent of industrial R&D; no major changes were observed in R&D expenditures in nonmanufacturing industries. Within manufacturing, R&D expenditures were particularly high in the transportation machinery sector and the information/communication electronics equipment sector. Intense R&D activities are considered a major reason why Japanese companies, notably those in the automotive industry, are competitive in the international market.

R&D expenditures are classified into basic research, applied research, and development. Since the 1990s approximately 15 percent of all R&D

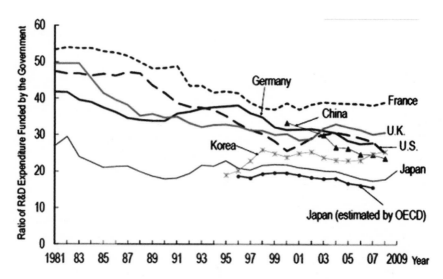

FIGURE 9.1   Ratio of R&D expenditure funded by government. (National Institute of Science and Technology Policy, *Japanese Science and Technology Indicators 2011* [Tokyo: Ministry of Education, Culture, Sports, Science and Technology, 2012], 23.)

expenditure in Japan has been for basic research, which is similar to the ratio in the United States.[23] Among major countries, the share of basic research is smallest in China (less than 5 percent), where development accounts for nearly 80 percent. By contrast, in France basic research accounts for almost 25 percent of total R&D expenditures. In the 1970s and 1980s Japan was often criticized, particularly in the United States, for "free-riding" on basic research in other countries. The empirical data suggest that at least since the 1990s Japan has devoted a comparable proportion of R&D to produce new scientific knowledge without direct commercial application.

Human resources are a key component of the science and technology system. The number of researchers in Japan has grown from approximately four hundred thousand in the early 1980s to six hundred thousand in 2010 and has steadily increased on a per capita basis (figure 9.2). The ratio has been higher than that of the United States and approximately twice as high as that of European countries. Approximately three-fourths of the researchers in Japan work in the private sector, the highest ratio among industrialized countries. The percentage of female researchers in Japan remains the lowest among major Organisation for Economic Cooperation and Development (OECD) members, although it has risen from 8 percent in 1992 to about 14

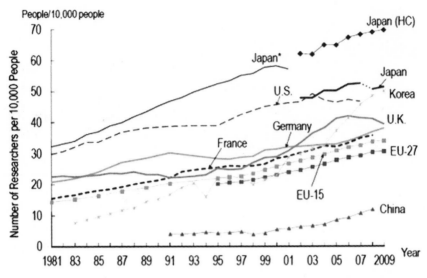

FIGURE 9.2   Number of researchers per capita. (National Institute of Science and Technology Policy, *Japanese Science and Technology Indicators 2011* [Tokyo: Ministry of Education, Culture, Sports, Science and Technology, 2012], 64.)

percent in 2010. These data suggest that Japan has successfully maintained rich human resources, especially in industry, but still needs to increase the number of female scientists and engineers because of the aging and shrinking labor force.

The declining trend in positions available for young researchers in Japan's universities will have a serious impact in the years ahead. Although the tenured and contract faculty at national universities has grown over the past thirty years from around 50,000 to 63,000, the number of faculty members under age thirty-five has dropped from more than 10,000 to 6,800.[24] The problem is partly demographic: people born during the Baby Boom after the World War II now occupy the senior positions at universities, which reduces the opportunities for younger researchers. While this is true in other countries as well, changes in government policy over the past two decades have made the situation in Japan much more severe.[25] During the 1990s, the government encouraged universities to expand their graduate schools, which hired more faculty and staff and churned out more PhDs. By 2001, however, the government had begun to force national universities to trim the number of full-time staff every year, and far fewer young researchers were employed.

Another challenge is the low international mobility of researchers in Japan and the low level of collaboration with counterparts abroad. A cross-country survey of research scientists in sixteen countries, while finding considerable variation in immigration and emigration patterns, showed that few foreign scientists study or work in Japan: their proportion is an extremely low 5 percent.[26] Japan also has the lowest percentage of emigrants at 3.1 percent; very few Japanese scientists seek employment abroad. The rate of return of scientists with international experience to their home country is the highest in Japan, at 92 percent. In short, foreign scientists are extremely rare in Japan, few Japanese researchers take positions abroad, and those who do are likely to return to Japan. This pattern stunts intellectual cross-fertilization and deprives Japanese scientists of rich international collaboration.

By contrast, universities and research institutes across the globe compete fiercely to attract the best scientists and engineers. Countries like Canada and Australia have migration policies designed to attract overseas talent. In the United States, for example, an immigration plan is under consideration that would award green cards to a huge pool of US-educated graduate students and PhDs in science and engineering. The very limited extent of international exchange and collaboration in Japan is a severe handicap in the global race for talent in science and technology. Scientists migrate in search of career opportunities and outstanding colleagues or research teams. The fact that only a small number of foreign scientists are attracted to work or study in Japan indicates that the country does not provide promising career opportunities for outstanding young researchers, or that excellent faculty and research teams are not easily accessible to outsiders, or that language, cultural, or other circumstances discourage foreigners from staying in Japan.

The Entrepreneurial University for Innovation

Many Japanese universities in the 1980s suffered from obsolete equipment, poor funding, and the loss of talented researchers to private companies. In 1990, while 27 percent of researchers were at universities, they spent only 12 percent of the nation's R&D expenditures, down from 18 percent in 1970. As a consequence, R&D expenditure per university researcher was nearly unchanged between 1970 and 1990, despite the increase in the ratio of national R&D expenditure to GDP from 1.59 to 2.77, an almost twofold increase in real GDP.[27] Over the same period the proportion of R&D spending by corporations increased from 69 percent to 77 percent. Major corporations had good research facilities such as state-of-the-art equipment for computing and experimentation, whereas many university researchers were struggling with outdated equipment in cramped quarters. In a survey conducted by the Science and Technology Agency in 1991, slightly more than half of university researchers said their research facilities were inferior to those in Europe and North America, while only 23 percent of researchers in companies echoed that complaint.

The relatively poor conditions in Japanese universities drove some desperate researchers to seek corporate resources to compensate for the shortage of government support. The inflow of research funds from the private sector to universities, in the form of joint research, research subcontracts, or grants, increased by more than five times during the 1980s. By the beginning of the 1990s the private sector was providing national universities with almost as much funding as the Grants-in-Aid for Scientific Research provided by the Ministry of Education (equivalent to the grants made by the US National Science Foundation). The inadequate physical, human, and financial resources available to universities raised doubts about their ability to generate scientific and technological knowledge for innovation in Japan.

The bursting of the bubble economy in the early 1990s coincided with growing concern that Japanese industry was threatened by the emerging economies. How could industrial competitiveness and innovation be reinvigorated? As noted above, the solution adopted was to promote the transfer of science and technology from academia to industry. The traditional role of universities—to produce and disseminate knowledge—changed; they were now expected to provide expertise to help achieve economic goals. The industrialization of scientific and technological knowledge in the service of the economy has resulted in a second academic revolution in which an "entrepreneurial university" contributes to an innovation-driven economic growth strategy.[28] The university is now supposed to transfer its scientific and technological knowledge through patents and licenses and to explore the commercial and economic development of academic inventions via spin-off firms or new ventures.

The government, with subsidies and other policy measures, encouraged universities to establish technology-licensing offices (TLOs) to help faculty members apply for and license patents, as well as to help corporations identify university research to be licensed and faculty members to tap for joint research. The Industrial Revitalization Law (1999) was dubbed the "Japanese Bayh-Dole Act" because it allowed university researchers to acquire patents for inventions based on government funding. As in the United States, the number of university patent applications increased in Japan, rising to 3,756 by 2004. Approximately one-third of the applications were in the fields of life sciences and biotechnology.[29] These institutional reforms in the 1990s also boosted joint research between national universities and private firms from 1,139 projects in 1990 to approximately 4,000 in 2000 and to more than 12,000 in 2008.[30] The number of new start-up companies based on university-invented technologies rose from 11 in 1995 to 135 in 2002, and 1,689 start-up firms were in operation in 2010. While nearly fifty TLOs have been established, few cases of licensing have been reported, which would suggest that most TLOs are not as profitable as was anticipated when these institutional reforms were implemented. In fact, the university share of R&D expenditures was a little more than 10 percent in 2010, while the ratio of researchers working in academia had declined to the lowest among the industrialized countries.

What have these policy initiatives and investment in human and financial resources produced? We can measure various types of output, such as scientific articles in academic journals, patents on inventions and technologies, and commercialized products and processes. According to a bibliometric analysis of scientific research in Japan, while the number of publications has been increasing since 1980, the growth rate in scientific papers in recent years is the lowest among the G7 countries.[31] Consequently, the global share of scientific papers produced by researchers in Japan has been declining. As the number of papers originating in the business sector fell, the role of universities expanded in the domestic structure of knowledge production, yet the number of papers from national universities has been flat recently. This relatively stagnant performance is at least partly attributable to the drop in positions for young researchers.

Compared with the number of scientific papers published in academic journals, research from Japan is relatively low in the international ranking of citation frequency. While the proportion of internationally coauthored papers has been rising significantly worldwide, there has been only a modest increase in such papers that include researchers in Japan.[32] Articles involving international collaboration tend to be read more widely in scientific communities and to be cited more frequently in academic journals than those written only by domestic authors. The implication for Japanese science is that research findings in Japan will have lower visibility, with negative consequences for its reputation and credibility at the global level.

Patents are also an important indicator of innovation. The total number of applications to the Japanese Patent Office continued to increase until the end of the 1990s and was the highest in the world until the mid-2000s (figure 9.3). Recently, however, the number of patent applications submitted in Japan has been decreasing and was overtaken by the number submitted in the United States in 2009. Applications by residents in Japan currently make up more than 85 percent of applications to the Japanese Patent Office, in contrast to applications to the US Patent and Trademark Office, half of which are from other countries. As the emerging economies rapidly developed, the relative position of the Japanese market declined globally, perhaps discouraging overseas applications for Japanese patents. Since the US market is the largest in the world, foreign individuals and organizations apply for patents there. Three Japanese companies—Panasonic, Sharp, and Toyota—were among the top ten in international patent applications in 2012.

Japan is relatively strong in the fields of nanotechnology, information and communication technology, and renewable energy. An analysis of patents granted by the US Patent and Trademark Office and applications to the European Patent Office shows that Japan maintains approximately a 20 percent share in these fields globally.[33] Japan's performance is particularly impressive in the area of technologies for climate change mitigation, producing 37 percent of the world's inventions. Japan ranks first in all fields except marine energy and accounts for more than 50 percent of the world's inventions in electric and hybrid energy, waste disposal, and lighting. Government investment in energy R&D since the 1970s helped establish Japan's strength in this field. The data on public R&D for low-carbon technologies in 2004, for example, shows that Japan spent US$220 million, almost twice the amounts for the United States ($70 million) and the EU15 (US$50 million) combined. On the other hand, Japanese patents in biotechnology have just a 10 percent share, suggesting that the biotechnology sector is relatively weak, especially compared with that in the United States.

Technology trade is a useful measure of technological competitiveness. Japan's technology trade balance, expressed as the ratio of exports to imports, was below 1 until the early 1990s. Since 1993 the balance has been in surplus and reached almost 4 at the end of the 2000s, although the scale is only a fifth that of the United States, which is still the largest technology exporter.[34]

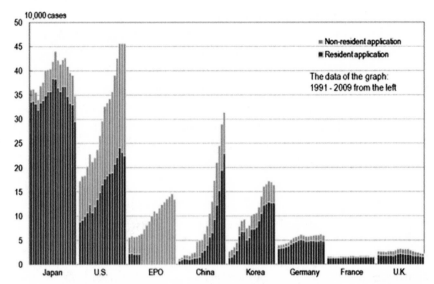

FIGURE 9.3   Number of patent applications (1991–2009). (National Institute of Science and Technology Policy, *Japanese Science and Technology Indicators 2011*, [Tokyo: Ministry of Education, Culture, Sports, Science and Technology, 2012], 135.)

The US technology trade balance has been gradually decreasing and has been below that of Japan since 2001.

Trade figures for high-tech industries are a strong indicator of scientific and technical knowledge applied to the development of commercial products. Japan has maintained a large surplus in radio, television, and communication equipment and medical, precision, and optical instruments, whereas the air-craft, spacecraft, and pharmaceutical sectors have consistently shown import surpluses. Although Japan's high-tech trade balance has never fallen below 1, it was surpassed by South Korea's in 2003 and by China's in 2009. Japanese industry is under pressure to innovate in ways competitors cannot easily match (see chapter 8 of this volume for further discussion of the implications of innovation on the future of manufacturing in Japan).

Recovering Public Trust in Science and Technology

Science and technology have been held in high esteem in Japan for their enormous contribution to the country's modernization and economic growth in the postwar period, and the public has lauded researchers for remarkable achievements in basic science and technology. Among the sixteen Japanese Nobel laureates in physics, chemistry, or medicine to date, nine have been awarded the prizes since 2000. The latest case is the creation of induced pluripotent stem (iPS) cells from mice in 2006 by Professor Shinya Yamanaka, Kyoto University, who was awarded the Nobel Prize in Physiology or Medicine in 2012, just six years after the first breakthrough. Fujitsu Limited and Riken, Japan's largest public research institution, together developed the K computer, which was ranked in 2011 as the world's fastest supercomputer until it was overtaken by IBM's Sequoia in 2012. Long a leader in high-speed bullet train transportation, Japan is developing next-generation magnetic levitation trains, is engaged in talks with the United States on cyber security and the Internet, and may host the Linear Collider Collaboration project.

Faith in science and technology, however, was shaken by the Great East Japan Earthquake, tsunami, and nuclear accident in March 2011. The series of disasters undermined the public's simple, optimistic view that highly trained experts can ensure proper decision making. It gradually became clear that scientists did not have sufficient knowledge about the fundamental mechanisms of ocean trench earthquakes and had not foreseen the possibility of such a megaearthquake in that region.[35] Underestimating the height of the tsunami, engineers produced a hazard map that turned out to be fatally inadequate on actual inundation. Furthermore, risk-communication measures failed to prepare citizens for what became a major disaster.[36] It is now evident that scientists reacted slowly and inconsistently after the Fukushima nuclear reactors melted down. The long list of failures includes missteps in establishing and adjusting evacuation zones, monitoring radiation and assessing the effects of radiation on human health, decontaminating the environment and food supply, communicating risk, and carrying out the difficult process of decommissioning reactors. Scientists differed over methodologies, procedures, and the measures to be taken, adding to the delay and confusion in policy circles.

Not surprisingly, public trust in science and engineering dropped. According to a survey conducted in December 2011, nine months after the earthquake, only 45 percent of respondents thought scientific experts should direct science and technology policy, compared to 79 percent in a similar survey in 2009.[37] A survey in April 2011 found that only 40.6 percent of respondents trusted statements by scientists, down from 84.5 percent in November 2010, although the number recovered to 65 percent in early 2012.[38] The involvement of scientists in policy making must be more open and transparent to the general public.[39] There was no system to enable competent scientists to advise political leaders in emergencies like a nuclear meltdown.[40] While science must be independent and objective, uncertainty and diverse views must be taken into account in policy making.

Regaining public trust is crucial for scientists and engineers in a much broader context. Scientific disciplines have traditionally been developed through institutionalization: establishing educational and research programs, forming academic societies and associations, and disseminating discoveries through textbooks and journals. The enormous advances in science have led to narrow specialization and fragmentation of knowledge. Many societal issues have become complex and global, with an appreciable degree of uncertainty and ambiguity. A survey of scientists and engineers in September 2011 (figure 9.4) found that fewer than 40 percent thought that R&D activities were contributing to solutions for social problems.[41] Much of the public shares that skepticism.

Under these circumstances, it was critically important to demonstrate the relevance of science to the general public. The Fourth Basic Plan (August 2011) scripted a national strategy for the next five years that includes sustainable growth and reconstruction from the Tōhoku disaster, a high quality of life for citizens, and leadership in the resolution of such global problems as large-scale natural disasters.[42] According to the plan, these objectives will be pursued through integrating science, technology, and innovation policies and giving a higher priority to human resources and their supporting organizations.

The traditional way to support science and technology—primarily through intensive R&D activities in universities and corporations—is not necessarily effective or appropriate for encouraging socio-technical innovation on pressing societal issues.[43] These issues include aging and population decline, as described by Sawako Shirahase in chapter 1 of this volume; a loss of economic vitality; a downward trend in industrial competitiveness; increasing competition for natural resources, energy, and food; and global issues such as climate change. To harness scientific and technological knowledge to the goal of building a sustainable society requires a different model that engages academia and industry with a variety of stakeholders. The new template is expected to stimulate social innovation and entrepreneurship and to encourage multistakeholder collaboration to address complex, interrelated problems.

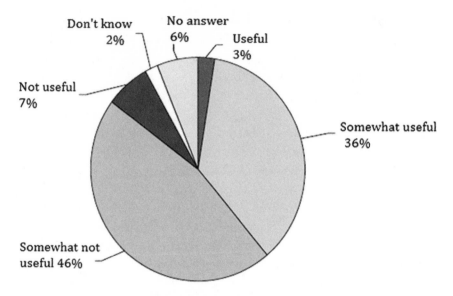

FIGURE 9.4 Are the outcomes of research and development useful to solve social problems? (National Institute of Science and Technology Policy, "Higashi Nihon daishinsai ni taisuru kagaku gijutsu senmonka e no anketo chōsa (dai 2-kai) Heisei 23-nen 9-gatsu jisshi" [Second survey on the Great East Japan Earthquake by science and technology experts, conducted in September 2011].)

Collaboration on societal issues such as environmental protection is already widespread. For example, the membrane ion exchange process replaced the mercury process for chlor-alkali production in the chemical industry, and lead-free solder was developed to eliminate the use of harmful material in electronic products.[44] Dense collaborative networks involving universities, public research institutes, and private firms were created that have influenced the direction and speed of scientific investigation and technological development.[45] In these cases, however, the R&D collaboration mainly centered on solving technical questions, not on addressing broad societal issues by engaging with multiple stakeholders.

Institutional conditions can impede or promote innovation when complex, interdependent societal issues must integrate diverse types of knowledge.[46] Many barriers—technical, economic, legal, and institutional—hinder effective integration.[47] Researchers in Japan and elsewhere are increasingly under pressure to publish scientific articles in academic journals in their own specialties, which is generally considered the path to tenure and promotion in academia. There is little incentive for scientists to collaborate with scholars in different fields and disciplines where activities are difficult to evaluate by conventional criteria. As a bibliometric analysis of the patterns of research collaboration on sustainability suggests, the creation, transmission, and sharing of academic knowledge tend to be confined to disciplinary and geographical proximities.[48] Industry-based researchers, on the other hand, basically pursue commercial objectives, which makes it difficult for them to lead in the development of these collaborative networks. In this era of new research, assembling the appropriate expertise for cross-cutting, interrelated societal issues will require that academic concepts, methodologies, and standards be clearly defined and robustly established. Inter- and transdisciplinary scientific approaches, coupled with institutional reforms in evaluation, promotion, and career paths, will be the key.[49]

Toward a New Paradigm of Science and Technology

Consider the case of electric vehicles. Their diffusion in Japan depends on major innovations in the electric grid to improve its control and management. Energy production, transmission, storage, and use must be improved. Smart batteries equipped to upload as well as download electricity can store energy, which is particularly important to absorb variations in power provided by renewables such as wind and solar. The relevant actors include utilities, manufacturers of electrical and electronic equipment, home building firms, and construction companies, many of which have never collaborated with automakers and whose interests and incentives may not be compatible. The large-scale deployment of electric vehicles hinges upon integrating the expertise of these stakeholders. In addition, regulations and standards must be coordinated for vehicle safety, road transportation, and a charging infrastructure.

In a search for an alternative model of innovation and cross-sector collaboration, leading universities in Japan have started to engage with business and local communities to design and implement social experimentation. These initiatives are funded by government agencies such as the Japan Science and Technology Agency and the Energy and Industrial Technology Development Organization. Multistakeholder platforms have been established to jointly design and implement demonstrations and pilot projects to create novel scientific and technological knowledge.[50] The vital parties include universities, private enterprises, local authorities, the national government, think tanks, nonprofit organizations, and citizens' groups. For instance, the main objective of one project is to draw up a blueprint for a low-carbon community that is friendly to elderly citizens and to demonstrate its feasibility via a comprehensive series of social experiments. Basic as well as applied research is conducted on such areas as housing, transportation, urban planning, and information systems. Technical development of solar heating, air conditioning, and compact electric vehicles is simultaneously explored with the establishment of policy and regulatory measures.

The integrated model of innovation through stakeholder collaboration will have valuable ramifications for science and technology in the future. Students and researchers from different academic backgrounds will participate in social experiments and learn inter- and transdisciplinary approaches to interwoven problems. They will also learn how to communicate with people and organizations that do not necessarily understand or share academic terminology and scientific curiosity, a function that can be extended to all stakeholders who will be able to monitor and appropriate results through open seminars, conferences, and publications. Still in an early stage, this model is encountering resistance, especially in institutional environments, which change only slowly compared with the rapid pace of scientific and technological progress. Nonetheless, this is a meaningful attempt to integrate scientific research and societal innovation through collaboration with stakeholders.

Looking back, Japan caught up with the West by initially importing scientific knowledge, adapting it to local circumstances, learning from trial and error, and then innovating better technologies. While government performed the crucial functions of navigation and support in the past, the private sector now has the human and financial resources to conduct R&D and innovate in many industries. With the rise of the emerging economies and intensifying global competition, however, Japan is hard pressed not to lose ground in industrial competitiveness, particularly in strategic sectors such as electronics. Some industries are hurting, drained of home-based manufacturing technologies because of the transfer overseas of production facilities and R&D activities. Globalization has increased competition for energy and natural resources and at the same time has exacerbated hazards such as climate change. Internally, the country's aging population and declining birthrate could result in a loss of social and economic vitality. Japan needs robust science and technology that spurs innovation.

The case of regenerative medicine illustrates the importance of institutional drivers in overcoming impediments to innovation. Although the creation of iPS cells prompted the government to provide substantial financial and organizational support for R&D, the poor alignment of institutional settings, public policies, and private initiatives undermined this promising field. Current guidelines and regulations for clinical trials in Japan are inadequate to examine the safety and risks of regenerative medicine applications. Moreover, the health insurance system does not encourage market formation. Disappointing outcomes have made private investors increasingly skeptical. Inappropriate regulations have delayed clinical applications, which have been few compared to other industrialized countries: only one commercialized product is on the market in Japan today. The institutional framework of basic and clinical research must be substantially reformed to expedite commercialization. Needless to say, ethical considerations have to be part of the dialogue.

Looking ahead, with its scientific prowess and technological capabilities Japan can be at the forefront of global efforts to cope with pressing societal problems. That will prompt Japanese academia to assimilate more junior people, more women, and more foreign researchers and will prompt Japanese industry to explore business opportunities in emerging markets in the promising fields of energy, environment, and health. The new paradigm will demand effective integration of necessary knowledge, going beyond the conventional boundaries. Public engagement of a diverse array of stakeholders in the coevolution of technology and institutions will be the key and a possible future for Japanese science.

Notes

1. I would like to thank the participants in the workshop on this book project for their comments on my presentation and Frank Baldwin for his very helpful comments and suggestions on this chapter. Any mistakes that remain are entirely my own.

2. Richard J. Samuels, *"Rich Nation, Strong Army": National Security and the Technological Transformation of Japan* (Ithaca, NY: Cornell University Press, 1994); Morris Low, Shigeru Nakayama, and Hitoshi Yoshioka, *Science, Technology and Society in Contemporary Japan* (Cambridge: Cambridge University Press, 1999); Tessa Morris-Suzuki, *The Technological Transformation of Japan: From the Seventeenth to the Twenty-First Century* (Cambridge: Cambridge University Press, 1994).

3. Hiroyuki Odagiri and Akira Goto, *Technology and Industrial Development in Japan: Building Capabilities by Learning, Innovation, and Public Policy* (Oxford: Clarendon Press, 1996).

4. Hiroyuki Odagiri and Akira Goto, "The Japanese System of Innovation: Past, Present, and Future," in *National Innovation Systems: A Comparative Analysis*, ed. Richard R. Nelson (New York: Oxford University Press, 1993), 81.

5. Wesley M. Cohen and Daniel A. Levinthal, "Absorptive Capacity: A New Perspective on Learning and Innovation," *Administrative Science Quarterly* 35, no. 1 (1990): 128–52.

6. Odagiri and Goto, "Japanese System of Innovation," 85.

7. Ibid., 87.

8. John M. Polimeni, Kozo Mayumi, Mario Giampietro, and Blake Alcott, *The Jevons Paradox and the Myth of Resource Efficiency Improvements* (London: Routledge, 2007).

9. Odagiri and Goto, "Japanese System of Innovation," 89.

10. Chalmers Johnson, *MITI and the Japanese Miracle: The Growth of Industrial Policy, 1925–1975* (Stanford, CA: Stanford University Press, 1982).

11. Odagiri and Goto, *Technology and Industrial Development*, 53.

12. Ibid., 55.

13. New Energy and Industrial Technology Development Organization [NEDO], *Eichi no hishō: NEDO 20-nenshi* [Soaring wisdom: Twenty-year history of NEDO] (Tokyo: NEDO, 2000), and *Heisei 17 nendo NEDO no purojekuto manejimento no hensen ni kakawaru chōsa* [Fiscal year 2005 report on the history of NEDO project management] (Kawasaki: NEDO, 2006).

14. Osamu Kimura, "Public R&D and Commercialization of Energy-Efficient Technology: A Case Study of Japanese Projects," *Energy Policy* 38, no. 11 (2010): 7358–69.

15. Hiroyuki Odagiri, Yoshiaki Nakamura, and Minoru Shibuya, "Research Consortia as a Vehicle for Basic Research: The Case of a Fifth Generation Computer Project in Japan," *Research Policy* 26, no. 2 (1997): 191–207.

16. Akira Goto and Hiroyuki Odagiri, *Innovation in Japan* (Oxford: Clarendon Press, 1997).

17. Lewis M. Branscomb, Fumio Kodama, and Richard Florida, *Industrializing Knowledge: University-Industry Linkages in Japan and the United States* (Cambridge, MA: MIT Press, 1999).

18. Dominique Foray, *The Economics of Knowledge* (Cambridge, MA: MIT Press, 2004). See also Dominique Foray and Bengt-Ake Lundvall, *Employment and Growth in the Knowledge-Based Economy* (Paris: Organisation for Economic Cooperation and Development, 1996).

19. Walter W. Powell and Stine Grodal, "Networks of Innovators," in *Oxford Handbook of Innovation*, ed. Jan Fagerberg, David C. Mowery, and Richard R. Nelson (Oxford: Oxford University Press, 2005), 56–85.

20. Henry Etzkowitz, Andrew Webster, and Peter Healey, *Capitalizing Knowledge: New Intersections of Industry and Academia* (Albany: State University of New York Press, 1998).

21. David C. Mowery, Richard R. Nelson, Bhaven N. Sampat, and Arvids A. Ziedonis, *Ivory Tower and Industrial Innovation: University-Industry Technology Transfer before and after the Bayh-Dole Act in the United States* (Stanford, CA: Stanford University Press, 2004).

22. National Institute of Science and Technology Policy, *Japanese Science and Technology Indicators 2011* (Tokyo: Ministry of Education, Culture, Sports, Science and Technology, 2012), 34.

23. Ibid., 41.

24. Cabinet Office, "Sōgō kagaku gijutsu kaigi, kiso kenkyū oyobi jinzai ikusei bukai, dai 1-kai kaigō, sankō shiryō (dētashū)" [Reference materials (data sets), first meeting, Committee on Basic Research and Human Resources, Council for Science and Technology Policy], May 22, 2012.

25. Ichiko Fuyuno, "Numbers of Young Scientists Declining in Japan," *Nature News*, March 20, 2012, DOI: 10.1038/nature.2012.10254.

26. Chiara Franzoni, Giuseppe Scellato, and Paula Stephan, "Foreign-Born Scientists: Mobility Patterns for 16 Countries," *Nature Biotechnology* 30, no. 12 (2012): 1250–53.

27. Odagiri and Goto, *Technology and Industrial Development*, 266.

28. Henry Etzkowitz, *MIT and the Rise of Entrepreneurial Science* (London: Routledge, 2002); Henry Etzkowitz, "Research Groups as 'Quasi-Firms': The Invention of the Entrepreneurial University," *Research Policy* 32, no. 1 (2003): 109–21; Henry Etzkowitz, "The Norms of Entrepreneurial Science: Cognitive Effects of the New University-Industry Linkages," *Research Policy* 27, no. 8 (1998): 823–33.

29. Masatoshi Kato and Hiroyuki Odagiri, "Development of University Life-Science Programs and University-Industry Joint Research in Japan," *Research Policy* 41, no. 5 (2012): 939–52.

30. Yasuo Nakayama, Mitsuaki Hosono, Koichi Hasegawa, and Akiya Nagata, *Sangaku renkei dētabēsu o katsuyōshita kokuritsu daigaku no kyōdō kenkyū / jūtaku kenkyū katsudō no bunseki* [Study on university-industry collaboration at Japanese national universities using the Database of University-Industry Collaboration] (Tokyo: Ministry of Education, Culture, Sports, Science and Technology, 2010); and Miyako Ogura and Kenichi Fujita, *Daigaku tou hatsu bencha chōsa 2011* [Academic start-ups survey 2011] (Tokyo: Ministry of Education, Culture, Sports, Science and Technology, 2012).

31. Ayaka Saka and Terutaka Kuwahara, *Kagaku kenkyū no benchimakingu 2011: ronbun bunseki de miru sekai no kenkyū katsudō no henka to Nihon no jōkyō* [Benchmarking

scientific research 2011: Bibliometric analysis on dynamic alteration of research activity in the world and Japan] (Tokyo: National Institute of Science and Technology Policy, 2011).

32. National Institute of Science and Technology Policy, *Japanese Science and Technology Indicators 2011*, 131.

33. Ibid., 138; and Antoine Dechezlepretre, Matthieu Glachant, Ivan Hascic, Nick Johnstone, and Yann Meniere, "Invention and Transfer of Climate Change–Mitigation Technologies: A Global Analysis," *Review of Environmental Economics and Policy* 5, no. 1 (2011): 109–30.

34. National Institute of Science and Technology Policy, *Japanese Science and Technology Indicators 2011*, 148.

35. Robert J. Geller, "Shake-Up Time for Japanese Seismology," *Nature* 472 (April 28, 2011): 407–9.

36. Ministry of Education, Culture, Sports, Science and Technology, *White Paper on Science and Technology 2012: Toward a Robust and Resilient Society—Lessons from the Great East Japan Earthquake* (Tokyo, 2012).

37. David Cyranoski, "Japanese Science Ministry Takes Partial Blame for Tsunami and Meltdown," *Nature News Blog*, June 20, 2012, http://blogs.nature.com/news/2012/06/japanese-science-ministry-takes-partial-blame-for-tsunami-and-meltdown.html.

38. National Institute of Science and Technology Policy, *Kagaku gijutsu ni taisuru kokumin ishiki no henka ni kansuru chōsa: Intanetto niyoru getsuji ishiki chōsa oyobi mensetsu chōsa no kekka kara* [Changes in public attitudes to science and technology: Findings from face-to-face interviews and from a monthly Internet survey] (Tokyo, June 2012).

39. Simon Perks, "Rebuilding Public Trust in Japanese Science," *Chemistry World*, September 6, 2012.

40. "Critical Mass," editorial, *Nature* 480 (December 15, 2011): 291.

41. Ministry of Education, Culture, Sports, Science and Technology, *White Paper on Science*, 85.

42. Government of Japan, Fourth Science and Technology Basic Plan, Cabinet Decision, August 19, 2011.

43. Masaru Yarime et al., "Establishing Sustainability Science in Higher Education Institutions: Towards an Integration of Academic Development, Institutionalization, and Stakeholder Collaborations," *Sustainability Science* 7, suppl. 1 (February 2012): 101–13.

44. Masaru Yarime, "Promoting Green Innovation or Prolonging the Existing Technology: Regulation and Technological Change in the Chlor-Alkali Industry in Japan and Europe," *Journal of Industrial Ecology* 11, no. 4 (2007): 117–39; Masaru Yarime, "Eco-Innovation through University-Industry Collaboration: Co-evolution of Technology and Institution for the Development of Lead-Free Solders," paper presented at the DRUID Society Summer Conference, Copenhagen, June 17–19, 2009.

45. Masaru Yarime, "Exploring Sustainability Science: Knowledge, Institutions, and Innovation," in *Sustainability Science: A Multidisciplinary Approach*, ed. Hiroshi Komiyama, Kazuhiko Takeuchi, Hideaki Shiroyama, and Takashi Mino (Tokyo: United Nations University Press, 2011), 98–111.

46. Masaru Yarime, "Understanding Sustainability Innovation as a Social Process of Knowledge Transformation," *Nanotechnology Perceptions* 6, no. 3 (2010): 143–53.

47. Stephen M. Maurer, "Inside the Anticommons: Academic Scientists' Struggle to Build a Commercially Self-Supporting Human Mutations Database, 1999–2001," *Research Policy* 35, no. 6 (2006): 839–53; Wesley Shrum, Joel Genuth, and Ivan Chompalov, *Structures of Scientific Collaboration* (Cambridge, MA: MIT Press, 2007).

48. Masaru Yarime, Yoshiyuki Takeda, and Yuya Kajikawa, "Towards Institutional Analysis of Sustainability Science: A Quantitative Examination of the Patterns of Research Collaboration," *Sustainability Science* 5, no. 1 (2010): 115–25.

49. Yarime, "Establishing Sustainability Science," 107.

50. Gregory Trencher, Masaru Yarime, and Ali Kharrazi, "Co-creating Sustainability: Cross-sector University Collaborations for Driving Sustainable Urban Transformations," *Journal of Cleaner Production* 50, no. 1 (2013): 40–55; Gregory Trencher, Masaru Yarime, Kes B. McCormick, Christopher Doll, and Stephen Kraines, "Beyond the Third Mission: Exploring the Emerging University Function of Co-creation for Sustainability," *Science and Public Policy* 41, no. 2 (April 2014): 151–79; Gregory Trencher, Xuemei Bai, James Evans, Kes B. McCormick, and Masaru Yarime, "University Partnerships for Co-designing and Co-producing Urban Sustainability," *Global Environmental Change* 28 (September 2014): 153–65.

CHAPTER TEN

Military Cooperation and Territorial Disputes: The Changing Face of Japan's Security Policy

Hiroshi Nakanishi

Japan's security policy, like many other aspects of the nation today, may appear to be in limbo, as exemplified by the quagmire of relocating the US Marine helicopter base at Futenma, Okinawa.[1] In 2009–10, under the new Hatoyama administration, trust between Tokyo and Washington nearly collapsed, and in June 2010, just after the prime minister resigned, Japan reacted in a confused way to assertive Chinese moves near the Senkaku Islands. Then, in March 2011, the country was struck by the Great East Japan Earthquake and accidents at the Fukushima nuclear plants. Revolving-door prime ministers and the relative decline in economic strength shown by China's displacement of Japan as the world's second-largest economy, a position it had kept since 1968, seem to substantiate this view. Nevertheless, Japanese security policy is undergoing arguably the most significant and smoothest transformation since the 1950s. This chapter explains the paradox and looks ahead to the near future.

Prime Minister Jun'ichirō Koizumi (2001–6) stepped down after an unusually long tenure by recent Japanese standards, and the country fell into political and economic confusion. Prime ministers were in and out of office quickly, the economy stalled again even before the global financial crisis started in 2007, and the rise of populist sentiment showed deep-seated problems. Foreign and security policy was not immune from the malaise. Even though relations with China and the Republic of Korea (ROK), strained by Koizumi's visits to Yasukuni Shrine, improved somewhat, ties with the United States deteriorated from the high point of mutual goodwill symbolized by the 2006 visit of the outgoing Koizumi to the United States, when

President George W. Bush warmly welcomed Koizumi (an Elvis Presley fan) by making a trip to Graceland with him.

The first administration of Shinzō Abe, Koizumi's successor, was the turning point. At fifty-two, Abe was the youngest prime minister of Japan since World War II and had been groomed for the job. Grandson of Nobusuke Kishi, prime minister from 1957 till 1960 and son of Shintarō Abe, foreign minister for four years in 1980s, Abe was outspoken, more conservative than Koizumi, and popular for his tough stand on the Democratic People's Republic of Korea (North Korea). Despite these credentials, Abe was unable to achieve his ambitious agenda—revision of the constitution and hardline policies toward North Korea and China. The Liberal Democratic Party (LDP) lost its majority in the 2007 Upper House election, and Abe, citing illness, suddenly resigned in September 2008. The next two LDP premiers, Yasuo Fukuda and Tarō Asō, lasted only a year each and could not turn the situation around. In early 2008, the *Economist* in an editorial entitled "Japain" pointed to the failure of Japanese politicians to cope with the nation's ills.[2]

Frustrated with the LDP's internal strife and leadership by the sons of past politicians, the public gave a landslide victory to the Democratic Party of Japan (DPJ) in the general election of August 2009. But DPJ rule resulted in foreign policy crises unprecedented in postwar Japanese history by weakening the trust between the leaders of Japan and the United States and worsening territorial disputes with neighboring countries, particularly China. Prime Minister Yukio Hatoyama turned out to be a softheaded visionary unable to back up idealistic talk with careful policy planning. Triumphant but inexperienced and divided, the DPJ could not overcome the premier's weakness. With little consultation within the party, Hatoyama pledged to scrap the 2006 deal between Washington and the LDP government to relocate the Futenma helicopter base to a new site at Henoko, Okinawa, which Hatoyama viewed as a symbolic example of the LDP's subservience to American demands. It is true that the Futenma Relocation Plan was never popular among Okinawans, many of whom thought the central government discriminated against the prefecture and resented hosting US forces. However, Hatoyama's bold rejection of the delicately crafted project just as the two governments were trying to persuade Okinawa not only stalled the relocation plan but created havoc in the overall relationship with Washington.

At the same time, Hatoyama embraced the idea of Japan leading the creation of an "East Asian Community" with other East Asian countries. The concept itself may not have upset the Obama administration, but the way Hatoyama did it—concealing his intentions from Washington while telling Chinese leaders Japan was too close to the United States—was unsettling. Japan's only ally is the United States, and the Japan-US security treaty is the keystone of Japan's defense. When the prime minister was unable to find a viable alternative to the Henoko site, top leaders in the Obama administration apparently lost confidence in him. Hatoyama was forced to revive practically the original plan in May 2010. That about-face broke up the DPJ's coalition with the leftist Japan Socialist Democratic Party, and Hatoyama had to resign.

Successor Naoto Kan faced another foreign policy challenge in September 2010 when Japanese Coast Guard patrol boats discovered a Chinese fishing boat in Japanese territorial waters close to the Senkaku Islands. Known as Diaoyu in Chinese, the islets have been claimed by China and Taiwan since 1971. The Chinese boat slammed into the Coast Guard vessels, which detained it and the crew. When Japan announced that charges would be filed against the boat captain, Beijing fiercely protested and demanded his release by imposing sanctions. China canceled invitations to Japanese students to attend the Shanghai Exposition, restricted exports of rare earth materials to Japan, and detained Japanese workers in China for allegedly entering military districts. In the midst of the uproar in Japan, Chief Cabinet Secretary Yoshito Sengoku suddenly announced that the local prosecutor's office in Ishigaki, Okinawa, had suspended legal action for insufficient evidence. The captain was released and returned to China to a hero's welcome, and the incident was closed. But the decision was ridiculed as weak-kneed in the Diet, by the media, and even within the government itself. Japan's and China's perceptions of each other had been steadily deteriorating for some time, according to a Cabinet Office poll (see figure 10.1), but this incident provoked a sharp turn for the worse. A separate poll showed that negative feelings toward China increased from 58.5 percent of respondents in October 2009 to 77.8 percent in 2010, a record high since the survey started in 1978.[3] Opposition parties fiercely attacked the Kan administration's handling of the incident, and the cabinet's approval rating slumped in the polls. In October Russian president Dimitry Medvedev visited Kunashiri, one of the disputed islands in the Northern Territories (Kurile Islands), for the first time as Soviet or Russian president, which added fuel to the attack on the Kan administration. This visit, combined with North Korea's bombardment of Yeonpyeong Island in November, made the Kan cabinet seem incapable of dealing with challenges to Japan's important interests. In January 2011, Kan was forced to reshuffle the cabinet and remove Sengoku.

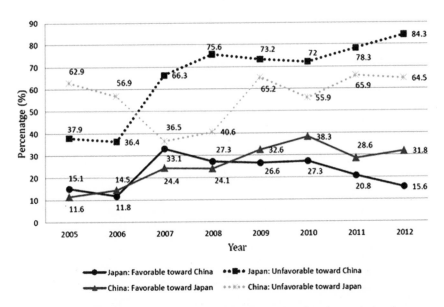

FIGURE 10.1   Public opinion in Japan and China. (Reproduced with permission from Genron-NPO, "Nitchyū ryōkokuni taisuru inshō" [Japanese and Chinese impressions of each other], 2012, www.genron-npo.net/pdf/forum2012.pdf.)

The 3/11 catastrophe was the coup de grace for the weakened Kan cabinet. The scale of the disaster and the danger of radiation from Fukushima temporarily halted politics as usual. But Kan soon came under fire for his handling of the emergency, the parties bickered over recovery funding for the Tōhoku area, and the continued use of nuclear power was contentious. Although the disaster invoked worldwide sympathy, assistance, and even respectful amazement at Japan's resilience, the enormous destruction and fear abroad of radiation contamination weakened the nation's international status. By late May 2011, divisions within the DPJ could no longer be papered over. Former prime minister Hatoyama and Ichiro Ozawa, the powerful founder of the DPJ, turned against Kan, while Katsuya Okada, Seiji Maeyama, and Yoshihiko Noda backed the cabinet. The showdown culminated in a no-confidence motion by the opposition in June that some DPJ members threatened to support. Fearful the DPJ would split up, Hatoyama opposed the motion and averted open revolt in the party but demanded that Kan resign, which he did on August 26. After a short campaign, Noda was elected president of the party and became the third DPJ prime minister in twenty-four months.

These interconnected events had far-reaching repercussions for Japan's foreign and security policy. The government seemed ineffective, unable to manage crisis after crisis. But behind the turmoil, new policies took shape that may drastically transform the domestic consensus on national security, if not replace it completely.

A New Defense Policy

The most conspicuous change was a new Defense Program Guideline (DPG) approved by the Kan cabinet in December 2010 that scrapped the Basic Defense Force Concept that had shaped security policy since 1976.[4] The new guideline is centered on a Dynamic Defense Force characterized by "readiness, mobility, flexibility, sustainability, and versatility." The Self-Defense Forces (SDF) are to maintain a higher degree of readiness with stronger intelligence, surveillance, and reconnaissance activities that enable quicker responses to various types of threats. The major missions cited by the guideline are to ensure the security of the sea and air space surrounding Japan and to respond to attacks on offshore islands, cyber warfare, attacks by guerrillas and special operations forces, and ballistic missiles. The SDF must be prepared for complex contingencies and consecutive or simultaneous events, as well as large-scale chemical, biological, radiological, or nuclear disasters.

The concept of a Dynamic Defense Force explicitly and radically changes the SDF mission from the Cold War, when it was defined as a supplementary deterrence capability against the Soviet threat in and around Japanese territory. The shift had been under way since the end of the Cold War era and was foreshadowed in the 1995 Defense Program Outline (DPO) and the 2004 DPG.[5] While the latter cited ballistic missiles, guerrillas, and special operations forces as the top threats, the 2010 DPG emphasizes maritime and air space security and the threat to offshore islands. The new DPG identifies the Okinawa Islands and the East China Sea as priority areas for "ISR [intelligence, surveillance, and reconnaissance], maritime patrol, air defense, responses to ballistic missile attacks, transportation, and command communications."[6]

The 2010 DPG imposes stringent limitations on fiscal and human resources and seeks to streamline forces and concentrate on acquisition of core equipment. For example, the number of tanks, howitzers, and rockets is reduced from about six hundred each to about four hundred each, while the number of the submarines is increased from sixteen to twenty-two (figure 10.2). Japan's military forces remain small compared to other countries in the

	Personnel		154,000
	Regular personnel		147,000
	Ready Reserve Personnel		7,000
Ground Self-Defense Force	Major Units	Regionally deployed units	8 divisions 6 brigades
		Mobile operation units	Central Readiness Force 1 armored division
		Surface to air guided missile units	7 anti aircraft artillery groups/regiments
	Major Equipment	Tanks	Approx. 400
		Howitzers and rockets	Approx. 400
Maritime Self-Defense Force	Major Units	Destroyer units	4 flotillas (8 divisions) 4 divisions
		Submarines units	6 divisions
		Minesweeper unit	1 flotilla
		Patrol aircraft units	9 squadrons
	Major Equipment	Destroyers	48
		Submarines	22
		Combat aircraft	Approx. 150
Air Self-Defense Force	Major Units	Air warning & control units	4 warning groups 24 warning squadrons 1 AEW group (2 squadrons)
		Fighter aircraft units	12 squadrons
		Air reconnaissance unit	1 squadron
		Air transport units	3 squadrons
		Aerial refueling/transport unit	1 squadron
		Surface to air guided missile units	6 groups
	Major Equipment	Combat aircraft	Approx. 340
		Fighters	Approx. 260
Assets capable of ballistic missile defense (BMD)*		Aegis equipped destroyers	** 6
		Air warning & control units	11 warning groups/squadrons
		Surface to air guided missile units	6 groups

* The numbers of units and equipment in this row are already included in the Maritime and Air Self Defense Forces' major units sections above.

** Additional acquisition of BMD capable, Aegis equipped destroyers, if to be provided separately, will be allowed within the number of destroyers set above after consideration of development of BMD related technologies and fiscal conditions in the future, among other factors.

FIGURE 10.2 Personnel and equipment of the Japan Self-Defense Forces. (Ministry of Defense, "National Defense Program Guidelines for FY 2011 and Beyond," December 17, 2010, www.mod.go.jp/e/d_act/d_policy/pdf/guidelinesFY2011.pdf, 19.)

region (table 10.1). The SDF has 247,746 personnel; China and North Korea have 2.2 million and 2.1 million, respectively.[7] Japan's defense budget stayed around ¥4.7 trillion from 2005 to 2012, roughly 1 percent of gross domestic product (GDP). The US Department of Defense estimates Chinese real defense spending in 2011 at between $120 billion and $180 billion, twice or triple Japan's.[8]

It is interesting to consider how a new DPG could be created in the midst of a political debacle. To some extent, it was possible because of, rather than despite, the turmoil. The Asō cabinet started the review of the 2004 DPG in early 2009. Customarily, the cabinet designates experts to write a report on security and defense policy, and the Ministry of Defense prepares a new DPG after that report is submitted. The Council on Security and Defense Capabilities was assembled in January 2009 and issued its report in August.[9] On balance, the report was a relatively conservative assessment of the 2004 DPG, saw global issues such as terrorism and the proliferation of weapons of mass destruction as most important for Japan's security environment, and recommended retention of the traditional Basic Defense Force Concept with some updating.

The review process was suspended by the change of government in August 2009. The Hatoyama cabinet formed a new expert committee, the Council on Security and Defense Capabilities in the New Era, in February 2010. There were two carry-over members, and there was not much difference ideologically between the two councils. But the domestic and international political environment had changed, and the DPJ government expected new policy initiatives that marked a departure from the LDP era. At the same time, the top leaders of the Hatoyama and Kan cabinets were too preoccupied with immediate issues such as Futenma and the Upper House election to pay close attention to the discussions and the council's final report. In addition, in the first half of 2010 Chinese naval activities near Japan caught the public's attention. In April, a contingent of ten Chinese naval vessels crossed the open sea between the main Okinawa island and Miyako Island, and a ship-borne helicopter flew close to the Japanese guided-missile destroyer *Suzunami*. Though the Chinese navy had been active in the South China Sea from some years earlier, the Japanese public interpreted this incident as a more assertive Chinese attitude backed by a growing military capability.[10] About the same time some Chinese officials reportedly began calling the South China Sea a "core interest" of China. In July, US secretary of state Hillary Clinton

TABLE 10.1 Defense Expenditures of Countries in the Asia-Pacific Region (2010)

	$US Billion	% of GDP
USA	600	3.70
China	112.2	1.24
Russia	68.2	3.09
Japan	51.0	0.99
ROK	31.8	2.52
Taiwan	10.3	2.08

Source: Compiled by permission from International Institute for Strategic Studies, *The Military Balance 2014* (London: IISS, 2014).

stated that the United States had a "national interest" in the South China Sea, countering the Chinese move.[11] These developments seem to have affected the focus and tone of the council report published in August 2010 and gave foreign policy and security experts leeway to formulate the 2010 DPG.[12]

The Noda cabinet made a series of important security decisions in late 2011. On December 20, the cabinet chose the F-35 as the next-generation fighter to replace the F-4E, a decision pending since 2007. (The Eurofighter and FA-18 lost out on the lucrative contract.) The same day the administration finally decided to send Ground SDF engineers on a UN-sponsored mission to the Republic of South Sudan.

A week later, Chief Cabinet Secretary Osamu Fujii announced new guidelines for the overseas transfer of defense equipment that replaced the three principles on arms exports established in 1967 (with revisions in the 1970s and 1980s). The principles had virtually prohibited arms sales abroad, requiring specific exemptions for cases such as the joint development of a missile defense with the United States. Under the new guidelines no specific exemption was required for the sale of military equipment in cases related to "peace contribution and international cooperation" and "international joint development and production of defense equipment" that contributed to Japan's security.[13] The defense establishment and arms industry had long sought removal of the ban on sales abroad, and there was an immediate policy impact. Japan and the United Kingdom announced an agreement on joint research, development, and production of military equipment.[14] Japan reportedly intends to provide patrol boats to the Philippines and Vietnam.[15]

Rescue Operations in the Great East Japan Earthquake

In the meantime, 3/11 provided an unexpected trial of the new defense posture. Some local governments were destroyed or not functioning, and transportation and communication networks were damaged. On March 14, Defense Minister Toshimi Kitazawa ordered formation of a Joint Task Force Tōhoku with the three SDF branches serving under one commander, General Eiji Kimizuka. It was the first joint task force and nearly full-fledged operation in SDF history. About one hundred thousand personnel were mobilized, as well as fifty-nine vessels and about 540 aircraft. The SDF was also engaged with the Fukushima nuclear power plant accident.[16] Although not a combat operation, the rescue and relief mission was close to the complex contingencies anticipated in the 2010 DPG. The SDF performed well, or at least that was the public perception. According to a survey by the Pew Research Center (figure 10.3), out of the major organizations that coped with the disaster-relief operations such as the media, the national government, Prime Minister Kan, and the Tokyo Electric Company, only the SDF were acclaimed for their performance after the earthquake.[17]

The United States quickly offered large-scale military help. At the peak of Operation Tomodachi, 24,500 personnel, twenty-four vessels, including the aircraft carrier USS *Ronald Reagan*, and 189 airplanes were deployed. Joint Coordination Offices were established at the Ministry of Defense, the US Yokota Air Base, and the Joint Task Force headquarters at Sendai.[18] It was the first combined operation of Japanese and American forces in the history of the bilateral alliance.

Operation Tomodachi demonstrated to the Japanese public the importance of the United States as an ally. Poll respondents reporting friendly feelings toward the United States reached a record high of 82 percent in October 2011. Operation Tomodachi may not have been the sole reason for appreciation of the US security role. During the short-lived Hatoyama period, the Ministry of Foreign Affairs commissioned a group of experts to examine archival records for "secret agreements" between Tokyo and Washington during the Cold War. Leaving aside whether "secret agreements" was the proper terminology, the group reported there were undisclosed agreements.[19] After these were made public, however, the foreign minister reaffirmed that Japan continued to rely on US nuclear deterrence. During the clash with China over the Senkaku fishing boat incident, Washington made clear that the islands were covered by the US-Japan Security Treaty.

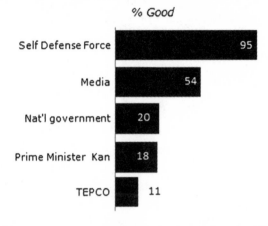

Self Defense Force Well-Regarded; Government, TEPCO Are Not

% Good

Self Defense Force	95
Media	54
Nat'l government	20
Prime Minister Kan	18
TEPCO	11

FIGURE 10.3   Public opinion about organizations' performance after 3/11. (Courtesy of Pew Research Center, Global Attitudes Project, "Japanese Resilient, but See Economic Challenges Ahead," June 1, 2011, www.pewglobal.org/2011/06/01/japanese-resilient-but-see-economic-challenges-ahead/.)

In addition to US forces, other countries provided assistance through military means. Australia sent C-17 transport planes, and the ROK and Thailand each dispatched rescue personnel or relief materials by C-130s.[20] This international help was a product of multilateral disaster relief cooperation started earlier. Indonesia and Japan had jointly organized under the Association of Southeast Asian Nations (ASEAN) Regional Forum an exercise at Manado, Indonesia, for mid-March 2011. Japan had to withdraw because of 3/11; some countries diverted their resources to help Japan. Disaster relief planning included the Pacific Partnership, an annual exercise led by the US Pacific Fleet. Several years of multilateral humanitarian cooperation paid off after 3/11.

Multilateral Security Architecture in the Asia-Pacific

Another new aspect of Japan's security policy is to create and reinforce a cooperative security network in the region.[21] The Abe cabinet called the "outer rim of the Eurasian continent . . . an Arc of Freedom and Prosperity" and a strategic area for Japanese diplomacy. Abe and Foreign Minister Tarō

Asō stressed security partnerships with democratic countries on the rim of the Eurasian continent, such as Australia and India. Japan and India issued a joint statement on a Strategic and Global Partnership in December 2006, and Japan and Australia announced a Joint Declaration on Security Cooperation in March 2007.[22] Japan has tried to make these bilateral schemes multilateral, for instance, in the Japan-US-Australia trilateral strategic dialogue that started in March 2006.[23] US secretary of state Condoleezza Rice rebuffed a proposal by the Abe administration for a Japan-US-Australia-India quadrilateral dialogue, but the United States has hosted a multilateral naval exercise, Malabar, since 2007 that includes Japan, India, Australia, and Singapore.[24]

The efforts to create regional security architecture continued despite the turnover in prime ministers and the transition from the LDP to the DPJ. In November 2010, Japan started to participate in the ASEAN Defense Ministers' Meeting-Plus, which includes eight non-ASEAN member states. The meeting in Hanoi that year discussed five areas of cooperation: (1) humanitarian assistance and disaster relief, (2) maritime security, (3) counterterrorism, (4) military medicine, and (5) peacekeeping operations, as well as issues related to the South China Sea.[25] Japan and the ROK held bilateral defense ministerial dialogues in 2009 and 2011, and a Japan-ROK-US defense dialogue also took place in 2009, 2010, and 2012. Japan and the ROK were observers at a joint exercise with the United States in 2010.[26] The first trilateral Japan-US-ROK exercise in June 2012 included the aircraft carrier USS *George Washington*. Because of territorial disputes and for historical reasons, there were few bilateral defense exchanges with China and Russia.

The US rebalance to the Asia-Pacific region was an expedient way out of the deadlock over Futenma. In April 2012 the Japan-US Security Consulting Committee agreed to separate the relocation issue from the rest of the US defense transformation process, though the two governments still wanted to implement the plan.[27] This change reflected a realistic assessment of antibase sentiment in Okinawa by US officials and input from members of Congress who thought the plan unachievable.[28] At the same time, US strategy had also evolved. Given China's attempt to acquire antiaccess and area-denial capability, the United States wanted to deploy and rotate its forces widely in the Pacific, including to Guam and Australia. In the same vein, the Security Consulting Committee agreed that the two governments should consider developing training areas in Guam and the Northern Mariana Islands.

For several years, Japan has sought to widen and deepen its security architecture in the Asia-Pacific. Though not quite explicit, the focus of Japanese security interest is shifting from Northeast Asia toward Southeast Asia, from a continental orientation to maritime security.

Historical Perspective: Is the Yoshida Doctrine Irrelevant?

Despite the apparent drift and stagnation in socioeconomic policies, Japan's security policy has been remarkably consistent the last few years. How was this possible with weak political leadership? Will it be sustained in the future?

During the Cold War, Japan generally followed the Yoshida Doctrine, named after Prime Minister Shigeru Yoshida (in office 1946–47, 1948–54), who signed the San Francisco Peace Treaty with the Western bloc in 1951. Yoshida established the basic framework of postwar Japan's foreign and security policy: (1) association with the West led by the United States under the bilateral security treaty, (2) limitation of Japan's military capability to an auxiliary force of US deterrence and avoidance of the threat or use of force in foreign policy, and (3) concentration on peaceful economic development and reliance on economic power to accomplish foreign policy objectives.[29] Yoshida himself never saw his decisions as worthy of the title "doctrine." Scholars and practitioners adopted the term *Yoshida Line* or *Yoshida Doctrine* in the 1960s as a convenient way to explain Japanese foreign policy strategy in the context of the international system, domestic politics, and ideational debate between the conservatives and the progressives.[30] By aligning with the United States, the dominant player in the Asia-Pacific region, Japan gained military security relatively cheaply and took advantage of Washington's promotion of Japanese interests to rehabilitate its diplomatic standing and benefit from decolonization and the liberal capitalist order. By accepting the Occupation's postwar reforms, including the pacifist constitution, and allowing limited rearmament, Yoshida balanced the traditional nationalist Right and the progressive Left. His successors, Hayato Ikeda and Eisaku Sato, controlled both groups by allying with the former, the conservative LDP that ruled Japan from 1955, and containing the latter as minority opposition parties in the Diet (parliament). The Yoshida Doctrine gained public acceptance by delivering economic prosperity, which provided alternative symbols for national pride and pacifist sentiment.

The high point of the Yoshida Doctrine was the first DPO adopted by the Miki cabinet in 1976, coupled with a ceiling on arms spending of 1 percent of GDP. The first systematic elaboration of the SDF's military objectives, the DPO defined them as defense and deterrence against limited, small-scale aggression directed at Japanese territory and stipulated dependence on the United States for protection against larger threats. The DPO was the culmination of years of debate and decisions such as accession to the nuclear nonproliferation treaty, the three non-nuclear principles, restraint on arms exports, nonresort to collective defense, and a virtual cap on the defense budget below 1 percent of GDP.

This security posture was criticized from the late 1970s to the end of the Cold War for various reasons. Japan's rise to the status of an economic giant brought complaints from the Western camp that Japan was a free rider taking advantage of other countries' defense efforts. Japan spent little on defense, the argument went, concentrating instead on economic development and amassing huge trade surpluses. Within Japan, as the Left weakened in domestic politics, neoconservative leaders like Yasuhiro Nakasone came to power who wanted Japan to play a larger role in world politics. Controversies with the ROK and China over the treatment of World War II in Japanese textbooks since the early 1980s stimulated the revival of an old-fashioned nationalism that denounced reforms carried out by the Allied Occupation and Japan's dependence on the United States for security. Still, until the end of the Cold War, the Yoshida Doctrine was not openly challenged. Although the ceiling on arms spending was abolished in 1986, the percentage stayed around the same level. The purpose of the Yoshida Doctrine in the 1980s was to enhance Asia-Pacific regionalism through economic interdependence and a regional division of labor.

The collapse of the Soviet Union and the First Gulf War (1990–91) dealt a severe blow to the Yoshida Doctrine. Aligned with the West but blocked from direct participation in a military conflict by popular pacifist sentiment and Article 9 of the constitution, the Kaifu administration provided equipment and aid worth US$13 billion to the UN-sponsored coalition efforts and rehabilitation in the Gulf area. Far from receiving credit for helping to rescue Kuwait, Japan's contribution was ignored or ridiculed as "checkbook diplomacy." Stung by this foreign policy setback, the ruling LDP was also hurt by a corruption scandal and lost power in 1993–94.

In the post–Cold War era, three schools of thought emerged in addition to the Yoshida Doctrine. The "normal Japan" orientation personified by Ozawa argued that Japan should have the same prerogatives as other nation-states and make security decisions on its own. Specific policy options ranged from a universalistic orientation—collective security under the UN system—to a nationalist assertion that Japan should step out from under the US security umbrella. A second approach, a Japanese-style neoconservatism, was advocated by Prime Ministers Koizumi and Abe in the first decade of this century. This line sought to integrate security policies with allies and friendly powers that shared similar "values"; it was held both by the liberal-leaning Koizumi, who was more market oriented and less ideological on history issues, and by Abe, who was more paternalistic and nationalistic. A third school of thought coalesced around the concept of Japan as a "global civilian power." Perhaps closest to the traditional Yoshida Doctrine, the proponents included journalists like Yoichi Funabashi and academics like Yoshihide Soeya, who sees Japan as a middle-ranking power. Current and former LDP members and leaders in the Kōmeitō Party like Hiromu Nonaka and Masayoshi Takemura share a similar view and are averse to overseas military involvement and a nationalistic tone toward East Asia.

Over the last two decades, these three policy strands were jumbled together while traditional pacifistic left-liberals were politically and ideologically marginalized. In the wake of the bitter disappointment at the international community's failure to recognize Japan's contribution to the First Gulf War and in line with the proposal by President George H. W. Bush in 1990 for a "New World Order," all three lines of thought supported Japan's involvement in peacekeeping operations under UN authorization. SDF participation in the UN peacekeeping operation in Cambodia in 1992–93 was generally regarded positively. As the notion of a new world order waned in the mid-1990s, the idea of Japan as a global civilian power and neoconservative ideas prevailed in the LDP-led coalition governments in 1994–2001 under Prime Ministers Tomiichi Murayma, Ryūtarō Hashimoto, Keizō Obuchi, and Yoshirō Mori.

During this period, the Japan-US alliance was redefined by the Hashimoto-Clinton declaration in April 1996, and the new US-Japan security guideline was issued in 1997. But there was tension within the Japanese government over the military threats posed by China and North Korea. Doves such as LDP secretary-general Kōichi Katō suggested that the new US-Japan guideline did not cover Chinese territory, including the Taiwan Straits. Later Seiroku Kajiyama, cabinet chief-secretary, countered that the Taiwan Straits were within the scope of the guideline. Beijing had conducted missile exercises in the Taiwan Straits in 1995 and 1996 and was wary of Japan's view on the issue. Premier Hashimoto took an ambiguous position.

New revelations of North Korean abductions of Japanese citizens, including of a thirteen-year-old schoolgirl, Megumi Yokota, surfaced in 1997 and became a rallying point for nationalists. North Korea launched a Taepodong missile over the Japanese mainland in August 1998 that the Japanese public saw as a concrete danger to their security. During a state visit to Japan in November 1998, Chinese president Jiang Zemin repeatedly spoke of Japan's guilt for the Pacific War, behavior that aroused nationalist anger in Japan. Right-wing political leaders like Shintarō Ishihara and Shingo Nishimura gained more influence. As China took the economic center stage in East Asia after the Asian financial crisis of 1997–98 and the United States became more unilateralist late in the Clinton administration, Japan tried a more Asia-oriented policy: the ill-fated proposal to create an Asian Monetary Fund in 1997 and the Chang Mai Initiative on a currency swap among Asian countries.

At the start of the new millennium, Japanese neoconservatives took the initiative. After 9/11 Koizumi quickly committed Japan to the "war on terrorism," while somewhat carelessly provoking a row with China and the ROK over Yasukuni Shrine.[31] Domestically, Koizumi's visits to Yasukuni helped advance his agenda. He spent political capital on the adventurous visit to North Korea to meet Kim Jong-il in a bid to normalize relations between the two countries. Koizumi made a breakthrough on the intractable issue of the abduction of Japanese citizens but could not establish diplomatic ties. Still, he was popular enough to win a resounding victory in the 2005 general election on the issue of postal reform.

Abe inherited Koizumi's neoconservative legacy and tried to put it into a more ideological mold—"value-oriented diplomacy"—with Japan part of a democratic coalition. Leading foreign observers such as Kenneth Pyle, Richard J. Samuels, Christopher W. Hughes, and Andrew Oros thought Japan might become a more assertive actor in security affairs.[32] This prediction was not shared by Japanese analysts, who were more cautious in evaluating the Koizumi era as structural change. They saw Koizumi's leadership as a blend of personal flair, effective balancing of the LDP old guard and the emergent DPJ, and the highly charged international atmosphere after the attack on the World Trade Center.[33] As the record shows, the relative stability and assertiveness on foreign policy under Koizumi were not continued by his successors. Abe had to resign with few tangible accomplishments, and the next two LDP premiers had little success or time in office.

The 2009 DPJ Manifesto (platform) called for a "close and equal" relationship with the United States but also mentioned revision of the Status of Forces Agreement and review of the Futenma agreement and advocated an East Asian Community. In short, the initial DPJ cabinet tried the "normal Japan" framework by combining nationalist and left-liberal ideology.

As we have seen, the DPJ fumbled Futenma, mainly because of Hatoyama's incompetence and inexperience, but the left-liberal nationalist policy line complicated Japan's relationship with the United States while yielding little progress with ties to China and the rest of Asia. Meanwhile, the international environment had changed. Chinese foreign policy was openly assertive, and the Obama administration was ready to rebalance its military forces to the Asia-Pacific area. Under Kan and Noda, neoconservative and global-civilian lines of thought converged into the new security policy.

The emerging policy coalition formed the structural base for the Dynamic Defense Force in the 2010 DPG and enhanced security architecture, particularly in the Asia-Pacific sea area. This policy line accords with a strategic landscape where the United States, the most powerful country in the world, tries to maintain the existing liberal order, including freedom of the seas, while China, the rising power in the last three decades, tries to create areas of denial in its vicinity. Japan sits on the strategic cleavage in this landscape and will have to take a position.

With radical pacifist ideas out of the picture, there is a consensus to put security considerations into the policy-making process. A case in point was the legislation on maritime and space policies. The Diet enacted the Basic Act on Ocean Policy and the Basic Act on Space Policy in 2007 and 2008, respectively, by large majority votes that included the LDP and DPJ. Basic policy plans that include security issues quickly followed.[34]Absent intense political and media attention, policies within the consensus tend to be quickly implemented, like the case of the arms transfer announcement in late 2011.

The new policy mixture seems more stable than a Japan deeply engaged in US global strategy or moving toward a deeper political engagement with Asia, particularly China and two Koreas. Japan's national interests are not always identical with those of the United States, notably in the Middle East. A global civilian stance that does not brandish force seems more acceptable to the

Japanese public. On the other hand, even though increasing economic interdependence may bring Japan closer to China and the two Koreas, including strategic partnership, there seem to be limits because of nationalistic friction as well as strategic and economic competition. Enhanced cooperation with the United States and other Pacific partners, combined with engagement with other Asian countries on an economic and functional basis that avoids contentious issues such as a military relationship, territorial disputes, and history, seems the most appropriate course for Japan. There will be domestic political support for this course as long as the neoconservative/global civilian policy lines can restrain the outright nationalism on both the right and the left.

The Future

Events from the summer of 2012 accelerated the shift to a new security paradigm. When the Noda administration bought several of the Senkaku Islands from a private Japanese citizen in September, China responded with intensive naval patrols close to Japanese territory and "reconnaissance" flights that violated Japanese air space. In August, the ROK dramatically reiterated its claim to Takeshima (Dokto) with a visit by President Lee Myung-bak, and Seoul has flatly rejected Japan's call for international arbitration. Finally, in December the LDP won a huge victory in the general election and Shinzō Abe became prime minister again. He condemned harassment of Japanese citizens and businesses in China over the Senkaku dispute and announced increased military spending to beef up Japan's maritime capability.

Japanese political leaders including Noda and Abe believe that Japan's relationship with the United States is its highest security priority. This oft-heard mantra in Tokyo deserves emphasis because economic indicators suggest to some that trade with China and other parts of East Asia is more important to Japan than the Tokyo-Washington nexus. That American leadership underlies peace and market economies in the region should not be undervalued. Abe is right to stress the importance of the security alliance with the United States. As maritime powers, Japan and the United States have a common interest in stable prosperity in the Asia-Pacific. But his evocation of the close personal relations with Washington enjoyed by Prime Ministers Nakasone and Koizumi is less credible. To the extent that his demand for constitutional revision rejects postwar democratic reforms under the US Occupation, the prime minister risks isolation not only from Washington but from East Asia as well.

The emerging security policy seems politically sustainable in the near future—for a decade or so—even though the second Abe administration has taken a tougher stance than the DPJ. Abe stopped the decline in real defense spending since 2012 and increased arms spending in FY 2013 by ¥40 billion yen, and the cabinet decided to revise the 2010 DPG. Abe also revived his earlier policy agenda of establishing a National Security Council and changing the current interpretation of the constitution, which bans the exercise of collective defense with the United States and other powers. Most of these policies are expected to be implemented, since a coalition of the LDP and the New Kōmei Party gained control of the Upper House in July 2013.

Even with public support for this daring approach to national security, implementation is likely to be limited by structural constraints. The international environment limits Japan's options, and the public, with a shared sense of crisis and risk, supports a broad pragmatic approach with more emphasis on security and military issues, although the public is not yet fully aware of the transformation adumbrated in the 2010 DPG and the other policy changes.[35]

Of the many pitfalls ahead, the most serious is the limited financial and human resources available to Japan. A negative ledger includes the huge national debt, annual budget deficits, a rapidly graying population and shrinking labor force, and a severe energy problem exacerbated by the nuclear accident at Fukushima. These constraints are discussed in other chapters in this volume (chapter 7 by Saori Katada and Gene Park, chapter 1 by Sawako Shirahase, and chapter 5 by Jacques E. C. Hymans). How many resources can be allocated to national security? Given the anticipated cutbacks in Pentagon spending, US pressure on Japan to bear more of the security burden may intensify. A breakdown in the domestic consensus to pay for security might lead to a major reformulation of Japanese foreign policy interests and objectives.

The second area of concern is the constitutional issue of collective defense. Flexible interpretation of the laws related to military affairs has been a hallmark of postwar Japanese jurisprudence. The government may be able to "finesse" the issue again. Still, there is widespread attachment to Article 9 and the pacifism symbolized in the constitution. Reinterpretation of Article 9, let alone outright revision of the constitution, as advocated by Prime Minister Abe, is certain to provoke a political storm.[36]

A third potential snare is the cross-current emanating from the West and the emerging economies. Western liberal capitalism is being challenged by the advent of a non-Western state capitalism. A crude binary perspective puts the United States on the Pacific side and China on the East Asian continent side as poles for different social philosophies as well as political and economic systems. Though a highly westernized society, Japan may in the future be torn by the gravitational forces of Western and Asian values such as communitarian orientation and a preference for domestic stability over international openness. Ideological and philosophical rivalries in domestic politics may deepen polarization and paralyze the political system.

Okinawa's function as linchpin of the new security policy remains problematical. The archipelago's strategic importance is rising—as the pivotal area for maritime operations for the United States, China, and Japan—but its troubled history of devastation in World War II, US military occupation until 1952, and the large US military presence make it inherently difficult for Okinawans to accept the role of strategic outpost. How to balance the military importance of Okinawa and the pacifistic sensitivity of its people, especially when the central government has less economic leverage, will remain a key challenge for Japanese leaders.

Nationalism in East Asia is becoming an increasingly dangerous factor. Since the 1980s, historical issues dating from World War II have been the salient rallying point for protests by China and the ROK against Japan and have sowed the seeds of nationalistic sentiment. In recent years, territorial rivalries over islands or islets have become flashpoints for nationalist sentiment. Japan's territorial claims over the Takeshima (Dokto) Islands held by the ROK and the Northern Islands held by Russia have attracted jingoistic support at home. Still, these are diplomatic issues with no possibility of military confrontation.

The case of the Senkaku Islands, which are under Japanese control but claimed by China (and Taiwan), is different. When the Japanese government decided to "nationalize" some of the islands by transferring ownership from a private citizen to the government in September 2012, China reacted vehemently. The response escalated from diplomatic protest, economic sanctions, and public protests to the dispatch of patrol vessels near the Senkaku area and harassment of Japanese Coast Guard ships. In addition, the Chinese government suddenly established an Air Defense Identification Zone in November 2013 that includes the Senkaku area. There have been repeated incidents when Chinese fighters flew close to the SDF reconnaissance planes. As Japan strengthens the SDF and Coast Guard, it also must hone crisis management skills and be sure responses are proportionate to the provocation in order to avoid inadvertent escalation.

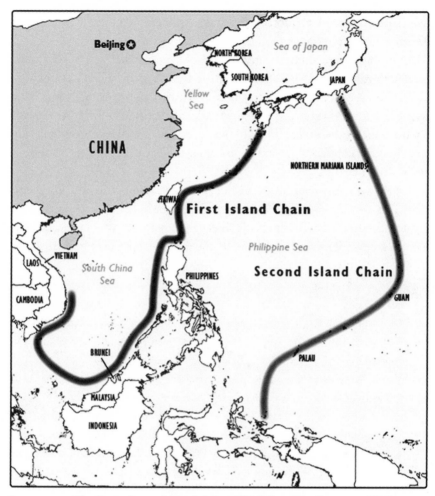

FIGURE 10.4   The first and second island chains. (US Office of the Secretary of Defense, *Annual Report to Congress: Military and Security Developments Involving the People's Republic of China 2012*, 2012, www.defense.gov/pubs/pdfs/2012_CMPR_Final.pdf, 40.)

In a longer-term perspective, China's desire to become a maritime power may be the most destabilizing factor in the region and possibly at the global level. Encircled by relatively close neighbors in the Northwest Pacific, Chinese naval doctrine to control the first and second island chain out from the continent (figure 10.4) is most likely to increase tension. Beijing's aspiration to become a maritime power dates from Deng Xiaoping in the 1980s, but it may be unattractive to President Xi Jinping. One of Japan's strategic objectives is to dissuade China, not by force but by persuasion, from indulging in the pipe dream of one day becoming a global maritime power.

In this age of uncertainty, other sudden large shocks to the world system cannot be ruled out. What if the North Korean regime suddenly collapses, or the Chinese Communist Party is wracked by a power struggle and loses control, or a war breaks out in the Middle East or South Asia, even possibly with nuclear weapons? The political and ideological consensus in Japan, already strained by socioeconomic problems, might be at risk if the country is embroiled in an international conflict.

Enormous challenges lie ahead, yet Japan has a long history of regeneration. The country withstood hardship and danger in the past not because of great leadership but thanks to the resilience of a populace who believed in the nation's future. Our fate will depend on the people's confidence in themselves.

Notes

1. I wish to thank Dr. Martin Jacques and participants in the conference "Possible Futures for Japan," June 30–July 1, 2012, for comments on an earlier version of this paper. I also wish to thank Frank Baldwin for his assistance.

2. "Japain," *Economist*, February 21, 2008, www.economist.com/node/10729998.

3. Cabinet Office, Government of Japan, "Chūgokuni taisuru shinkinkan" [Friendliness to China], under "Public Opinion Polls," Diplomacy home page, http://survey.gov-online.go.jp/h26/h26-gaiko/zh/z08.html (accessed June 25, 2012). The percentage of Japanese who did not have a favorable impression of China decreased to 71.4 percent in October 2011 but was still the second highest since figures were compiled.

4. For the Japanese version of the DPG, see Ministry of Defense of Japan, "Aratana bōei taikō (Heisei 23 nendo iko-ni kakawaru bōei taikō [New defense program guideline: Defense guideline since 2011], www.mod.go.jp/j/approach/agenda/guideline/2011/taikou_new.pdf. For the provisional English translation, see Ministry of Defense of Japan, "National Defense Program Guidelines for FY 2011 and Beyond," December 17, 2010, www.mod.go.jp/e/d_act/d_policy/pdf/guidelinesFY2011.pdf. For the Dynamic Defense Force, see p. 7; for missions, see p. 10. The commitment to the offshore islands seems intentionally vague and includes the Senkakus and islands in Japan's exclusive economic zone.

5. Links to these documents are on the Ministry of Defense home page, www.mod.go.jp/j/approach/agenda/guideline/index.html (accessed June 23, 2012).

6. See Ministry of Defense of Japan, "National Defense Program Guidelines," 13.

7. International Institute for Strategic Studies, *The Military Balance 2012* (London: IISS, 2012), 251, 233, 256.

8. See Ministry of Defense of Japan, "National Defense Program Guidelines," 19.

9. For both Japanese and English versions of the council report, see Council on Security and Defense Capabilities, "Capability Report," Executive Summary, August 2009, www.kantei.go.jp/jp/singi/ampobouei2/dai11/siryou1.pdf.

10. A recent detailed report by the National Institute for Defense Studies analyzes Chinese naval activities; see NIDS China Security Report 2011 (Tokyo: National Institute for Defense Studies, 2012), www.nids.go.jp/english/publication/chinareport/pdf/china_report_EN_web_2011_A01.pdf.

11. The initial agreement on return of the Futenma base was in April 1996. Satoshi Morimoto, *Futenma no nazo* [The puzzle of Futenma] (Tokyo: Kairyusha, 2010), 48. Morimoto, who became defense minister in 2012, suspects that the initial proposal was from the US military in Okinawa.

12. For Japanese and English versions of the council report, see Council on Security and Defense Capabilities in the New Era, "Japan's Vision for Future Security and Defense Capabilities in the New Era: Toward a Peace-Creating Nation," August 2010, www.kantei.go.jp/jp/singi/shin-ampobouei2010/houkokusyo.pdf.

13. For the guidelines, see "Bōei sōbihin toiu no kaigai iten ni kansuru kijun ni tsuite no naikaku kanbōchōkan danwa" [Statement by the chief cabinet secretary on guidelines for the transfer of defense equipment overseas], December 27, 2011, www.kantei.go.jp/jp/tyokan/noda/20111227DANWA.pdf. For a provisional English translation, see "Statement by the Chief Cabinet Secretary on Guidelines for Overseas Transfer of Defense Equipment Etc.," December 27, 2011, http://japan. kantei.go.jp/noda/topics/201112/20111227DANWA_e.pdf. On April 1, 2013, the Abe cabinet formally replaced restrictions on arms sales with "Three Principles on Transfer of Defense Equipment and Technology" (English translation on the Cabinet Office site at www.cas.go.jp/jp/gaiyou/jimu/pdf/bouei2.pdf). Arms sales will now be approved unless (1) the transfer violates obligations under treaties and other international agreements that Japan has concluded, (2) the transfer would violate obligations under UN Security Council resolutions, or (3) the defense equipment and technology are destined for a country that is party to a conflict regarding which the UN Security Council is taking measures to maintain or restore international peace and security.

14. "Joint Statement by the Prime Ministers of the UK and Japan," April 10, 2012, Ministry of Foreign Affairs of Japan, www.mofa.go.jp/region/europe/uk/joint1204.

html, and "Memorandum between the United Kingdom Ministry of Defence and the Japan Ministry of Defense relating to Defence Cooperation," May 28, 2012, Ministry of Defense of Japan, www.mod.go.jp/j/press/youjin/2012/06/03_memo. pdf.

15. See "ASEAN gun e no nōryoku shien taishōkoku kakudai e Filipin nado o kentō" [The Japanese government is considering increased support for ASEAN military forces such as the Philippines] *Sankei Shimbun*, October 7, 2014, www.sankei.com/ politics/news/141007/plt1410070012-n1.html.

16. Kazumasa Imai, "Higashi Nihon daishinsainiokeru Jieitai no katsudō/Nichibei kyōryoku" [Activities of the SDF and Japan-US cooperation in the Great East Japan Earthquake: Lessons learned from SDF disaster relief operations and Operation Tomodachi by US forces], *Rippo to Chosa*, June 2012, www.sangiin.go.jp/japanese/annai/chousa/rippou_chousa/backnumber/2012pdf/20120601061.pdf.

17. For survey results, see Pew Research Center, "Japanese Wary of Nuclear Energy," June 5, 2012, www.pewglobal.org/2012/06/05/japanese-wary-of-nuclear-energy/.

18. Imai, "Higashi Nihon," 63. For a comprehensive analysis of US activities under Operation Tomodachi, see Richard J. Samuels, *3/11: Disaster and Change in Japan* (Ithaca, NY: Cornell University Press, 2013).

19. For the report of the commission headed by Shinichi Kitaoka, see Ministry of Foreign Affairs of Japan, "Iwayuru 'mitsuyaku' mondai-ni kansuru yushikisha iinkai hokokusho" [Report of the experts' committee on the "secret agreement"], March 9, 2010, www.mofa.go.jp/mofaj/gaiko/mitsuyaku/pdfs/hokoku_yushiki.pdf.

20. Imai, "Higashi Nihon," 64.

21. Ken Jimbo, *Ajia Taiheiyō-no anzenhoshō akitekutya: Chiiki anzenhoshō-no sanso kōzō* [Security architecture in the Asia-Pacific: The three-layered structure of regional security] (Tokyo: Nihon Hyoronsha, 2011).

22. For the Japan-Australia Declaration, see Ministry of Foreign Affairs of Japan, "Japan-Australia Joint Declaration on Security Cooperation," March 13, 2007, www.mofa.go.jp/region/asia-paci/australia/joint0703.html. For the Japan-India Joint Statement, see Ministry of Foreign Affairs of Japan, "Joint Statement towards Japan-India Strategic and Global Partnership," December 15, 2006, www.mofa.go.jp/region/asia-paci/india/pdfs/joint0612.pdf.

23. Records of the ministerial and official meeting are at Ministry of Foreign Affairs of Japan, "Nichi-Bei-Gō senryaku taiwa" [Japan-US-Australia strategic dialogue], ministerial meetings (March 2006, November 2006, June 2008, September 2009, October 2013) and official meetings (July 2007, December 2007, April 2009, July 2010), www.mofa.go.jp/mofaj/area/jau/index.html.

24. The Maritime SDF participated in the Malabar exercise in 2007, 2009, and 2014. Ministry of Foreign Affairs, Southwest Asia Division, "Saikin no Indo jōsei to Nichi-Indo kankei" [Recent developments in India and Japan-India relations], February 2015, 2.

25. Ministry of Defense of Japan, *Defense of Japan 2011* (Tokyo, 2011), 315, www.mod. go.jp/e/publ/w_paper/e-book/2011/_SWF_Window.html.

26. Ibid., 331–33.

27. US-Japan Security Consultative Committee, "Joint Statement of the Security Consultative Committee," April 27, 2012, Ministry of Defense of Japan, www.mod. go.jp/j/approach/anpo/js20120427.html.

28. Travis J. Tritten, "On Okinawa, Webb Says DOD Missing Deadlines for Study on Marines Realignment," *Stars and Stripes*, April 3, 2012, www.stripes.com/mobile/news/pacific/okinawa/on-okinawa-webb-says-dod-missing-deadlines-for-study-on-marines-realignment-1.173452, and Senator Jim Webb, "Observations and Recommendations on U.S. Military Basing in East Asia," May 2011, http://webb.senate.gov/issuesandlegislation/foreignpolicy/Observations_basing_east_asia.cfm.

29. For an in-depth analysis of the Yoshida Doctrine, see Kenneth B. Pyle, *The Japanese Question: Power and Purpose in a New Era* (Washington, DC: AEI Press, 1996).

30. The term *Yoshida rosen* (Yoshida Line) was first used by Kosaka Masataka, *Saishō Yoshida Shigeru* [Prime Minister Shigeru Yoshida] (Chuo Koronsha, 1957). The term *Yoshida Doctrine* came into use in Japan and the United States from the late 1970s to the early 1980s. Yoshihide Soeya, "Yoshida rosen to Yoshida dokutorin" [The Yoshida Line and Doctrine], *Kokusai Seiji* 151 (March 2008): 1–17, https://www.jstage.jst.go.jp/article/kokusaiseiji1957/2008/151/2008_151_1/_pdf.

31. Koizumi paid tribute to the war dead, but he did not deny Japan's responsibility for the Pacific War. For Koizumi's visits to Yasukuni Shrine and relations with China, see Yomiuri Shinbun Seijibu, *Gaikō o kenkanishita otoko* [Confrontational diplomacy] (Tokyo: Shinchosha, 2006), chap. 3.

32. Kenneth B. Pyle, *Japan Rising: The Resurgence of Japanese Power and Purpose* (New York: Public Affairs Books, 2007); Richard J. Samuels, *Securing Japan: Tokyo's Grand Strategy and the Future of East Asia* (Ithaca, NY: Cornell University Press, 2007); Andrew L. Oros, *Normalizing Japan: Politics, Identity, and the Evolution of Security Practice* (Stanford, CA: Stanford University Press, 2008); Christopher W. Hughes, *Japan's Remilitarization* (London: International Institute for Strategic Studies, 2009).

33. Yomiuri Shimbun Seijibu, *Gaikō o kenkanishita otoko*, chap. 3, and Hideo Ohtake, *Koizumi Junichirō popyurizumu no kenkyū* [Jun'ichirō Koizumi: A study on populism] (Toyo Keizai Shinposha, 2006). On the other hand, some scholars see Koizumi's era as a significant turning point for policy making because the prime

minister and his staff took the initiative from the ministries. Tomohito Shinoda, *Kantei gaikō* [The prime minister's diplomacy] (Osaka: Asahi Shimbunsha, 2004), and Satoshi Machidori, *Shushōseiji-no seidobunseki* [An institutional analysis of the prime minister] (Tokyo: Chikura Shobo, 2012).

34. For the act and basic plan on ocean policy, see "Kaiyō kihon hō ni tsuite" [Basic act on ocean policy], April 27, 2007, www.kantei.go.jp/jp/singi/kaiyou/konkyo6. pdf; "Kaiyō kihon keikaku" [Basic plan on ocean policy], April 2013, www.kantei. go.jp/jp/singi/kaiyou/kihonkeikaku/130426kihonkeikaku_je.pdf. For documents on space policy, see "Uchū kihon hō" [Basic law on space], www.kantei.go.jp/jp/ singi/utyuu/kihon.pdf, and "Uchū kihon keikaku" [Basic policy for the space plan], 2009, 2013, and 2015, www.kantei.go.jp/jp/singi/utyuu/keikaku.html.

35. The cabinet formed by the LDP–New Kōmeitō coalition in December 2012 quickly reviewed the 2010 DPG. After establishing the National Security Council (dubbed as Japan's NSC or JNSC) in November 2013, the Abe cabinet issued the new DPG as well as the National Security Strategy, the first of its kind by a Japanese government. For an English translation of the 2013 DPG, see National Defense Program Guidelines for FY 2014 and Beyond (Summary), December 17, 2013, www. cas.go.jp/jp/siryou/131217anzenhoshou/ndpg-e.pdf; for the National Security Strategy, see "National Security Strategy December 17, 2013," www.cas.go.jp/jp/ siryou/131217anzenhoshou/nss-e.pdf. The general thrust of these documents is not significantly different from the 2010 DPG, but the series of changes more forthrightly reinforces the SDF and strengthens US-Japan security arrangements.

36. In February 2013, Prime Minister Abe reassembled the expert commission to review the legal basis of security policy that he had formed in his first term and directed it to again examine the issues, including collective defense. The commission published a report on May 15, 2014. (For the English version of the report, see "Report of the Advisory Panel on Reconstruction of the Legal Basis for Security," www.kantei.go.jp/jp/singi/anzen-hosyou2/dai7/houkoku_en.pdf.) After several weeks of consultation between the LDP and the New Kōmeitō Party, on July 1, the cabinet decided on a resolution that overturned the previous constitutional interpretation and enabled Japan to engage in collective defense overseas. (For an English translation of the cabinet decision, see "Cabinet Decision on Development of Seamless Security Legislation to Ensure Japan's Survival and Protect Its People, July 1, 2014," http://japan.kantei.go.jp/96_abe/decisions/2014/__ icsFiles/afieldfile/2014/07/03/anpohosei_eng.pdf.)

CHAPTER ELEVEN

Economic and Strategic Leadership in Asia: The Rivalry between China and Japan

Claude Meyer

"To have a good neighbor is to find something precious," says the proverb, and despite the wary ambivalence between China and Japan, these mighty economies plus India will make Asia preeminent in global growth by 2030.[1] China's rise is without historical precedent. In a mere thirty years this country of 1.3 billion people has pulled itself out of underdevelopment and become the world's second-largest economy, destabilizing the world system and reordering the hierarchy of the great economic powers. China's gross domestic product (GDP) accounts for 11.5 percent of global output and is larger than Japan's; only a decade ago it was only a quarter the size of Japan's GDP. Supplanting Japan in 2010 as the world's second-largest economy was foreseeable, given a Chinese labor force more than ten times that of Japan. However, the suddenness of this shift epitomized the contrast between the tremendous momentum of China's growth and near stagnation in Japan.

In March 2011, *annus horribilis*, Japan suffered its biggest crisis since World War II with three combined disasters—a massive earthquake, a devastating tsunami, and the world's worst nuclear accident since Chernobyl. These came amid what is widely viewed as an irreversible decline for a country handicapped by many structural weaknesses, in particular demographic challenges, skyrocketing public debt, and political paralysis. Although not surprising in itself, surpassing Japan in terms of GDP is symbolic revenge for China and marks a major turning point for both countries.

To many observers, Asia's future is already mapped out with the overwhelming ascent of China and the inexorable decline of Japan. This view of future leadership in Asia is probably misleading, just as the perception of an unstoppable Japan proved to be at the end of the 1980s. Indeed, it fails to take into account the two rivals' ambitions as well as their strengths and weaknesses. While the transfer of economic power to Asia is well under way, especially since the global financial crisis of 2008, China and Japan share the same aspiration to become the dominant force in an integrated Asia. Their quest for supremacy is structured by the dialectical relationship between economics and strategic power. For China, the priority is to accelerate growth in the economic sphere in order to consolidate its strategic influence as a regional leader and global power. Japan seeks to safeguard its economic leadership through technological supremacy while "normalizing" its strategic position in Asia and the world. The evolution of this standoff between China and Japan will shape the future of Asia over the next two decades. On the one hand, China has strategic advantages in international politics and military matters; on the other, a resilient Japan will probably maintain its economic leadership, so they will have to share regional leadership.

Interlinked Fates in a Troubled History

To understand the present and to forecast possible futures, it is worth examining how the paths followed by Japan and China have intersected at certain times in the past. The troubled history of Sino-Japanese relations may be summarized in five stages: kinship, emancipation, "betrayal," aggression, and recognition. These have structured Japan's relations with China and, conscious or not, have deeply marked the national psyche.

Japan's religious and cultural kinship with China dates from the sixth century, when Buddhism and Confucianism spread to Japan from the continent via Korea. Japan came under the cultural sway of the Middle Kingdom, borrowing ideograms, institutions, and social etiquette. The matrix of this mother culture shaped the Japanese people's linguistic, artistic, and spiritual universe, though they adapted it to their own cultural environment. The sixteenth century saw Japan's emancipation from the Chinese world order based on the Hua-Yi tribute system that regulated China's relations with its neighbors. In the imperial cosmogony, China was under heaven at the center of the world as the only civilized place. The emperor was the Son of Heaven, while barbarous neighboring regions could only be his vassals. Peace and the development of trade depended on the tributary system imposed on neighboring countries. However, Japan rejected Chinese suzerainty, paying tribute only for a short period in the fifteenth century and thereafter refusing any form of allegiance to China. This rejection of the Asian tributary system based on Chinese hegemony was of crucial importance for Sino-Japanese relations and should be kept in mind when envisaging what they could be in the future.

With the Meiji Restoration in 1868 Japan chose Western modernity over Chinese tradition, a decision interpreted in China as a kind of betrayal. In fact, the Meiji Restoration inspired the nationalist revolution that led to the overthrow of the Qing dynasty in 1911. For the Chinese revolutionaries seeking to end China's political and economic deliquescence, Japan was a source of inspiration, if not a model. Japan's aggression in the second Sino-Japanese War (1937–45) and the crimes committed by its military forces continue to weigh heavily on bilateral relations.[2] Japan expanded into Manchuria in 1931 and invaded northern China in July 1937. After a bloody battle for Nanjing, Imperial Army troops massacred thousands of Chinese soldiers and civilians in the worst atrocity of the invasion. By 1939, Japanese forces occupied northeastern China and a large portion of its coastal areas. World War II ended in August 1945, and China fell into a civil war won by the communists in 1949. This chapter of the benighted relationship closed when Japan recognized the People's Republic of China in 1972. Six years later the two neighbors signed a treaty of peace and friendship and renounced any hegemonic ambitions.[3]

This complex history illustrates how the two countries were linked in a dialectical movement of fascination and resentment that still affects their relations. From the outset Japan rejected a subordinate status with its larger neighbor with universalist claims, though Japan's cultural universe still bears the imprint of imperial China. Japan took advantage of China's weakness to invade the country, a humiliating experience deeply ingrained in the Chinese consciousness. The suffering that militarist Japan inflicted on the Chinese population left deep scars, and, despite the apologies made by Tokyo several times, resentment against the former invader reappears at the slightest incident. Large anti-Japanese demonstrations took place in China after the Japanese government "nationalized" the Senkaku/Diaoyu Islands in September 2012. The violence of these protests was evidence again of the underlying differences in historical memory that divide the two countries.

A Booming Chinese Economy but Severe Challenges Ahead

China's meteoric economic development over the past thirty years has registered an average annual growth rate of 10 percent; domestic output and income per capita have increased by more than ten times since 1981. The proportion of the population living below the poverty line (one US dollar a day) has fallen from 63 percent to 8 percent, whereas in sub-Saharan Africa it has remained more or less unchanged at around 40 percent over the same period. Among developed countries, however, Beijing's success causes more concern than admiration. The new industrial power became the biggest exporter in 2009 with a market share of 9 percent, compared with only 1 percent in 1980, and China threatens whole industrial sectors across Europe and the United States. Yet these impressive achievements should be seen in historical perspective. As the leading economic power for centuries, China still represented over 30 percent of world GDP in 1820 compared with 23 percent for Europe and only 3 percent for Japan.[4] Although China's achievements look phenomenal because of the size of the country and the length of the growth cycle, they are in fact comparable to those of other countries in the region that have experienced similar growth rates. Japan, of course, achieved 10 percent average annual growth between 1955 and 1973, as did later the Little Dragons (South Korea, Hong Kong, Singapore, and Taiwan) and then the Tigers (Malaysia, Thailand, Indonesia, the Philippines, and Brunei).

Furthermore, China faces challenges and dangers in the future. The first constraint on Chinese growth is a triple dependency on natural resources, technologies, and markets overseas (at least, in the near term). Although China is a leading producer of many minerals, the explosion of industrial demand has resulted in massive imports, worth a net $70 to $80 billion a year. China already uses more than 20 percent of the world's primary energy output, a proportion that is likely to double by 2030. China is self-sufficient only in coal, its first energy source, and is becoming increasingly dependent on oil, now importing half its requirement. That rate could rise to 80 percent by 2030, when the number of cars in the country is expected to reach 270 to 300 million. China is also highly dependent on foreign technologies, which according to some estimates represent 60 to 70 percent of the technologies used in the country by either foreign multinationals or Chinese companies, the latter through licensing agreements or acquisition of foreign companies with high technological value. The third dependence is the overreliance of

Chinese growth on exports, half of which are to Europe and the United States. The drivers of growth are unbalanced, with excessive investments and exports and insufficient domestic consumption.[5] This imbalance requires a reversal of China's development model, one of the objectives of the Twelfth Plan (2011–15).[6] The Third Plenum of the Eighteenth Chinese Communist Party Congress held in November 2013 decided on far-reaching reforms to attain this goal.

In addition to this triple dependency, the Chinese economy is plagued with constraints on growth, starting with social inequalities. Rapid growth has spectacularly reduced poverty in China but has also created a double rift: social inequalities are increasing, and regional disparities are becoming more apparent.[7] The income gap between cities and the countryside has almost doubled in twenty years,[8] and these income inequalities at the national level are compounded by regional disparities between the coastal provinces and the interior.[9] Growing inequality coupled with endemic corruption nourishes popular frustration that often culminates in revolts and "large-scale incidents"; the government fears instability could threaten rapid growth.

Ecological disaster from intensive industrialization and rapid urbanization is also an ominous possibility. More than a third of river water is unfit for any type of use; three hundred million rural dwellers drink unsafe water. With coal supplying 64 percent of primary energy needs, China overtook the United States as the world's biggest emitter of carbon dioxide. China's demand for energy is likely to almost double by 2030.

Increased social security costs and support of the banking system could be a major constraint on public finances. According to one estimate, only half of urban workers and only 25 percent of workers in the countryside have full coverage (health, unemployment, and pension). The official goal is to have a basic system in place by 2020, at a total cost of about US$850 billion. The cost will become increasingly onerous as the population ages and as the labor force shrinks between 2015 and 2020.[10] In short, China could well find itself "old before it gets rich." The fragile banking sector will be another financial burden. The four large state banks had to be rescued in 2000, and massive bank lending to companies weakened by the crisis in 2008–9 will probably lead to new bad debts and further write-offs, brought about by the excessive borrowings of some local governments and the brisk development of a nonregulated shadow banking sector. On the bright side, China's current budgetary situation is relatively sound. The deficit is in the range of 3 percent of GDP, and central government debt, at 20 percent of GDP, is at an enviable level. However, that figure rises to 60 percent and probably higher if one includes the indebtedness of the provinces, whose financial condition is quite difficult to assess and may be far weaker than estimated.

Last but not least, China must deal with the rapid erosion of its comparative advantages—low labor costs and an undervalued currency. Labor costs will soar over the next ten years as a result of substantial wage increases and higher social security charges.[11] Productivity gains will make up for much of the additional outlay, but developed countries might shift their imports from China to lower-cost emerging economies. This trend will be further aggravated by the evolution of the yuan exchange rate, which has already appreciated by 30 percent since 2005 and should continue at a moderate pace, in sync with gains in productivity.[12]

Chinese authorities are well aware of the internal and external challenges ahead. On the domestic front, China will have to cope with a polarized society, an environmental crisis, and heavy financial obligations. External constraints include restrictions on raw material supplies and gradual erosion of the comparative advantages that have stimulated explosive export growth. Together, these could undermine government legitimacy, adding political uncertainty to the mix of factors liable to hinder growth.

Strengths and Weaknesses of a Resilient Japan

Those who see the decline of Japan as ineluctable point to the many weaknesses afflicting its economic and political situation: deflation, demographic decline, a huge public debt exacerbated by the Tōhoku disaster, dependence on imported resources, and, most important, a chronic absence of true political leadership, if one excludes Jun'ichirō Koizumi (2001–6) and Shinzō Abe since December 2012.[13] However, the Cassandras fail to take into account the strengths and resilience of Japan, which still holds a commanding economic and financial position in Asia. Despite having virtually no raw materials and only 2.2 percent of the world's labor force as against China's 27 percent, Japan still produces about 8 percent of world GDP, compared to 11.5 percent for its giant neighbor. This simple fact says much about an economic colossus that combines industrial competitiveness with commercial vigor and financial power.

Japan's industrial and technological prowess remains its trump card. Unlike China, Japan has already entered the postindustrial era and become a knowledge economy; industry accounts for only 26.5 percent of GDP compared with 72 percent for services. Yet Japan is still a top-tier industrial power, in third place behind the United States and China. One of the many factors underlying the success of Japanese industry was the strategy implemented under the aegis of the Ministry of International Trade and Industry based on the targeting of products with substantial technological value added and strong global demand. That is why Japan is at the forefront of the automobile industry and the world leader in machine tools and industrial robots. It leads the field in some of the most advanced segments of electronics and biotechnologies and is preparing the technologies of the future. Two pillars support this offensive strategy: the abandonment or relocation of unprofitable activities and innovation in buoyant industries.

Japan's commercial vigor seems to have weakened in the face of China's aggressive export drive, since over the last ten years Japan's share of world trade fell from 8 percent to 5 percent. This apparent loss of commercial power to China does not mean that Japan is less competitive but rather that its manufacturing sector has become more international. Exports alone are not a true yardstick of Japan's global market share, which is three times larger when the production of Japanese companies overseas is included. Financial strength is another mainstay of Japan's economic power. This seems like a paradox for a country with the highest public debt among members of the Organisation for Economic Co-operation and Development (OECD), but national investors finance 95 percent of domestic debt. In spite of China's rising foreign exchange reserves, Japan remains the world's largest creditor nation, with US$3.1 trillion net assets held in other countries at the end of 2013 against US$2 trillion for China.

On the basis of these industrial, technological, and financial strengths, Japan has imposed its economic supremacy in Asia. Despite the scars of history, Japan is the benchmark for the region, most of which has borrowed its economic model. Since the 1980s, Japanese multinationals have played a leading role in the vertical division of labor in Asia by developing a dense network of production facilities across the region. These multinationals and their subcontractors have spread throughout Asia in successive waves and now have some ten thousand subsidiaries, including five thousand in China. Japan has had a decisive influence on the structure of industry in Asia. Vertical integration between Japan, China, and the rest of Asia owes much to Japanese production networks. The Japanese model combines fragmented manufacturing processes with highly centralized control of subsidiaries by the parent company. This form of industrial organization has done much to shape the "Asian integrated circuit," distinguished by a high level of intrafirm exchanges. With its strict hierarchies, this industrial model gives Japanese firms supremacy in Asia because it is based on technological leadership and exceptional control over methods of production.

In finance, too, Japan wields overwhelming power in Asia. As the world's leading creditor nation, it is a major donor to multilateral institutions and has the capital, institutions, and expertise to reign supreme in Asia. The size of its financial markets dwarfs those in the rest of the region, and its big financial institutions are among the world's largest. The expansion of private sector financial players has been compounded by the highly active economic diplomacy pursued by Tokyo in Asia over the last thirty years, especially through Official Development Assistance. Japan became the world's largest donor nation in 1989 and until the early 2000s directed more than half of its foreign aid to developing Asian countries. Japan is still the biggest donor to countries in the Association of Southeast Asian Nations (ASEAN) and was long the leading donor to China. At the multilateral level, Japan has a decisive influence on the policy pursued by the Asian Development Bank; Tokyo nominates the president and has 17 percent of the voting rights. Additionally, in the aftermath of the 1997–98 Asian financial crisis Japan has played a leading role in monetary coordination between the countries of the region.

Japanese leadership in Asia rests on a third foundation of "soft power" that influences the countries of the region through a value system, ideas, and culture. Japan elicits ambivalent feelings in many Asian countries: mistrust of the former oppressor mixed with fascination at its success. Japan exerts a kind of soft power as an economic model and cultural trendsetter, although it is in competition with South Korea for the latter. Its development model has greatly enhanced Japan's prestige in the region as other countries have replicated its export-oriented growth strategy, adjusted to their own circumstances. The spread of Japanese cultural goods—films, manga, music—in Asia has almost doubled in ten years and helps to reinforce the "Cool Japan" image among young people. Tokyo is well aware that soft power is another weapon in the battle for prestige and influence in Asia. Japan can boast not only democratic institutions that contrast with China's authoritarian regime but also attractive economic and cultural models.

Although exceptionally resilient in successive crises, including the Tōhoku triple catastrophe, Japan faces daunting challenges over the next decades. Structural weaknesses will undermine future performance. Compared with China's potential, the prospects for long-term growth are poor. Productivity gains decelerate in a mature economy like Japan's: markets for many products are saturated, and domestic demand is small in comparison with other economies in the region such as India and China. Setting aside chronic political inertia, three other factors also cloud the economic horizon: demographics, public sector debt, and dependence on energy sources abroad. Demographic decline is the most serious of these handicaps because it is irreversible unless the birthrate picks up from its very low present level. Indeed, the demographic challenge is the result of a scissors effect that produces an ever-widening gap between a low fertility rate and rising life expectancy.[14] The total population has begun to shrink, and the decline in the labor force will be even more spectacular.[15] An aging population will inevitably cost more in health care and pensions, which will have to be funded from a shrinking base. A solution could be found within the broader region, which has abundant skilled labor. Encouragement of immigration from other parts of Asia would enable Japan not only to preserve its economic vitality but also to enhance its image in the region. However, the population is culturally hostile to immigration, and this has so far deterred the authorities from taking vigorous measures, which will be unavoidable in the long term.

The economy is also handicapped by gross public sector debt, approaching 238 percent of GDP at the end of 2013, compared with 173 percent in 2008. A significant part of the massive debt overhang is attributable to the numerous stimulus plans introduced during the crisis of the 1990s, costing a total of US$1 trillion. Even if almost all the debt is financed by domestic investors and the net debt, after stripping out holdings of financial assets, is a more reasonable 130 percent of GDP, this massive debt is a sword of Damocles hanging over growth. Very strong corrective measures, including tax increases, will be needed in the next decade to reduce it to more acceptable levels. The increase of the consumption tax from 5 percent to 8 percent in April 2014 and probably 10 percent in October 2015 is a first step in the right direction, but this rate will have to be significantly increased over the medium term to bring about a substantial reduction of the public debt. Dependence on imported raw materials and energy is another weakness, although the economy is very energy efficient.[16] Tokyo's energy policy has been based on three interwoven strands: energy savings, sustainable development, and diversification of sources of supply. Japan's experience in reducing energy consumption dates from the first oil shock in 1973. The constant quest for energy efficiency is coupled with ambitious environmental protection goals, especially against the greenhouse effect. The only Asian country bound by the Kyoto Protocol, Japan had set a target of reducing CO_2 emissions 25 percent by 2020 compared to 1990.[17] But post-Fukushima Japan is now facing a severe dilemma concerning the reactivation of some of its fifty-five nuclear reactors, which provided 29 percent of its electricity needs. The nuclear accident will have far-reaching consequences for energy policies in place since the 1970s. Increased imports of fossil fuels, especially liquid natural gas, will raise the energy bill, aggravate the dependency on other countries for an energy mix, and considerably increase pollution. Consequently, Japan withdrew from the Kyoto Protocol in November 2012 and decided to reduce its CO_2 emissions only 3.8 percent by 2020 compared to 2005.

As a result of all these impediments, the Japanese economic recovery will be quite modest in the coming years. According to the International Monetary Fund, real GDP should increase by 1.7 percent in 2014 and 1 percent in 2015. In the longer run, the current forecast is that the economy will grow at a 1.1 percent annual rate over the 2010–19 decade, and 0.8 percent in the following decade through 2029. But the potential growth could be boosted by the ambitious economic plan implemented by Prime Minister Abe starting in the beginning of 2013. This program, dubbed "Abenomics" by the media, is composed of short-term monetary and fiscal measures coupled with far-reaching structural reforms. Some of these reforms will be in any case required by Japan's participation in the Trans-Pacific Partnership. Abe's plan is discussed in chapter 7 by Saori Katada and Gene Park in this volume.

Complementary and Interdependent Economies

China and Japan are closely linked by similar development models and increasing integration through complementarities and mutual dependencies. Whatever the differences in their political systems, a high degree of convergence is apparent in their growth patterns. Of course, China can point to the unique nature of its development experience, but the way the economy has taken off since 1978 has much in common with Japan's initial stirrings during the Meiji period and then the formidable industrial expansion in 1955–73.

Whether in China's thirty golden years (1980–2010) or Japan's high-growth era, the same four elements—savings, education, government policy, and private enterprise—played key roles. There are also some differences. The first is to be found in the classic growth factors of labor, capital, and technological innovation. The twin drivers of Japan's rapid-growth period were capital investment and technological progress; labor made a negligible contribution, since there was virtually no increase in the labor force or the number of hours worked. For China, too, investment was the main driver of growth, but labor made a greater contribution than technological progress, for employment grew by 2 percent a year whereas technological progress advanced more slowly.

In both countries the state has been a "developer" through government policy, but in China it also has an entrepreneurial role through direct involvement in the production system. The state sector still accounts for a third of domestic output. The two models show similarities in external commercial relations and in their approach to globalization; both take a neomercantilist approach that protects the domestic market and promotes exports, leveraged at certain times by an undervalued currency. Yet there are two striking differences.

First, China saw openness to foreign investment as the quickest way to overcome its technology lag. Conversely, Japan has always preferred to acquire foreign technologies in order to protect its own market and safeguard its socioeconomic system. The door has opened just a crack since the mid-1990s, but the stock of foreign investment still represents only 4 percent of GDP compared with 25 percent in China and 38 percent in the United States.

Second, China, which does not yet have a large domestic market, is also much more open to international trade. Exports rose from 20 percent of GDP in the 1990s to an average of 32 percent since China joined the World Trade Organization (WTO) in 2001, compared with less than 10 percent for Japan in the 1960s and 1970s. Whatever the differences, the models that underpin the economic "miracles" in Japan from 1955 to 1973 and in China from 1978–80 to 2008 have many common features: educated labor forces, low wages, still largely administered economies, abundant personal savings to fuel industrial investment, selective openness to international trade, and above all a common national resolve to gain economic supremacy and thereby erase past humiliations.

The two economies are closely connected. China and Japan together account for more than three-quarters of East Asia's GDP, while China alone accounts for over half of emerging Asia's GDP. The economic relations between Asia's two giants are therefore the key to assessing the true extent of Japan's supremacy in the region. The structure of those relations is determined by mutual dependence in trade, investment, and finance. The extensive integration of the two dominant economies, at once complementary and interdependent, marks a major turning point in regional configuration. China's accession to the WTO in 2001 massively boosted its foreign trade. Japan was the main beneficiary, as China has become its major trade partner. Just as Japan needs the Chinese market, China needs the technology imported from Japan in the form of machinery, components, and so forth. Bilateral trade reflects the vertically integrated production networks in Asia. China depends on the technology of Japanese companies, which have tripled the number of their Chinese subsidiaries in ten years. Most of the top thousand Japanese industrial firms have factories in China, yet only 8 percent of Japan's foreign direct investment worldwide is there, against 27 percent in Europe and 32 percent in the United States. That cautious approach to investment in China is matched by a highly selective relocation of activities, which generally exclude research and development. Extremely mindful of intellectual property issues, Japan is the leading foreign investor in terms of patents filed in China.

About 20 percent of Japan's total trade is with China, up from 13 percent in 2000 and 7 percent in 1995. On the Chinese side, trade with Japan, its leading supplier, represents 10 percent of the total. Unlike the United States and Europe, Japan's trade with China/Hong Kong is balanced. Trade integration between the two Asian giants stems from the broader process of regional integration, which here achieves its full effect, since the development gap between the two economies makes them complementary in terms of both markets and products. Japan exports goods with a high technological content, such as electronic components and machine tools, and imports products with less value added, such as consumer electronics, textiles, and agricultural products. This complementarity results from the two countries' comparative advantages in an almost ideal configuration, with advanced technology on one side and low-cost labor on the other. Consequently, there is still little competition between their products in markets in the developed world. On closer examination, however, China's trade positions appear to be growing very rapidly at Japan's expense. Chinese exports (manufactured goods only) rose from 6 percent to 14 percent of the world market between 1995 and 2005, while Japan's market share fell by four points, from 14 percent to 10 percent, over the same period.[18] However, these customs statistics give only a partial account of the real situation because Chinese export figures includes products manufactured by Japanese companies in China.

Given the levels of development in the two countries, their interdependence is asymmetrical. At first sight it looks as though Japan is more dependent, since 18 percent of its exports go to China whereas Japan absorbs only 8 percent of Chinese exports, considerably less than the United States and Europe (18 percent each). But while the Chinese market is essential for Japan's growth, China is probably more reliant on Japan than vice versa. China's industrial and commercial expansion relies to a considerable extent on technology from Japan in the form of intermediate goods (components) or capital goods (machinery).

China and Japan have not signed a free trade agreement (FTA), even though they are keen to conclude FTAs with many other countries in the region. Instead, they are considering a tripartite FTA with South Korea. The agricultural component of any such agreement would be an obstacle for Japan because of the poor productivity of its farmers. More importantly, both Tokyo and Beijing fear a relentless competition in each other's domestic markets. Head-to-head competition between Chinese and Japanese exporters, currently slight in the developed countries, is already keen in emerging markets and will intensify as China reduces the technology gap. The Japanese market will not be immune from Chinese competition, so Tokyo has no interest in opening it up too soon. At present, Sino-Japanese competition is strongest in access to natural resources, under way now over oil in Siberia and exploitation of hydrocarbon deposits in the East China Sea. In the future, that competition will play out in the arena of technology. At least that is China's intention and the greatest threat to Japan's supremacy.

The Battle for Technological Supremacy

Japan remains indisputably Asia's leading economy, but China seeks to close the gap in double-quick time and be the region's only global power capable of projecting its influence in both the economic and the strategic spheres. Japan cannot contest China over the size of their economies—that battle has already been lost—but it can contend in terms of innovation and creativity. Japan is almost six times more productive than China, a ratio that carries over to the disparity in income per capita, US$38,000 for Japan against US$6,800 for China. Japan will soon be just a medium-sized economic power, but it has no intention of relinquishing its lead in technology. China has set itself highly ambitious objectives in that area for 2020.

Indeed, technology is the main reason for Japan's leadership, and China is determined to catch up. Currently, Japan's global domination is outstanding, as can be seen from the amounts devoted to research and development and number of patents. Its R&D expenses represent 3.6 percent of its GDP, compared to an average of 2.3 percent by OECD members. These expenditures pay off in patents. Japan ranks first in number of patents per capita, obtaining each year 29 percent of the world total of triadic patents (recorded at the same time in Japan, the United States, and Europe), and receives 22 percent of the patents granted in the United States. These figures refer to annual flows. Japan's global technological standing is even more striking when compared with Japanese companies' patents in force worldwide, expressed in millions at the end of 2010. According to World Intellectual Property Indicators, Japan was first with 2.03, followed by the United States (1.46), South Korea (0.56), Germany (0.30), and China (0.27).[19] The efficiency of Japanese R&D is confirmed by the ratio of patent applications per US$ million of research and development expenditure. Japan is second behind South Korea and well above the United States (fifteenth). Japan's strength is concentrated in high-technology sectors—electronics, mechanical engineering, fine chemicals, new nanostructure materials, energy, and the environment. It excels also in the fusion technologies that combine different elements, such as mechatronics or optronics. Japanese firms do more than develop new products: they are also expert at optimizing industrial processes through *monozukuri*, the quintessence of science, technology, and skill to make things.

China's vision, as outlined in the fifteen-year Science and Technology Plan (2006–20), is to transform itself rapidly into a major technological power and become the world's laboratory, not just its workshop. Beijing intends to develop the capacity for independent innovation in key sectors and ultimately to increase spending on R&D from 1.4 percent to 2.5 percent of its GDP, which would mean a quadrupling in value, taking into account the foreseeable increase in the GDP. Promising progress has already been made in several industries: aviation, aerospace, railway, and information technology. Yet there is a very long way to go before China can reduce its heavy reliance on foreign technologies, especially Japanese. R&D spending has more than quadrupled in eight years, but it still seems paltry in comparison to the Japanese figure. Although the number of researchers in China has doubled since 2000, it is one-tenth the figure in Japan in relation to the workforce. Chinese researchers already rank third in the world for total articles published and are almost on a par with Japan. In 2012 China was number one in patent applications with 27.8 percent of the world total (against 1.8 percent in 1995), ahead of the United States (23.1 percent) and Japan (14.6 percent), but the number of Chinese patents filed abroad remains very small.[20] The rapid results in some sectors and the vast resources putatively allocated are evidence that China has embarked on its quest to catch up.

According to specialists, technological progress in Chinese industry remains a mixed picture. China is gaining ground in certain sectors with a high international profile, such as automobile production, space, shipbuilding, railways, and renewable energy sources. Chinese car makers aim to catch up soon with their Japanese rivals in the clean-car segment. Great strides have been made in applied research, but basic research remains rather underdeveloped and fails to produce genuine innovation, even in priority sectors like space and electronics. So China's race to catch up in innovation will be a marathon, not a sprint. Moreover, the outcome is uncertain because Japan, the leader of the pack, is stepping up the pace. China is playing for very high stakes: technology is the key to economic supremacy in Asia, which in turn is a precondition for overall leadership in the region. It would seem difficult for Beijing to achieve this objective before 2025–30.

Strategic Issues: China's "Peaceful Rise"?

China's pursuit of power, masked by the mantra of a "peaceful rise," is matched by Japan's aspiration to a "normalization" that would enable Tokyo to assert itself vigorously in strategic matters on the regional and global stage. For the neorealist John Mearsheimer, China is an example of a nation seeking to establish hegemony in its own region in order to extend its sphere of domination and ultimately control the entire global system. As for the political and strategic dimensions of its action in Asia, China plays the role of an enterprising and "benign" regional player with two objectives: to maintain stability in the region, necessary for its own economic expansion, and to increase its influence by allaying fears of a "Chinese threat." This policy has three main strands: stable borders, regional security, and economic diplomacy.

China has settled eleven territorial disputes since 1998 and has concluded agreements with almost all its neighbors. Some disagreements over land frontiers remain with India, but more worrying are China's escalating disputes over maritime rights in the China Sea, both with Japan in the eastern part (Diaoyu/Senkaku Islands) and with neighboring countries in the south, particularly Vietnam and the Philippines.[21] Deeply scarred by past foreign domination, China is extremely prickly on matters of territorial integrity and sovereignty, as in Tibet and Xinqiang, while Taiwan remains the cloud on the horizon.

Security in Asia is a prime objective of Chinese foreign policy: Chinese diplomats are very active in the ASEAN Regional Forum and try to exercise a kind of tutelage over ASEAN countries. However, tensions in the South China Sea have been increasing since 2010, as China asserts more and more strongly its territorial claims, especially over rights to exploit the region's possibly extensive reserves of oil and gas. Freedom of navigation, notably in China's two-hundred-mile exclusive economic zone, is also a contentious issue because Beijing seems to consider the South China Sea a region of core interest. Furthermore, China's ambitions in Asia come up against US strategic domination of the region. Beijing feels encircled by a mighty American network of military bases and alliances. Consequently, China's diplomatic action focuses on Central Asia and the Korean peninsula, the latter through the Six-Party Talks.[22]

The third strand of Chinese regionalism is economic diplomacy through FTAs in Asia, which some commentators have compared to the old tribute system tinged with neomercantilism. China's cooperation with ASEAN, more advanced than that of Japan or South Korea, has already culminated in a free-trade area that came into effect in 2010. China is also increasingly influential in monetary and financial cooperation within the ASEAN+3 and at meetings of the Asian Development Bank.

In using its influence in Asia to consolidate its international stature, China has two key advantages that Japan lacks: permanent membership in the UN Security Council and nuclear weapons. To achieve its ambitions, China is engaging in very dynamic diplomacy and modernizing a "purely defensive" army of over two million whose budget has more than tripled since 2000. China's greater openness to the rest of the world has a dual dimension: economic, through its accession to the WTO, and political, through its conversion to multilateralism. China's proactive global diplomacy, sometimes contradictory, seeks to promote bilateral trade and to contribute to the stability of the global system on a multipolar basis. Bilateral economic partnerships are important, especially in Africa and Latin America, to secure raw materials and diversify export markets, but Washington remains the primary focus of bilateral diplomacy, as this relationship is vital for both economies. China needs the US market and the United States needs Chinese savings. More broadly, Beijing feels driven to speak for the developing countries in a world run by the developed nations and has already used the Group of Twenty masterfully for this purpose. China has the potential to become a great power and, unlike Japan, has a clear vision of its place in tomorrow's world. Yet China's multilateralism is ambiguous, and its foreign policy is subject to a dialectical tension between ambitions as a responsible great power and the priorities of economic diplomacy and policy of nonintervention in the internal affairs of other countries, as evidenced in its stance on Syria.

Which "Normalization" for Japan?

Precluded constitutionally from certain options available to China, Japan occupies a very peculiar position both geographically and strategically. Although located in Asia, Japan borrowed the Western development model to modernize during the Meiji Restoration and thus "left Asia" to "join Europe" as Fukuzawa Yukichi put it in "Goodbye Asia."[23] In the 1947 Constitution Japan renounced war, an essential attribute of power. Tokyo's foreign policy is often difficult to interpret because it oscillates between contradictory demands. To cope with this complex positioning, Tokyo has built its foreign policy on a renewed focus on Asia and an active pacifism that tries to reconcile a military alliance with Washington and a commitment to multilateralism centered on the United Nations. The strategic return to Asia was marked in 1992 by a highly symbolic event: participation in a UN peacekeeping operation in Cambodia. This sent the message that Japan wanted to be a responsible and useful regional power, not only anxious to protect its economic interests but also willing to work for stability and peace. If the mission in Cambodia was already a significant change in Tokyo's defense policy, Prime Minister Abe's plan, announced in July 2014, of a new interpretation of the constitution is a major turning point: under the right of a "collective self-defense," Japan could come to the aid of allies attacked by a common enemy, even if Japan is not itself under attack. Japan is more and more involved in regional security issues as threats grow in the region, from North Korea but also potentially from China, whose military expenses have exploded in recent years. Japan wants to be a "normal" country that takes diplomatic action and develops defense capabilities commensurate with its economic strength. Tokyo's dilemma is how to reconcile the pacifism imposed by its constitution with the desire to be recognized as a global power like China, albeit on a different level. Benefiting from American military protection, Japan wants to assert itself as a great civilian power that serves the cause of peace and global public goods within the UN framework. In other words, it has switched from a passive pacifism to an active one. Japan believes in international cooperation rather than confrontation, in disarmament rather than deterrence. Without any universalist pretensions, Tokyo draws on its economic power and the moral legitimacy of its pacifism to promote global public goods, human security, peace-building, and respect for the environment, for which it has an unrivaled legitimacy, attributes that would qualify it to be a permanent member in a reformed UN Security Council. Admission to the inner circle would be recognition that Japan had achieved great power standing through economic and technological leadership combined with active pacifism committed to the promotion of public goods worldwide.

Shaping the Future of Asia

The idea of an Asian Community is gaining traction even if it will take decades to achieve because of the disparities within the region. Currently neither of the two dominant powers fulfills all the conditions for undisputed hegemony in the region. Japan is the leading economy, but its pacifist constitution deprives it of strategic options. Conversely, China is still an economic power in the making, and it will take two decades or so to surpass Japan, particularly in the technological field. Until then, the two regional powers presumably will have to share leadership in the region. In the coming years, their relations will be structured by a very unstable mix of rivalry and pragmatic cooperation. Co-leadership is already emerging in regional bodies such as ASEAN+3, but this shared leadership is bound to be quite antagonistic. Indeed, mistrust runs very deep, rooted in history and exacerbated by the dispute over the Senkaku/Diaoyu Islands, China's unilateral decision in November 2013 to impose an Air Defense Identification Zone in the East China Sea, and Abe's visit to Yasukuni Shrine the following month. Furthermore, on both sides, the new leaders—Prime Minister Abe and President Xi Jinping—display assertive stances about the roles of their own countries. Their visions of regional architecture are incompatible.

Two scenarios can be envisaged for an Asian Community. Should the Asian Community comprise not only ASEAN+3 but also Australia, India, and New Zealand (the so-called ASEAN+6), Japan will find its place as part of a cooperative arrangement with both China and India in a kind of triumvirate. India's huge population and strategic clout will limit China's influence, and the Asian Community will be inspired by the democratic values shared by most of its members. This scenario would certainly be best for the harmonious development of the region.

On the other hand, if this community comprises, as Beijing wants, only ASEAN+3 (China, Japan, and South Korea), the grouping will be entirely under the sway of China. By 2030, China's economy will be four times as big as Japan's, and Beijing will probably be in a position to impose both economic and political dominance on the rest of Asia. Japan will refuse to become a satellite of China and will endeavor to find a new position for itself, combining economic power, financial wealth, strong conventional defense, and international influence through the promotion of global public goods. In short, Japan will become a large Asian Switzerland, prosperous and pacifist. Given the ascent of a more and more powerful and assertive China during the next fifteen years or so, this scenario appears to be the most probable.

Notes

1. For a comprehensive study of the Sino-Japanese rivalry through 2011, see Claude Meyer, *China or Japan: Which Will Lead Asia?* (New York: Oxford University Press, 2012).

2. Japan won the first war in 1894–95.

3. In September 2012, in protest against Japan's policy toward the Senkaku/Diaoyutai Islands, China canceled commemorative activities to mark the fortieth anniversary of the restoration of diplomatic relations. "Opportunity Lost as Hard-Liners in China Gain Support," *Asahi Shimbun*, September 24, 2012.

4. Angus Maddison, *Chinese Economic Performance in the Long Run, 960–2030*, 2nd rev. ed. (Paris: Organisation for Economic Co-operation and Development, October 2007), 50. GDP is expressed in purchasing power parity.

5. Consumption as a proportion of GDP fell from 47 percent in 1996 to 32 percent in 2011. *China Statistical Yearbook* (Beijing: National Bureau of Statistics of China), various issues.

6. This reorientation of the economy is one of the main topics of *China 2030: Building a Modern, Harmonious, and Creative High-Income Society*, by World Bank and

Development Research Center of the State Council of the People's Republic of China (Washington, DC: World Bank, 2012).

7. The Gini index, which measures income inequality on a rising scale from 0 to 1, was 0.28 in 1980 and 0.474 in 2012. "Inequality: Gini out of the Bottle," *Economist*, January 26, 2013, www.economist.com/news/china/21570749-gini-out-bottle.

8. The multiplier is now about 4, rising to 6 if access to health care and education is included. Rural inhabitants account for 55 percent of China's population but only 11 percent of national wealth. *China Statistical Yearbook 2011*.

9. Income per capita in the richest provinces is six times greater than in the poorest, against four times ten years ago. Most growth centers are located in the coastal provinces, which account for 60 percent of GDP and 90 percent of foreign trade with only 38 percent of the population. *China Statistical Yearbook 2011*.

10. From 6.8 percent of the population in 2000, those over sixty-five are expected to be 12 percent in 2020 and 16 percent in 2030. The number of workers per retiree will fall from its current level of nine to four by 2030. See United Nations, *World Population Prospects: The 2008 Revision* (New York: United Nations, 2009).

11. Wages have increased by 15 percent a year on average between 2001 and 2007, and 20 percent thereafter. *China Statistical Yearbook*, various issues.

12. Economists diverge on the appropriate level of the yuan. Some opine that in 2012 it reached its equilibrium rate, while others think it is still undervalued by 20 to 25 percent.

13. The cost of reconstruction from the Tōhoku disaster is estimated at about US$250 billion or 5 percent of GDP. After the 2011 recession, economic growth resumed in 2012. *OECD Economic Outlook* 2012, no. 1 (2012).

14. The fertility rate is 1.37 children per woman, compared with 1.65 in the OECD countries as a whole. Life expectancy is eighty-two years on average, compared with seventy-four in Europe and seventy-seven in the United States. Ibid.

15. The working-age population is projected to fall from eighty-two million in 2010 to sixty-nine million in 2030 and fifty-two million in 2050. Those over sixty-five will account for 31 percent of the population in 2030 and 38 percent in 2050. OECD, *OECD Family Database*, April 2011, www.oecd.org/social/family/database.

16. With comparable GDP, Japan consumes 4.7 percent of world energy against China's 15 percent. Japan is the world leader in energy efficiency. International Energy Agency, *World Energy Outlook 2011* (Paris: IEA, November 2011).

17. The two main polluters of the planet, the United States and China, are not parties to the Kyoto Protocol.

18. European Commission, *Global Europe–EU Performance in the Global Economy* (Brussels: European Commission, October 2008).

19. World Intellectual Property Organization, *World Intellectual Property Indicators 2011* (Geneva: World Intellectual Property Organization, 2011).

20. In 2012, China ranked eighth for patents filed abroad (twenty-six thousand against around two hundred thousand each for Japan and the United States). Ibid.

21. China's dispute with Vietnam concerns the Spratly and the Paracel Islands, while the issue with the Philippines is the Scarborough Shoal.

22. The six participants are China, Japan, North Korea, Russia, South Korea, and the United States.

23. Fukuzawa Yukichi, the most influential Japanese intellectual of the time and founder of Keio University, coined the motto in an unsigned article denouncing the inertia of a conservative China that refused to embrace progress. See "Datsu-A Ron" ["Goodbye Asia"], *Jiji Shinpo*, March 16, 1885.

CHAPTER TWELVE

Possible Futures of Political Leadership: Waiting for a Transformational Prime Minister

Ellis S. Krauss and Robert J. Pekkanen

Japan faces a host of serious challenges: demographic decline that is the steepest in the world; economic stagnation and yawning public deficits; the future of Japan's energy policy; the rise of a militarily powerful neighbor with territorial issues and bitter wartime memories in China; a hostile, unstable, and probably nuclear-armed North Korea; and unresolved and potentially hugely disruptive base issues with its sole ally in the world, the United States.[1] However, many lament that leadership to solve or manage these problems seems to be in short supply in these tough times, pointing to the seemingly endless number of prime ministers shuffling through the turnstile in Nagata-chō and the nearly monotonic and precipitous rot in popularity and public support that sets in from the instant a new prime minister is anointed. At the time when leadership is more needed than ever, it is harder to find.

We do not believe that strong leadership is inevitably good, or even needed to solve all problems.[2] Nor can the long-term consequences of policies necessarily be known at the time. However, there is a widespread public dissatisfaction with the state of Japan's leadership, and a sound case can be made that the real challenge facing Japan has been political leadership itself. In other words, the country's challenges can be met with astute and creative political leadership but cannot be managed even adequately without it. Does Japan's near future include such leaders? We envision a few possible futures for political leadership in Japan. We see a number of institutional constraints that reduce the likelihood that leaders will succeed. But we argue that, contrary to the naysayers' expectations, there are reasons to believe that a transformational leader may emerge from Japan's party politics, and indeed one potentially transformative leader seems to have recently emerged. We will deal later with whether the transformations he might bring are for better or worse.

We proceed in our analysis by first clarifying what we mean by *leadership* and then reviewing the postwar terrain for Japanese leaders. We contend that relatively low stakes characterized Japan's leadership before around 1994; a weak Prime Minister's Office meant little policy influence, and the PM's popularity was relatively unconnected with the party's fate at the polls. Most PMs were classical "transactional" leaders, distributing appointments in exchange for support. Nevertheless, stability and a degree of effectiveness in policy making and problem solving were provided by an institutionalized system of the national bureaucracy and the veteran politicians in the Liberal Democratic Party (LDP) who were also experts at policy and policy making. The political success of Yasuhiro Nakasone showed, however, that even under these conditions a relatively strong and successful—if not a fully "transformational"—leader could emerge.

On the other hand, beginning in the late 1980s and especially after various electoral and administrative reforms of the 1990s, several social and political trends combined to make it more important to have the right person in the PM's office. These new circumstances could enable a skillful leader to exploit them to provide popular and transformative leadership; they could also doom others to nasty, brutish, and short terms in office. These structural changes produced substantial instability, and today obstacles abound to thwart effective and stable leadership in Japan.

In this article we document the changes that have brought us to the present conditions of political leadership in Japan. On the basis of this analysis, we then offer different scenarios to answer the question: What are the possible alternative futures for leadership in Japan?

Defining *Leadership*

We are centrally concerned here with investigating leadership as *position*.[3] In our mind, this means focusing on the leadership of the prime minister: the legal head of government in Japan and, for many, the "face" of the country. The extent of the PM's power can certainly be debated, as can be the issue of his influence over, or with, the public (as his recent decision to cut back nuclear energy by 2040 calls into question—a decision said to have been influenced by the public sentiment against nuclear energy and by antinuclear protests). Yet there is no other single figure in Japan who is more widely recognized as a leader both inside and outside the country. For that reason, we focus on the position of the prime minister, considering the structural or institutional factors that affect the exercise of leadership, as well as individual qualities that come into play in assuming (or not) the role of leader.[4] In this approach, we recognize the importance of both individual "statecraft" and the structure of institutions.[5]

James MacGregor Burns poses a useful distinction between what he calls "transactional" and "transformational" leadership.[6] Simply put, most leaders are "transactional" types whose leadership involves an exchange between leaders and followers such that the follower gets payments (wages, prestige, or, in our case, government or party positions) for complying with the leader's wishes. This neatly fits the PMs of the '55 system, as we explain below, because most of them traded posts for votes in the party presidential election. In contrast, transformational leaders do not simply play the game well enough to win or merely get compliance. Rather, they change beliefs or the institutional rules of the game of political possibilities. Samuels might say that they "stretch constraints."[7] We argue below that there are greater possibilities for a transformational leader these days than under the '55 system. As a caveat, we want to make clear that we do not see a sudden discontinuous or step change, and we are certainly not saying that there were no powerful leaders until 1993 or that all PMs are now colossi.[8] Rather, we argue that the conditions or the prerequisites for what made a great leader were different in the two periods.

Leadership under the '55 System

The '55 system—as the period from the formation of the perennially ruling LDP until it lost power to a coalition of several reforming smaller opposition parties in 1993 was commonly known—was characterized by weak prime ministerial leadership and very decentralized and fragmented vote gathering, party leadership, and policy-making processes of the party.[9] Some political scientists see these characteristics as the result of the multimember district electoral system whereby several candidates of the LDP competed in the same district. Others attribute more weight to the internecine conflicts and rivalries among party leaders and between them and the party's rank-and-file representatives. But all agree that, whatever its cause, the party had arguably not only the most decentralized but the largest organization of the industrialized parliamentary democracies.[10]

Votes were mobilized by individual representatives' personal vote-gathering district organizations; bargaining among the five powerful personal leadership factions determined who became prime minister as well as all appointments to party, parliamentary, and leadership positions; and veteran midlevel LDP representatives (who served in its intraparty policy-making group, the Policy Affairs Research Council) constituted "policy tribes" (*zoku giin*) that, along with the powerful national bureaucrats, were the major shapers of party and government policy. For these reasons, the party leader, who automatically became prime minister with the LDP's perpetual majority, was a relatively weak leader. As Kenji Hayao argues, the PM's major influence on policy was to provide extra impetus to select proposals already on the policy agenda.[11] Japan's decentralized party and bottom-up policy-making process contrasted sharply with centralized parties and systems, as for example in the United Kingdom and New Zealand.

Almost all the prime ministers in this system headed party factions. These factions were organized along personalistic—not ideological—lines to win the party presidential election. The faction head commanded the loyalty of the representatives in their factions in a few ways: by providing aid in getting official party nominations (especially valuable the first time representatives ran); furnishing them with funding; and obtaining party, legislative, and government posts for followers through bargaining with other factions, thus controlling their political career advancement. By forming coalitions with other faction leaders, a faction head could obtain a minimum winning coalition at the party's convention, selecting its leader, since representatives constituted the great majority of votes in this selectorate.

Once that leader was in office, he (Japanese prime ministers have always been male—an issue of note in and of itself) would contract obligations to the supporting factions in the winning coalition to appoint some of their leaders to the cabinet and to prevent the rival coalition factions from being able to completely resist government policy. The PM would also need to appoint some of his supporters to the cabinet, leading to what became the eventual party norm of awarding cabinet posts to senior members of factions in proportion to a faction's strength among the party's MPs. In effect, prime ministers were literally "first among equals"; with limited ability to choose even their own cabinet members, they were constantly vulnerable to being replaced and continually badgered by time-consuming consensus building among faction leaders.

There was not even a legal basis for the prime minister to introduce policy proposals to his own cabinet. Cabinets did not formulate policy (and by party rules all policy had to be first approved by the party); rather, policy started in the bureaucracy and then bubbled up from the lower echelons of the party. In practice, this meant policy originated from the divisions of the party's Policy Affairs Research Council where the designated specialists had the greatest influence. Under Japan's multimember district electoral system, candidates were not greatly dependent on the party leader or the party image for their seats. They were much more dependent on their own local organization and constituent service skills, and on their factions who funded them and provided them with the party posts from which they could direct pork to their constituents.

Under these conditions, strong prime ministerial leadership exerting strong policy entrepreneurship was extremely rare. Indeed, as Anthony Mughan has aptly characterized the Japanese PM: "When coalitional and factional politics coincide, then, the emergence of 'grey,' insipid prime ministers becomes almost a certainty; the position of chief executive will be filled by individuals who command no particular authority with voters or within their own party. . . . They are denied the ability of, for example, a Margaret Thatcher or a Tony Blair to set the political agenda and dominate its debate. Their predicament is perfectly illustrated by the Japanese experience . . . that produced rapid cabinet turnover and 'grey,' insipid prime ministers."[12]

Japan Reformed

Institutional Reforms

Between 1994 and 2001, two major reforms—the most significant since the American Occupation ended in 1952—fundamentally changed the institutional context in which the ruling party and the prime minister operated. Thirty LDP members bolted from the party in 1993. This led to a snap election after which a coalition of all the opposition parties except the Japanese Communist Party took power from the LDP for the first time in fifty years. Upon gaining power, the new coalition partners then pushed through electoral reform and campaign finance bills.

The new electoral system was a hybrid or "mixed" system. Voters cast one ballot for one representative in three hundred local districts and a second ballot for a party with 180 seats distributed proportionally to their party choice. The tiers were parallel, not linked or compensatory, but candidates could both run in the district and be listed in proportional representation.[13]

The second major reform was an administrative reform that changed the relative influence of politicians vis-à-vis national bureaucrats, of the cabinet vis-à-vis the bureaucracy and the LDP, and of the prime minister within his own cabinet.[14] Its purpose was to streamline government and decrease bureaucratic influence on policy making. First, it reduced the number of cabinet ministerial positions from twenty by about a third. It created, however, a few new "councils" of cabinet rank within the Cabinet Office (formerly Prime Minister's Office), the most important of which was the Council on Economic and Fiscal Policy to advise the prime minister on budget and other economic matters. Second, these administrative reforms explicitly gave the prime minister the authority to initiate policy within the cabinet, making him more than a "first among equals" within his own cabinet, and they also undermined some of the bottom-up nature of policy making within the LDP and government. Third, it explicitly encouraged more involvement of politicians and less of bureaucrats in policy making by creating new subcabinet positions of deputy minister and secretary to give younger politicians more experience in policy making and to give cabinet ministers more help.

These two reforms alone would have at least somewhat altered the potential position of the prime minister. The new mixed electoral system also greatly increased the importance of the prime minister to the party, particularly to the backbenchers, because party image and the party leader's image became more important to voters (and thus to the candidates). In the proportional representation tier, the closed nature of the party lists also gave the prime minister more leverage within the party as he could influence ranks on that list. The administrative reform bolstered greater capability in policy making (and policy became more decisive to voters).

These reforms, taking place at the level of the political office of the prime minister, were also multiplied and reinforced by two other social changes occurring outside politics per se. One was the increasing influence of television, a trend that began in the mid- to late 1980s and took off in the early 1990s. Former prime minister Nakasone (1982–87) was the first PM to use television to his advantage, circumventing his weak factional position in the party by using it to successfully cultivate a personal leadership image among the public separate from the party. Although subsequent prime ministers would revert to the insipid backroom politician image, a few others also skillfully used their own media image. For example, the transitional prime minister Morihiro Hosokawa, leader of the anti-LDP reform coalition that passed electoral reform—handsome, dashing, and a scion of a family as old as the Imperial family—effectively managed the media and cultivated an appealing television image for the short time he was in office. The growing importance of visual media now gave some prime ministers and other influential politicians the ability to use it to their advantage. This also meant that leaders with a poor television image were weakened both with the public and within their own party.

The second social trend that influenced politics was the large increase in "floating voters": independent voters who were not loyal to any particular political party or to any particular candidate (floating free from, for example, membership in politician support groups). Many of them were male and female office workers in urban areas who voted on the basis of their current perceptions of the issues and the parties at the time of the election and who could switch their vote in the next election. These voters had first been noticed as a growing trend as early as the 1970s. By the 2000s their numbers had progressively increased to constitute as much as 50 percent of the electorate.[15]

The complex interaction between the new electoral system, television, and the rise of the independent voters has yet to be completely disentangled. At the very least, it is certain that all these factors have been complicit in producing a new—and growing—political phenomenon. This includes a new electoral system, the subsequent rise of new parties, and the growing influence of television, which has made policies and the party leader's image more important to voters while diminishing the role played by party identification and personal ties to the individual candidate.

Koizumi

The two LDP prime ministers in office from 1998 to 2001 were typical faction leaders; they came to power through the traditional prereform method of factional bargaining and governed in the same prereform style. And then came Koizumi.

Jun'ichirō Koizumi was a third-generation representative, but he also was one of the least likely veteran LDP politicians to become prime minister.

Something of a loner, divorced, and a passionate fan of rock music and opera, Koizumi came to power only after his mentor and faction leader Yoshirō Mori proved a disastrously unpopular prime minister. Fearing huge losses in the upcoming Upper House election in summer 2001 and desperate for a popular party head, party prefectural branches rebelled and forced party leaders to hold a primary among party members. Koizumi won handily. Then, in the runoff among LDP Diet Members, a majority voted for him in the primary election rather than former prime minister Hashimoto.

Koizumi's popular appeal lay in much more than his unusual image; he was well known for his calls for reform of the country and of his own party. Indeed, he promised to either reform or destroy the LDP. The targets of his reform drive were reforming the economy (especially its massive and often wasteful pork barrel expenditures) to restore initiative and to help Japan emerge from its decade-long recession, and—a longtime pet project—splitting up and gradually privatizing Japan's postal system. The latter was far more than mail delivery, as it included postal savings, a three-trillion-dollar enterprise that constituted the largest financial institution in the world, as well as a large insurance operation.

Koizumi immediately demonstrated his intent to change the way politics operated by appointing cabinet members without relevance to factional balance: a change that ripped out the heart of the old transactional leadership arrangement. He further proposed various cutbacks in wasteful pork barrel budget expenditures such as unnecessary road construction and privatized several public corporations. Although he had to compromise because of resistance from the party forces that benefited from this pork, he pushed through more in the way of such reforms than any of his predecessors.[16]

When he tried to impose postal privatization on the party, the conflict between old- and new-style politics came to a head. Rebel LDP representatives came close to defeating the bill in the House of Representatives (HOR) and then voted it down in the Upper House. Koizumi faced a dilemma. If he did nothing, he would be a lame-duck prime minister and accomplish nothing else before his term ended the next year. While he couldn't dissolve the fixed-term Upper House, he could dissolve the Lower House that had passed his bill.[17]

This is what he did. Koizumi gambled, kicked the rebels out of the party, and dissolved the Lower House. He and his chief adviser personally picked "assassins," many of them women, to run against the rebels in their districts and ran a campaign focused exclusively on the need for postal reform to accomplish further changes and to help him remake the LDP. The opposition Democratic Party of Japan (DPJ), which had been steadily gaining on the LDP in previous postreform elections, ran a campaign centering on disparate issues other than postal reform (which they had voted against). Koizumi's strategy involved the manipulation of issue framing to narrow the alternative the public would consider—postal privatization and continuation of reform, or no reform in the future. The media concentrated on the rebels versus assassins' races and on Koizumi's appeals for reform. In the election, urban independent voters who normally tended to vote for the DPJ turned instead to Koizumi's message of reform while the LDP kept its rural base. The surprising result was an overwhelming victory for Koizumi and the LDP.[18]

Koizumi finished out his term as LDP president and then, in another uncharacteristic action for a politician, resigned even though many voters (and many within his own party) preferred that he go for another term and stay on as prime minister. There is a widespread consensus that Koizumi, because of his domestic economic reforms and most especially his attempts to change Japanese politics, was one of the two most important postwar prime ministers. This is despite a controversial record in foreign policy, due to his sending Japanese troops to Iraq and his visits to Yasukuni Shrine.

Koizumi's strength as a national leader stands out even more when his successors are taken into account. In the years since Koizumi left office, Japan has had six prime ministers, each lasting only one year. The first three of these were LDP politicians, but none capitalized on Koizumi's greater centralization of the party and policy making, and each of them backtracked from Koizumi's reform agenda. Consequently all saw their popularity drop precipitously. Finally, in a historic election in August 2009, the LDP lost its first general election—drubbed by the DPJ, which quickly formed a coalition government with some smaller parties (to secure a majority in the Upper House). The fact that within four years after one of its greatest electoral victories, and just three after Koizumi retired as prime minister, the LDP could overwhelmingly lose an election is a testimony to Koizumi's status as the one leader who could manipulate the new capabilities that political and administrative reform (as well as the media and an increased number of floating voters) brought to the prime minister.

The three DPJ prime ministers did not fare any better—in the sense of being long-lasting or perceived as effective—than their last three LDP predecessors. Even PM Yoshihiko Noda too, in the end, fit this pattern. The DPJ's first prime minister, Yukio Hatoyama, resigned after an incompetent handling of the Okinawa base relocation issue (Futenma) and allegations of scandals involving a political contribution. His successor, Naoto Kan, quickly lost seats and a majority for his party's coalition in the Upper House election of July 2010 because of an ill-advised remark about raising the consumption tax. He then was accused of tragically mishandling the government's response to the Great East Japan Earthquake, tsunami, and nuclear plant crisis in March 2011. Yoshihiko Noda succeeded Kan and quickly began to decline in popularity, facing grave challenges inside and outside the party and continuing low public support rates. In the first five years after Koizumi retired, Japan experienced six prime ministers, three each of the two major parties. Shinzō Abe, starting his second stint as prime minister in 2012, has already bested those tenures and, with a 2014 election victory, may be poised to last.[19]

It is clear that since the electoral reform of 1994 the criteria for being a successful and thus long-lived political leader have greatly changed.

The New Political Leadership "Game" in Japan

Because of the changes discussed above, policy making gradually shifted from the government bureaucracy and the veteran leaders within the party to the cabinet and the prime minister. As a result, the prime minister and the cabinet have become more visible to the voters, and their image and that of the party and its policies have become more important in voting decisions and in policy making. As a result, the significance of having popular or unpopular political leaders has increased enormously. Leaders who are popular and seen as effective, in charge, and willing to fight for change and popular policies, like Koizumi, may last more than a year or two. But the large majority since electoral and administrative reform do not fall in this camp. Instead, those who are perceived as incompetent (Mori, Abe, Hatoyama), weak (Fukuda), not pushing reform and surrounded by corrupt cabinet members (Abe in his first term), or ineffective (Kan) become a huge liability to the party and its representatives in their attempts to maintain themselves in power and be reelected.

This much is clear. What is less clear, however, is why it has become so difficult for political leaders to seem to be competent, effective, in charge, and able to bring about popular policies. And the question also must be raised as to whether, or for whom precisely, a strong prime ministership is indeed advantageous. What are the obstacles to both effective and popular political leadership in Japan these days that would explain why so few since reform have been able to satisfy these new expectations, given how manifest the new "mandates" for political leadership now are and how much more influence the prime minister and cabinets have in policy making?

One difficulty confronted by all prime ministers is the frequency of elections in Japan. The elections for the House of Councillors (HOC) are held every three years on a fixed schedule (e.g., 2001, 2004, 2007, 2010). Nationwide local elections for prefectural assemblies and for mayors and governors are held every four years on a fixed schedule (e.g., 1999, 2003, 2007, 2011). In between these elections, or simultaneously in the case of the Diet, are the general elections for the HOR (e.g., 2000, 2003, 2005, 2009).

There was an election for one or the other of these bodies every year in the last thirteen years with the exception of 2002, 2006, and 2008—that is, for ten out of the past thirteen years. And a major party loss in any one of these elections, or the fear of an impending large loss, especially a large loss in one of the Diet elections, can be the excuse that the ruling or major opposition party needs to dump an already weak leader or for him to take responsibility and resign. Thus six of the past ten prime ministers since the implementation of electoral reform in 1996 lost power because of a recent actual, or pending possible, election loss (and Obuchi died in office).

Another severe structural problem is Japan's flawed bicameral system, in particular the consequences for governance of divided government, known in in Japan as *nejire kokkai* or a "twisted Diet." Bicameral legislatures anywhere, of course, face this possibility of different parties controlling different houses. In Japan, however, the problem is exacerbated by the diverging nature of electoral systems, and the nature and norms of the two houses.

Japanese voters confront four different electoral systems in choosing their representatives in the two houses. The HOR system tends to produce majoritarian results from its three hundred single-seat districts, with one party likely to capture a majority or plurality, and with proportional representation tending to encourage votes for a party. The HOC system tends to produce a "personal vote" for candidates and not necessarily a majoritarian result. When these features are combined with the different timing of elections and the severely malapportioned electoral districts in the HOC, the odds are increased that each house may produce different winning parties or coalitions of parties.

After the 2000, 2003, and 2009 HOR elections an Upper House election took place the next year, and after the 2005 HOR election an Upper House election took place two years later. In effect, a prime minister often only has a year or perhaps two at most to produce policy results before he is subject to another election. If he disappoints in that year or two, or because of the vastly differing electoral system in each house even if he doesn't, his party may lose the HOC election (or he may have to resign to take responsibility for his party's defeat), producing a "twisted Diet." This makes it even more unlikely that he will succeed, since he confronts an opposition party or coalition in the other house that has little incentive to cooperate to help him pass legislation. His party needs a two-thirds majority in the HOR to override the decision of the Upper House (except in budgets and treaties, where a majority suffices). There is a provision for conference committees of the two houses to reconcile bills, as in the US Congress, but in Japan these have rarely been used.

Another Diet practice often inhibits the prime minister from speedy action on bills. The Japanese Diet is in session less than almost any other major legislative body in the democratic world. It has only 150 days in session; an extension requires the cooperation of the opposition. The average number of days in session is about 200 per year. But plenary sessions and committee meetings are held only three days per week, and there are a large number of holidays as well, meaning that the actual working days are about 100 or fewer per year (this compares to almost double that in the United States, United Kingdom, or Italy).[20] Further, these working days require a prime ministerial policy address and interpellations from the floor that further reduce real working time. Adding to the problems of a ruling party is that, by rules, no legislation is automatically carried over to the next session. In Germany, for example, legislation can be carried over indefinitely, but in Japan it must be reintroduced. All this gives opposition parties the ability to delay bills they don't like (in either house) and thus operates as a de facto weapon to persuade the prime minister and his party either to shelve the legislation or to compromise on it. As a result, the Japanese Diet passes only between 80 and 150 of the bills submitted by the cabinet per calendar year,[21] smaller numbers than most national legislatures.

Complicating the interinstitutional and interparty obstacles to effective leadership are the intraparty fissures in Japan's two largest political parties since reform. Even before reform, when the LDP was in power there was a severe conflict between reformers and nonreformers, leading to the 1993 split that in turn led to electoral reform.

Pro- versus antireform differences in the party also led indirectly to the downfall of Prime Ministers Abe and Asō in 2007 and 2009, respectively. Most of the "rebels" whom Koizumi had kicked out of the party for opposing his postal privatization bill but who had been reelected as independents petitioned Abe to be reinstated in the LDP. Under pressure from the antireform members of his party and Upper House members afraid they would not do well in the forthcoming HOC elections in 2007, Abe caved and allowed them back in. Nothing could have signaled more clearly to the many voters who had voted for reform in the 2005 election under Koizumi that the party was now backtracking on this key valence issue. Abe, who, like all prime ministers after him, started out with an approval rating of over 60 percent, saw that figure drop precipitously as a result. In combination with a huge pension debacle—about fifty million national pension records were found to have gone missing or to be inaccurate—and several of his cabinet ministers were involved in corruption scandals, his party lost the HOC election, and Abe, under pressure from the media and within the party, resigned. Asō's administration seemed to represent the epitome of antireform and reversion to the old LDP. He and his party paid the price for this in the 2009 election, although the global financial crisis also mattered greatly.

The pro- versus antireform cleavage in the party is probably closely correlated with its urban-rural division. Although a large majority of Japanese live in urban areas, especially the megalopolises in the Tokyo and Osaka regions, they receive less representation than their fellow citizens in rural areas. Both houses' districts have been malapportioned for many years. The Supreme Court prior to electoral reform allowed such inequality to stand in the HOR as long as it did not exceed 3:1. It ruled that the malapportionment was unconstitutional if it exceeded that ratio; in these cases, however, it did not order the Diet to reapportion but rather left it up to the Diet itself to decide.

With electoral reform, however, the malapportionment was reduced to 2:1 in the HOR on average. This provided more incentives for political leaders to reduce pork barrel policies that are very unpopular with urban residents, since they have benefited the rural areas most, and to cater more to urban residents. Koizumi understood the logic of this change, and his postal privatization plans were particularly popular with urban "floating voters."

But this in turn produced a reaction among rural residents, who saw themselves as the greatest victims of Koizumi's policy reforms: decreasing pork barrel, fewer post offices, and greater income inequality from economic liberalization. Whereas the prereform LDP and its leaders could straddle the urban-rural divide and stay in power as long as they satisfied their rural voters with pork barrel projects, agricultural subsidies, and other policies that heavily favored their overly powerful rural constituency, this is no longer the case. Reform has revealed an urban-rural split that is difficult for any party to straddle. In the meantime, we see the urban-rural divide play out in the DPJ as well. The LDP had adopted new agricultural policies to help rationalize Japanese agriculture over the long term to allow Japan to make concessions in international negotiations in the World Trade Organization. Because these policies (rightly) favored larger farmers, smaller farmers were dissatisfied with them. In a successful attempt to curry favor with rural voters, the DPJ pushed an alternative policy that would treat small farmers more like bigger ones. Economically irrational but politically rational, this policy enabled the DPJ in 2009 for the first time ever to win more seats in rural areas than the LDP.

Formerly an urban party, the DPJ faces its own urban-rural divide. The party is split over the current issue of whether Japan should join the Trans-Pacific Partnership, a free trade agreement among a number of Pacific Rim countries that is being pushed by the United States. While the LDP after its 2009 defeat has become a rural rump of a party dominated by veteran and older representatives from safe rural seats, the DPJ has begun to move toward trying to win rural areas as well as urban ones and intensifying its *intra*party divisions. This in turn makes it exceedingly difficult for leaders of either party to gain a consensus on policy in their parties.

Waiting for the Next Koizumi?

So what are the possible futures of Japan? Broadly speaking, we see three paths forward.

Let's start with the path of weak leadership. Let's call this one the "Koizumi was sui generis" scenario. It is certainly possible that Japan will be plagued by a string of mediocre leaders who fail to solve its pressing problems. The DPJ learned how to be an obstructionist opposition party after 2007. Dwarfed in the Lower House by the LDP, the DPJ used the Upper House to thwart the LDP at every turn. Unfortunately for the DPJ, the LDP has studied the DPJ playbook well. Now the LDP knows how to kill policies in the HOC, carp and criticize at every opportunity, and repeat constant demands for an immediate election. Unfortunately for the LDP, even if it wins an HOR election, as in 2014, the DPJ may be able to repay the favor (in 2016). With an election every year, the chance to score political points may prove irresistible. This is smart opposition politics but does not portend good governance for Japan. Exploiting the division between the two houses of parliament can make Japan almost ungovernable (recall there's no president or use of conference committees to pressure compromise), but at the same time it is difficult to win both the HOC and the HOR.

There is always a middle path, and there are always different scenarios. Perhaps the most likely is that good and popular leaders emerge intermittently but are overcome by the institutional problems. In this telling, a leader emerges, wins an election, claims a mandate, and quickly gets to work. Some legislation is passed in the honeymoon months, but the situation sours—or perhaps courage or his party support fails—before fundamental issues can be addressed. There are enough midrange successes, such as Noda's raising of the consumption tax, or some modest innovations in energy policy, that Japan muddles through the next decade or two even with revolving-door prime ministers, but the opportunity to transform the country is missed.

The best-case scenario is that a transformational leader rides a wave of popularity into office and then remakes some of Japan's dysfunctional institutions and achieves policy successes in critical areas such as those at the beginning of this article. The availability of new policy tools to the prime minister means that he can do more these days than ever before. Shielded by popularity, this prime minister would also have great power inside the party. After all, Koizumi in 2005 probably had more power vis-à-vis the party than any LDP leader ever, even if his immediate successors failed to follow suit and wasted his victories. The public's appetite for reform has fueled every election in the past decade. The success of flash parties such as the Osaka Renovation Party in 2011 shows that there is a huge opportunity for a popular leader to change the country.[22]

As we see it, these new leaders must reframe issues in a way that transforms politics. Here is one example of how those transformations might happen. The increasing malapportionment stemming from the depopulation of the countryside creates one of the best political reform openings in contemporary Japan. The basic problem is that there are no districts larger than a single prefecture for the Upper House, but some prefectures have become so depopulated that they do not "deserve" even a single HOC seat, for example

Tottori Prefecture. This creates a conflict between the need to have a Tottori seat and the fact that even a single Upper House seat in Tottori would make it overrepresented to an unconstitutional degree. One resultant solution to the "twisted Diet" problem, of course, is to abolish the HOC, making Japan effectively a unicameral system more like Sweden or New Zealand. Since this would require a constitutional amendment or the HOC voting for its own abolition, other solutions may have to be sought. A less extreme solution would be to change the way in which seats in the HOC are distributed to reduce the inequalities.

Much of the attention by media and citizens for reducing malapportionment has targeted the Lower House, and the Supreme Court in recent cases has become stricter about reducing the inequalities. Should the Supreme Court become equally attentive to the problem in the HOC and strongly urge the Diet to reform the system, perhaps making the HOC elections more similar to those in the HOR, the outcomes of elections for the two houses, even if they were to be held within a year or two of the other, might result in the same party or coalition of parties controlling both houses. This could be the wedge to reform the HOC and end its chronic impasse with the HOR and the resulting gridlock. Alternatively, both parties might become so afraid of public disgust and reaction to the stalemates that they could more frequently and effectively use the option of conference committees and learn to compromise on them.[23]

Another fundamental reform that we can see having a possibility of emerging is radical change to the party system. Both the LDP and DPJ are catch-all parties with an often incoherent assemblage of views. Strong intra-party divisions complicate the policy-making process. Koizumi was able to turn this to his electoral advantage in 2005, and perhaps a DPJ leader could pull off the same trick. It is commonplace to suggest that Japan might be better served if the two parties split up and then reformed around more ideologically coherent groupings. Some observers felt Koizumi might do this himself early in his term as prime minister.

Beyond institutional, electoral, or party reform, there are plenty of other areas such as immigration or energy policy that seem ripe for creative and transformative solutions.[24] Indeed, readers will be able to connect political leadership in some way or another to possible futures explored in almost every chapter of this book. So there is no reason to believe that some of the major problems facing leadership in Japan are beyond solution. But who might be the one to solve them?

In September 2012, Shinzō Abe, erstwhile failed prime minister following Koizumi, surprisingly defeated a more popular rival for the presidency of the LDP just in time to lead the party to a landslide victory in an election that was a manifestation of the depths of disappointment in the DPJ after three years in power.[25] Even more surprisingly, Abe proceeded to capture the public's imagination with his new approach to the economy, quickly dubbed "Abenomics" by the media on both sides of the Pacific. His goals to stimulate economic growth again through a combination of monetary, fiscal, and structural reform policies (the "three arrows") were immediately popular with a public tired of recession or sluggish expansion for two decades. He also forthrightly restated his plans to use his majority to revise Japan's "Peace Constitution" in a conservative direction, though retaining its purely defensive orientation, and in other aims went beyond anything that previous constitutional revisionists, including Abe, had ever proposed. In July of 2013, his party, with its coalition partner, the Kōmeitō, also won a majority in the HOC, followed by a crushing victory in the HOR in December 2014. Abe now has the electoral basis to become a transformative leader, perhaps even more so than Koizumi.[26] Abe won a second time not because his policies are particularly popular but because Japanese voters are still disaffected with the opposition DPJ, which has not recovered from its very disappointing three-year term in office 2009–12, and the opposition camp was also divided.

Early in Abe's term, he acted on this new capability, forcing his reluctant party to accept his bringing Japan into the Trans-Pacific Partnership being negotiated by the United States and other countries and passing a needed but vague and draconian version of a State Secrets Law that may intimidate even the news media from publishing certain types of information. In July 2014 his cabinet passed a proposal to reinterpret the constitution to allow "collective defense" for the first time. Here Abe had to compromise on the details a bit with his coalition partner, the Kōmeitō, which has less conservative views on foreign policy.

Constitutional revision has never been clearly popular with a majority of Japanese, who remain divided over any defense and alliance issues, and a bare majority supports his collective defense proposal. As expected, his poll numbers did drop, but they still remain relatively high for a Japanese prime minister in the postwar era. In a context where Japanese have high (albeit diminished) expectations for "Abenomics" and increasingly perceive both a newly assertive China, with whom they are in a tense situation over the

Senkaku/Diaoyu Islands, and an erratic North Korea as threats to Japan, this is not surprising.

Some of these changes, particularly the move toward collective defense, may make sense in the increasingly tough neighborhood of Northeast Asia. Abe and some of his appointees' statements about the history of the Pacific War, however, are another matter. Although few Japanese except for the extreme right wing support this historical revisionism, these statements intensify the tension and conflict with Japan's neighbors. The law on national secrets also went beyond what was probably needed. Abe may be becoming a transformative leader—and he is surely the strongest candidate for this role in the years since Koizumi stepped down—but naturally not everyone will like the way he is transforming things.

Abe's leadership thus raises an important issue regarding political leadership in Japan. The lack of effective leadership in Japan aside from Koizumi has been a major problem for Japan for much of the postwar period. In many established democracies, there is an increasing contradiction and dilemma in the television and Internet age of politics between the need for leaders to mobilize the popular support of voters decreasingly connected to political parties to gain power and the need for the experience and knowledge to wield it once in power to accomplish policy goals. Perhaps because the influence of visual media on Japanese politics is relatively recent and the full capabilities of the prime minister's office are also relatively new, this dilemma and contradiction seems to have been particularly acute for Japanese political leaders in recent years. Veteran politicians may know how to play party politics but may not be able to mobilize and maintain the popular support needed to win elections and keep their parties happy; new and rising popular "stars" in the political firmament may excite the public briefly but prove incapable of wielding or understanding how to wield the levers of power once they govern in Japan's complicated institutional processes. In other words, there is an imperfect match between the skills needed to win influence within the party and those needed to maintain popular support (those versed in the US primary system may find this has a familiar echo). The implication of our analysis in this chapter is that the need for an overlap in these skills in Japanese political life has grown.

Abe thus far has been surprisingly able to accomplish both mobilizing public support and pushing his ideas on his party and government—whether those ideas are particularly popular or not. He may well now have the means to transform Japan as Margaret Thatcher was able to transform Britain after her 1983 election victory.[27]

The *content* of the transformation matters as much as the ability to carry it out, however. Like Thatcher, Abe may transform the country he leads, but these transformations will have supporters and detractors, as well as winners and losers. The ultimate outcomes and consequences of a transformation are never easy to predict and can lead to partial counter-reactions. Blair and a revived Labour Party came to power soon after Thatcher. With a few years of breathing space after the 2013 HOC and 2014 HOR elections and a divided opposition that seems unlikely to threaten the LDP even in 2016, Abe has perhaps the longest time horizon of any prime minister for several decades. Although no counter-reaction or effective opposition to Abe's transformations is on the horizon now, possible futures are difficult to predict and transformative leadership can result in unforeseen consequences.

Notes

1. The authors thank Mindy Tadai for greatly advancing their thinking through her committed intellectual engagement on this topic. The authors also gratefully acknowledge that this chapter benefited from discussions with John Campbell, Robbie Feldman, Yoso Furumoto, Yukio Maeda, Michio Muramatsu, Naoto Nonaka, Ken Pyle, Scott Radnitz, Dan Smith, Chris Winkler, and Nobuo Yoneyama. Finally, the authors thank for comments and advice all participants of a workshop held June 30–July 1, 2012, at Hayama, Japan, and the audience for a presentation at the International House of Japan on July 2, 2012, in celebration of the twentieth anniversary of the Abe Fellowship, at which an earlier version of this chapter was discussed. Of course, none of those thanked above are responsible for or necessarily share the views of this chapter.

2. Unlike authors such as James MacGregor Burns, we do not argue for a "moral dimension" requisite to leadership. Rather, we see leadership as succeeding in achieving results. Naturally, many policies have unintended consequences, but these do not mean that leadership failed. A failure of leadership would mean a failure to accomplish goals. We realize also that some things can be achieved without leadership, but to probe deeply into this (as well as the relative merits of collective versus individual leadership or of presidential versus parliamentary systems, etc.) is beyond the scope of this chapter. It is also an open question we do not address here whether accomplishing any particular set of goals is "good" (or "good" for some and not others, etc.). We ourselves do not take a position on whether, for example,

Koizumi's policies were "good" for the country; we do try to gauge his success in accomplishing his goals within Japan's democratic parliamentary framework. Similarly, we do not take a position here on whether Noda's success in raising the consumption tax in 2012 was "good" for Japan (or for some subset of Japanese), but rather count it only as a policy goal accomplished by Noda. In the same way, we do not take a position on whether Abe's success in advancing his agenda, for example by passing the State Secrets Law, is "good" for Japan. See James MacGregor Burns, *Leadership* (New York: Harper Perennial, 1978).

3. Neatly summarized by Kevin Grint, *Leadership: A Very Short Introduction* (New York: Oxford University Press, 2010).

4. These can include the institutional levers that give the PM influence over the bureaucracy. However, we are interested in how this affects the PM rather than how it shifts an abstract balance between politicians and bureaucrats.

5. For an eloquent discussion of the importance of agency, see Richard J. Samuels, *Machiavelli's Children* (Ithaca, NY: Cornell University Press, 2003). Note, however, that our focus outside "agency" is on structure rather than "conditions."

6. Burns, *Leadership*.

7. Samuels, *Machiavelli's Children*.

8. The authors thank Hiroshi Nakanishi for his cogent comments on this point. Also, although we think that it is self-evident that leadership matters, a theoretical investigation of that assumption is not the goal of this chapter. However, we believe that most other chapters in this book describe futures in which political leadership looms large. In addition, we show elsewhere the effects of bad leadership. See Ellis S. Krauss and Robert Pekkanen, "Profiles in Discourage: Prime Ministerial Leadership in Post-war Japan," in *Poor Leadership and Bad Governance*, ed. Ludger Helms (London: Edward Elgar, 2012).

9. Earlier versions of certain parts of this section were originally drafted for an unpublished paper presented at the Conference on Political Leadership, Rothermere American Institute, Oxford University, Oxford, June 28–30, 2010.

10. See our discussion in Ellis S. Krauss and Robert J. Pekkanen, *The Rise and Fall of Japan's LDP* (Ithaca, NY: Cornell University Press, 2010).

11. Kenji Hayao, *The Japanese Prime Minister and Public Policy* (Pittsburgh, PA: University of Pittsburgh Press, 1993).

12. Anthony Mughan, *Media and the Presidentialization of Parliamentary Elections* (New York: Palgrave, 2000) 14.

13. See Krauss and Pekkanen, *The Rise and Fall of Japan's LDP*, for a broader inquiry into the effects of electoral system change.

14. On administrative reform, see Tomohito Shinoda, *Leading Japan: The Role of the Prime Minister* (Westport, CT: Praeger, 2000), 183–200.

15. Ethan Scheiner, *Democracy without Competition in Japan: Opposition Failure in a One-Party Dominant State* (New York: Cambridge University Press, 2005), 36. Estimates of "floating voters" as well as the definition vary. Some include percentage of all eligible voters, some only the percentage of those who actually vote, some weak party supporters and some not; traditionally a "floating voter" in Japan was someone who was not a member of a *kōenkai* or tied into a candidate's personal support network, but recently the definition seems to have approached much more the Western definition of "independent" voter not supportive of a particular political party. All agree, however, that the number of independent voters not necessarily tied into voting for one political party has increased greatly in the last twenty years.

16. Our point here is not to laud the content of Koizumi's policies, which naturally not all Japanese are enamored of, but rather to highlight successful policy change in an era where ineffective leadership has drawn anguished complaints from the public. Another example would be to indicate that Noda finally succeeded in raising the consumption tax, but whether it will have good or bad consequences for the economy is still in doubt; the point is that unlike previous leaders he did at least succeed in pushing through his policy.

17. On the postal privatization attempts and aftermath, see Ellis Krauss and Robert J. Pekkanen, "Reforming the Liberal Democratic Party," in *Democratic Reform in Japan: Assessing the Impact*, ed. Sherry L. Martin and Gill Steel (Boulder, CO: Lynne Rienner, 2008), 11–39.

18. On the 2005 election and its potential consequences, see ibid., 29–36.

19. For book-length analyses of Abe's two HOR electoral victories, see Robert Pekkanen, Steven R. Reed, and Ethan Scheiner, eds., *Japan Decides 2012: The Japanese General Election* (London: Palgrave, 2013) and *Japan Decides 2014: The Japanese General Election* (London: Palgrave, forthcoming).

20. Mikitaka Masuyama and Benjamin Nyblade, "Japan: The Prime Minister and the Japanese Diet," *Journal of Legislative Studies* 10, nos. 2–3 (2004): 257.

21. Ibid., figure 1, 258.

22. On the other hand, the Japan Innovation Party or other new movements that then try to compete at the national level might also make it more difficult for any party to gain a majority, creating even more stalemate, but that is part of a more pessimistic scenario.

23. Shinichi Kitaoka, "Breaking the Political Deadlock with Bold Reforms," Tokyo Foundation, January 12, 2012, www.tokyofoundation.org/en/topics/politics-in-persepctive/bold-reforms.

24. For an interesting take on immigration policy and incentives for politicians, see the working paper by Adam Schiffer and Michael Strausz, "What Are Zombies Afraid Of? Public Opinion, Replacement Migration, and Japan's LDP," n.d.

25. See the analyses of the LDP by Endo, Pekkanen, and Reed in Pekkanen, Reed, and Scheiner, *Japan Decides 2012* and by Endo and Pekkanen in Pekkanen, Reed, and Scheiner, *Japan Decides 2014*.

26. We acknowledge Steven R. Reed as the originator of this apt analogy.

27. For more on Abe's policies, see Gregory Noble, "Abenomics," Llewelyn Hughes, "Energy Policy," Saori Katada and Scott Wilbur, "Trade Policy," Ellis S. Krauss, "Foreign Policy," Jeffrey Kingston, "Nationalism," and Robert Pekkanen and Steven R. Reed, "Japanese Politics from 2012 to 2014," all in Pekkanen, Reed, and Scheiner, *Japan Decides 2014*, as well as Robert J. Pekkanen and Saadia M. Pekkanen, 2015, "Japan in 2014: All About Abe" in Asian Survey 55, no. 1 (2015): 1–16.

CHAPTER THIRTEEN

State Power versus Individual Freedom: Japan's Constitutional Past, Present, and Possible Futures

Lawrence Repeta and Colin P. A. Jones

The Liberal Democratic Party versus the Constitution

An assessment of Japan's possible futures must consider the likelihood that the present constitution, which took effect on May 3, 1947, will be significantly amended or even replaced.[1] This is especially true in light of the extensive slate of constitutional amendments proposed by the Liberal Democratic Party (LDP) in 2012 (the "LDP Proposal").

Since its formation in 1955 the LDP has advocated the adoption of an "autonomous constitution" (*jishu kenpō*). *Autonomous* reflects the view that Japan's current constitution (the 1947 Constitution) was forced on the country by the United States during the Allied Occupation (1945–52) after World War II. LDP leaders believe the 1947 Constitution does not reflect Japan's history and culture and should be revised to do so.

The LDP has published proposed constitutional amendments on several occasions, beginning with a report released in April 1956. The party's ideas were presented in fine detail in a "Draft New Constitution" adopted at the annual party congress in November 2005 and again in the LDP Proposal. So far, none of these proposals have led to change. The text of the constitution is exactly the same today as it was in 1947.

Someday these words may be amended. Vigorous leadership by Prime Minister Shinzō Abe following the LDP's victory in the December 2012 House of Representatives election suggests that the time may come soon. In this chapter, we discuss the past and present of the 1947 Constitution and possible futures under an "autonomous" constitution of the type contained in the LDP Proposal, which was formally approved on April 27, 2012, and released the following day.[2] The date was symbolic: sixty years previously, on April 28, the Treaty of San Francisco had taken effect, occupation by the Allied Powers had formally ended, and the country had recovered sovereignty.

But had it? The United States continued to exercise dominion over Japanese territory for two more decades (the Ogasawara Islands until 1968, Okinawa until 1972). Even on the main islands the United States has continuously maintained military bases under a one-sided military alliance signed the same day as the peace treaty. By the time Japan formally regained its sovereignty in 1952, the United States was already using these bases to fight the Korean War. Six decades later, it retains significant military bases in Japan, funded largely by Japanese taxpayers and existing largely outside the jurisdiction of Japanese law.

This is the past from which Japan's constitution was born and the present in which it has existed—without formal amendment—for over half a century. Any self-respecting nationalist would reasonably find this situation objectionable, all the more so because of the charter's remarkable provenance.

The 1947 Constitution

The document that became the postwar constitution was first drafted in English over the space of about a week in February 1946 by a team of American Occupation officials working in great secrecy and under tremendous time pressure. After their draft was presented to a stunned Japanese government, there followed an intense process of translation and backroom negotiations in which the Americans had the upper hand. Yet both sides shared the goal of presenting to the world a "Japanese" initiative that would both protect Emperor Hirohito and forestall interference by other Allied powers in constitutional reform.[3] An outline of the draft was announced by the Japanese government in March 1946, and the draft itself was presented to a newly elected Diet (its members having won elections in which women voted for the first time) as a proposed amendment (*in toto*) of the Meiji Constitution of 1889. The Diet (parliament) made a number of changes (including adding some of the social rights contained in Chapter III) to the proposal before approving it. The resulting charter was promulgated by Emperor Hirohito on November 3, 1946 (the Meiji emperor's birthday) and came into effect on May 3 of the following year.

Much effort went into disguising the constitution's foreign provenance, including the unusual tactic of drafting it in vernacular Japanese rather than the dense, highly technical classical Japanese used in statutes at the time. Nonetheless, the document showed much foreign influence. To understand this one need look no further than the preamble, which was drafted by an American army lawyer and is probably much more inspiring when read in the original English than in the Japanese into which it was painstakingly rendered.

The significance of the 1947 Constitution can be understood only in contrast to its predecessor, which was bestowed upon the Japanese people as a gift of Mutsuhito, the Emperor Meiji. In fact, many of the provisions of the present constitution represent clear refutations of the Meiji Constitution, starting with Article 1, which declares sovereignty to be vested in the people, not the emperor. The Meiji Constitution did acknowledge that the emperor's subjects held some rights—freedom of religion and speech, for example—but declared them to be subject to whatever limits might be imposed by the Diet through law.

Reaction to the 1947 Constitution

Revising the 1947 Constitution first took a prominent place on the national political agenda soon after the end of the Occupation. Over the decades since, it has been a constant theme in Japanese politics, though often in the form of background noise, with much debate and repeated proposals for change but little concrete progress.

Although the LDP and its allies have ruled Japan throughout most of this period, they have failed to achieve their long-standing goal of transforming the constitution into a document that matches their vision of Japan. Why? Under Constitution Article 96, amendments must be approved by "concurring vote of two-thirds or more of all the members of each House" of the Diet and must thereafter be approved by a majority of all persons voting in a national referendum. Perhaps this hurdle is simply too high: the LDP has never controlled the necessary supermajority of seats in both houses of the legislature.

Another reason might be that enough Japanese have *liked* the constitution as it is, or at least have liked some of the new things it stood for when it was announced to a country still struggling to emerge from the rubble of a disastrous war. Thereafter, a significant part of the population has remained supportive or at worst ambivalent with respect to the constitutional status quo, particularly when it comes to the pacifist provisions of Article 9. A 2007 opinion poll taken by NHK, Japan's national public broadcaster, revealed that while 41 percent of those surveyed thought constitutional change was necessary, 24 percent felt no change was necessary, and a further 30 percent could not say either way.[4] A 2013 poll by the broadcaster showed 39 percent of those polled agreeing that "some" provisions of the constitution needed to be changed, with 21 percent feeling that no changes were necessary.[5]

Abe's "Technical" Amendment

We have not found any record that the LDP has ever submitted an amendment proposal to the Diet. Indeed, it was not until 2007, during Abe's first term as prime minister, that a law (the Constitutional Amendment Referendum Act) was passed establishing the procedures for the national referendum mandated by the constitution as part of the amendment process.

Following the LDP victory in the December 2012 elections that awarded the party and its allies control of two-thirds of the House of Representatives, Prime Minister Abe promised that a proposed amendment would be submitted to the Diet, though his approach may be considered deceptive, even mendacious. Rather than moving forward with the LDP Proposal in its entirety, he instead offered just one amendment: a change to Article 96 that would lower the bar for approving further amendments to majorities of both houses plus the approval of a majority of those citizens voting in a national referendum.[6]

This seemingly transparent ploy, characterized by one critic as an invitation to come into a restaurant with no menu, might nonetheless work on a populace that may have long been vaguely aware of the need to amend *something* about the American-tainted constitution and might agree with the abstract notion of making amendments easier. But such a change might have profound effects. It would empower simple majorities to change any part of the constitution, including protections for free speech and other fundamental rights.

Moreover, the referendum requirement is likely to provide little real protection, since the Constitutional Amendment Referendum Act seems carefully structured to minimize actual debate over proposed amendments once they have been approved by the Diet, something most people are likely to learn only when it is too late. With no minimum turnout required by the act and only about 60 percent of voters participating in most national elections, if the LDP gets amendments through the Diet they could be approved by as little as 30 percent of the citizenry.

After the LDP and their coalition partners further strengthened their control of the Diet through victory in the House of Councillors' election in the summer of 2013, the debate on amending Article 96 died down. Prime Minister Abe instead turned his energy and political capital to using a cabinet resolution to "reinterpret" Article 9 to allow Japan to participate in collective self-defense activities in foreign lands. The Abe cabinet formally adopted such a resolution on July 1, 2014.

Changing the constitution through either amendment or interpretation is clearly an important agenda for Abe and his party. A closer look at the rest of the changes desired by the LDP shows the sort of constitutional future awaiting Japan if the party remains in power.

The LDP Proposal

The extensive changes included in the LDP Proposal can be divided into three categories. The first consists of technical changes such as adding paragraph numbers and titles to articles (already included in most commercial reproductions of the constitution, but not technically a part of it as promulgated), fixing quirky language, and other fine tuning.

The second category consists of substantive changes unlikely to be controversial because they would merely make the constitution reflect what the government already does or courts already allow. For example, the current constitution does not provide for dissolution of the House of Representatives except upon a no-confidence vote. Nor does it clearly accord any formal role to the cabinet in the legislative process.[7] Yet in actuality the great majority of legislation passed by the Diet is proposed by the cabinet, and prime ministers have dissolved the House of Representatives on numerous occasions without a no-confidence vote. Neither of these practices is unusual in a parliamentary system.

The LDP Proposal would also clearly designate the emperor as head of state. Unlike the Meiji Constitution, the 1947 Constitution contains no clear designation of such status, which would arguably be inconsistent with the constitutional principle of popular sovereignty.[8] Yet for all intents and purposes the emperor is treated as head of state in practice, and many foreign diplomats probably already labor under the misconception that he is. In a similar vein, LDP proposals for what might be called the "boring" parts of the constitution to allow budgeted expenditures to be continued over multiple fiscal years would arguably remedy the significant restrictions that the annual budgeting process imposes on fiscal flexibility.

In this second category, one might even include the LDP's proposal to recognize the existence of a National Defense Force (*kokubōgun*). This would be accomplished through a drastic rewriting of Chapter II of the constitution, which contains the charter's famous Article 9 and would be entitled "National Security" rather than the current "Renunciation of War." Although there is significant popular opposition to changing Article 9, Japan already has a formidable military—the Self-Defense Forces (SDF).[9] So to provide for it in the constitution may amount to nothing more than an acknowledgment of the status quo. Over the decades the nation's leaders have had to ponder a variety of potential military threats: the Soviet Union in the Cold War era; more recently a bellicose North Korea, an increasingly assertive China, and a vaguely defined "war on terror" that has placed demands on Japan to commit military support in places as far away as Afghanistan and Iraq. Arguably the real issue is not so much the existence of the SDF as the ability of the government to react decisively in emergencies, whether to external threats or to natural disasters of the type discussed in some of the previous chapters. It is here that the LDP proposals become more specific and potentially significant.

This brings us to the third category of amendments proposed by the LDP. As the previous paragraph suggests, there is some overlap between the second and third categories. For decades, the principal controversy surrounding Article 9 has concerned not Japan's possession of military forces but the constitutional authority to use those forces collectively with the militaries of other countries and thereby to fulfill an important role in global and regional security. Having emerged as an economic superpower that enjoys the commercial benefits of a relatively peaceful world, Japan has been increasingly pressured to share the burden of maintaining peace in regions outside Japan by participating in "collective self-defense" operations recognized by Article 51 of the UN Charter. Japan's Cabinet Legislation Bureau has consistently interpreted Article 9 to prohibit participation in collective self-defense, a significant limitation on Japan's ability to contribute to multinational military campaigns involving the use of force.[10]

Here the LDP Proposal would make a real, substantive constitutional change by unambiguously permitting the deployment of the National Defense Force internationally. The revised Chapter II would also clearly commit Japan to protecting national territory, airspace, waters, and resources. This is not an insignificant commitment at a time when Japan is engaged in an increasingly hostile dispute with China over the Senkaku (Diaoyu) Islands, situated between Okinawa and Taiwan. Furthermore, when taken in conjunction with a provision to be added elsewhere obligating the state to assist Japanese nationals abroad in emergencies (LDP Proposal, Art. 25-3), Article 9 as revised could serve as grounds for active, even constitutionally required, foreign military interventions.

State of Emergency

The single proposal that may have the greatest impact on Japan's future course would be an entirely new chapter of the constitution. The LDP would label this new Chapter IX "State of Emergency" and grant the prime minister and his cabinet extraordinary powers. A new Article 98 would enable the prime minister, acting through the cabinet, to declare a state of emergency "in the event of armed attacks on the nation from abroad, disturbances of the social order due to internal strife [*nairan*], etc., large-scale natural catastrophes due to earthquakes, etc., or other emergency situations as designated by law." This is a broad range of potential situations, enhanced with the Japanese equivalent of "et cetera," apparently to ensure that the prime minister would have broad latitude in judging when to act. Although emergency declarations are subject to some post facto control by the legislature, these amendments would result in a dramatic expansion of executive powers, notwithstanding the preservation of the constitutional designation of the Diet as the "highest organ of state power" and sole legislative body.

Under Chapter IX (LDP Proposal Art. 99[1]), emergency cabinet orders would have the same effect as laws, thus eliminating the ordinary requirement for Diet deliberations of government action, including opportunities for opposition politicians to debate proposed declarations and for the news media to report on such deliberations. The entire process could take place in secret. Moreover, the prime minister would be empowered to issue orders to mayors and prefectural governors.[11] The analysis of Japan's disaster management system by William Siembieda and Haruo Hayashi in chapter 6 of this volume indicates that at least in the case of natural disasters this authority is unnecessary.

Moreover, a new Article 99(3) would state that everyone "must comply with the directives of national or other public institutions . . . to protect the lives, persons or property of the people." What fate would befall civil liberties and other fundamental rights during a state of emergency?

Language is included mandating that constitutional provisions "relating to fundamental rights shall be respected to *the greatest extent.*" These words may sound reassuring, but when one considers the lax attitude of Japan's Supreme Court in protecting individual rights (described below) and another LDP proposal (also described below) that would subordinate individual rights to the "public order," there is good reason to fear that emergency powers might be abused.

The Meiji Constitution also granted the emperor emergency powers, similarly subject to parliamentary restraints that proved ineffective. The lack of an effective safeguard on the abuse of these powers by officers acting in the emperor's name was a key factor leading to Japan's slide into militarism and total war.

Back to the Present: The Role of the Courts

The prospect of limits imposed on fundamental rights in emergencies naturally raises the issue of the judicial role in overseeing the actions of the executive branch of government. The American authors of the constitution's first draft looked to the courts to serve as the ultimate defenders of the individual rights guaranteed in the constitution. They eliminated control by the Ministry of Justice over judges and the courts, created a new Supreme Court with administrative authority over lower court judges, and granted the Court the power of "judicial review," the authority to judge the constitutionality of actions by other branches of government.

The failure of the Supreme Court to effectively use its judicial review power ranks as one of the greatest disappointments of the 1947 Constitution. Despite being clearly vested with the power of judicial review and the independence necessary to exercise it, Japan's Supreme Court has been extremely deferential to other branches of government. For the most part it has used procedural techniques such as highly restrictive notions of standing or ripeness and substantive doctrines such as "political question" to avoid using the power.

When it has not avoided the issue, the Court has overwhelmingly upheld laws or government acts in cases where they conflict with individual rights and freedoms. Moreover, the Court has failed to develop comprehensible standards to explain its judgments in these cases, often relying on poorly articulated reasons such as the broad "public welfare" concept of Articles 12 and 13.[12] Instances when the court has issued judgments holding the act of another agency of government unconstitutional can be counted on the fingers of both hands. Furthermore, with the exception of a handful of rulings on the subject of voting rights, the Court's unconstitutionality judgments have involved relatively minor issues, such as striking down restrictions on pharmacy licensing and the subdivision of forested land.[13] By failing to exercise its power of judicial review, the Court has allowed other branches of government to determine the law governing issues of widespread importance throughout Japanese society.

Supreme Court acquiescence to most government actions and programs is no surprise. Supreme Court appointments are controlled by the cabinet, and LDP politicians have controlled the cabinet almost continuously since the party was formed. LDP satisfaction with the performance of the Supreme Court to date is suggested by the lack of any significant LDP proposal to amend Chapter VI of the constitution, which creates the judicial branch and defines its powers.[14]

Change as Ideology

Except for Article 9's restraint on the use of military force, the 1947 Constitution has not been a significant hindrance to the exercise of power by LDP politicians. If the constitution has not been an obstacle, why do LDP leaders seek the comprehensive changes embodied in the LDP Proposal?

Other than the obvious and long-standing example of national defense, few of the constitutional changes proposed by the LDP have actually been justified as responses to identified social or political problems attributable to defects in the current charter. The lack of concrete reasons may explain why Abe and his followers focus on attacking the constitution's provenance and pushing the largely abstract idea of amendment itself as their initial goal.

Thus it seems that ideology rather than any practical dissatisfaction with life under the 1947 Constitution drives Abe and the LDP to seek constitutional change. The ideology underlying the LDP Proposal appears to be more important than the actual words of either the present constitution or the new one they propose. For this reason, regardless of whether the LDP

Proposal is ever implemented in whole or in part, it is worth attention as an indicator of the ruling party's vision for the future of Japan.

Yet since the proposal's authors do not expressly declare their ideology it must be divined from the substance of their proposals. There are two primary characteristics. First, it is nationalistic: the LDP asserts that Japan's constitutional rights are different from rights in other countries, the product of Japan's unique "history, tradition and culture." Second, it is authoritarian: the paramount value is *not* individual freedom and the "pursuit of happiness," as it may be in Western countries and elsewhere, but "public order." According to the LDP Proposal, when individual rights conflict with public order, they must give way. In the following sections, we will show how this ideology infuses the LDP proposals for constitutional change.

From "Universal" Rights to "Native" Rights

The nationalistic thread in the LDP Proposal is apparent from the express rejection of both the universal nature of human rights and the "Western theory of natural rights." The party intends to expunge these foreign influences and replace them with a system of native rights based on Japan's past.

Japan's 1947 Constitution was drafted, revised, and adopted during an era of revolutionary change in global human rights, between the founding of the United Nations in 1945 and UN General Assembly adoption of the Universal Declaration of Human Rights in 1948.[15] The list of rights declared in Japan's 1947 Constitution closely parallels the Universal Declaration and several human rights treaties that Japan signed and ratified thereafter.[16]

"Promoting and encouraging respect for human rights and for fundamental freedoms for all" is one of the primary purposes of the United Nations.[17] These rights and freedoms are defined in the Universal Declaration. The UN General Assembly proclaimed the Universal Declaration to be "a common standard of achievement for all peoples and all nations" and described its purpose to be securing these rights and freedoms' "universal and effective recognition and observance."[18]

Japan joined the United Nations in 1956, one year after conservative factions joined to found the LDP. From that time until the present, government representatives have consistently voiced enthusiastic support for the protection of universal rights. Japan has ratified several international human rights conventions whose goal is the protection of universal rights.[19] Drafters of these instruments were well aware of differences in culture and traditions among the more than 150 nations that have ratified them.[20] Nonetheless, regarding the "universality" of these rights, the UN High Commissioner on Human Rights is uncompromising. The commission's website declares: "The principle of universality of human rights is the cornerstone of international human rights law."[21]

LDP leaders disagree. They declare that rights are *not* universal, and they propose restrictions on individual rights that will pull Japan in a direction that would surely undermine and contradict Japan's obligations under international human rights law. This would constitute a radical change to Japan's fundamental policy and its position in the United Nations' human rights system.

Rejecting the "Western Theory of Natural Rights"

The authors of the LDP proposals do not directly challenge Japan's obligations under international human rights instruments. They aim their fire solely at the 1947 Constitution and would replace universality with its opposite, uniqueness. The first sentence of the LDP Constitution would read: "Japan is a nation with a long history and unique culture, with a *tennō* [emperor] who is a symbol of the unity of the people."

Regarding the issue of universality versus uniqueness, the LDP Q&A explains, "Rights are gradually formulated through the history, tradition, and culture of each community. Therefore, we believe that the provisions concerning human rights should reflect the history, culture, and tradition of Japan. The current constitution includes some provisions based on the Western theory of natural rights. We believe these provisions should be revised."[22] What elements of "history, culture, and tradition" should provide the basis for human rights in Japan? The Q&A's authors do not tell us directly, but several proposed changes in constitutional wording and statements in the Q&A pamphlet indicate a clear direction.

The express rejection of the "Western theory of natural rights" is a good place to start. Natural rights theory holds that everyone is endowed with various rights at birth. Nearly a century before the American and French Revolutions, John Locke wrote that all men are by nature free and equal and that all have rights, such as the right to life, liberty, and property. Locke declared that the people grant only limited powers to government. His ideas found expression in the American Declaration of Independence, which refers specifically to the "laws of nature" and announces that all men "are endowed by their Creator with certain unalienable Rights, that among these are Life, Liberty and the pursuit of Happiness." In 1946, these very words found their way into Article 13 of Japan's new constitution, which tells the world that "all citizens shall be respected as individuals. Their rights to life, liberty, and the pursuit of happiness shall . . . be the supreme consideration in legislation and in other governmental affairs."

Phrases like these are the core of the Western concept of natural rights. The Q&A is certainly correct in saying that many provisions of Japan's 1947 Constitution reflect this thinking. But the American authors who planted the words of Locke and Jefferson in Article 13 also diluted their impact by inserting a limitation: citizens' right to life, liberty, and pursuit of happiness would be the supreme consideration only "to the extent that it does not interfere with the public welfare." As noted above, when interpreted by the Supreme Court of Japan this phrase has operated as a significant limitation on individual rights.[23]

Whether the individual rights protected by the 1947 Constitution are described as derived from "Western natural rights theory" or from "universal principles," for nationalistic LDP leaders the problem is the same: the source of such rights is not uniquely Japanese and therefore they are subject to interpretation by reference to standards and definitions that are outside their control. By recasting rights in nativist terms, LDP leaders can preserve for themselves the authority to dictate how human rights should be understood and interpreted in Japan.

LDP Opposition to Individual Rights

Opposition to individual rights is a central theme of the LDP Proposal. Perhaps the most obvious example is Article 13, which begins with the statement that "all citizens shall be respected as *individuals*" (emphasis added). The LDP authors are so opposed to recognizing individual rights that they would delete the word *individual* (*kojin*) and replace it with the term *people* (*hito*).[24] Thus all citizens would be respected not as *individuals* but in some other undefined status, perhaps as members of families or communities overseen by a paternalistic state.

Constitutional scholars frequently note the historic importance of the guarantee of individual rights in the 1947 Constitution. Kazuyuki Takahashi explains that the hostility of Japan's political leaders toward individual rights was apparent long before the creation of the 1947 Constitution. "Traditionalists who felt nostalgia for the ancient regime of Kokutai [national polity]," he writes, "abhorred the individualist ideas and ideals they sensed the new Constitution embodies."[25] The term *kokutai* was closely tied to imperial sovereignty and was "presumed to preexist the [Meiji] Constitution,"[26] which described the sovereign emperor as the descendant of "a line of Emperors unbroken for ages eternal."

Yōichi Higuchi, a leading opponent of the LDP Proposal, emphasizes the significance of individual rights: "The Constitution designed a society around an intellectual value—respect for the individual—that replaced veneration for the emperor."[27] The celebration of individual rights in the 1947 Constitution was thus a direct affront to the ideals of Japan's political elite.

We have seen no evidence indicating that LDP leaders seek a wholesale revival of the Meiji Constitution or of imperial sovereignty. However, any consideration of constitutional change begins with the Meiji Constitution, the immediate predecessor to the "imposed" 1947 Constitution. The Meiji Constitution was composed by Japanese drafters after their careful study of legal systems abroad.[28] In the early stages of the occupation, Japan's leaders sought to preserve as much of the Meiji Constitution as possible until the American draft was "forced" upon them.[29] It is therefore the most important reference—other than the 1947 Constitution itself—to understanding Japan's modern constitutional tradition. While the LDP Proposal does not call for an outright revival of the Meiji constitutional system, its hostility toward individual rights and its imposition of new duties on the people are consistent with the ideals of the Meiji Constitution.

LDP Opposition to Constitutional Limits on Government Power

Because individual constitutional rights are limitations on government control over human behavior, opposition to those rights implies a desire for increased government control. The idea that government power should be limited is a core feature of both natural rights theory and modern constitutionalism, a concept with which the LDP has struggled for decades while ruling in their shadow. Takahashi has described the entrenched opposition to constitutional limits on government power:

We commit ourselves to constitutionalism, which, we believe, is the strategy for freedom, destined to ensure that political power is exercised in conformity with the constitution, guaranteeing fundamental rights and the separation of powers. . . . The problem is that the idea of constitutionalism is a foreign concept to us Japanese; that is, it is not endogenous to our own soil. Before we learned the idea from Westerners, we did not know the idea of imposing law on rulers. Law had always come from rulers; obedience to the law had been a virtue of the people; rulers had *ruled* by law instead of *being ruled* by law [emphasis added].[30]

Legal historians agree that constitutionalism and the rule of law, founded on the central idea that government is limited by law, did not evolve on their own in East Asia but were imported from the West. Until the adoption of the 1947 Constitution, Japan employed what scholars have labeled a "rule-by-law" regime in which law was a tool used by government to control the people. Tom Ginsburg summarizes the comparison: "In contrast with Western legal traditions organized around the notion of the autonomous rights-bearing individual, the Imperial Chinese tradition is usually depicted as emphasizing social order over individual autonomy and responsibilities over rights. Law exists not to empower and protect individuals from the state, but as an instrument of governmental control. Any rights that do exist are granted by the state and may be retracted."[31] This was certainly the case under the Meiji Constitution, which allocated sovereign power to the emperor (*tennō*). Dan Fenno Henderson explains that by vesting sovereignty in the emperor and making all individual rights subject to laws passed by the Diet, the Meiji system "clearly rejected anything like the French natural right theory or the American social contract theory as a limitation on the constitutional policymakers. Rather, as the preamble of the constitution states, these rights were bestowed on the subjects as a benevolent act."[32]

Resistance to constitutionalism and limitations on government power run throughout the LDP Proposal. Rule-by-law concepts like "social order over individual autonomy" and law as "an instrument of government control" are alive and well in the LDP.

"Public Order" over Individual Rights

As described above, the Supreme Court has interpreted the 1947 Constitution in a manner that imposes very few restraints on government power. But

LDP leaders would nonetheless revise the constitution to further constrain the Court's power to rule in favor of individual rights. They propose to revise Article 12 to indicate that "public order" overrides individual rights. The LDP version of this article would read that the people "shall be aware that duties and obligations accompany freedoms and rights and shall *never violate the public interest and public order* [emphasis added]."[33]

The LDP would also go so far as to make it doubly clear that the "public interest and public order" qualification applies to the Article 21 guarantee of freedom of expression. The present resounding declaration that "freedom of assembly and association as well as speech, press, and all other forms of expression are guaranteed," would gain a new proviso: "Notwithstanding the provisions of the preceding paragraph, activities intended to harm the public interest or public order and associations for such purposes are not allowed."[34]

Even under the present constitution the law is selectively applied against individuals and groups perceived to be opponents of the established political regime. The police targeted antiwar activists who opposed the deployment of an SDF contingent to Iraq;[35] in at least one case they arrested an individual for exhorting attendees not to stand during a school graduation ceremony; and they have consistently surveilled and arrested Communist Party supporters engaged in distributing newsletters and other campaign literature.[36]

The kind of government action shown in these cases—direct attacks on spokespeople for competing policies and ideologies—would gain a constitutional imprimatur as acts that protect public order. Moreover, this LDP revision would restrict not only speech activities but also the right of association, empowering the police to take action against both organizations and individual members. Elevating public order over free speech and association in the constitutional text would put the police in a legally unassailable position when they surveil, arrest, or take other actions against individuals or organizations they deem threats to public order.[37]

How does the LDP itself define "public order"? It doesn't! In the Q&A, the LDP authors merely explain that "our use of the term 'public order' is not intended to refer to 'regulating activities challenging the state.' 'Public order' here refers to 'social order' [*shakai chitsujo*]; it means peaceful social life [*heibon na shakaiseikatsu*]. There is no question that individuals who assert human rights should not cause nuisances to others."[38]

According to the LDP Proposal, social order is superior to individual freedom. Threats to freedom arise not from the actions of state authorities but from individuals who assert constitutional rights and thereby inconvenience (*meiwaku*) and threaten the "peaceful social life" of others. Labeling those who exercise constitutional rights as troublemakers sets the stage for government action to rein them in. The LDP shifts a core constitutional function from limiting state power to limiting individual behavior. What is the source of this kind of thinking?

Constitutional Rights or "Human Rights"?

The term *human rights* is frequently used in Japan when there is no constitutional nexus at all. Government admonitions to the public to "respect the human rights of others" are commonplace, even in contexts not generally associated with human rights as they are understood in other countries—school bullying, for example.[39] When Japan's new constitutional order replaced "veneration for the emperor" with "respect for the individual" and raised individual rights to a universal level, the government, news media, educational institutions, and others faced a tall order in educating the people about the significance of their new rights. One major initiative centers around a "Human Rights Protection Bureau" (*jinken yōgo kyoku*) newly created within the Ministry of Justice in 1948. The bureau is charged with promoting awareness of human rights among the people at large and mediating disputes with the help of lay "human rights commissioners."[40]

Through this kind of program, the government has consistently promoted the idea that a "human rights violation" is an incident that involves private individuals and organizations. The role of the government in this context is to act as a benevolent overseer, counseling victims and perpetrators and seeking to defuse confrontations while limiting the damage and improving behavior.

Needless to say, this may be valuable work. In most cases, however, these types of violations have little or nothing to do with constitutional rights. According to the government's 2011 report, the most common incidents come within categories labeled "assault, maltreatment," "infringement on the security of residence and living," and "bullying in schools."[41] Many serious matters may be addressed through this program, but unless they involve complaints against action by government authorities they do not raise constitutional issues. The law provides that disputes between individuals are to be resolved according to Japan's civil code, not the constitution.

In international forums, the government has often put forth its human rights commissioner system as evidence of its efforts to fulfill duties under international human rights treaties. But international human rights bodies do not agree that a voluntary program to mediate disputes between private parties is sufficient. They have repeatedly recommended that Japan establish "an independent national human rights institution outside the Government, in accordance with the Paris Principles . . . with competence to consider and act on complaints of human rights violations by public authorities."[42]

Japan has not followed this recommendation. An LDP cabinet did propose a bill to establish a new human rights commission in 2002, but the body would have been under the Ministry of Justice, and its primary charge would have been to monitor the acts of private parties, especially the news media, *not* the acts of government agencies. One provision of that bill would even have prohibited "excessive reporting." The bill was severely criticized by Japan's bar associations and other groups concerned with human rights. After reviewing this proposal, UN High Commissioner on Human Rights Mary Robinson sent a letter to Prime Minister Jun'ichirō Koizumi explaining why it utterly failed to meet the United Nations' recommendation.[43]

"Constitutional Duties"

Another category of LDP revisions would lay the foundation for more direct government control of the people by expanding the range of "constitutional duties."[44] The salient proposal in this regard is amendment of the constitution's Article 99, which currently reads: "The Emperor or the Regent as well as Ministers of State, members of the Diet, judges, and all other public officials have the obligation to respect and uphold this Constitution." This duty is a direct corollary of the principle that government powers are created and limited by the constitution. The LDP would flip this idea on its head with new language declaring that "all of the people must respect this constitution."[45] This would lay the foundation for government to both define and enforce those duties through law and other official acts. Regarding specific new duties, the most obviously inflammatory proposal is new wording that would mandate respect for the national flag and anthem. Together with the emperor himself, these are the most powerful symbols of Japanese nationalism and have been a flash point for much of the postwar period.

LDP efforts to raise their status reached a landmark in 1999 with passage of a law formally establishing them as Japan's national flag and anthem (*kimigayo*, a paean to the imperial lineage). At the time government spokesmen assured the public that the new law would not lead to mandatory ceremonies. But the spotlight then moved to local governments, led by Tokyo governor Ishihara Shintaro, which adopted rules requiring public school teachers to participate in school ceremonies involving the flag and anthem. This action incited a rare example of public civil disobedience, as hundreds of teachers defied orders to stand and sing. They were punished with official reprimands, pay cuts, and removals from classrooms. These sanctions were challenged in court, leading to a series of Supreme Court decisions in 2011 that vindicated Ishihara and his followers by dismissing the teachers' claims for protection under Constitution Article 19, which declares a right to belief and conscience.

Insertion of these duties into the constitution would enable government leaders to impose discipline and restrict freedom of belief and expression. Obligatory veneration of nationalistic symbols could be extended to all persons subject to the constitution, including the descendants of Korean, Chinese, and other victims of Japanese militarism.

Other proposed new duties would also create government power to control behavior. Of special interest is the proposed new Article 19-2: "No person shall improperly acquire, possess, or use information concerning individuals."[46] This language imposes new constitutional duties with potentially extremely broad applications. "Information concerning individuals" is a virtually limitless category, including not only names, photographs, and vital data but potentially any type of information describing any aspect of specific people. This duty would apply to news organizations, bloggers, and writers of all kinds, as well as a vast range of businesses and voluntary organizations whose actions might be deemed "improper." For example, debate on public policies and social issues might be suppressed in the name of protecting privacy, and it could be very risky for anyone but the government to publicly attribute responsibility for any problem to any identifiable individual.

Another new duty concerns the family. The LDP proposes a provision that reads: "The family shall be respected as the natural and fundamental unit of society. Family [members] must mutually support each other."[47] A provision like this would put the state in position to define family duties. It also raises the question whether one specific goal in the LDP campaign is revival of the patriarchal household system. As Ayako Kano explains in chapter 4 on gender in this book, new forms of family and household in Japan defy traditional categories.

Other proposals reinforce the suspicion that the LDP goal is to formally reestablish a "rule-by-law" system in which the role of law, including the constitution, is to provide tools to enable the state to control society. Examples include language proposed for Article 12 that would require people to "realize that freedoms and rights are accompanied by responsibilities and duties" whose scope is undefined. Presumably it will be left to the government to define them as it deems necessary.

Our analysis shows that the ideology displayed in the LDP Proposal for constitutional change contradicts fundamental notions of democratic government. Rather than limiting the power of government, the LDP would use the constitution to limit the rights of the people. The LDP Proposal is not the result of a quick or halfhearted committee process. It is the culmination of more than fifty meetings carried out over a period of nearly two and a half years.[48] Four former LDP presidents including Shinzō Abe were "supreme counselors" to the primary committee charged with preparing these changes.[49] The LDP Proposal is the product of a powerful and determined political force.

In contrast to the standard understanding of popular sovereignty, in which the people create and oversee government, the LDP proposes a different dynamic. According to this dynamic, the people, rather than the source of sovereign power, are the source of problems to be managed by government authority through the constitution in the first instance and through potentially sweeping legislation in the second. We view the LDP Proposal as a sort of "anticonstitution" in which the roles of the state and the people are reversed.

The LDP Proposal is based on an ideology that is nationalistic and authoritarian. Nationalistic political leaders like Shinzō Abe have borne a deep animosity toward the 1947 Constitution since it was adopted, but so far they have been unable to change a single word. By their words and actions, they have demonstrated their commitment to change the constitution, by amendment if possible, by their interpretation if not.

In chapter 12 of this volume, Ellis Krauss and Robert Pekkanen query whether Japan will produce a new "transformational leader." We can only wonder whether Abe or someone like him will become such a leader and whether the LDP Proposal will be the core of their plan for Japan's future.

Notes

1. All translations of LDP constitutional proposals and of excerpts from the LDP Q&A pamphlet are by the authors, who have sole responsibility for their accuracy.

2. See LDP, Nihonkokukenpō kaisei sōan Q&A [Draft reform to Japan's constitution, Q&A], October 2012, 2, www.jimin.jp/activity/colum/116667.html (hereafter cited as LDP Q&A). This pamphlet includes a complete text of the LDP revision proposals, together with brief commentaries in Q&A format. There have been many proposals by many parties for constitutional change over the years. See Reischauer Institute of Japan Studies, "Constitutional Revision Research Project," http://rijs.fas.harvard.edu/crrp/eresources/showa.php (accessed February 12, 2015), for a valuable collection of this material. This chapter will focus on the 2012 LDP proposals. The Sankei Shimbun also published a thorough set of proposals in April 2013. Sankei shinbun 80shunen "kokumin no kenpō" yōkō/zenbun [Sankei Shinbun eightieth-year anniversary "People's Constitution" summary/preamble] April 26, 2013, http://sankei.jp.msn.com/politics/news/130426/plc13042610310034-n1. htm (accessed February 13, 2015).

3. Public opinion in many Allied countries demanded that Hirohito be tried as a war criminal. For a history of this era, see Ray A. Moore and Donald Robinson, *Partners for Democracy* (New York: Oxford University Press, 2002), 36–49.

4. On the subject of amending Article 9, only 28 percent expressed support for change, with 41 percent opposed and 26 percent undecided. The survey results are discussed in Koji Shioda, *Kenpō kaisei giron to kokumin no ishiki* [Public political consciousness and the debate over constitutional revision], *Hōsō kenkyū to chōsa*, December 2007, 72–80, www.nhk.or.jp/bunken/summary/yoron/social/025.html.

5. Reiji Yoshida, "Amending Constitution Emerges as Poll Issue," *Japan Times*, May 3, 2013, www.japantimes.co.jp/news/2013/05/03/national/amending-constitution-emerges-as-poll-issue/#.UbLKgpxu3tM.

6. A group of scholars led by Yōichi Higuchi was formed in May 2013 to oppose this move. See "Gakushara '96jōnokai' kessei, san'insenmuke kaisei hantai yobikake" [Scholars and others form "Article 96 Group," call for opposition to revision as House of Councillors election looms], May 23, 2013, Doko e iku, nihon [Where are you going, Japan?], http://blog.livedoor.jp/gataroclone/archives/27376713.html.

7. The English version of the constitution is misleading in this respect, since in Article 72 it says, "The Prime Minister, representing the Cabinet, submits bills . . . to the Diet," which seems clear. However, the Japanese version does not use the term meaning "proposed law" (i.e., bill) that is used in Article 59, which sets forth the

legislative process. Since Article 41 declares the Diet to be the *sole* lawmaking organ of the state, the important role the cabinet actually plays in the legislative process may conflict with the constitution's intent.

8. Insofar as the roles typically associated with a head of state, particularly in the area of international relations, are, under the current charter, performed by the cabinet, with the emperor providing only an attesting role, constitutional theory generally holds that he should not be considered the head of state. See, e.g., Nobuyoshi Ashibe, *Kenpō* [The constitution], 5th ed. (Tokyo: Iwanami Shoten, 2011), 47; Kōji Satō, *Nihonkokukenpō* [The constitution of Japan] (Tokyo: Seibundoh, 2011), 511–12; Hideki Shibutani, *Kenpō* [The constitution] (Tokyo: Yuhikaku, 2007), 58–59.

9. The most prominent citizens' group devoted to protecting Article 9 is the Article Nine Association, launched in 2004 by Nobel Prize winner Kenzaburō Ōe and other well-known writers and public intellectuals. See their website at www.9-jo.jp.

10. The role played by the Cabinet Legislation Bureau—a central-government bureaucracy attached to but independent from the cabinet—presents an interesting example of the balance of power between elected and unelected government organs. See Richard J. Samuels, "Politics, Security Policy, and Japan's Cabinet Legislation Bureau: Who Elected These Guys, Anyway?," Japan Policy Research Institute Working Paper 99, March 2004, www.jpri.org/publications/workingpapers/wp99.html.

11. The prime minister would also be empowered to "make such disbursements and dispositions as are fiscally necessary," thus eliminating Diet budgetary approval.

12. Craig Martin has compared the failure of Japan's Supreme Court to pronounce clear standards to be used in cases involving conflicts between government action and individual rights with the work of courts in other countries where they have final authority. See Craig Martin, "The Japanese Constitution as Law and the Legitimacy of the Supreme Court's Constitutional Decisions: A Response to Matsui," *Washington University Law Review* 88, no. 6 (2011): 1527 and its citations.

13. Malapportionment in both houses of the Diet resulting in great disparities in the number of voters represented by different seats has generated a steady stream of constitutional litigation. The Supreme Court found the apportionment scheme unconstitutional in two cases but stopped short of declaring the elections invalid. See, e.g., Shigenori Matsui, *The Constitution of Japan* (Portland, OR: Hart, 2011), 50–54. The Court has also invalidated an electoral statute that limited the rights of Japanese voters overseas; see Supreme Court (Grand Bench), September 14, 2005, 59 Minshū 2087, www.courts.go.jp/app/files/hanrei_jp/338/052338_hanrei.pdf (in Japanese, accessed February 13, 2013; we have deleted the reference to an English

translation because this seems to have disappeared.). It should be noted that at the time of writing, the December 2012 election that brought Abe to power was the subject of constitutional challenges before the Supreme Court, with lower courts finding unconstitutional levels of inequality and one even declaring the election itself to be void on such grounds.

14. The LDP Proposal would allow for postappointment ratification of Supreme Court justices to be defined by statute. It would also relax restrictions on reducing judicial compensation and would allow the tenure of lower court judges to be set by statute instead of the ten-year terms currently mandated in Article 80.

15. Lawrence Beer notes, "Most rights contained in the 1948 Universal Declaration were guaranteed to Japanese a year earlier." Lawrence W. Beer, "Human Rights Commissioners (Jinken Yōgo Iin) and Lay Protection of Human Rights in Japan," in his *Human Rights Constitutionalism in Japan and Asia* (Kent: Global Oriental, 2009), 154.

16. The Universal Declaration was followed by a series of international human rights conventions that converted the aspirational statements of the declaration into binding legal commitments. The most important of these conventions is the comprehensive International Covenant on Civil and Political Rights (ICCPR), which Japan signed and ratified in 1979. The ICCPR has been ratified by more than 160 countries; see United Nations, "The Universal Declaration of Human Rights," 1979, www.un.org/en/documents/udhr/index.shtml.

17. United Nations Charter, Article 1.

18. United Nations, "Universal Declaration."

19. For a recent example of a passionate statement in support of universal human rights by a Japanese representative, see "Statement by Ms. Yaeko Sumi, Alternate Representative of Japan on item 69 (a): Implementation of Human Rights Instruments, Third Committee, 67th Session of the General Assembly," October 23, 2012, www.mofa.go.jp/announce/speech/un2012/un_121023_en.html.

20. There is an ongoing global debate among anthropologists, political leaders, constitutional scholars, and others about the relationships between universal rights and local cultures and traditions. See Henry J. Steiner and Philip Alston, *International Human Rights in Context, Law, Politics, Morals*, 2nd ed. (New York: Oxford University Press, 2000), 372–402.

21. It goes on to say: "This principle, as first emphasized in the Universal Declaration on Human Rights in 1948, has been reiterated in numerous international human rights conventions, declarations, and resolutions. The 1993 Vienna World Conference on Human Rights, for example, noted that it is 'the duty of States to promote

and protect all human rights and fundamental freedoms, regardless of their political, economic and cultural systems.'" See United Nations, Office of the High Commissioner for Human Rights, "What Are Human Rights?," www.ohchr.org/en/issues/Pages/WhatareHumanRights.aspx (accessed January 28, 2015).

22. LDP Q&A, 14.

23. It seems quite unlikely that the Americans who participated in making the original draft could foresee the transformation of the words *public welfare* into a restriction on individual rights. Their own experience was shaped by a very different problem—the actions of an aggressive US Supreme Court which had repeatedly declared "public welfare" legislation such as restrictions on working hours to be violations of the US Constitution. For a very readable account of this era in American constitutional history, see Noah Feldman, *Scorpions: The Battles and Triumphs of FDR's Great Supreme Court Justices* (New York: Grand Central Publishing, 2011). The attitude of Japan's nationalist politicians must have caught them by surprise. During 1946 Diet debates, political leaders were already declaring that the "public welfare" clause would restrict individual rights. See William Marrotti, *Money, Trains, and Guillotines: Art and Revolution in 1960s Japan* (Durham, NC: Duke University Press, 2013), esp. 67–70.

24. A linguistic problem with the standard English translation of the 1947 constitution is that it frequently uses the term *the people* where the Japanese version uses *kokumin*, which would be better translated "citizens." The LDP Proposal is thus better translated as "Citizens shall be respected as people" in the sense of "Each citizen shall be respected as a person." Note that the use of the term *kokumin* in defining constitutional rights has left numerous uncertainties as to the degree to which the rights of non-Japanese are protected. The LDP Proposal does not seek to remedy this deficiency.

25. Kazuyuki Takahashi, "Why Do We Study Constitutional Law of Foreign Countries, and How?," in *Defining the Field of Comparative Law*, ed. Vicki C. Jackson and Mark Tushnet (Westport, CT: Praeger, 2002), 45.

26. Takahashi also explains: "The word Kokutai is not found in the Meiji Constitution. It was created to express the nature of the existence of the Japanese polity, which was presumed to preexist the [Meiji] Constitution. The [Meiji] Constitution reflects the distinguishing feature of Kokutai to the extent that the legal terms can give expression to it, but there is more to Kokutai than can be translated into legal terms. The word is heavily loaded with emotion, and it is extremely difficult to confine it to the legal sphere." Ibid., 40.

27. Yōichi Higuchi, ed., *Five Decades of Constitutionalism in Japanese Society* (Tokyo: University of Tokyo Press, 2000), 5. On July 29, 2012, Deputy Prime Minister Tarō

Asō, speaking before an ultraconservative group in Tokyo, said Japan should change the constitution stealthily as the Nazis did with the Weimar Constitution. After a public outcry, Aso said he had been misunderstood and withdrew the suggestion.

28. There was an especially strong German influence. For a description of the creation of the Meiji Constitution, see Marius B. Jansen, *The Making of Modern Japan* (Cambridge, MA: Belknap Press, 2000), 389–95.

29. For an account of the February 1946 presentation of the American draft to the Japanese government, see Moore and Robinson, *Partners for Democracy*, 108–10.

30. Takahashi, "Why Do We Study."

31. Tom Ginsburg, *Judicial Review in New Democracies* (New York: Cambridge University Press, 2003), 12.

32. Dan Fenno Henderson, "Law and Political Modernization in Japan," in *Political Development in Modern Japan*, ed. Robert E. Ward (Princeton, NJ: Princeton University Press, 1968), 421.

33. LDP Q&A, 44.

34. Ibid., 46.

35. For a discussion of prosecution of peace activists, see Lawrence Repeta, "Limiting Fundamental Rights Protection in Japan: The Role of the Supreme Court," in *Critical Issues in Contemporary Japan*, ed. Jeff Kingston (London: Routledge, 2013).

36. For a description of these prosecutions, see Nihon Kokumin Kyuenkai [Japan People's Relief Organization], "Tokyo-kokkōhōdan'atsu horikoshi jiken" [Tokyo—The Horikoshi case: Repression through national public law], www.kyuenkai.org/index.php?%B9%F1%B8%F8%CB%A1%C3%C6%B0%B5%CB%D9%B1%DB %BB%F6%B7%EF (accessed February 12, 2015).

37. See National Police Agency, "Keibi keisatsu 50nen no ayumi" [The fifty-year history of the Security Police], n.d., www.npa.go.jp/archive/keibi/syouten/syouten269/sec01/sec01_0301.htm (accessed February 12, 2015). A surprising amount of Japan's postwar constitutional jurisprudence is derived from cases involving government efforts to suppress the Communist Party of Japan. One showcased significant abuse of police powers, including an intensive undercover investigation to prove that the defendant, a low-level bureaucrat, was distributing Communist Party literature on his days off. See Nihon Kokumin Kyuenkai, "Tokyo-kokkōhōdan'atsu horikoshi jiken."

38. LDP Q&A, 14.

39. Late in 2012 one of the authors came across a small sign posted in a public restroom in a train station. It was sponsored by both the Legal Affairs Bureau and the Prefectural Federation of Human Rights Committees and carried the imprimatur

of the MOJ's human rights mascot characters. The sign warned whoever had previously written offensive, discriminatory graffiti on the bathroom wall that such behavior infringed rights protected by the constitution! This is perhaps an extreme example of the way in which government actors trivialize human rights and reinforce the notion that citizens themselves, not the government, present threats to human rights.

40. See Ministry of Justice, "Activities of the Human Rights Organs of the Ministry of Justice," 2006, www.moj.go.jp/ENGLISH/HB/hb-02.html.

41. Ibid.

42. UN Office of the High Commissioner for Human Rights, "Concluding Observations of the Human Rights Committee," October 30, 2008, www.google.com/url ?sa=t&rct=j&q=&esrc=s&source=web&cd=1&ved=0CCAQFjAA&url=http% 3A%2F%2Fwww2.ohchr.org%2Fenglish%2Fbodies%2Fhrc%2Fdocs%2Fco%2FC CPR-C-JPN-CO.5.doc&ei=eKHJVJ6DKc-uogSttoG4AQ&usg=AFQjCNERF RQalsmNyplSgP11P6-izefoxQ&bvm=bv.84607526,d.cGU.

43. "Jinken hōan—kokuren ga mondaishi" [Human rights bill: The United Nations sees problems], *Asahi Shimbun*, July 2, 2002. For an English-language commentary, see "JCLU Comment on the Bill," *Jinken Shimbun*, March 30, 2002, no. 335, trans. Laura Becking and Ueno Satoshi, Japan Civil Liberties Union, www.jclu.org/katsudou/universal_principle/articles/335nhrc.html.

44. Currently the constitution provides for only three such duties: to educate children (Article 26), to work (Article 27), and to pay taxes (Article 30).

45. LDP proposed Article 102(1), in LDP Q&A, 64.

46. Ibid., 45–46.

47. Ibid., 46.

48. Ibid., 4.

49. Ibid., 79.

About the Contributors

Anne Allison is Professor of Cultural Anthropology at Duke University and is the author of four books on contemporary issues in Japan. Her most recent book is *Precarious Japan* (2013).

Frank Baldwin represented the Social Science Research Council in Japan and is an independent editor and researcher. He is the translator of Haruki Wada's *The Korean War* (2013).

Takahiro Fujimoto is Professor of Economics at the University of Tokyo. He is the author of *The Evolution of a Manufacturing System at Toyota* (1999) and *Monozukuri kara no fukkō* [Manufacturing and economic growth] (2012).

Haruo Hayashi is a Professor at the Disaster Prevention Research Institute, Kyoto University. He is a coeditor of a special issue of the *Journal of Disaster Research* (August 2012) entitled "Sustainability/Survivability Science for a Resilient Society Adaptable to Extreme Weather Conditions."

Jacques E. C. Hymans is Associate Professor of International Relations at the University of Southern California. He is the author of *Achieving Nuclear Ambitions: Scientists, Politicians, and Proliferation* (2012), winner of the American Political Science Association's 2013 award for Best Book in Science, Technology and Environmental Politics.

Colin P. A. Jones is a Professor of Law at Doshisha Law School in Kyoto. He is the author of four books on law in Japanese as well as numerous scholarly articles in both Japanese and English, and writes regularly on Japanese law for the *Japan Times*.

Ayako Kano is Associate Professor in the Department of East Asian Languages and Civilizations at the University of Pennsylvania. She is the author of *Acting Like a Woman in Modern Japan: Theater, Gender, and Nationalism* (2001).

Saori N. Katada is Associate Professor in the School of International Relations at the University of Southern California. She is the author of *Banking on Stability: Japan and the Cross-Pacific Dynamics of International Financial Crisis Management* (2001).

Jeff Kingston is Professor of History and Director of Asian Studies, Temple University, Japan. He is the author of *Contemporary Japan: History, Politics, and Social Change since the 1980s*, 2nd ed. (2012).

Ellis S. Krauss is Professor of Japanese Politics and of US-Japan Relations at the School of International Relations and Pacific Studies, University of California, San Diego. His most recent book (coauthored with Robert Pekkanen) is *The Rise and Fall of Japan's LDP: Political Party Organizations as Historical Institutions* (2010).

Claude Meyer is Associate Professor of International Economics at the Paris School of International Affairs, Sciences Po, Paris. His most recent book is *La Chine, banquier du monde* [China, banker of the world] (2014).

Hiroshi Nakanishi is Professor of International Politics at Kyoto University. He is coauthor of *Kokusai Seijigaku* [Textbook on international politics] (2013).

Machiko Osawa is Professor of Labor Economics at Japan Women's University. Her most recent books are *Nihongata wākingu pua no honshitsu* [Working poor] (2010) and *Josei wa naze katsuyaku dekinai no ka?* [What's holding Japanese women back?] (2015).

Gene Park is Assistant Professor of Political Science at Loyola Marymount University. He is the author of *Spending without Taxation: FILP and the Politics of Public Finance in Japan* (2011).

Robert J. Pekkanen is Associate Professor at the University of Washington. He is the coeditor of *Japan Decides 2012: The Japanese General Election* (2013).

Lawrence Repeta is a Professor on the law faculty at Meiji University in Tokyo. His recent publications include "Reserved Seats on Japan's Supreme Court" (*Washington University Law Review*, 2011).

Sawako Shirahase is Professor of Sociology at the University of Tokyo. She is the author of *Social Inequality in Japan* (2013).

William J. Siembieda is Professor of City and Regional Planning at California Polytechnic State University–San Luis Obispo. He is coeditor of *Contemporary Urbanism in Brazil: After Brasilia (2009).*

Masaru Yarime is Project Associate Professor of Science, Technology, and Innovation Governance at the University of Tokyo. He is the editor of the *Routledge Handbook of Sustainability Science* (forthcoming).

Index

Comprehensive Survey of People's Living Conditions, 33n41

computers, 7, 226

Confucianism, 262

Constitutional Amendment Referendum Act, 307–8

constitutional reform, Japanese, 298, 304–22; Abe's "technical" amendment, 307–8; change as ideology, 312–13, 322; constitutional duties, 320–22; LDP Proposal, 304–5, 308–22; limits on government power, 316–17; National Defense Force proposal, 309–10; reactions to 1947 Constitution, 306–7; rights issues, 313–15, 317–20; state of emergency proposal, 310–11; technical changes proposed, 308; uncontroversial substantive changes proposed, 308–9. *See also* Peace Constitution (1947)

consumer culture, Japanese, 12–13, 37–38, 46–47

corporations, Japanese: competitiveness, 3, 173; contributions to relief efforts, 154–55; globalization of, 202; R&D activities and investment, 215, 216–17, 218–19

Council on Economic and Fiscal Policy, 287

Council on Security and Defense Capabilities, 242

Council on Security and Defense Capabilities in the New Era, 242

counterterrorism, 8, 250–51, 309

couple-only households in Japan, 11, 20, 99; pension distribution, 22, 23*fig*

crime in Japan, 71, 88–89

crisis management: definition of, 140; by

local leadership, 140, 157, 160, 191. *See also* disaster management in Japan

cultural goods, Japanese, 268

cyber security technologies, 226

Czech Republic: nuclear policy, 120*t*

Daiichi Kangyō Bank, 174

debt, Japan's: denomination of, 180; domestically held, 172–73, 176, 267; foreign-held, 6, 167, 180; future prospects, 178–82; public debt accumulated, 167, 172–73, 175–78, 253, 266, 269

Defense Program Guideline (DPG), 240–43, 260n35

Defense Program Outline (DPO), 240, 248

Democratic Party of Japan (DPJ): family policies, 16–17, 96; fiscal policies, 171–72, 179, 295; fissures, 239, 297; foreign policy, 237, 251; Manifesto, 251; nuclear and energy policies, 112–13, 115; obstructionism of, 295; prime ministers, 290–91; social welfare policies, 61; strategy against Koizumi, 290; voter disaffection, 298

demographics, Japanese, 11–30; blended society and, 3, 29–30; changes in, 3–4, 9–10, 11, 181–82, 266, 269; changes since World War II, 22, 24; disaster management and, 5–6, 141–42, 162; gender equality and, 17–19, 92–93; household savings and, 181, 182; immigration and, 26–30, 71–73; life expectancy, 280n14; population projection, 24–26, 25*fig*, 77n1, 280n15; rural, 26; social services and, 2, 58, 167,

172; socio-technical innovations for, 227–28; trends chart, 143*fig. See also* birthrate, Japanese

Deng Xiaoping, 255

Denmark, gender equality in, 95

Disaster Countermeasures Basic Act (DCBA), 144

Disaster Management Agency, 154

disaster management in Japan, 5–6, 10, 139–62; after Kobe Earthquake, 148–49; alternative models, 158–59; building structures and, 144, 157; decentralization of, 144–45, 146*fig*, 147, 162; demographic shift and, 141–42; development of, 141, 163n5; evolution of system, 143–48; flexibility in, 147, 166n46; holistic approach, 6, 139, 140, 159, 161–62; infrastructure resilience, 191; lack of multihazard approach, 147; minister of state for, 145, 147; objectives, 148; operational continuity concept, 139; planning for future, 147, 155–58, 160–62, 191; social collectivity and, 50–54, 142, 153; state of emergency powers proposed, 310–11; trends chart, 143*fig*

Disaster Relief Act (1947), 143

Dispatched Manpower Business Act (1999), 59

Dog Who Protects the Stars, The (film), 49–50

Doi, Takako, 104n17

Doi, Takeo, 41

domestic savings rate, Japanese, 6

Domestic Transmission Trading Scheme, 204

domestic workers, importing, 97

Dōmoto, Akiko, 104n17

Dynamic Defense Force, 240, 251

earthquakes, Japanese: Ansei-Tōkai, 155; comparative damages, 149*t;* disaster management plan, 144; Great Kanto Earthquake, 141; Nankai, 143; predicted, 5–6, 141, 145, 155–58, 159–60; threat areas, 156*fig;* threat underestimation, 160–61. *See also* 3/11 triple disaster; Kobe earthquake

"East Asian Community" concept, 237–38, 251

East China Sea, 240, 278

economy, Chinese, 261–62, 264–66, 270–73. *See also* manufacturing, Japanese

economy, Japanese, 167–84; Big Bang financial reform, 174–75; challenges, 269–70; Chinese interdependence, 270–73; cost-cutting, 1980s, 169–70; cultural goods, 268; defense spending and, 253; disaster management and, 5–6, 141–42, 161–62; financial balance, 1998–2011, 177*fig;* fiscal balance, 1975–2012, 171*fig;* fiscal-financial connection, 175–78; fiscal policies, 6, 168–72, 175–84; fiscal stimulus, 1990s, 170; fiscal stimulus, 2000s, 171–72; fiscal stimulus, current, 183–84; gender inequality and, 4–5; global recession and, 1, 42, 168, 189; "lifetime employment" system, 12, 36–37, 38–39, 41; national employment plans, 27; neoliberal policy consequences, 59–61, 68–69; neoliberal reforms, 41–45, 58–59; pessimism and, 189, 192–95; postwar "enterprise society," 37–38, 40;

economy, Japanese (*continued*)
precarity of, 3–4, 189, 261–62, 266–70; security and, 236; spending gap, 168–72; strengths of, 3, 6, 168, 172–73, 261, 264, 266–68; sustainability, 178–82; trends chart, 143*fig;* yen appreciation and, 189, 195, 197. *See also* banks and financial institutions, Japanese; employment policies in Japan; manufacturing, Japanese

education in Japan: costs of, 16, 39; female higher education enrollment, 82n42; jobs and, 69; research positions, 220, 231; workers' training, 207

elderly population, Japanese, 2, 3–4, 10; caregiver shortages, 66, 70, 72–73; electoral politics and, 100; family household changes, 21–22; gender inequality and, 92–93; household savings, 181, 182; proportional growth of, 11, 25–26, 42, 72, 74, 77n1, 141–42, 170, 253; social inequality and, 19–24, 62; social welfare for, 6, 33n45, 58, 169, 182; socio-technical innovations for, 227–28, 230

electrical power companies (EPCOs), 113; fuel cycle technologies and, 126, 130; nuclear policy veto power, 125*t,* 128–32. *See also* Tokyo Electric Power Company (TEPCO)

electronics industry, 216, 218, 229, 230, 267, 274–75

Emergency Management Agency, 152

employment policies in Japan: changing paradigm, 58–77; chimera of reform, 74–76; cross-trained workforce, 190, 191–92, 194, 201, 206–7; current

and projected job market, 74–75; immigrants and, 26–29, 71–73; insecurity costs, 69–71; labor contract law, 75–76; "lifetime employment" system, 12, 36–37, 38–39, 41, 90, 190; neoliberal policy consequences, 59–61, 68–69; neoliberal reforms, 41–45, 58–59; plans, 27; possible futures, 76–77; R&D positions, 219–20; "results-based," 41–42, 43–44; retraining programs, 196; temporary and irregular workers, 41–42, 43–44, 46, 58, 59, 60–62, 66–67, 74; training programs, 74; women's marginalization, 63–67, 74; worker mobility and, 78n7

Energy and Environment Council, 115

Energy and Industrial Technology Development Organization, 229

energy policy, Japanese, 2, 10; future mix, 113–16, 150, 269–70, 297; hard choices in, 121–22, 209, 253, 270; neoliberal reforms, 126, 129–30, 132; R&D projects, 216. *See also* nuclear policy, Japanese

entrepreneurial university, 7, 222

environmental policies, Japanese, 5, 7, 150, 203–5, 227, 270. *See also* energy policy, Japanese; nuclear policy, Japanese

Equal Employment Opportunity Law (EEOL), 66–67, 76, 90–91

ewoman Inc., 64

exchange rates, 179, 194–95, 198–201, 202, 266

exports, Japanese, 8, 168, 179, 193–94, 209, 224, 243, 248, 267, 271–73

family-care leave system, 14, 81n37, 91, 97, 100

family-corporate system, 3–4, 18, 36–37, 38–41; disintegration of, 37, 41–42, 53–54, 76, 90; as "hidden capital," 40; "reproductive futurism" principle, 39

family structure in Japan, 3–4; alternative, 3, 99–100; breadwinner/housewife model, 17, 18, 36–37, 38, 39–40, 46–47, 97–98, 99, 107n51; centrality of, 46–47, 48, 49–50; changes in, 11, 12, 20, 43, 52–54; constitutional reform and, 321–22; gender inequality and, 5, 17, 65–66; post-disaster, 50–54; postwar, 37–38; social inequality and, 20–21; welfare system premises, 11–12

Fast Retailing (Uniqlo), 65

fast track/permanent resident visa program, 72

Filipino immigrants to Japan, 26, 73, 99

financial assets, Japanese, 3, 10, 168, 172–73, 184n2

Financial Services Agency, 174–75, 187n49

Financial Supervisory Agency, 174

Finland: nuclear policy, 135n43

Fire and Disaster Management Agency, 145, 163n10

Fire Services Act (1948), 143–44

First Gulf War, 248, 249

Fiscal Investment Loan Program (FILP), 169, 170

Fiscal Structure Reform Law (FSRL), 170, 174–75

Flood Control Act (1949), 143

foreign policy, Japanese. *See* security policy, Japanese

fossil fuels, 114, 121, 179, 209

Fourteenth National Fertility Survey, 18–19

Foxconn Technology Group, 201

France: nuclear policy, 120*t;* R&D expenditure, 219

"freeters," 42, 43, 44, 46, 69, 88–89, 90

Fuji Bank, 174

Fujii, Osamu, 243

Fujimoto, Takahiro, 6, 179, 199

Fujitsu Limited, 226

Fuji-Xerox, 206

Fukasawa, Maki, 89

Fukuda, Yasuo, and administration, 237, 291

Fukushima, Mizuho, 96

Fukushima Daiichi nuclear plant meltdown, 10; casualties, damages, and costs, 1, 50–51; government distrust and, 52–53, 153–54; international impact, 118–21; post-incident policy gridlock, 5, 110–32; scientists' failures after, 226; security issues, 150, 236; TEPCO bankruptcy and nationalization, 128–32. *See also* 3/11 triple disaster

Fukuyama, Francis, 41

Fukuzawa Yukichi, 277, 281n23

Funabashi, Yoichi, 249

Furuichi, Noritoshi: *Happy Youth in the Country of Despair*, 68, 69

genba (manufacturing sites), 189, 209n2

Genda, Yūji, 48, 78n7

Gender Equality Bureau, 91

gender equality in Japan, 4–5, 10; 3/11 triple disaster gendered dimensions, 87; alternative family structures and, 99–100, 321–22; assumptions and, 90; backlash, 93–97, 98; biological essentialism, 98; breadwinner/

gender equality in Japan (*continued*)
housewife division of labor and,
17–18, 36–37, 38, 39–40, 46–47, 97–98,
99, 107n51; child care and, 17, 40–41,
44, 65–66, 77, 100; class and, 102n3;
demographics and, 17–19; domestic
feminism and, 92, 95–96; female
researchers, 219–20, 231; future of,
97–102; gender as category, 88–90;
government gender policy, 90–93;
higher education enrollment, 82n42;
IMF on, 77; immigration policy and,
98–99; impact of internationalism,
92; Japanese discourse, 104n16; lack
of female political leaders, 285; macho
culture and, 64–65; male economic
disparity discourse, 89–90, 96–97;
marginalized women, 63–67, 103n9;
mentoring and, 65; nationalism and, 93;
pre-1945 militarism and, 95; proposals,
100; surnames of married couples,
93–94, 96; transnationalism and, 101–2;
wage disparity, 44, 63; "weak man" and
"herbivorous male" discourses, 89–90,
94; women's marital aspirations and,
19; work/life balance, 5, 44, 65–66, 74,
87–102; workplace and employment, 18,
39–40, 43–44, 47, 60, 63–67, 74, 77, 90
General Motors, 203
Germany, nuclear policy of, 5, 120*t*, 130
Ginsburg, Tom, 317
globalization: competitiveness and, 213,
230–31; globalized households, 99;
labor conditions and, 58–59, 103–4n12;
low wages and, 198, 199, 201
global recession, 1, 42, 168, 180, 189,
192–93, 199

global warming, 203–5
government bonds, Japanese (JGBs),
6, 168, 172, 173, 175–78, 180–82, 184,
184n4
Grants-in-Aid for Scientific Research, 222
Great East Japan Earthquake. *See* 3/11
triple disaster
Great Kanto Earthquake, 141
Greece, sovereign debt crisis, 172, 181
Group of Twenty, 277
Guam, 246

Hashimoto, Ryūtarō, and administration,
170, 174, 195, 249, 250, 289
Hashimoto, Tōru, 101
Hatoyama, Yukio, and administration:
child welfare, 16; environmental
policy, 204; fiscal policy, 172; foreign
policy, 236, 237–38, 239, 242, 244, 251;
resignation, 291
Hayakawa, Takashi, 27
Hayao, Kenji, 285
Hayashi, Haruo, 5–6, 310
Henderson, Dan Fenno, 317
"herbivorous male" discourse, 89–90
Higuchi, Yōichi, 316, 323n6
hikikomori (social withdrawal), 39, 48
Hirohito, Emperor, 305, 323n3
historical revisionism, 93, 248, 299
homelessness, 4, 48
homogeneity of Japanese society, 13, 27–28,
62, 71
Hong Kong, 181, 264, 272–73
Hoshi, Takeo, 186n22
Hosokawa, Morihiro, and administration,
116, 288
House of Councillors (HOC), 2, 9, 169,

Securities and Exchange Law, 174, 185n13

security policy, Japanese, 3, 7–8, 10, 236–56; active pacifism stance, 277–78; Asia-Pacific multilateral security architecture, 245–47; defense expenditures, 243*t;* defense policy changes after 2010, 240–43; earthquake rescue operations, 244–45; economy and, 167; future, 252–56, 275–77; history of Sino-Japanese relations, 262–63; public opinion toward China, 239*fig;* recent foreign policy, 236–40, 248–52, 298–99; Yoshida Doctrine and, 247–52

Self-Defense Forces (SDF), 309; earthquake rescue operations, 244–45; mission changes, 7–8, 240; overseas peacekeeping operations, 8, 243, 249, 277, 308; personnel and equipment, 241*fig,* 242; Senkaku incidents and, 254

Sengoku, Yoshito, 238

Senkaku/Diaoyu Islands, 3, 7, 8, 236, 238, 244, 252, 254, 263, 276, 278, 279n3, 299, 310

Serizawa, Shunsuke, 48, 52

share-houses, 53

Sharp, 224

Shimizu, Katsutoshi, 186n22

Shintarō, Ishihara, 321

Shiozawa, Yoshinori, 199

Shirahase, Sawako, 3, 38, 92, 142, 167, 182, 206, 227, 253

Siembieda, William, 5–6, 310

Singapore, 181, 264

Sino-Japanese relations, history of, 262–63. *See also* China

Sino-Japanese War, 263

social connectedness in Japan, 3–4, 36–54; disintegration of, 37; family-corporate system and, 36–37; government distrust and, 52–53; immigrants and, 71; individual responsibility and, 41–42; local initiatives, 53; myth of social cohesion, 62, 71; nostalgia and, 37, 44–45, 46–47, 97–98; post-disaster collectivity, 50–54, 142, 153, 158; precariat's threat to, 71; relationless society, 45–50; withdrawn youth, 39, 42, 47, 53, 94

Social Democratic Party, 104n17

social inequality, Japanese: birthrate and, 3, 70; child poverty rate, 62; debates about, 13, 61; family household structure and, 20–21, 21*fig,* 33n45; generational imbalance and, 19–22, 24; regular vs. irregular employment wage disparity, 43; relative poverty, 4, 12, 62, 79n15; rise in, 2, 12–14, 61–63, 74; trends in, 19–20, 20*fig;* underemployment and, 4, 58, 88–89

Socialist Democratic Party, 238

social media: connectedness and, 53; crisis management and, 152–53

social security system, Japanese, 1, 4; familial structure and, 11–12; funding, 6, 22, 170; privatization of, 42; strains on, 11, 26, 167

Social Stratification and Mobility Survey, 78n7

Social Welfare Council, 154

social welfare in Japan: cuts in, 169; eligibility criteria, 60; family support and, 70; growth in recipients, 59, 72, 74, 172, 182; science and technology applied to, 227–28